T0319821

Joint Venture Strategies

Design, Bargaining, and the Law

Zenichi Shishido

Professor, Hitotsubashi University, Japan

Munetaka Fukuda

General Manager, Internal Audit Division, Solar Frontier K.K., Japan

Masato Umetani

Senior Manager, Fuji Xerox Co. Ltd, Japan

Edward Elgar
PUBLISHING

Cheltenham, UK • Northampton, MA, USA

Published by
Edward Elgar Publishing Limited
The Lypiatts
15 Lansdown Road
Cheltenham
Glos GL50 2JA
UK

Edward Elgar Publishing, Inc.
William Pratt House
9 Dewey Court
Northampton
Massachusetts 01060
USA

A catalogue record for this book
is available from the British Library

Library of Congress Control Number: 2015945464

This book is available electronically in the Elgaronline
Law subject collection
DOI 10.4337/9781783475049

ISBN 978 1 78347 503 2 (cased)
ISBN 978 1 78347 504 9 (eBook)

Typeset by Columns Design XML Ltd, Reading
Printed and bound in Great Britain by
TJ International Ltd, Padstow, Cornwall

Contents

Preface   viii

1 Introduction   1
  1.1 Overview   1
  1.2 The structure of incentive bargaining in joint ventures   2
  1.3 Synergies and intellectual property   3
  1.4 Staged bargaining   5
  1.5 The success and future of joint ventures   7

PART I   INCENTIVE BARGAINING

2 Conflicts and risks in joint ventures: premises of incentive
  bargaining   11
  2.1 Conflicts in joint ventures   12
  2.2 Risks of participating in a joint venture   24
  2.3 Methods of motivating partners to provide capital to
     one another   27

3 Bargaining over sharing control   29
  3.1 Bargaining over voting rights   29
  3.2 Bargaining over composition of the board of directors
     and management appointments   31
  3.3 Bargaining over sharing of veto rights   32
  3.4 Bargaining over rights to information disclosure   34
  3.5 Bargaining over exit rights   35

4 Bargaining over sharing total return   37
  4.1 Three types of return   37
  4.2 Return on investment   38
  4.3 Return from transactions   40
  4.4 Ancillary return   48

5 Bargaining over exit rights   52
  5.1 The significance and idiosyncrasies of exit rights in
     incentive bargaining   52
  5.2 Grounds for exit   55

5.3 Bargaining over exit conditions   58
5.4 Methods of exit provided by law   58
5.5 Valuation of ownership interests   60
5.6 Post-exit arrangements   63
5.7 Case analysis   66

PART II   SYNERGIES AND INTELLECTUAL PROPERTY

6 **Synergies**   71
   6.1 Definition of synergies   71
   6.2 Classification of joint ventures by objective   75
   6.3 Antitrust law   82
   6.4 Reasons for creating a JV company in addition to a
       contractual alliance   84

7 **Intellectual property and incentive bargaining**   87
   7.1 Planning related to human capital contributions to
       joint ventures   87
   7.2 Acquisition of control through IP rights   96
   7.3 IP rights as a means of sharing total return   97
   7.4 IP rights and exit   101
   7.5 License agreements   103

PART III   STAGED BARGAINING

8 **Pre-contract bargaining**   115
   8.1 Joint venture lifecycle: four stages   115
   8.2 Preparatory stage: pre-contract bargaining   116
   8.3 Establishment stage   126

9 **Legal measures for finalizing bargains**   132
   9.1 Joint venture agreement   132
   9.2 Ancillary agreements concerning transactions with
       the joint venture   134
   9.3 Agreement regarding joint venture governance and
       organizational law   135
   9.4 Joint venture's charter/articles of incorporation   140

10 **Post-contract bargaining**   144
   10.1 Monitoring during the operational stage   144
   10.2 Need for renegotiation between partners   145
   10.3 Renegotiation during the operational stage   149

10.4 Renegotiation at the termination stage 153
10.5 Joint venture funding methods and renegotiation 155

**11 Cost-centers, profit-centers, and human capital provider
autonomy** 158
11.1 Cost-center versus profit-center 158
11.2 Monitoring and the autonomy of human capital
providers 163

12 Termination of the joint venture 169
12.1 Termination by agreement 169
12.2 Termination without agreement 169
12.3 Practical issues relating to joint venture termination 174

PART IV   THE SUCCESS AND FUTURE OF JOINT VENTURES

**13 Successful joint ventures: avoiding common joint venture
pitfalls** 185
13.1 Types of joint venture failure 185
13.2 Causes of organizational management failure 187
13.3 Preventing and resolving organizational management
failures 189
13.4 The bottom line: creating a sustainable joint venture 192

**14 New trend: hybridization of joint venture agreements and
venture capital investment agreements** 194
14.1 Contractual organizations 194
14.2 Comparison between joint venture agreements and
venture capital investment agreements 195
14.3 Strategic alliances in pursuit of technological innovation 197
14.4 Strategic alliances between venture capitalists and
large corporations acting as strategic investors 204

Appendix 1 208
Appendix 2 211
References 302
Index 307

Preface

Although everyone will agree that a joint venture is organized to create synergies that are unavailable to joint venture partners individually, very few people try to define synergies seriously. It seems that most people vaguely think of synergies as an increased social welfare by partnering. It is, however, not the case for joint ventures. A joint venture is a strategic alliance between two or more business companies. A business company will never participate in a joint venture to improve public welfare, but only for maximizing its own payoff (as a result, public welfare will be improved).

This book defines synergies as total return for each partner. The total return is comprised of three types of payoffs, i.e., return on investment, return from transactions, and ancillary return. This definition is not only realistic from a practitioner's point of view, but also makes it possible to analyze incentive bargaining in a joint venture from a game-theoretic point of view. In a successful joint venture, each partner is satisfied with its total return. If a partner is dissatisfied with its total return, its incentive to provide its monetary and human capital to the joint project will be lost. As a result, the other partner will not obtain sufficient synergies in the long run. Partners will bargain with each other for maximizing their own payoff.

A joint venture is a risky project, almost always with in-built conflicting interests. Partners predict opportunistic behavior of the other partner and easily lose their incentive to cooperate. Many joint ventures fail, not necessarily because of operational management failure, but because of organizational management failure, i.e., incentive bargaining failure.

Partners will confront various tradeoffs in incentive bargaining. Therefore, the key point of successful bargaining strategies is to maintain a good balance between partners' incentives. Partners can more easily reach a good balance by taking complementarities into consideration. For example, a partner may be satisfied with less control but greater return. Another partner may be satisfied with less monetary return but more ancillary return, such as a learning effect.

Joint venture is a typical long-term relational contract. Incentive bargaining in joint ventures is not a one-shot game but a staged bargaining, the pattern of which will change depending on the stage of the joint venture lifecycle. Typically, when a cost-center joint venture turns into a profit-center joint venture, two-player bargaining between the JV partners will be changed into three-player bargaining including management of the joint venture.

The pursuit of synergies in joint ventures will inevitably raise various legal issues, particularly intellectual property law, antitrust law, and corporate law. This book will cover critical legal issues of joint ventures. Legal analysis is basically premised on U.S. law (Delaware corporate law in particular) with occasional references to Japanese law.

This book is actually the result of a "joint venture" among a scholar and two practitioners. Zenichi Shishido has studied joint ventures from a law and economics point of view. Munetaka Fukuda and Masato Umetani have worked for the legal departments of two different international joint ventures, and have not only created and monitored many joint ventures, but have also solved their disputes. We have got together and discussed these issues on a monthly basis for the last 15 years and have finally reached a shared view on joint ventures. As a result, this book is based on Shishido's theoretical framework with rich details in practice provided by Fukuda and Umetani. Our study is based on many real cases both experienced by Fukuda and Umetani, and publicized by the media. This book has a list of joint venture cases reported by NIKKEI newspaper for the last 15 years as an appendix.

Although this book shares the basic analytical framework of our previous book published in Japanese (ZENICHI SHISHIDO, MUNETAKA FUKUDA & MASATO UMETANI, JOINTO BENCHA SENRYAKU TAIZEN: SEKKEI, KOSHO, HOMU NO SUBETE [JOINT VENTURE STRATEGY: DESIGN, BARGAINING, LAW] (Toyokeizai, 2013)), all chapters are re-constructed and rewritten for international readers.

The authors wish to acknowledge the helpful comments of Bruce Aronson, Richard Buxbaum, Mark Ramsayer, and Roberta Romano. Anthony Bertero, Alexander Coley, Lexi Rubow, and Yu Tanebe provided skillful research assistance. Masako Yamada provided helpful administrative assistance.

Zenichi Shishido, Munetaka Fukuda, Masato Umetani

1. Introduction

1.1 OVERVIEW

The goal of this book is to provide a clear set of analyses that demonstrate how joint ventures are founded upon a sort of "incentive system." Each partner company ("player") participates in a joint venture in order to maximize its own payoff. In order to do so, each player needs to incentivize its partners to provide capital to a joint project. This is a game-theoretic scenario. This book presents three important concepts relating to joint ventures: incentive bargaining;[1] synergy (i.e., three kinds of payoff); and staged bargaining from each partner company's point of view.

A joint venture is a strategic alliance to which each partner company contributes not only a substantial amount of monetary capital but also relation-specific human capital. Each partner company participates in the management of the joint venture. Therefore, each player is both the principal and agent of the other, creating a double moral hazard problem that must be considered. Unless proactive measures are taken, a player may hesitate to provide its own capital, either monetary or human, because of the risk of the other acting opportunistically.

Although there is potential for synergy, the joint venture is a risky project. This book takes a close look at each relevant stage involved in the incentive bargaining between the partner companies, indicating what the successful bargaining strategies are from each partner company's point of view.

This book is divided into four parts. Part I (Chapters 2–5) concerns incentive bargaining: why partner companies need to motivate each other and how they bargain. Then, in Part II (Chapters 6 and 7), synergy is

---

[1] Incentive bargaining is the bargaining between the indispensable capital providers of the firm, motivating them to provide the capital they own to the joint project. *See* Zenichi Shishido, *Introduction: The Incentive Bargain of the Firm and Enterprise Law: A Nexus of Contracts, Markets, and Laws, in* ENTERPRISE LAW: CONTRACTS, MARKETS, AND LAWS IN THE US AND JAPAN 1 (Zenichi Shishido ed., 2014).

explored: how synergies are created in practice and how intellectual property (IP) is relevant to creating synergies and to incentive bargaining. Part III (Chapters 8–12) deals with staged bargaining. The form of the partners' incentive bargaining changes as the joint venture progresses through each stage of its lifecycle. Each chapter in Part III describes the important points of incentive bargaining from the practitioner's stand-point, from the pre-contract stage to the termination stage. Finally, Part IV (Chapters 13 and 14) considers the points of joint ventures' success and the future of joint ventures.

1.2 THE STRUCTURE OF INCENTIVE BARGAINING IN JOINT VENTURES

When two or more players start any joint project, they each need to incentivize each other in order to maximize their own payoff. In venture capital-backed firms, monetary capital providers (venture capitalists (VCs)) and human capital providers (entrepreneurs) are categorically separate. The incentive bargaining in venture capital-backed firms involves entrepreneurs trying to incentivize VCs to provide monetary capital while VCs try to incentivize entrepreneurs to provide human capital. The goal is to strike a good balance between the autonomy of human capital providers and monitoring by monetary capital providers.

On the other hand, in joint ventures, each player (partner) provides both monetary and human capital; therefore, monetary capital providers and human capital providers are not separated in the same way. Imbalances between monetary contributions and human capital contributions will inevitably occur, thereby causing an imbalance between the proportion of human capital contributed and the share of the return on investment, leading ultimately to an incentive distortion. Accordingly, the major objective of incentive bargaining is to adjust for this imbalance and provide proper incentives to the partner who provides the more important human capital.

One risky aspect of participating in a joint venture is that conflicting interests between partner companies often arise in situations of self-dealing, corporate opportunity, and disclosure. Because of these potential conflicting interests, each player expects opportunistic behavior of its partner and feels wary about providing its capital to the joint project. From a synergy perspective, one can see how such a risky situation leads to each player pushing incentives to the other so that each provides capital to the joint project. The balance then typically results in the sharing of control, which mitigates risks, and sharing total return as a positive incentive. Making certain exit methods available provides an additional bargaining point related to both sharing control and total return.

Bargaining over how to share control includes making determinations as to the division and sharing of voting rights, board member seats, veto rights, information rights, and exit rights. If the result of this division is that one partner lacks equal control, it will be at risk of a squeeze-out. If both partners have equal control, such as in a 50/50 joint venture, there is a risk of deadlock, although the risk of squeeze-out is eliminated. Therefore, designing the optimal balance of control is important to forming a functional cooperative relationship.

Joint venture partners bargain over sharing total return to maximize synergies realized by each joint venture partner (JV partner), which herein is defined to include return on investment, return from transactions, and any ancillary return. Return on investment is the payoff from equity holdings, consisting of dividends and capital gains. In stock corporations, return on investment is determined by a given partner's share of the total monetary capital investment. The share of human capital is, however, not the same as the share of monetary capital. Without any adjustment, the incentives of the partner that provides the more important human capital will be distorted. In most cases, adjustments are made through return from transactions. Ancillary return, such as "learning effects," also could play the role of a substitute. Each partner company must consider the sum of the three types of return worthy before providing capital, which will, in turn, create the potential for a cooperative relationship.

Bargaining over exit rights is particularly important in joint ventures. Partners should be concerned not only with the amount of capital that the retreating party can recoup, but also with the effect that a threat of exit may have on the sharing of control within the joint venture. So, although it is too risky for partners to contribute resources without any exit rights, granting easily exercised exit rights distorts all partners' incentive to commit to a joint venture because of the excessive risk of one partner exiting in a way that will inevitably be detrimental to the other. Delicate bargaining is required to maintain a good balance between these two extremes.

1.3 SYNERGIES AND INTELLECTUAL PROPERTY

The objective of forming a joint venture is to realize synergies. We define synergies as the sum total of return on investment, return from transactions, and ancillary return for each partner. By this definition, we can discuss maximization of synergies in a game-theoretic context. The three types of return constitute returns or synergies that are unavailable to JV partners individually. They can only be realized by partnering with each other.

Joint ventures can be classified into 11 types based on the JV partners' objectives as described in Chapter 6. These 11 types generally fall into one of two broad categories: joint ventures that are intended to achieve greater efficiencies between incumbent businesses, or those that aim to enter a new business or market.

The cooperation that is required to realize synergies will almost inevitably be accompanied by some competition-restraining effects. This makes antitrust law a key legal obstacle for partners in a joint venture. It becomes necessary to assert that the pro-competitive effects of the joint venture are higher than the anticompetitive effects, and the partners must also comply with the *ex ante* procedural regulations of the jurisdiction where the joint venture is to be established.

Why the partners create a joint venture company (JV company) rather than just entering into a contractual alliance to realize synergies is an important question. Although most synergies can alternatively be realized through a mere contractual alliance, creating a company increases exit costs and the mutual commitment between partners, incentivizing each partner to provide capital to the joint project. Also, where technology licensing is involved, the licensor partners can prevent technology transfer to the licensee partner, and also secure ongoing rights to the products based on the development of the licensed technology, by licensing technology to a joint venture, instead of directly licensing it to the licensee. However, it is not always more advantageous to establish a JV company instead of entering a contractual alliance. Each partner must carefully compare the two alternatives depending on the unique situation.

Intellectual property plays a critical role both in realizing synergies and in incentive bargaining. In most joint ventures, synergies will be realized by combining the parent companies' respective IP, including technology, know-how, and trademarks. The benefits of this human capital investment include financial return in the form of royalties and greater control that stems from the licensing partner's ability to define conditions on the joint venture's use of the IP. The non-licensor partner also benefits from the joint venture, in that the venture may give it the opportunity to profit from the combination of technologies that the licensing partner would not feel comfortable licensing to the other partner[2] directly. However, non-licensor partners should be aware of the fact that a partner licensing indispensable IP rights additionally has strong bargaining power, due to the threat of exit. Finally, when engaging in incentive bargaining over IP licensing, partners should keep in mind the potential tax and antitrust implications of any agreement.

1.4 STAGED BARGAINING

In order to maximize synergies, JV partners must motivate each other to provide monetary and human capital to the joint project, not in a one-shot game, but as part of an ongoing process, typical of long-term relational contracts.

The subject matter and method associated with incentive bargaining changes with the stage that the joint venture is then undergoing. The joint venture lifecycle can be divided into four stages: the preparatory stage; the establishment stage; the operational stage; and the transformation and termination stage.

1.4.1 Pre-Contract Bargaining: The Preparatory and Establishment Stages

Pre-contract bargaining at the preparatory stage generally takes a significant amount of time. Potential JV partners negotiate step by step and commit to each other by exchanging memorandums of understanding (MOU) and/or letters of intent (LOI) to mark areas where they have reached agreement throughout the bargaining process. During this stage, they discuss and make decisions about basic matters, such as the joint venture's business model, the scheme for establishing the joint venture, ways to maximize the three types of return, and basic policies on sharing control and total return. When agreement on these key matters has become sufficiently well defined, the partners create and sign a legally binding joint venture agreement.

JV partners next follow the steps for establishing the joint venture laid out in the joint venture agreement. This "establishment stage" includes the legal establishment of the JV company, the transfer of assets required

---

[2] The term "the other partner" is generally used herein to describe the other partner in the typical case where there are two partners in the joint venture. However, the same principles would apply in situations where there are more than two partners.

by the joint venture, and the finalization and execution of ancillary agreements.

In these stages, the legal method of finalizing a bargain is practically important. Partners may finalize the result of their incentive bargaining in various contracts, including a corporate charter/articles of incorporation, shareholder agreements and ancillary agreements. As the form and interpretation of these contracts will vary based on the compulsory and default rules of the legal entity that the JV partners choose (e.g., rules regarding charter autonomy and exit option limitations), the choice of legal entity affects the durability of the agreements between partners.

1.4.2   Post-Contract Bargaining: Operational and Transformation/ Termination Stages

Incentive bargaining between JV partners continues after the joint venture is established. Post-contract bargaining includes both monitoring and renegotiation. JV partners need to monitor each other to make sure that monetary and human capital are provided as promised, in addition to ensuring that the decision-making process complies with the joint venture agreement. Further, because it is generally impossible for the joint venture agreement to include provisions for every future contingency, JV partners are often forced to renegotiate when new situations arise, such as a change in the market environment, a change in the nature of the joint venture, or a change in the JV partners' relationship. This renegotiation may take various forms, including an additional financial contribution to the joint venture and dispute resolution between the partners. Although renegotiation is indispensable to the survival of a joint venture experiencing a changing environment, expectations that renegotiation will take place may create a hold-up problem.

One important change that may occur during the life of a joint venture is the transformation of its character from a cost-center to a profit-center. Cost-center joint ventures perform cost-cutting functions for the partners, with management strictly monitored by JV partners. On the other hand, profit-center joint ventures are primarily intended to earn profit from third parties and are therefore necessarily given more managerial autonomy. If a cost-center joint venture transforms into a profit-center joint venture, the form of the incentive bargaining changes from two-player bargaining between JV partners to three-player bargaining between JV partners and the joint venture management.

The final stage of post-contract bargaining occurs upon termination of the joint venture. Joint ventures can terminate either by agreement or without any agreement. JV partners may agree to an exit by one or both partners while keeping the joint venture in operation. Dissolution of the joint venture may also be agreed to depending on the situation. Even when conflicts prevent an agreement, a joint venture may be terminated through a buyout/sellout, arbitration, judicial dissolution, or bankruptcy. There are many practical issues for JV partners to consider at this stage.

1.5 THE SUCCESS AND FUTURE OF JOINT VENTURES

1.5.1 Avoiding Common Joint Venture Pitfalls

Although a joint venture can potentially result in synergies that benefit each partner, the success rate for joint ventures is quite low. Successful joint ventures are created when the incentive bargaining between partners provides sufficiently balanced incentives and each partner is satisfied with its total return. Conversely, joint ventures typically fail as a result of a failure in organizational and/or operational management. This book examines some of the major reasons why organizational management fails, so that partners seeking to create a successful joint venture can avoid such pitfalls.

Organizational management failure occurs in several scenarios, such as when there is insufficient incentive to provide capital *ex ante*, *ex post* dissatisfaction with the share of total return, and often times, when there is opportunistic behavior by a dominant partner.

Although several practical and legal measures have been developed to prevent or resolve organizational management failure, the bottom line is that both partners can potentially exit or threaten to do so, and therefore an ongoing relationship of trust between each other is vital, as it allows for a greater possibility of constructive dialog in cases of conflicts.

1.5.2 Looking to the Future of Joint Ventures

The final chapter reviews the major issues of incentive bargaining in joint ventures by comparing similarities and differences between joint venture agreements and venture capital investment agreements. From the incentive bargaining point of view, joint ventures and venture capital agreements both have characteristics typical of a "contractual organization": a relationship among a relatively small number of contractual parties (investors) that wish to incentivize each other to contribute capital through shared ownership and shareholder agreements. In both types of contractual organization, the parties engage in incentive bargaining over the sharing of total return separate from the sharing of control. They demonstrate, however, distinguishing characteristics as they have been used in completely different ways in practice.

The following are the major characteristics of incentive bargaining in joint ventures which are distinguishable from incentive bargaining in venture capital investments: (1) in joint ventures it is necessary to reconcile the imbalance between monetary capital contributions and human capital contributions; (2) built-in self-dealing transactions, which play an important role in reconciling the imbalance contributions, create conflicts; (3) staged financing schemes are rarely used; (4) the parties rarely intend to exit through an IPO (initial public offering) or M&A (mergers and acquisitions); and (5) the reputational mechanism rarely provides much incentive to refrain from opportunistic behavior.

Interestingly, in recent years, the above-listed distinctions have been blurred, resulting in a hybrid-form contractual organization. This form is most frequently used when large corporations seek to form a relationship with technologically innovative start-up companies. For example, in a strategic alliance of a mega-pharmaceutical company and a biotech start-up company, the mega-pharmaceutical partner often acts as both a VC and a JV partner, and its role evolves as the subject drug development progresses.

Another typical example of a hybrid contractual organization is a strategic alliance between VCs and large corporations acting as strategic investors. Although large manufacturing corporations have historically made direct investments of venture capital on occasion (corporate venture capital), conflicting interests prevent them from creating true synergies. Attempting to ease these conflicts, large corporations have started to form alliances with professional VCs. The characteristics of these alliances place them somewhere in between joint ventures and venture capital agreements. They can be called "joint venture capitals." Some of them are more like joint ventures, and others are more like traditional venture capitals.

In practice, the joint venture is a creature of trial and error. Although there is potential for synergy and the same incentive bargaining problems have been a constant for a long period, adaptations/modifications to incentive bargaining are still being attempted and the characteristics of future joint ventures may differ from what we see today.

PART I

Incentive bargaining

2. Conflicts and risks in joint ventures: premises of incentive bargaining

This chapter discusses risks associated with joint ventures that are derived from the inevitable conflicts between JV partners upon the establishment of a joint venture, and the concerns of JV partners over these risks. Since potential partners are generally aware of the conflicts inherent in joint ventures, they are naturally wary of each other's intentions. Accordingly, such concern makes partners hesitant to contribute capital.[1]

Joint ventures must deal with conflicts concerning self-dealing, corporate opportunity, competition, and disclosure. Each of these can pose corporate law problems relating to conflicts of interest and directors' fiduciary duties.[2]

The main risks faced by prospective JV partners aiming to establish a joint venture include: the risk of being squeezed out, the risk of opportunistic behavior by the other partner, as well as a pair of two-sided risks. The first is the risk of the other partner refusing to renegotiate and, conversely, the risk of being forced to renegotiate to one's own detriment. The second is the risk of the other partner exiting and, conversely, the risk of being unable to exit oneself.

If both partners are hesitant to contribute capital and neglect to alleviate each other's concerns, their planned joint venture will never become reality. As such, both partners must engage in incentive bargaining over the sharing of control, sharing total return, and methods of exit, so as to ensure their mutual willingness to contribute capital. This imperative increases the costs of establishing a joint venture in comparison to a solely owned business.

---

[1] *See* ZENICHI SHISHIDO, DOKIZUKE NO SHIKUMI TOSHITENO KIGYO: INSEN-TIBU SHISUTEMU NO HOSEIDORON [THE FIRM AS INCENTIVE MECHANISM: THE ROLE OF LEGAL INSTITUTIONS] 28–33 (2006).

[2] In this book, a "conflict" refers to a situation where JV partners' interests actually or potentially conflict with each other, and a "conflict of interest" refers to a situation where the position of either JV directors or JV partners actually or potentially raises a corporate law problem of fiduciary duties.

2.1 CONFLICTS IN JOINT VENTURES

As will be discussed in Chapter 6, joint ventures are established to realize synergies through combining the respective strengths of their parent companies. The resulting situation is that joint ventures tend to have transactional relationships with their parent companies but also a competitive relationship with at least one parent. Transactional relationships entail conflicts with respect to self-dealing, while competitive relationships entail conflicts involving corporate opportunities and competition. Additionally, if a joint venture aims to realize synergies by combining the parent companies' respective technologies and/or know-how, the parents will have conflicts with respect to disclosure of that technology/know-how to the venture. Parents may also have conflicts with respect to disclosure related to self-dealing and/or corporate opportunities. In other words, if the aim is to realize synergies in some form or another, it is impossible to design a joint venture that is immune from inter-partner conflicts. These conflicts are the subject of corporate law conflict-of-interest problems when a joint venture is organized as a standalone enterprise, such as a stock corporation or LLC (limited liability company).

When a JV company's interests conflict with at least one of its parent company's interests, the fiduciary duties of the parent company and the directors of the joint venture appointed by the parent raise issues of corporate law.[3] Given that the purpose of establishing a joint venture is maximization of the parent companies' profits, directors appointed to the joint venture by each parent should theoretically be permitted to act in the interests of their parent company over the interests of the joint venture. Under corporate law, however, joint venture directors owe fiduciary duties to the JV company.[4] Further, under US case law, even if a joint venture is organized as a corporation, a parent company may be charged with a fiduciary duty to a co-partner to the extent that its actions affect the co-partner's interests.[5] In contrast, Japanese law has no such concept of fiduciary duty owed by a shareholder to fellow shareholders, either in case law or statutory law.

---

[3] *See* Zenichi Shishido, *Conflicts of Interest and Fiduciary Duties in the Operation of a Joint Venture*, 39 HAST. L. J. 63, 64 (1987).

[4] *Id.*, at 71.

[5] *See* WILLIAM A. KLEIN & JOHN C. COFFEE, JR., BUSINESS ORGANIZATION AND FINANCE: LEGAL AND ECONOMIC PRINCIPLES 168 (10th ed. 2007); Shishido, *supra* note 3, at 73.

Parent companies could make a tacit agreement to mutually allow their respectively appointed directors to act with preference for the appointing parent company's respective interests. From this standpoint, suits claiming damages on grounds of breach of a joint venture director's fiduciary duty to the joint venture should arguably be barred by estoppel. However, this argument does not completely eliminate the legal risk of joint venture directors being held liable to pay damages for breach of their fiduciary duty to the joint venture.[6]

This issue of a director's fiduciary duty to a corporate joint venture can be largely avoided by organizing the joint venture as an LLC. Delaware state law allows LLC members and/or managers to contract out of fiduciary duties through specific language in the LLC agreement.[7] Even in Japan, LLC agreements may limit or eliminate LLC managers' fiduciary duties, provided that the LLC members unanimously consent to the release in advance.[8]

However, there is no overwhelming incentive for JV partners to completely avoid the fiduciary duties imposed by corporate law. Instead, they face opposing incentives – because they are exposed not only to the risk of being sued for breach of a fiduciary duty, but also to the risk of opportunistic behavior by the other partner. LLC agreement provisions that lead to such conflicting incentives may require judicial interpretation and the default fiduciary duty could still apply regardless of either party's intent or desire.[9]

---

[6]   *Id.*, at 81–82.

[7]   6 Del. Code §18-1101(c). *See* Zimmerman v. Adhezion, 62 A.3d 676, 702 (Del. Ch. Jan. 31, 2013).

[8]   Under Japanese law, this is treated as exculpation from the consequence of the breach of fiduciary duty, rather than the elimination of the duty itself. *See* Zenichi Shishido, *Goben Godo Kaisha [Joint Venture LLCs]* in KIGYOHO KINYUHO NO SHINCHORYU [NEW TREND OF ENTERPRISE LAWS AND FINANCIAL LAWS] 211, 222 (Atsushi Koike et al. eds., 2013); Zenichi Shishido, *Dai 3 Hen (Mochibun Kaisha) Zenchu [General Comments to Part 3 (Membership Companies)]*, *in* 14 KAISHA-HO KONMENTARU [14 COMMENTARY ON THE COMPANIES ACT] 5, 10 (Hideki Kanda ed., 2014); Zenichi Shishido, *Legislative Policy of Alternative Forms of Business Organization; The Case of Japanese LLCs, in* RESEARCH HANDBOOK ON PARTNERSHIPS, LLCS AND ALTERNATIVE FORMS OF BUSINESS ORGANIZATIONS Ch. 22 (Robert W. Hillman & Mark J. Lowenstein eds., 2015).

[9]   Zimmerman (*supra* note 7) is a classic example. *See id.* On the concept of default fiduciary duties, *see* Myron T. Steele, *Freedom of Contract and Default Contractual Duties in Delaware Limited Liability Partnerships and Limited Liability Companies*, 46 AM. BUS. L. J. 221 (2009); Moshen Manesh, *What is the*

As a starting point for discussion, the following is a summary of the conflicts that commonly arise in joint ventures. Even where such conflicts appear to involve the joint venture and one of its parent companies, these situations ultimately boil down to a conflict between parents.

2.1.1 Conflicts with Respect to Self-Dealing

One example of conflicts arises in cases of self-dealing. From a supply-chain standpoint, joint ventures usually have a vertical relationship with both of their parent companies. Transactions between the joint venture and its parents are generally programmed into the joint venture setup in advance. In such cases, the co-partners have a conflict in terms of how transaction terms are determined. For example, joint ventures often purchase raw materials from one parent and supply finished products to the other parent for resale.[10] It is also common for them to hold technology licenses and rights to use the brand name of one or both of their parents.

JV partners, by definition, contribute both monetary capital and human capital to their joint ventures. Imbalances inevitably occur between contributions of monetary and human capital. Return on investment,[11] or cash flow rights, are ordinarily shared according to the share of monetary capital contribution. As a result, the share of return on investment and the share of human capital contribution are imbalanced. And if such imbalances[12] are not rectified, the partner slated to contribute the greater

---

Practical Importance of Default Rules under Delaware LLC and LP Law?, HARV. BUS. L. REV. Online 121 (2012); Leo E. Strine, Jr. & J. Travis Laster, *The Siren Song of Unlimited Contractual Freedom, in* RESEARCH HANDBOOK ON PARTNERSHIPS, LLCS AND ALTERNATIVE FORMS OF BUSINESS ORGANIZATIONS Ch. 1 (Robert W. Hillman & Mark J. Lowenstein eds., 2015).

[10] A typical example of such a joint venture is NUMMI, an erstwhile joint venture between Toyota and GM. *See* ZENICHI SHISHIDO & ATSUSHI KUSANO, KOKUSAI GOBEN: TOYOTA · GM JOINTO BENCHA NO KISEKI [INTERNATIONAL JOINT VENTURES: A CASE STUDY OF THE JOINT VENTURE BETWEEN TOYOTA AND GENERAL MOTORS] (1988).

[11] In this book, "return on investment" refers to the sum total of dividends and capital gains that shareholders receive based on their respective ownership percentages in a JV company. We will use the term to distinguish from "return from transactions" and "ancillary return." *See infra* Ch. 4.

[12] In this book, "imbalance" is an important concept that refers to the gap between the share of human capital contribution and the share of return on investment of a JV partner, which will cause a distortion.

human capital may feel that the deal is unfair and become reluctant to make the necessary contribution. In practice, such imbalances are often rectified through return from self-dealing transactions.

Take a hypothetical case in which Partner A is prepared to contribute relatively important human capital to a joint venture but cannot earn an adequate return on this capital based solely on its share of the joint venture's profits and/or pro-rata self-dealing transactions.[13] To rectify this imbalance and incentivize Partner A to contribute its human capital, Partner B may agree to non-pro rata self-dealing transactions[14] between the joint venture and Partner A where profits are directed to Partner A alone. Distribution of return through self-dealing transactions to rectify imbalances poses a number of risks, including (1) problems in terms of the self-dealing transaction being challenged as invalid under corporate law and the fiduciary duties of the director(s) who authorized the transactions, (2) tax consequences, and (3) potential antitrust violations.

Delaware corporate law permits self-dealing subject to two require-ments: fair process and fair price.[15] The Companies Act of Japan, in contrast, dictates that the validity of a self-dealing transaction may be challenged after the fact, and the responsible director(s) could potentially be found to have breached a fiduciary duty.[16] Regardless of the terms of a transaction between a joint venture and one of its parents, the transaction will pose no conflict-of-interest problems under corporate law if all of the joint venture's parents consent to the terms. However, the transaction can still be challenged on the grounds of defective consent if the information disclosure upon which all of the partners' consent was premised was incomplete or otherwise deficient. To avoid such a risk, JV partners should take two precautions. First, when the joint venture is established, the partners should agree to a list of mandatory disclosures for self-dealing transactions expected to occur in the future. Second, whenever self-dealing occurs, the joint venture should obtain the consent of any parent companies not party to the transaction after making the mandatory disclosures agreed to in advance. Where such precautions have been taken, a parent company not party to the transaction will likely be estopped from subsequently suing for damages. At the very least, the plaintiff would bear the burden of proving that the transaction was unfair.[17] JV partners must also be careful that information disclosure

---

13　*See infra* Ch. 4, 4.3.3.
14　*See infra* Ch. 4, 4.3.4.
15　8 Del. Code §144.
16　Shishido, *supra* note 3, at 82.
17　*Id.*, at 87.

related to self-dealing transactions does not run afoul of antitrust prohibitions against collusion.

Additionally, under tax law, profit distributions that are deemed not to be at arm's length may be treated as a receipt of taxable income or a taxable gift, or there may be other unintended tax consequences (e.g., taxation of transfer pricing between domestic and offshore affiliates). Accordingly, when JV partners seek to rectify imbalances through preferential transaction terms, the terms must effectively be set within an arm's-length price range.

From the incentive bargaining standpoint, JV partners face two key issues. The first is how much information should be disclosed on manufacturing costs and terms of transactions with third parties (duty of notification, audit rights) in the course of obtaining consent for non-pro-rata self-dealing transactions. The second is the extent to which consent rights (veto rights) should come into play.[18] However, no matter how thoroughly transaction terms are negotiated between JV partners in advance, one partner's relative bargaining power vis-à-vis the other's changes over time. If inequitable transaction terms were negotiated due to one partner's superior bargaining power at the time of a joint venture's inception, such terms pose a risk of sparking a dispute between partners post inception.[19]

2.1.2 Conflicts with Respect to Corporate Opportunities and Competition

A second area in which conflicts are common is corporate opportunities and competition. When presented with an opportunity to acquire a company or enter a new market, JV partners typically have conflicting

---

[18] Although a corporate law problem of conflicts of interest arises due to joint ventures' status as independent enterprises, transaction prices are set by inter-partner negotiation in joint ventures where each partner has adequate monitoring authority through veto rights or other means. Similar pricing would presumably result even if the partners had not structured their business dealings as a joint venture.

[19] For example, in a construction machinery manufacturing joint venture between Mitsubishi Heavy Industries (MHI) and Caterpillar, Caterpillar gained the exclusive right to supply engines to the joint venture even though both companies had been manufacturing engines until a 1979 revision of the joint venture agreement. This inequitable transaction term became a source of dissatisfaction for MHI. *See* SHIN CATERPILLAR MITSUBISHI CORPORATE HISTORY COMPILATION COMMITTEE, SHIN KYATAPIRA MITSUBISHI 25-NENSHI [NEW CATERPILLAR MITSUBISHI'S 25-YEAR HISTORY] (1991).

interests in terms of whether to individually seize the opportunity and operate it on a solely owned basis or give the opportunity to their joint venture to operate.[20]

To effectively avoid the risk of fiduciary breach under corporate law with respect to corporate opportunities, JV partners can enter into an agreement limiting the corporate opportunities that their joint venture may undertake before establishing the joint venture. They also have the option to contractually agree in advance to mutually waive their respective rights to claim damages on the grounds that the other partner usurped a corporate opportunity from the joint venture.[21] Delaware corporations may waive corporate opportunities in their articles of incorporation or through a board resolution, thereby allowing shareholders or directors to avail themselves of waived opportunities without worrying about being sued for fiduciary breach down the road.[22]

Be aware, however, that even though JV partners may be able to avoid the risk of lawsuits for fiduciary breach, if one partner individually appropriates a corporate opportunity that rightfully should have gone to the joint venture, such opportunism could distort the incentive of the other partner and ultimately lead to an outcome contrary to the opportunistic partner's own long-term interests.[23]

As an example, say that P1 and P2 establish a joint venture to manufacture television LCD panels. In light of market trends and technological considerations, the joint venture's technology team proposes entering the market for LCDs used in smartphones as well. P1 is in favor of the idea but the joint venture's directors appointed by P2 oppose it because P2 has the potential to independently enter the smartphone LCD market in the future. What type of conflict problem does this scenario pose?

In terms of conflicts with respect to corporate opportunities and competition in the context of a joint venture, it is important to delineate the business domains of the parent companies and their joint venture. The key issues are (1) the definition and scope of the joint venture's business

---

[20]   Shishido, *supra* note 1, at 74. Conflicts with respect to corporate opportunities between joint ventures and their parent companies tend to be more common in the case of horizontal joint ventures that have a competitive relationship with one or both parent companies.

[21]   Shishido, *supra* note 3, at 106.

[22]   8 Del. Code §122(17). *See* ROBERT R. KEATINGE, ANN E. CONAWAY & BRUCE P. ELY, KEATINGE AND CONAWAY ON CHOICE OF BUSINESS ENTITY: SELECTING FORM AND STRUCTURE FOR A CLOSELY-HELD BUSINESS 252 (2013).

[23]   Shishido, *supra* note 3, at 106–108.

purpose, (2) parent company's and joint venture's duties not to compete with each other, and (3) how new business opportunities are to be shared among the parties. During the process of establishing a joint venture, the JV partners agree on the purpose and scope of the business to be operated by the joint venture. Such agreements typically specify the objective scope of the jointly operated business (types of goods and services in which it will deal, technologies it will use, etc.), geographic scope (commercial rights, territorial restrictions), and temporal scope (duration of the venture). Defining the business as jointly operated by the JV partners is extremely important. To the extent possible, this definition should be included in the business purpose section of the articles of incorporation. In Japan, however, a corporation's original articles of incorporation cannot be certified if they contain geographic restrictions (territorial division of markets) or name specific goods not listed under standard industry classification. Consequently, some matters (e.g., licensing agreements, supply of goods agreements) are covered solely by agreements between JV partners or between partner(s) and joint venture.[24]

It is important for JV partners to clearly demarcate their jointly owned business and respective solely owned businesses.[25] They must be vigilant of opportunistic behavior, whereby one partner's solely owned business branches into a line of business that is the joint venture's rightful domain,

---

[24]   In addition to contractual provisions regarding a joint venture's business purpose, contractual provisions that impose a duty not to compete on the parent companies and contractual provisions that stipulate how new business opportunities are to be shared among the joint venture and its parent companies may also be used (*See* Ihara Hiroshi, *Gobengaishi no Yakuin Jinji wo Meguru Funso* [*Disputes Regarding Joint Venture Director Appointments*], 974 NBL 40, 45 (2012)). However, non-compete clauses pose a risk of antitrust problems, and reaching an agreement on how to share potential future business opportunities is not necessarily easy. Even if the opportunity-sharing issue is resolved contractually, if one partner subsequently becomes dissatisfied with how business opportunities are shared, the resultant distortion effect could undermine the joint venture's continued existence. Shishido, *supra* note 3, at 91–112.

[25]   One approach is for the partners to spin off their respective competing businesses as separate companies and then merge the spun-off companies into a joint venture. An example of such a joint venture is Mitsubishi Chemical Hoechst, the parent companies of which avoided conflict problems by merging their paint businesses into a joint venture and unifying their paint sales channels. NIHON KEIZAI SHIMBUN, October 26, 1992; NIKKEI SANGYO SHIMBUN, December 19, 1990.

and of competitive behavior, whereby the joint venture enters a line of business that is the rightful domain of a partner's solely owned business.

In cases where goods manufactured by a joint venture are processed further and sold by one parent company under its brand name, the duty not to compete imposed on the joint venture and the parents becomes an issue. A former joint venture between Meiji Dairies and Borden is one case in point. Meiji entered into competition with the joint venture by launching its own ice cream brand, Aya. In response, Borden canceled its joint venture agreement with Meiji in 1992 and established a solely owned subsidiary in Japan with the aim of building its own sales channels.[26]

Another example of a joint venture that was deprived of an opportunity by competition from one of its owners is TNK-BP, a 50:50 joint venture between British oil major BP and Russian investment group AAR. When BP formed an operational and capital alliance with Rosneft, a Russian state-owned oil company in competition with TNK-BP, it was sued by its Russian JV partner for breach of the joint venture agreement (specifically, its duty to give precedence to TNK-BP in its Arctic oil operations and to obtain consent before conducting joint operations with a third party in Russia).[27]

JV partners impose upon their joint ventures a duty to notify them of actions by the joint venture that may stray beyond the scope of its business. Meanwhile, they also monitor their joint ventures for such actions. One way to prevent majority partners from passing directors' resolutions in violation of inter-partner joint venture agreements is to require minority partners' advance consent to the matters that are to be voted on by the board of directors and grant veto rights to minority

---

[26] In this case, Borden sued for injunctive relief on the grounds of breach of its licensing agreement in response to Meiji Dairies' launch of its own new ice cream brand in anticipation of the licensing agreement's expiration. NIHON KEIZAI SHIMBUN, February 7, February 20, 1991; NIHON KEIZAI SHIMBUN, April 11, 1991. When Häagen-Dazs entered the Japanese market, it selected Suntory, which did not have an ice cream business, as its partner. According to case studies of joint venture dissolutions presented in Shiro Takeda, *Nihon Kigyo no Kokusai Teikei Kaisho ni Kansuru Ichikosatsu* [*Study of Dissolutions of Japanese Companies' International Alliances*], 17 YOKOHAMA NAT'L UNIV. MGMT RES. REV. 31 (1996), competition between joint venture companies and their parents seems to be one common source of conflict. http://kamome.lib.ynu.ac.jp/dspace/bitstream/10131/753/1/KJ00000160245.pdf.

[27] *See* NIHON KEIZAI SHIMBUN, August 23, 2011, at 7. TNK-BP was subsequently dissolved following litigation and mediation.

partners.[28] Conversely, to deter opportunistic behavior that encroaches upon a joint venture's business domain by the other partner, a JV partner may impose a duty of notification on the other partner or on the joint venture and monitor the other partner's behavior.[29]

Additionally, conflicts with respect to financing a joint venture are similar in nature to conflicts with respect to corporate opportunities. Suppose, for example, that a JV partner whose interests are more aligned with the joint venture's interests (often the local partner) wishes to expand the joint venture's operations, therefore favoring retaining earnings over distributing profits as dividends. Alternatively, the partner may want to fund capital expenditures with debt or equity financing. Meanwhile, the other partner (often an offshore company) dissents because its own interest is to quickly recoup invested capital rather than expanding the joint venture's operations.[30] If the offshore partner blocks expansion of the joint venture's operations by exercising its veto rights, the local partner may become dissatisfied. Such dissatisfaction could distort the local partner's incentive to contribute human capital to the joint venture.[31]

2.1.3   Conflicts with Respect to Disclosure

A third area in which interests often conflict is disclosure. A joint venture's directors or officers typically possess confidential information on the joint venture and one parent company. If disclosure of the parent

---

[28]   For an example of a case in which a minority partner's veto rights were ruled invalid because a material matter requiring advance, unanimous approval (director appointments, in this case) had not been stipulated in sufficiently specific terms, *see* Ihara, *supra* note 24, at 40, Chizai-Kosai (Tokyo High Court, November 30, 2010, Case No. Heisei22-10040) www.courts.go.jp/hanrei/pdf/20101202113443. The case involved a dispute over whether director appointments in a joint venture owned by four companies (ownership was split 25.6%: 25.4%: 24.6%: 24.6%) constituted a material matter requiring advance, unanimous approval of the four partners (matters over which even minority shareholders have veto rights) pursuant to the joint venture agreement, or whether the appointments only required majority approval pursuant to the Board of Directors Regulations (as a consultation report stipulated in the management agreement).

[29]   Regarding corporate opportunity and competition in joint ventures, *see* Shishido, *supra* note 3, at 76.

[30]   *Id.*, at 79–80.

[31]   Joint ventures whose termination was reportedly at least partially attributable to this problem include Yamazaki Nabisco, Ajinomoto-CPC (Knorr), and GM Daewoo. NIKKEI SANGYO SHIMBUN, May 14, 1992.

company's information to the joint venture would be beneficial to the joint venture but detrimental to the parent company, the joint venture and parent company will have conflicting interests with respect to disclosure. A joint venture director's or officer's failure to disclose information beneficial to the joint venture may constitute a breach of fiduciary duty to the joint venture. Conversely, disclosure of the information may constitute a breach of fiduciary duty to the parent company. Moreover, exchanging information could constitute an antitrust violation.[32]

The only way for joint venture directors to deal with disclosure-related conflicts is to balance the joint venture's interests against their parent company's interests in light of three factors: the nature of the information, the interests of the other parent companies, and the extent of the disclosure.[33]

Instances in which disclosure would be beneficial to a joint venture but detrimental to a parent company involve various types of information. Foremost is information pertaining to technology or know-how. Such information is typically a key constituent of a company's competitive advantage and partners are concerned about the risk of misappropriation of leaked confidential information and the potential loss of intellectual property. Joint venture directors do not have the duty to unconditionally disclose their parent company's technological information to the joint venture. Even if directors refrain from disclosing their parent company's technological information, they are unlikely to be chargeable with breach of their fiduciary duty to the joint venture, whereas disclosure of the information would be a breach of their fiduciary duty to their parent company.[34]

In many cases, however, joint ventures are unable to realize synergies without combining the parent companies' respective technologies and/or know-how. JV partners tend to face a prisoner's dilemma in deciding how much information to disclose. Specifically, they have to weigh the benefits of the synergies that can be derived through the information disclosure against the loss of competitive advantage that would result from dilution of the value of their proprietary technology through direct photocopying of disclosed information or development of substitute know-how.[35] To resolve such dilemmas, JV partners agree in advance on

---

[32] Shishido, *supra* note 3, at 112–113.
[33] *Id.*, at 113.
[34] *Id.*, at 113.
[35] *See* Zenichi Shishido, *The Strategy behind the Organizational Game: A Comparison between the Joint Venture Negotiation and the Venture Capital Negotiation*, *in* STRATEGIC ALLIANCES AND JOINT VENTURES: LAW, ECONOMICS

items such as limitations on patent licensing, attribution of improvement inventions (which is also a competition issue), and the duty to make new technologies available to the joint venture.

On a related note, the issue of whether a joint venture may conduct research and development is often renegotiated after the fact. JV partners that license technology to a joint venture typically refuse to permit the joint venture to conduct research and development independently out of concerns of excessive dissemination of their technology. However, new technological applications based on an existing patent that are discovered in the course of a joint venture's operations require a new patent application for competitive reasons. It is often more efficient for the joint venture, which is closer to the market, to file the new application than for the licensor partner to do so. Licensor partners typically stipulate in advance that any improvement inventions are to be granted back, which effectively transfers ownership back to the licensor partner.[36] Meanwhile, the other JV partner may be dissatisfied that, although it also is contributing capital to the joint venture, the total return from the joint venture will effectively be shared inequitably due to free-riding on the joint venture's R&D investments. Such situations may also give rise to antitrust issues.

A second area in which conflicts often arise is material information related to transactions between a joint venture and one parent company. Such information includes, for example, the cost of products that the parent company sells to the joint venture and the terms of its sales to third parties. If, without disclosing such material information, a JV director leads the joint venture to engage in disadvantageous transactions with the parent company that appointed that director, the director would likely be chargeable with breach of fiduciary duty to the joint venture. However, if such information is a corporate secret of the parent company and the information's disclosure would be adverse to the parent company's interests, the director would not necessarily be duty bound to fully disclose the information. Partial disclosure of the information or even-handed use of the information without disclosure should suffice to ensure the joint venture is not subjected to disadvantageous transaction terms.[37]

AND MANAGEMENT (Joseph A. McCahery & Erik P. M. Vermeulen eds., forthcoming, available at: http://ssrn.com/abstract=2629019).

[36] On grant back, *see infra* Ch. 7. *See also* CYNTHIA CANNADY, TECHNOLOGY LICENSING AND DEVELOPMENT AGREEMENTS, 424 (3d ed. 2013); IAN HEWITT, HEWITT ON JOINT VENTURES, Ch. 17 (5th ed. 2011).

[37] Shishido, *supra* note 3, at 113–114.

A third category of information often giving rise to conflicts is information related to corporate opportunities. Such information includes JV partners' own plans and profit forecasts with respect to business opportunities where conflicting interests are at play. In most cases, such information will be a corporate secret, disclosure of which would be adverse to the JV partner's interests. Accordingly, directors appointed by that JV partner would likely be able to withhold or at least avoid full disclosure of the information.[38]

Meinhard v. Salmon,[39] a landmark case regarding the fiduciary duties of partners in a joint venture (albeit one organized as a partnership), highlights the subtleties of the duty to disclose information regarding corporate opportunities. The facts of the case are as follows. Two individuals formed a partnership to operate real property leased to one of the partners for 30 years. Profits were split equally between the partners. When the lease was nearing expiration, Partner A, the nominal lessee, renegotiated with the leased property's owner to renew the lease under modified terms and with modified subject matter, unbeknownst to partner B. Upon learning that a new lease had been signed, Partner B sued for a one-half interest in the leasehold. The New York Court of Appeals ruled in favor of Partner B by a 4:3 majority on the grounds that Partner A's actions constituted a breach of a fiduciary duty ("duty of finest loyalty"). The three dissenting justices issued a minority opinion arguing that because the partners had never discussed continuing the business beyond the initial lease's 30-year term and the new lease's subject matter differed substantively from the initial lease, (1) the new lease did not qualify as a business opportunity of the partnership, (2) Partner A did not breach his duty of loyalty to Partner B, and (3) Partner A had the right to appropriate the opportunity to himself.

Today, even when a joint venture is organized as a corporation or LLC, the joint venture agreement should expressly stipulate that the JV partners have the right to freely take advantage of business opportunities outside the scope of the joint venture's purpose.

Dealing with joint venture conflict problems related to information disclosure requires reconciliation of conflicting interests not only between the joint venture and the conflicted JV partner, but also between the JV partners. Because information that a JV partner discloses to a joint venture is typically disclosed to the other JV partner as well, a JV partner will open itself up to even greater detriment upon disclosing information

---

[38]   *Id.*, at 114–115.
[39]   249 N.Y. 458, 164 N.E. 545 (1928).

if the other JV partner is a competitor.[40] Another point to keep in mind is that when two JV partners are competitors, information disclosed to the joint venture by a partner may give rise to antitrust issues as well.[41]

2.2 RISKS OF PARTICIPATING IN A JOINT VENTURE

Given inter-partner conflicts such as those discussed above, each JV partner tends to be wary of the other's intentions. As long as they remain wary of each other, there will be hesitation to contribute the necessary monetary and human capital. To ensure success of a joint venture, prospective partners must negotiate in advance not only to eliminate their own concerns, but also to minimize the concerns of the other partner, thereby incentivizing both partners to contribute capital without reservation.

Four risks that often cause prospective partners to be wary of each other are discussed below. The discussion is limited to risks posed by future action by the other partner, not risks related to the success or failure of the joint venture's business.

2.2.1 Risk of Squeeze-out

A joint venture is by definition an arrangement where both partners are supposed to participate in management. However, if a minority partner contributes capital without some sort of contractual protection of its right to participate in management, it is at risk of being excluded from management (squeezed out) by the majority partner based on the majority rule principle of corporate law.

As noted above, JV partners often plan to transact business with the resulting joint venture from the outset. If a minority partner is squeezed out, it faces substantial risk that such pre-programmed transactions will be discontinued. Thus, the risk of a squeeze-out includes the risk of being deprived of return from transactions.[42] Consequently, companies that contribute capital to a joint venture as minority partners typically secure veto rights over material matters, either contractually or through the

---

[40]   Shishido, *supra* note 3, at 115–116.

[41]   *Id.*, at 117–120.

[42]   As used herein, "return from transactions" includes both return proportionate to the recipient's ownership interest that is treated as constructive dividends and disproportionate return obtained at the expense of the other partner. *See* infra Ch. 4, 4.1.2.1.

issuance of multiple classes of shares, in addition to the right to appoint directors in a proportion that is at least equal to their ownership interest.

2.2.2 Risk of Other Party Refusing to Renegotiate/Risk of Being Forced to Renegotiate to One's Own Detriment

If a minority partner's participation is essential, the majority partner will have to grant considerable veto power to the minority partner to lessen the risks inherent in the minority-partner status in order to incentivize the minority partner to contribute its capital. To completely eliminate both partners' risk of being squeezed out, JV partners often decide to share ownership equally. Equal ownership means that both partners possess absolute veto rights.

However, possession of veto rights by both partners means that no decisions are made unless both partners agree. While 50:50 ownership eliminates the risk of decisions being made against one partner's interests, it gives rise to the risk that the other partner will refuse to renegotiate when changed circumstances necessitate renegotiation. This, in turn, poses a risk of management deadlock, where renegotiations break down over a certain matter and decision-making paralysis ensues for the joint venture as a whole.

There is a trade-off between the risk of the other partner refusing to renegotiate, which stems from the difficulty of revising incomplete contracts,[43] and the risk of being forced to renegotiate to one's own detriment. In cooperative projects like joint ventures, the need to renegotiate in response to future changes in circumstances is foreseeable from the outset. Equally foreseeable is that when renegotiation occurs, the weaker partner in terms of bargaining power will likely be forced to agree to disadvantageous concessions. The prospect of such an outcome gives rise to the hold-up problem, where prospective JV partners are hesitant to make relationship-specific investments from the outset.[44]

2.2.3 Risk of Opportunistic Behavior by the Other Partner

A risk common to all JV partners is that the joint venture may prove fruitless because, while one partner fully contributes its human capital, the other partner intentionally withholds human capital beneficial to the joint venture. The nature of the human capital that is withheld and the

---

[43] On incomplete contracts, *see generally* PAUL MILGROM & JOHN ROBERTS, ECONOMICS, ORGANIZATION AND MANAGEMENT 129–140 (1992).

[44] On the hold-up problem, *see generally id.*, at 136–139.

nature of the losses incurred when the other partner behaves opportunistically differ depending on the nature of the joint venture's business.

In joint ventures, the key challenge tends to concern the provision of
human resources or the disclosure of technology/know-how to the joint
venture by the JV partners. In either case, the partners typically enter into
a very detailed agreement before establishing a joint venture, but the
ultimate outcome hinges on how committed each partner is to contributing human capital. When the other partner behaves opportunistically,
there is a high risk that the partner(s) that disclosed technology/know-
how to the joint venture will lose competitive advantage in the marketplace as a result of said disclosure. The likelihood of such a loss poses a
substantial risk of hold-up. If a joint venture's synergistic benefits do not
sufficiently outweigh these costs, the at-risk partner faces a classic
prisoner's dilemma.[45]

Joint ventures that are both unlikely to yield large synergistic benefits
and pose a high risk of a prisoner's dilemma scenario arguably should
never be undertaken in the first place, but the prisoner's dilemma can
sometimes be avoided by increasing the share of profits payable to the
partner that provides the more-important technology.[46] Alternatively, an
effective balance could be reached through a repeated-game approach,[47]
whereby the partners disclose information to each other incrementally.
However, this approach is not a universal solution, and will only work in
some, but not all, situations, depending on the type of business involved
as well as the business practices of each partner.

Moreover, in industries where companies repeatedly form joint ventures,[48] companies that engage in opportunistic behavior will incur a high
cost in the form of loss of trust and damaged reputation. When such a
reputational element is added to the aforementioned game approach, a
Pareto-optimal outcome becomes attainable in some cases. In joint
ventures, however, such reputational constraints are seldom operative.

---

[45]   The threat of exit is one means of dealing with the hold-up problem. *See*
Shishido, *supra* note 35.

[46]   *See* Shishido, *supra* note 1, at 84; Shishido, *supra* note 35.

[47]   On repeated game, *see* ROBERT GIBBONS, GAME THEORY FOR APPLIED
ECONOMISTS 82 (1992).

[48]   A good example is the pharmaceutical industry where bio venture companies and mega pharma companies have repeatedly created drug-development
joint ventures. *See infra* Ch. 14, 14.3.

2.2.4 Risk of the Other Partner Exiting/ Risk of Not Being Able to Exit Oneself

In a joint venture, the partner that needs the other partner more is exposed to the risk of the other partner exiting the joint venture. Conversely, threat of exit gives the other partner substantial bargaining leverage. This threat may distort the needier partner's incentive to contribute capital to the joint venture. One potential way to alleviate the risk of the other partner's untimely exit is to impose exit restrictions through such means as a contractual prohibition on stock transferability within a certain time frame. Another way to alleviate the needier partner's risk is for the other partner to make a sufficient commitment to the joint venture, such as a large relation-specific investment that will yield return based solely on pre-programmed trade with the joint venture.

However, use of exit restrictions to alleviate this risk of exit gives rise to a trade-off between the risk of the other party exiting and the risk of not being able to exit. It is important to strike an appropriate balance between these two risks because there is a possibility that a prospective partner possessing resources indispensable to the joint venture will be hesitant to make a relation-specific investment in the joint venture.

2.3 METHODS OF MOTIVATING PARTNERS TO PROVIDE CAPITAL TO ONE ANOTHER

Companies seeking to participate in joint ventures aim to maximize the total return (synergies)[49] that they respectively derive from the joint venture. Synergistic-driven joint ventures inevitably entail conflicts between partners. Given such conflicting interests, prospective JV partners are wary of relation-specific investments. Accordingly, to maximize synergies for both partners, prospective JV partners must negotiate joint venture agreements that reduce their own risk enough to enable them to contribute capital to the joint venture. At the same time, they must also offer the other partner incentives to contribute both monetary and human capital; JV partners consequently engage in incentive bargaining with each other.

Incentive bargaining concerns the sharing of management control and total return. Bargaining over sharing control of a joint venture specifically addresses (1) how ownership, directorships, and veto rights will be

---

[49]   In this book, "synergies" refers to total return for each JV partner realized by participating in a joint venture. *See infra* Ch. 6, 6.1.

shared, (2) the partners' respective rights to information disclosure, and (3) exit rights.

In bargaining over sharing total return, issues that are particularly important in the context of joint ventures are (1) reconciliation of imbalances between the share of human capital contributions and the share of return on investment,[50] (2) allocation of cash flows between dividend distributions and retained earnings, (3) exit conditions, and (4) valuation of an existing partner's ownership interest.

Although exit conditions fall within the purview of both bargaining over sharing control and bargaining over sharing total return, the issue of bargaining over exit conditions will be discussed in detail in Chapter 5 because it is an especially significant aspect of incentive bargaining in a joint venture.

---

[50] *See supra* note 12.

3.   Bargaining over sharing control

For both publicly traded companies and venture companies, the biggest issue related to bargaining over how to share control is the balance between the monetary capital providers' monitoring rights and the human capital providers' autonomy with respect to the use of funds.[1] In joint ventures, however, the monetary capital providers and human capital providers are identical because all JV partners contribute both monetary and human capital. Consequently, in joint ventures in which all partners participate in management, all partners want a combination of managerial autonomy as human capital providers and monitoring rights as monetary capital providers.[2]

3.1 BARGAINING OVER VOTING RIGHTS

The first step in negotiating a joint venture agreement is deciding how to share equity control (partners' ownership percentages). In a joint venture between two parties, each partner has three options for dividing up control. First, the partner can assume majority control of the joint venture. Second, the partner can allow the other partner to have majority control and settle for minority shareholder status for itself. Third, the partner can share control equally with the other partner. The option chosen will largely determine the future course of the joint venture.[3]

---

[1]   *See* ZENICHI SHISHIDO, DOKIZUKE NO SHIKUMI TOSHITENO KIGYO: INSENTHIBU SHISUTEMU NO HOSEIDO RON [THE FIRM AS AN INCENTIVE MECHANISM: THE ROLE OF LEGAL INSTITUTIONS] 99–102, 181–188 (2006).

[2]   However, a JV partner that is a non-managing partner that does not contribute much human capital would want monitoring rights as a monetary capital provider.

[3]   *See* Zenichi Shishido, *The Strategy behind the Organizational Game: A Comparison between the Joint Venture and the Venture Capital Investment Negotiation, in* STRATEGIC ALLIANCES AND JOINT VENTURES: LAW, ECONOMICS AND MANAGEMENT (Joseph A. McCahery & Erik P. M. Vermeulen eds., forthcoming, available at: http://ssrn.com/abstract=2629019).

If one partner has majority control and a management disagreement arises between the partners, the controlling partner has the power under corporate law to impose its will by excluding (squeezing out) the other partner from management. Likewise, if a company is a minority shareholder in a joint venture, it is at risk of being squeezed out. In contrast, if the two partners share control equally, neither needs to worry about being squeezed out. Instead of the risk of a squeeze-out, each partner faces a higher risk of a management deadlock where the other partner refuses to renegotiate on the joint venture.[4]

In any case, prospective JV partners must create an environment in which each partner can confidently contribute capital by minimizing concerns that cause the other partner to hesitate to contribute capital.

The optimal control-sharing arrangement for a joint venture can be determined by identifying which partner possesses the human capital most crucial for operating the joint venture. This is because a partner possessing human capital indispensable to the joint venture must be given a strong incentive to contribute that human capital.[5] A financially weaker partner may therefore be able to negotiate a 50/50 joint venture if it possesses irreplaceable human capital (e.g., indispensable management resources).

Additionally, management control and payoffs need not be shared in equal proportion. For example, a partner that contributes the more important human capital may have equal voting rights but receive a majority share of distributions of dividends and residual assets. To establish this kind of disproportional sharing arrangement under corporate law, the partners could set up the joint venture as a corporation with nonvoting stock or multiple classes of stock, or as a limited liability company.[6]

Furthermore, control rights need not be shared in a way that mimics the proportion to partners' ownership percentages. One partner can be granted complete control of a portion of the joint venture's operations. For example, one partner may operate and have sole decision-making authority over the joint venture's product development and production

---

[4]   *See* Shishido, *supra* note 1, at 78.

[5]   *See id.*, at 84. If partners share payoffs in proportion to their ownership percentages, a partner's return on investment would increase in proportion to any increase in the partner's ownership interest, but the sum total of the three types of payoff is not necessarily proportional to a partner's ownership interest. Accordingly, partners can be incentivized to contribute key human capital by receiving return from programmed trade that is not limited by ownership percentages.

[6]   *See* IAN HEWITT, HEWITT ON JOINT VENTURES Ch. 8-16 (5th ed. 2011).

functions. Such an arrangement can be legally achieved by stipulating basic rules (e.g., the business operations assigned to each partner) in the joint venture agreement and stipulating specific rights and obligations in separate (e.g., R&D outsourcing) agreements between the joint venture and individual partners. Additionally, each partner can strengthen its influence over the joint venture's management through indirect means such as involvement in key personnel appointment/dismissal decisions and establishing reporting lines from the joint venture to its parent companies.[7]

3.2 BARGAINING OVER COMPOSITION OF THE BOARD OF DIRECTORS AND MANAGEMENT APPOINTMENTS

In joint ventures, the principle of the majority-shareholder rule is almost invariably modified to alleviate the minority partner's concerns about being squeezed out.

First, seats on a joint venture's board of directors are typically allocated between partners in approximate proportion to their respective ownership percentages in a manner analogous to proportional representation in politics.[8] If the joint venture has issued only common stock, the method of allocating directorships may be stipulated in an agreement between the shareholders. However, such contractual provisions may prove difficult to enforce when a dispute arises between the shareholders. Other methods for allocating directorships include issuing different classes of stock and utilizing class voting. These approaches are enforceable under corporate law so long as the joint venture's articles of incorporation dictate that an election for the board of directors shall take place at each shareholder class meeting.

In addition to giving the minority partner a certain number of seats on the board, other safeguards to ensure a minority partner's rights to participate in management include: (1) ensuring that the minority shareholder's appointed directors are necessary to meet the quorum requirement for board meetings, (2) granting the minority partner the right to veto decisions by the board of directors to delegate their authority to

---

[7] On indirect control and operational influence, *See id.*, at Ch. 8-17.

[8] *See id.*, at Ch. 8-18. In joint ventures, unlike venture capital agreements, minority partners are as a general rule never allocated a majority of seats on the board of directors (and vice versa) due to the nature of joint businesses. *See* Shishido, *supra* note 1, at 88.

specific corporate officers, (3) requiring advance notice of matters to be discussed at board meetings, (4) granting the minority partner a right of advance approval of board meeting agenda items, and/or (5) prohibiting board resolutions on matters not on the agenda.[9]

The partner responsible for managing the joint venture on a day-to-day basis is determined by which partner has the right to appoint the joint venture's CEO. However, the other partner may bargain to gain the right to veto specific management directives or to be consulted before management decisions are made.[10]

3.3 BARGAINING OVER SHARING OF VETO RIGHTS

Another important modification of the principle of the majority-shareholder rule in joint ventures is the sharing of veto rights. Because both partners maintain veto rights in a 50/50 joint venture, the veto is more of an issue in joint ventures that involve a minority partner. Even in 50/50 joint ventures, both partners' consent is generally required to pass a resolution on a matter subject to veto rights at both the shareholder general meeting and board of directors' levels to mitigate the risk of important matters being decided without both partners' representatives in attendance.[11]

3.3.1 Matters Subject to Veto Rights

In addition to fundamental changes to a JV company (e.g., merger, dissolution, divestment of business operations, revision of articles of incorporation), matters often subject to veto rights include decisions related to expansion of the previously agreed-upon scope of the joint venture's operations and changes in partners' ownership percentages in conjunction with additional investments, such as equity capital contributions or large loans.[12]

---

[9]   *See* Hewitt, *supra* note 6, at Ch. 9-09.
[10] *See id.*, at Ch. 8-36.
[11] *See id.*, at Ch. 9-11.
[12] *See id.*, at Ch. 9-10. For examples of cases in which partners should secure veto rights, *see id.*, at Ch. 8-31. Stock transferability restrictions are one type of veto right. Membership restrictions that restrict third parties from participating in a joint venture sometimes may be in violation of antitrust law as a form of competition-restrictive agreement, but the necessity of assuming such a risk is often justified as rational.

Other matters sometimes subject to veto rights include the execution of material agreements regarding disbursements of funds by the joint venture (with materiality determined based on the amount of the disbursement or the technology involved), political contributions, and any execution or revision of an agreement between the JV company and an individual partner that may pose a conflict of interest.

3.3.2 Risk of Deadlock

The allocation of veto rights between partners is ultimately determined by the minority partner's bargaining power, but granting excessive veto rights increases the risk of a management deadlock and distorts incentive of the majority partner. Problems arise when a minority partner is granted veto rights over matters that preclude maintenance of the status quo, such as the appointment of directors or approval of financial statements.

From a motivational standpoint, it is also in the best interests of the minority partner to retain minimal veto rights after ceding day-to-day management control to the majority partner, letting the majority partner make decisions on all matters not subject to veto rights. The minority partner's bargaining power with respect to monitoring the majority partner depends on the magnitude of the threat of exit by the minority partner. Additionally, granting veto rights over a larger number of matters limits the JV management team's autonomy and poses a risk of lowering managerial efficiency by distorting incentive of the management team.[13]

One conceivable approach to balancing minority partner veto rights is to grant the majority partner a call option to buy out the minority partner if the minority partner exercises its veto rights more frequently than had been agreed upon in advance. Another approach is to grant the minority partner a put option in exchange for agreeing to accept relatively weak veto rights.[14] However, the first approach creates the risk of the majority partner using its call option to squeeze out the minority partner by repeatedly scheduling votes on, for example, resolutions to increase the joint venture's equity capital.

3.3.3 Methods of Gaining Veto Rights

A JV partner's veto rights over specific matters are initially granted by the shareholders' agreement. For matters that are within the purview of the articles of incorporation, veto right provisions identical to those in the

---

[13] *See id.*, at Ch. 8-30.
[14] *See id.*, at Ch. 9-12.

shareholders' agreement are included in the articles of incorporation. When the joint venture has issued only common stock, the enforceability of shareholders' agreements becomes questionable in relation to matters not included in the articles of incorporation. Shareholders' agreements are enforceable under corporate law if a joint venture issues classified stock with veto rights and stipulates the matters subject to shareholder approval at shareholder class meetings in its articles of incorporation.

Matters subject to veto rights may require shareholder approval or may be subject to approval by the joint venture's board of directors through special resolution.[15] Matters involving management of the joint venture generally fall into the latter category. Shareholder approval is often required for matters relating to: (1) the joint venture's equity ownership structure, (2) changes in the joint venture's purpose, and (3) long-term investment plans.[16]

3.4 BARGAINING OVER RIGHTS TO INFORMATION DISCLOSURE

Even in 50/50 joint ventures it is rare for partners to share management responsibilities equally, let alone in joint ventures with majority and minority partners. Typically, one of the partners takes charge of managing the joint venture. If this is the case, the right to demand disclosure of information is essential for the non-managing partner to monitor the managing partner.

Among the non-managing partner's disclosure-related rights, the most important is the right to attend meetings of the board of directors. In addition to securing seats on the board, the non-managing partner also has the power to exercise a veto, by requiring the presence of a director appointed by the non-managing partner as a requirement of a quorum or resolution, or by requiring pre-agreement from the managing partner on agenda items subject to resolution by the board. Additionally, the

---

[15]   With respect to veto rights, even if one partner has more seats on the board of directors than the other partner, if the board meeting quorum and number of votes required to pass board resolutions are set at the equivalent of the majority partner's total number of board seats (e.g., five) plus one (six in total), the other partner would be able to ensure its veto right if only one of its directors attended board meetings and voted against any resolutions to which the partner is opposed. In practice, resolutions at joint ventures' board meetings are usually approved or rejected unanimously.

[16]   *See id.*, at Ch. 8-32.

frequency of board meetings and other governance structures to monitor the joint venture operations are important. Having the right to appoint the CFO and/or accounting officer (i.e.,treasurer or corporate controller) is another effective monitoring method. Partners may also choose to dispatch a team to audit the joint venture or appoint an external accounting auditor to permanently oversee the joint venture.

Regarding the content and frequency of periodic disclosures, in addition to disclosure of statutory financial statements and the minority partner's unconditional rights to visitation and on-site inspection of the joint venture's books, the majority partner and/or joint venture should be charged with the duty to periodically report to the minority partner. A minority partner should also provide the right to demand disclosure of information in the shareholder agreement and/or in the articles of incorporation.[17]

Finally, the joint venture agreement should explicitly provide that a director may disclose information about the joint venture to the partner that gave them the position. Otherwise, directors could be accused of violating their duty of confidentiality.[18]

3.5 BARGAINING OVER EXIT RIGHTS

The right to exit is related to both sharing of control and sharing of payoffs.[19] In terms of sharing control, the threat of exit is sometimes more important than ownership percentages or the composition of the board. If the minority partner's human capital (including technology and know-how) is to the joint venture and cannot be substituted, that minority partner will have a great amount of bargaining leverage over the other partner. Further, there is no need for such a minority party to worry about being squeezed out because the joint venture itself would not be viable in the absence of the partner company. In this case, the threat of exit will exist even without a contractual right to exit. Even the threat of refusing to cooperate (e.g., refusing to contribute human capital) constitutes a dire threat to the joint venture's continued existence.[20]

---

[17] *See id.*, at Ch. 9-22.
[18] *See id.*, at Ch. 9-22.
[19] *See* Shishido, *supra* note 1, at 68.
[20] However, there is no assurance that indispensable human capital will retain its competitive advantage forever. The other partner may completely master the requisite technology/know-how or a new substitute technology may be developed. From this perspective, it is important to secure a right of exit in the form of withdrawal of financial capital.

Effective strategies for maintaining a meaningful threat of exit include licensing intellectual property to the joint venture instead of transferring, or structuring the joint venture so that it is dependent on the continuous provision of human capital. Conversely, for partners that do not possess indispensable human capital, retaining a contractual right to withdraw financial capital is extremely important from the standpoint of sharing control. Even if a partner cannot meaningfully threaten to withdraw human capital, the threat of withdrawing monetary capital plays a counterbalancing role.

4. Bargaining over sharing total return

4.1 THREE TYPES OF RETURN

The purpose of bargaining over sharing total return is to maximize synergies realized by each JV partner. Such synergies include three types of return: return on investment, return from transactions, and ancillary return. Whichever form the return from a joint venture takes, the joint venture is a success if the sum total of the three types of return is maximized for each partner and exceeds initially planned return. Bargaining over sharing of total return is the process of setting rules for sharing the three types of return between partners.

In bargaining over sharing total return, partners first determine return on investment. Return on investment takes the form of profits derived from the joint venture and is shared in proportion to the partners' respective ownership percentages. As such, it is generally not susceptible to disagreements during incentive bargaining.[1] Partners can determine return on investment through a comparative analysis of the possible courses of action: (1) unilateral market entry, (2) market entry through a joint venture, and (3) forgoing market entry completely. Next, they should design an incentive framework and utilize return from transactions to rectify any imbalances.[2] Lastly, individual partners should identify opportunities for capturing private gains, or ancillary return, from participation in the joint venture. If they follow this process, they should be able to rationally justify their decision to establish a joint venture to their shareholders and stakeholders (e.g., creditors, suppliers). As part of this process, the partners should make sure that they quantify synergies net of the transaction costs associated with forming the joint venture.

---

[1] *See* IAN HEWITT, HEWITT ON JOINT VENTURES, at Ch. 7-13–14 (5th ed. 2011).
[2] On imbalances, *see* Ch. 2, 2.1.

4.2 RETURN ON INVESTMENT

4.2.1 Definition of Return on Investment

Return on investment refers to the sum total of dividends and capital gains that shareholders receive based on their respective ownership percentages in a JV company. As a general rule, return on investment is shared in proportion to the partners' ownership percentages.[3]

4.2.2 Bargaining over Sharing Return on Investment

To increase return on investment, JV partners must "maximize the size of the pie" by increasing the joint venture's net present value. Inter-partner bargaining over return on investment is a non-zero-sum game.

In bargaining over sharing return on investment, it is important to first agree on how to allocate the cash flows that factor into return on investment. Some JV partners place priority on long-term growth in enterprise value fueled by internal retention and reinvestment of profits. Others place priority on short-term cash dividends to recoup their investment in the joint venture as early as possible.

Such different priorities give rise to conflicting interests between partners. Joint venture agreements or business plans appurtenant thereto often include provisions on dividend policies (e.g., dividend payout ratio), compulsory accumulation of capital reserves, and other restrictions on the use of profits (e.g., internal retention of profits within the joint venture through dividend limits, investments in designated objectives, prioritized repayment of borrowings). Dividend policies should be reviewed in light of the joint venture's profitability and are subject to renegotiation.[4]

Second, once ownership percentages (partners' shares of return on investment) have been set, they are difficult to change. This difficulty is due to restrictions in corporate law and joint venture agreements that lock in the JV partners and maintain constant ownership percentages, such as

---

[3] Under both Japanese and US corporate law, returns on investment can also be shared disproportionately to percentage ownership interests. In Japan, for example, the Companies Act grants flexibility in sharing returns among partners when different classes of shares are used (Article 108) or when a joint venture is organized as an LLC (Articles 575–675). However, sharing returns in disproportion to ownership percentages can raise tax issues.

[4] *See* Hewitt, *supra* note 1, at Ch. 9-20.

stock transferability restrictions and pre-emptive rights granted to share-holders. If a joint venture is organized as a stock corporation, its owners cannot get their equity capital contributions back until the joint venture is dissolved.

A key concern for JV partners is whether the other partner(s) will contribute resources necessary for the joint venture's growth once it is up and running. One way to incentivize the other partner to provide human capital indispensable to the joint venture is to grant the other partner a share of profits in excess of its ownership percentage. Methods of doing so include issuing dividend-paying preferred stock and organizing the joint venture as an LLC. When joint ventures are organized as a stock corporation, however, the partners' respective shares of return on invest-ment tend to equal their respective ownership percentages. In such cases, a more practical way to incentivize the other partner by disproportion-ately sharing total return is to adjust the other partner's share of return from transactions instead of its return on investment.

In establishing a joint venture, partners draft joint venture agreements that include provisions on their rights and duties to contribute additional monetary capital. In some cases, however, one partner lacks the where-withal to contribute additional capital.[5] Partners are typically granted the right to veto capital increases,[6] but the risk of missing out on business opportunities is difficult to avert.

Unless a joint venture is a publicly traded company, JV partners have limited means of recouping their invested capital because their joint venture's stock is not salable in a public equity market. The ultimate means by which a partner can realize its share of return on investment is to sell its ownership interest to the other partner or a third party through a bilateral transaction or, if the joint venture is dissolved and liquidated, to collect its share of the residual assets distributed to shareholders after all creditors have been paid off in full. The ways in which partners may exit a joint venture and valuation of their ownership interests are issues related to exit bargaining, discussed in Chapter 5.

---

[5] In the case of venture capital investment, contractual provisions are drafted on the assumption that ownership percentages will change with each successive growth round. With joint ventures, however, ownership percentages are generally assumed to remain constant.

[6] *See* Hewitt, *supra* note 1, at Ch. 9-10; Ch. 9-16.

4.3 RETURN FROM TRANSACTIONS

4.3.1 Definition of Return from Transactions

Return from transactions is contractual return that a partner directly receives from goods, services, and/or rights transactions between itself and the joint venture. Transactions between joint ventures and their parent companies are generally planned before the joint venture is established. Return that a JV partner earns from such transactions is separate from and additional to return on investment. Transaction contracts between joint ventures and their parent companies are an important determinant of the viability of the joint venture's business model and the partners' total return.[7] Return from transactions is return available to partners by virtue of their participation in a joint venture. They are an incentivizing tool and subject to both contractual bargaining and monitoring.

If a joint venture requires non-substitutable management resources possessed by one of its parent companies, operation of the joint venture's business as originally planned is contingent on the parent company providing those resources to the joint venture. Conversely, if management resources required by a joint venture are highly substitutable, the joint venture can procure equivalent goods or services from a third party in the marketplace instead of from its parent companies.

If a joint venture and one of its parent companies conduct transactions on arm's-length terms (with respect to, e.g., price, quantity, time frame), both the cost to the joint venture and the profit earned by the parent company will be the same as if the transactions had been conducted with a third party instead of between related parties.[8]

Nonetheless, the ability to stably conduct transactions within the same group, even on arm's-length terms, is beneficial to the transacting partner. Also note that, as used herein, return from transactions does not mean a transfer of the joint venture's property to one JV partner at the expense of the other partner(s) through transactions more advantageous to the transacting partner than an arm's-length transaction.

---

[7] *See id.*, at Ch. 6.

[8] In effect, the company does not incur any detriment as a result of transactions that generate such returns, but the transactions formally meet the criteria for self-dealing transactions and therefore require both JV partners' consent and are subject to monitoring by the partners as to whether they are necessary, their terms are customary, and they are priced at arm's length.

Finally, if a joint venture is operated as a cost-center, the JV partners will generally seek to earn return from transactions instead of return in the form of dividend distributions.[9]

4.3.2   Considerations in Structuring Return from Transactions

When structuring return from transactions, JV partners should take the following into consideration:

(i)   division of their roles and responsibilities within the joint venture (e.g., identify synergies realizable through mutually complementary competitive advantages, such as division of production/development and marketing functions between the partners);

(ii)   business model and its legal structure (compare with other available legal means to achieve the same economic objectives and decide, for example, between earning a 3 percent royalty on products manufactured and sold by the joint venture or a 5 percent operating margin on products manufactured by the partners themselves and sold to the joint venture);

(iii) economic advantages and disadvantages of related-party transactions in comparison to third-party transactions;

(iv)   the need for exclusive rights (e.g., exclusive distribution rights, exclusive drawing rights); and

(v)   determination of transaction consideration such as goods prices, service fees, and intellectual property licensing royalties[10] (e.g., decide on a fixed-markup cost-plus pricing formula for goods). In the course of a joint venture's actual operations, even formally arm's-length transactions sometimes end up distributing return from transactions to one JV partner. Partners therefore typically have the right to approve material transactions between the joint venture and the other partner, as well as the terms thereof.

4.3.3   Pro rata Self-Dealing Transactions

Transactions from which JV partners derive return could be pro rata self-dealing transactions or non-pro rata self-dealing transactions, the

---

[9] In joint ventures treated as a cost-center, product sales prices (or service fees) charged by the joint venture to its parent companies are typically set by a cost-plus formula, whereby the joint venture earns a fixed markup on the sum of its raw material and processing costs. On cost-center joint venture, *see* Ch. 11.

[10] *See* Hewitt *supra* note 1, at Ch. 6-38; Ch. 6-39.

latter of which aim to rectify imbalances. Return from pro rata self-dealing transactions is distributed to partners in proportion to their respective ownership percentages. To the extent possible, partners should conduct transactions with their joint ventures on a pro rata basis to ensure that they receive their fair share of return in relation to the other partner(s).

If both partners contribute non-substitutable management resources essential to realization of mutual synergies and they elect to individually enter into transaction agreements with the joint venture as a means of contributing such resources, the transactions are specific to the joint venture and therefore not substitutable with third-party contractual arrangements. When both partners engage in this type of transaction with their joint venture, return from the transactions is generally shared on a pro rata basis to equitably share total return relative to the partners' respective total contributions of both monetary and human capital.

Pro rata self-dealing transactions are a method of distributing de facto return to partners based on an agreement by the partners entered into before the joint venture's operating profitability is known for certain. Such transactions therefore pose a risk of creating inequities among partners if, for example, actual transaction volumes differ from forecasted volumes. Another potential concern is that return from pro rata self-dealing transactions is essentially equivalent to hidden dividends if the transactions' pricing inordinately detracts from the joint venture's profits. In such cases, return from pro rata self-dealing transactions is at risk of being taxed as a gift or gratuity or subject to transfer pricing taxation.[11]

The classic case in which pro rata self-dealing transactions succeed is where a joint venture and its parent companies have a vertical relationship with each other within a product value chain and the joint venture is able to transact equally with all of its parent companies. One hypothetical example is a 50:50 joint venture that manufactures and supplies equal quantities of a product to both of its parent companies at the same price and on the same schedule. In practice, however, pro rata self-dealing transactions are difficult to realize because of variability of prices or sales volumes caused by factors such as market changes or intensification of competition. Thus, the failure to effect a pro rata self-dealing transaction is often caused by an unintentional distribution to one JV partner of a disproportionately large share of return from transactions.

---

[11] For example, transactions in which both JV partners earn management service fees in proportion to their ownership percentages in exchange for management know-how provided to the joint venture pose relatively high taxation risk despite being pro-rata self-dealing transactions.

4.3.4   Return from Non-Pro rata Self-Dealing Transactions

The second type of return from transactions is not proportional to JV partners' ownership percentages. Only the partner that engages in the transaction, subject to the consent of the other partner(s), is entitled to such non-pro rata return from the joint venture.[12]

Because JV partners' shares of contributed human capital never coincide with their ownership percentages, sharing of total return in proportion to ownership percentages results in an inequitable division of total return between partners.[13] Imbalances arise between partners' human capital contributions and their ownership stakes in the joint venture as a result of each partner providing different human capital in accord with the joint venture's objective of pooling management resources to compensate for each individual partner's resource deficiencies.

If not rectified, such imbalances act as a disincentive against human capital contributions by the disadvantaged partner. The partner with the most human capital to contribute must be incentivized to contribute its resources by being entitled to earn total return in proportion to its outsized capital contribution. For example, a JV partner that contributes human capital in the form of a patent licensed to the joint venture typically receives royalties plus all profits from the grant-back of any invention patent granted to the joint venture that is directly related to the licensed technology. In comparison to return earned by its co-partner(s), the licensor partner exclusively earns the return attributable to the human capital it contributed in disproportion to its ownership interest. The terms of such transactions are freely negotiable between the partners in theory. In actuality, however, they are constrained by tax law. Transaction terms consequently must be set within an arm's-length price range.

To the extent that one partner receives a larger share of return from transactions than the other partner(s), total return from the joint venture is shared unequally, as are opportunities to benefit from joint venture synergies. Accordingly, if only one partner conducts transactions with the joint venture, it must first obtain the consent of the other partner, even if the transactions are made at arm's length. The other partner must bargain from the standpoint of total benefits (i.e., including other types of return) to realize a share of total return proportionate to their shares of

---

[12]   If one JV partner and a joint venture engage in transactions that increase the joint venture's assets as a result of the partner agreeing to transaction terms disadvantageous to itself, the transactions would have the character of an additional equity capital contribution by the partner to nurture the joint venture.

[13]   *See supra* Ch. 2, 2.1. *See* also Hewitt, *supra* note 1, Ch. 2-36.

contributed monetary and human capital. Doing so requires complex business planning regarding rules for sharing prospective unrealized return.

4.3.5 Specific Examples of Return from Transactions

Methods of realizing return from transactions include transfers of monetary consideration from the joint venture to partners in the form of markups (transfer price minus cost of goods sold) in goods supply contracts, royalties based on intellectual property licensing agreements,[14] service fees in outsourcing agreements related to the provision of services (e.g., manufacturing, sales, administrative) to the joint venture,[15] interest payable on loans,[16] rent payable on leased real estate, remuneration of officers appointed to the joint venture by partners, and management fees.[17]

4.3.6 Monitoring

In terms of sharing return from transactions, JV partners may evade the other partner's oversight and engage in opportunistic behavior with the aim of earning more than their agreed-upon share of total return (i.e., capturing return from transactions to which they are not rightfully entitled). To prevent such opportunism, a partner should monitor the other partner's transactions with the joint venture and must be able to exercise veto rights. In the particular case of transactions intended to rectify imbalances, a partner must monitor transaction agreements between the other partner and the joint venture and sharing of return from transactions.

However, when conducting transactions with the joint venture, one partner may deal with a director that it appointed to the joint venture and conceal the nature of the transactions from the other partner(s). A formal resolution by the joint venture's board of directors consequently may not

---

[14]   *See* Hewitt *supra* note 1, at Ch. 17.

[15]   *See id*, at Ch. 6-42.

[16]   *See id*, at Ch. 7-20.

[17]   On Management Agreements, *see id.*, at Ch. 6-36. For example, in cases in which a joint venture is managed by personnel assigned to the joint venture by its parent companies, the joint venture is sometimes charged management fees calculated by each parent company as the personnel's compensation for full-time employment (including a cost-plus markup) multiplied by the percentage of time the personnel spend working at the joint venture.

be an effective monitoring mechanism. It is therefore important for a partner to impose a duty of advance notification on the joint venture and secure a right to information disclosure and right of prior approval of the joint venture's material transactions with the other partner.

Key points that a partner should look into when monitoring the other partner for opportunistic or duplicitous behavior with respect to return from transactions include the following:

(i)   Are the transactions reasonably necessary for the joint venture? For example, is the joint venture paying the other partner royalties derived from an unneeded patent on an obsolete technology?

(ii) Is any partner engaging in surreptitious self-dealing transactions not sanctioned by the joint venture's board of directors?

(iii) Is the joint venture fulfilling its notification duties to the partners? Is information being adequately provided to the joint venture's board of directors?

(iv) Is any partner in breach of contract? For example, is any partner appropriating an unduly large share of resources to itself in violation of a pro rata sharing agreement or, in the case of a cost-plus pricing agreement, improperly manipulating costs while ostensibly abiding by the agreed-upon markup?

(v)   Is pricing reasonable and economically rational?

4.3.7 Stakeholder and Tax Issues Related to Return from Transactions

Sharing return from transactions to rectify imbalances entails a number of risks, including (1) the risk of self-dealing,[18] (2) taxation risks,[19] and (3) the risk of antitrust violations.[20] Figure 4.1 shows the web of

---

[18] On conflicts of interest, *see id.*, at Ch. 6-13; Ch. 8-57; Ch. 8-60.

[19] *See id.*, at Ch. 15.

[20] *See id*, at Ch. 16. Federal Trade Commission and U.S. Department of Justice, *Antitrust Guidelines for Collaborations among Competitors* (April, 2000) www.ftc.gov/os/2000/04/ ftcdojguidelines.pdf; *Horizontal Merger Guidelines* (August, 2010) www.justice.gov/ atr/public/guidelines/hmg-2010.pdf. *See* Section 1 of the US Sherman Act (prohibition against contracts, combinations and conspiracies in restraint of trade or commerce) and Article 101 of the Treaty on the Functioning of the European Union (prohibition against agreements and concerted practices restrictive of competition). If a joint venture is a full-function joint venture possessing all functions of an autonomous business entity on a long-term basis, the EU Merger Regulation and Horizontal Merger Guideline

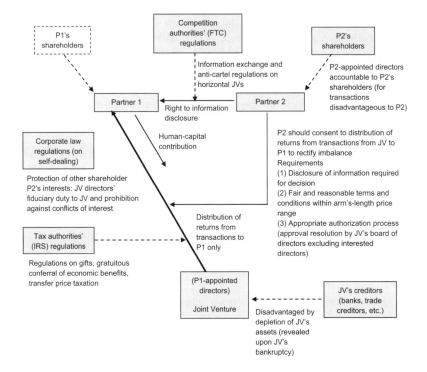

Figure 4.1   Correlation diagram among stakeholders

stakeholders with an interest in how return from joint venture trans-actions are shared.

Taxation risk is an important consideration with respect to return from transactions. When JV partners structure return from transactions, they need to look at after-tax cash flows and consider the tax treatment of and foreign tax credits for purchases and sales of goods, provision of services (service fees), dividend income from overseas subsidiaries, interest, tangible asset usage fees (e.g., rent), and intangible asset licensing fees (e.g., royalties) to ensure that the transactions do not run afoul of tax laws.

When JV partners assess international taxation risks, it is important for them to identify: (1) the party or parties obligated to pay taxes; (2) the country or countries to which taxes are payable; (3) the transactions

would apply to the joint venture if it constitutes a "concentration." *See* Commission notice on the concept of full-function joint ventures under Council Regulation (EEC) No. 4064/89 on the control of concentrations between undertakings, OJ C66, 02.03.1998, p. 1.

subject to taxation (including the identity of party or parties that recognize profit/loss, the benefit and consideration, the functions/roles fulfilled by parties to the transactions, the identity of party or parties that bear the risk of expenses exceeding revenues, and relevant contracts and their implementation status); and (4) the various types of applicable taxes and taxable events (taxability of income, deductibility of expenses/losses, tax withholding related to incoming and outgoing funds).

The following are examples of Japanese tax law provisions pertaining to joint ventures that transfer income to their parent companies through such means as transactions of goods, dividends, and interest payments. First, when a joint venture formed as a subsidiary in Japan receives funding from its foreign parent company, it may be subject to an undercapitalization tax that eliminates deductions for interest payable on "excessive debt."[21] The undercapitalization tax aims to prevent a foreign company from reducing the tax burden of its subsidiaries, including joint ventures, by thinly capitalizing them and increasing their dependence on debt financing from the majority parent company. A second such provision eliminates deductions for interest payments on a joint venture's excess interest expense when the joint venture's majority parent company earns "above-market profits" by charging a higher-than arm's-length interest rate on its loans to the joint venture.[22] The excess interest tax is intended to prevent tax avoidance through related-party interest payments that are excessive relative to income.

Regarding cases where parent companies transfer income to joint ventures, Japan has adopted an anti-tax haven rule (unitary taxation of foreign subsidiaries), which applies to income transfers from parent companies to their joint ventures.[23] Under this rule, if profits earned from a joint venture are retained by a special-purpose corporation (SPC) domiciled in a tax haven for the purpose of tax avoidance by a joint venture's majority parent company, those profits are taxable to the Japanese parent company.

Transfers of income between a joint venture and one of its parent companies have special tax implications in three scenarios regardless of the direction of the transfer. First, in the case of a gratuitous transaction between a joint venture and one of its parents, the economic benefit

---

[21] On Thin Capitalization Rule, *see* www.mof.go.jp/tax_policy/summary/international/180.htm.

[22] On Japanese Earnings Stripping Rules, *see* www.nta.go.jp/shiraberu/ippanjoho/pamph/hojin/kaisei_gaiyo2012_5/pdf/c.pdf.

[23] On Anti-Tax Haven (Controlled Foreign Company) Rules, *see* www.mof.go.jp/pri/publication/financial_review/fr_list5/r94/r94_074_096.pdf.

gratuitously transferred is treated as a gift and the donor is prohibited from deducting expenses (e.g., usage fees) related to the benefit (Corporation Tax Act, Article 37). Second, when assets are gratuitously transferred, their fair value is taxed as income to the recipient in the fiscal year of the transfer (Corporation Tax Act, Article 22(2)). Third, if a joint venture and its majority parent company are foreign related parties, the difference between arm's-length prices and actual-transaction prices are subject to transfer price taxation if the transactions are a reciprocal exchange of value. If, for example, a joint venture is prohibited from deducting a portion of expenditures paid to an overseas parent company (that is, revenues are taxable but expenses are not fully deductible), it may face a huge tax bill. It would also be subject to de facto double taxation to the extent that its taxes are not refundable under a bilateral tax treaty.[24]

4.4 ANCILLARY RETURN

4.4.1 Definition of Ancillary Return

Ancillary return is return specific to an individual JV partner. It is neither return on investment nor return from transactions. Rather, it includes the other benefits that accrue to a partner by virtue of its participation in the joint venture.

Ancillary return belongs directly to the recipient partner. It generally does not require the consent of or need be shared with the other partner. Because a partner has no specific claim on the other partner's ancillary return and directly incurs no loss as a result thereof, ancillary return is not subject to the other partner monitoring. Ancillary return typically takes the form of joint venture synergies that are difficult to value in monetary terms. They arise from business combinations that are greater than the sum of their parts.

---

[24] *See*   www.nta.go.jp/shiraberu/zeiho-kaishaku/jimu-unei/hojin/010601/00. htm. Regarding artificially low-priced transfers, *see* Japan Supreme Court Third Petty Bench judgment of December 19, 1995, at *Minshu* Vol. 49 No.10: 3121. For an example of a case in which use of foreign tax credits was found not to be abusive (tax evasion), *see* Japan Supreme Court Second Petty Bench judgment of December 19, 2005, at *Minshu* Vol. 59 No.10: 2964.

4.4.2 Methods of Realizing Ancillary Return and Specific Examples

Examples of ancillary return include: knowledge gained beyond the scope of a licensing agreement (e.g., know-how acquired from personnel on temporary assignment from the other partner), enhancement of a company's public image (e.g., increase in brand value due to the joint venture, improved public image), reductions in cost of sales, overhead expenses, and/or cost savings from closure of facilities due to consolidation of operations,[25] and expectations of future transactions. Improvement in a joint venture's asset efficiency means growth in return on investment, but improvement in a JV partner's own asset efficiency as a result of operating the joint venture is an ancillary return. In some cases, ancillary return constitutes a major factor behind the management decision to form a joint venture.

JV partners are not necessarily assured of benefiting from knowledge gained from their joint ventures. For example, in the NUMMI joint venture between GM and Toyota, GM successfully transplanted the Toyota production system (TPS) to its Brazilian plant but failed in its attempt to apply the TPS to its Saturn subsidiary. GM as a whole was unable to master the TPS. Toyota, by contrast, gained a US supply chain and built a relationship with the United Auto Workers labor union.[26]

4.4.3 Nature of Ancillary Return

Ancillary return is by nature a de facto payoff not shared with the other partner. A JV partner has no right to claim ancillary return derived from either the joint venture or the other partner. Ancillary return usually cannot be transferred to or assumed by third parties even in the event of the joint venture's dissolution and liquidation. While ancillary return increases one partner's return, it does not do so at the expense of any other party. Ancillary return therefore expands the Pareto frontier.

Although ancillary return is sometimes quantifiable in monetary terms, its valuation involves uncertainties, including forecast accuracy, when

---

[25] Other conceivable forms of ancillary return include reduction of a JV partner's personnel expenses due to secondment of employees to the joint venture and increased financing capacity as a result of appreciation of a JV partner's share price by virtue of a favorable market response to the joint venture.

[26] *See* ZENICHI SHISHIDO & ATSUSHI KUSANO, KOKUSAI GOBEN: TOYOTA – GM JOINTO BENCHA NO KISEKI [INTERNATIONAL JOINT VENTURES: A CASE STUDY OF THE JOINT VENTURE BETWEEN TOYOTA AND GENERAL MOTORS] (1988).

valuation inputs are limited to subjective expectations based on JV partners' individual circumstances. In such cases, ancillary return is valued by the recipient partner's best managerial judgment.

4.4.4 Interests between Partners

Ancillary return cannot be shared between partners. They generally do not give rise to directly conflicting interests between partners. However, when a joint venture is effectively used as an alternative to licensing intellectual property (e.g., know-how gained via the joint venture), the resultant ancillary return of one partner would be indirectly disadvantageous to the other partner. Conflicts therefore may arise if the partners are in competition to acquire know-how ahead of one other.

Additionally, if a partner operates a solely owned business that competes with the joint venture, conflicts can arise between the partner and the other partner(s) when know-how gained from the joint venture is used by the solely owned business to compete with the joint venture.[27]

4.4.5 Bargaining over Sharing Ancillary Return

A JV partner has no obligation to explain or even disclose the existence of ancillary return to the other partner. Additionally, ancillary return is not subject to inter-partner bargaining over sharing of return. Absent exceptional circumstances, ancillary return is best not disclosed to a prospective partner during the bargaining process because such disclosure could convey the impression that return will be shared inequitably, thereby distorting incentive of the other partner. However, insight into a prospective partner's ancillary return is an asset in the bargaining process. Additionally, one party may be amenable to making concessions in terms of sharing of other return if aware of its own prospective ancillary return.

4.4.6 Relationship to Internal Approval

JV partners have a duty to justify their investments in their joint venture to their own shareholders and creditors. For example, when NUMMI was established, Toyota cited acquisition of knowledge from GM about labor

---

[27] The issue of a JV partner's use of the fruits of a joint venture in the partner's solely owned business is sometimes dealt with by defining the scope of the joint venture's business and imposing a duty not to compete. *See* Hewitt *supra* note 1, at Ch. 11-7.

management at US plants as an ancillary return from the joint venture.[28] In the process of gaining internal approval of a joint venture, ancillary return is often explained as a justification for subjective or strategic decisions on the grounds that they compensate for shortfalls in return on investment and return from transactions.

4.4.7 Tax Benefits and Subsidies

Tax benefits represent another type of ancillary return from a joint venture. JV partners should therefore employ careful tax planning to maximize such benefits.[29] Before establishing a joint venture, the prospective partners should investigate the requirements for and expected benefits of any government subsidies, preferential access to infrastructure, and tax breaks (incentives) available to the joint venture and confirm the resultant return that would accrue both to the joint venture and directly to the partners.

---

[28] Regarding ancillary returns from Toyota and GM's NUMMI joint venture (*see supra* note 26), GM said that the knowledge it had gained of the TPS was beneficial to its worldwide plants' production systems. Meanwhile, in addition to easing trade friction, Toyota subsequently succeeded in the North American market as a result of building overseas production operations and cultivating personnel as a precursor to internationalization and solo overseas expansion (ASAHI SHIMBUN, February 14, 2004, pages 8 and 12). NUMMI was subsequently dissolved in conjunction with GM's bankruptcy in 2009.

[29] *See* Hewitt, *supra* note 1, at Ch. 15.

5.   Bargaining over exit rights

5.1   THE SIGNIFICANCE AND IDIOSYNCRASIES OF EXIT RIGHTS IN INCENTIVE BARGAINING

5.1.1   Importance of Bargaining over Exit Rights

Available avenues for JV partners to exit a joint venture is an important topic that should be incorporated into the joint venture agreement.[1] As such, exit rights are subject to pre-contract bargaining (*see* Chapter 8). Although partners are naturally hesitant to negotiate conditions of termination when first setting up the joint venture,[2] methods of exit are an important topic in preliminary bargaining because they can influence incentive bargaining strategies that depend on the threat of exit.

JV partners must be cognizant of three points when bargaining over methods of exit. First, a partner that contributes resources essential to the joint venture's operation may be able to gain an upper hand in bargaining over the sharing of control of the joint venture and/or the sharing of total return.[3] Second, bargaining over the sharing of total return is influenced by the terms that govern partner recovery of invested capital at the time of exit.[4] Third, the manner in which partners contribute resources to a joint venture may differ depending on whether contributed assets can be extracted when exiting the joint venture.[5]

---

[1]   *See* Zenichi Shishido, Dokizuke no Shikumi toshiteno Kigyo: Insen-thibu Shisutemu no Hoseido Ron [The Firm as an Incentive Mechanism: The Role of Legal Institutions] 59, 90 (2006). *See* Ian Hewitt, Hewitt on Joint Ventures, at Ch. 13 (5th ed. 2011).

[2]   *See* Hewitt, *supra* note 1, at Ch. 13-51.

[3]   Exit rights are a means of monitoring the other partner's contractual performance via the threat of exit. They also influence sharing of control. *See* Shishido, *supra* note 1, at 35, 69.

[4]   In a closed joint venture with no market in which partners can sell their equity interests, exit rights are also important from the standpoint of sharing of total return (i.e., recovering invested capital). *See id.*, at 59.

[5]   For example, a partner may decide to contribute capital in the form of a loan instead of equity, or vice versa.

When partners bargain over exit conditions, they must decide on specific procedures for various matters, including: (1) termination of their relationship in the joint venture, (2) termination of the joint venture agreement and/or ancillary contracts, (3) termination of the JV company's status as a legal entity (dissolution/liquidation), (4) partner succession through transfer of a partner's ownership interest (stock) to a third party or the other partner, and (5) termination of shareholder rights through the repurchase of an equity stake (treasury stock) by the JV company.

Key issues that should be addressed in bargaining over partners' exit rights include: (1) grounds for exit (i.e., causes of termination of the joint venture), (2) ways of exit, (3) valuation of ownership interests at the time of exit and (4) post-exit arrangements.

5.1.2 Reasons for Exit

One reason that partners exit joint ventures is that the joint venture has failed. Freedom to withdraw from an insufficiently profitable business is therefore important. If a joint venture's business fails, the JV partners must make an economically rational business decision in regard to transforming the joint venture's business model, exiting the joint venture, or winding up the joint venture.

A second reason that a partner may consider exiting a joint venture, even a successful one, is that the joint venture requires additional capital in excess of the partner's maximum loss tolerance.

Third, exit may be a rational business decision for a JV partner when the other partner has captured a disproportionately advantageous share of total return (i.e., an organizational management failure).

5.1.3 Threats of Exit

While exit rights incentivize partners to contribute capital to a joint venture, the flipside is that each partner has to worry about the threat of exit wielded by the other. In general, the risks of contractual organization (*see* Chapter 1) include the risk of the other partner exiting the joint venture. Exit rights are therefore an effective constraint on the other partner's behavior. JV partners are sometimes forced to make concessions to prevent the other partner from exiting a joint venture. If one partner has greater ability to exit than the other partner, it is in an advantageous bargaining position because it can threaten to exit the joint venture if the other partner does not renegotiate in a manner that satisfies the partner with more exit capability. Accordingly, when bargaining before establishing a joint venture, partners have an incentive to restrict the other partner's ability to exit while securing exit rights for themselves.

5.1.4   Risk of the Other Partner Exiting/ Risk of One's Own Inability to Exit

For JV partners, the risk of exit involves the risk of the other partner exiting and the risk of not being able to exit.

Without exit rights, JV partners face commitment risk – i.e., the risk of not being able to exit a joint venture once it has been established, of being forced to endlessly and unpredictably contribute additional capital to the joint venture. Partners consequently have no incentive to contribute resources unless there is an accessible right to exit.[6]

Preserving the threat of exit confers strong bargaining power over the other partner and can be a means of inducing the other partner to contribute resources on a continual basis instead of merely at the joint venture's inception. On the flip side, a partner has a disincentive to contribute resources when the joint venture is established if it faces excessive risk of the other partner exiting. Once a joint venture is operational, a partner will be hesitant to contribute additional capital and will seek to maintain the status quo if the risk of the other partner exiting exceeds a certain critical threshold. Excessively lenient exit conditions distort the incentives of all partners to commit to a joint venture. Accordingly, JV partners must be mindful of preserving the other partner's incentives to contribute resources to the joint venture by refraining from exercising the threat of exit too liberally.

---

[6]   Partners are sometimes unwilling to contribute capital to a joint venture unless they have exit rights. For example, if a partner operates a business identical or similar to the joint venture's business and it needs to regain intellectual property or specific tangible assets contributed to the joint venture when it exits the joint venture, exit rights will be a prerequisite for the partner to contribute resources to the joint venture. Additionally, in the case of a project-type joint venture based on a multi-phase business plan, partners may refuse to contribute resources unless they have the right to exit the joint venture through a phase-gate mechanism in the event that the joint venture's business proves unprofitable. Otherwise, the partner will be unable to recover its investment at the scheduled end of the joint venture's life, when the JV company's residual value is distributed to the partners.

5.2 GROUNDS FOR EXIT

5.2.1 Planned Terminations

The planned termination of a joint venture can be triggered by (1) achievement of the joint venture's objectives or (2) expiration of the joint venture's term.

Joint ventures terminate upon the achievement of objectives established at the outset.[7] A typical example is a construction joint venture that terminates upon completion of the subject construction project.[8] Mining joint ventures that terminate when their mineral reserves have been fully depleted are another example of termination upon the achievement of objectives.

Joint ventures of a predetermined duration include those with a scheduled termination date incorporated into their business plans.[9] In some cases, the joint venture's lifetime is limited by law – for example, a joint venture may terminate upon expiration of a fixed-term commercial leasehold or drug patent.

Limiting a joint venture's lifetime in advance is significant in two respects. First, it imposes a time limit on directors' managerial decision-making ability with respect to business decisions involving the lifetime of the joint venture. Second, investment decisions at the time of the joint venture's inception will be based on the joint venture's projected value at the time of its scheduled termination date.

5.2.2 Termination upon Unforeseen Events

5.2.2.1 A joint venture's bankruptcy or inability to accomplish its business plan

JV partners typically conduct reviews of a joint venture's operations using milestone targets that are established upon the joint venture's

---

[7] *See* Hewitt, *supra* note 1, at Ch. 13-32.

[8] Construction joint ventures are typical contractual joint ventures.

[9] Hilton International and Tokyo Electric Express Railway (now Tokyu Corporation) established a JV company (Tokyo Hilton Hotel Co., Ltd.) pursuant to a 20-year joint venture agreement. The JV company went out of business upon expiration of the joint venture agreement's initial term on December 31, 1983. Its hotel reopened from January 1, 1984 as the Capitol Hotel Tokyu, part of the Tokyu Hotel chain. *See* ILO, *Definitive Report – Report No 343* (November 2006) www.ilo.org/dyn/normlex/en/f?p=1000:50002:0::NO:50002: P50002_COMPLAINT_TEXT_ID:2908466.

inception. On the basis of these reviews, joint ventures that underperform operationally and fail to meet financial targets are sometimes restructured and/or renegotiated with the aim of improving performance.[10] Underperforming joint ventures are typically dissolved when efforts to improve their performance prove unsuccessful; when they incur cumulative losses in excess of a certain threshold; when they are deemed incapable of achieving their operational objectives; or if they become bankrupt due to insolvency or default.

5.2.2.2 Management deadlock

Deadlock is the inability to reach agreement on key management decisions. It occurs when a joint venture is unable to make institutional decisions (at the board of directors level), when the JV partners are unable to reach an agreement (at the shareholder general meeting level), or when one partner exercises its veto rights or refuses to attend meetings of a decision-making body. If the means of resolving deadlock prove ineffective, the joint venture is likely to fail.[11] Potential options for resolving deadlock in a joint venture include consultation between the JV partners' chief executives.

5.2.2.3 Bankruptcy or insolvency of a JV partner

Insolvency and especially bankruptcy of a JV partner are typically stipulated as grounds for termination of joint venture agreements.[12]

5.2.2.4 Change in control of a partner

In the event of a change in control of a JV partner, the partner's business strategy with respect to the joint venture is also subject to change. This is especially likely when the partner comes under the control of a shareholder that is in competition with the other partner in the joint venture.[13] For a joint venture to succeed, trust and communication between partners and mutual cooperation among employees seconded from both partners are important factors. A change of control in a partner company tends to have a material impact on the relationship of trust between partners, and therefore it is often stipulated as grounds for termination in joint venture agreements.[14]

---

[10] *See* Hewitt, *supra* note 1, at Ch. 13-33.
[11] *See id.*, at Ch. 10; Ch. 13.
[12] *See id.*, at Ch. 13-26.
[13] *See id.*, at Ch. 13-28–31.
[14] *See id.*, at Ch. 1-22, Figure 1.7. According to Hewitt, one of the key success factors for joint ventures is a relationship of trust between JV partners.

Just as there are various modes of M&A, a change of control can take multiple forms, including (a) a merger in which one partner is absorbed into another company, (b) acquisition of one partner accompanied by a change in the partner's management resulting from a change in the partner's controlling shareholder, (c) transfer, by a partner to a third party, of a business through which the partner provides resources to the joint venture (or the split-up of that partner into multiple companies), (d) a change in management policy in conjunction with a change in one partner's controlling shareholder in the course of corporate reorganization proceedings, and (e) transfer to a third party of all or a material part of the assets that one partner has allowed the joint venture to use in its operations.[15]

5.2.3   Possible Grounds for Termination of Joint Ventures

5.2.3.1   Material breach of the joint venture agreement
If one JV partner materially breaches the joint venture agreement or an ancillary contract, and its co-partner rescinds the joint venture agreement in response, the joint venture will terminate. Types of contractual breach that pose a relatively high risk of impairing the relationship of trust between partners include: a resolution by the board in violation of a voting agreement, breach of a duty of confidentiality, breach of a duty not to compete, and breach of a duty to renegotiate by a partner that has engaged in opportunistic behavior.[16]

5.2.3.2   Change in a partner's business policy
JV partners sometimes decide to convert a joint venture to a solely owned business of a single partner or one partner may withdraw from a joint venture as a result of a change in the business policy of the other partner.

---

[15]   For examples of contracts, *see Business Contracts from SEC Filings*, http://contracts.onecle.com/type/22.shtml. Regarding research on capital lock-in clauses in joint venture agreements, *see* Robert Hauswald & Ulrich Hege, *Ownership and Control in Joint Ventures: Theory and Evidence*, AMERICAN. EDU (February 2009) www1.american.edu/academic.depts/ksb/finance_real estate/rhauswald/papers/Ownership%20and%20Control%20in%20JVs.pdf.

[16]   Regarding contractual breaches by partners, *see* Hewitt, *supra* note 1, at Ch. 13-22. Regarding breaches of confidentiality and non-compete duties, *see id.*, at Ch. 11-06–13. Regarding breaches of the fiduciary duty of good faith, *see id.*, at Ch. 11-15–27.

Additionally, if a partner becomes unable to provide essential human resources to a joint venture on an ongoing basis, the joint venture may terminate.

5.3   BARGAINING OVER EXIT CONDITIONS

In bargaining over exit conditions, a key issue is whether to grant unconditional exit rights that permit partners to terminate the joint venture agreement at their convenience.[17] Unconditional exit rights destabilize joint ventures, put both partners at risk of the other partner exiting, and cause partners to be hesitant about contributing financial and human capital. Conversely, exit conditions that are too restrictive pose a significant barrier to exiting a failed joint venture and cause minority partners to be hesitant to contribute capital due to the risk of being locked into a joint venture or being unable to exit or recover invested capital.[18]

While exit clauses and termination clauses reduce both the risk of being unable to exit an unprofitable business and the risk of another partner withholding resources from the joint venture, they also create the risk of the other partner exiting. If a joint venture agreement provides for unconditional exit rights, the risk of the other partner exiting increases. This increased risk reduces partners' incentive to contribute human and monetary capital to a joint venture and their willingness to renegotiate a joint venture agreement. JV partners also want to avoid the risk of a race to exit. Consequently, joint venture agreements virtually never grant unconditional termination rights or put options that grant partners the unconditional right to be bought out by the other partner(s). Instead, joint venture agreements provide for conditional exit rights. However, if negotiations between partners become deadlocked, resolution often requires arbitration or litigation.

5.4   METHODS OF EXIT PROVIDED BY LAW

5.4.1   Types of Exit Method

When a joint venture is organized as a stock corporation and the joint venture agreement stipulates grounds for termination and ways of exiting the joint venture, one way for a partner to terminate the joint venture is

---

[17]   *See id.*, at Ch. 13-09.
[18]   *See* Shishido, *supra* note 1, at 60.

by selling its ownership interest in the joint venture. Sale of a partner's ownership interest is a means by which the partner can wholly or partially exit the joint venture while allowing the JV company to remain in existence. Variations include (a) conversion of a joint venture into the other partner's wholly owned business through the sale of all ownership interest to the co-partner, (b) replacement of a partner through sale of the partner's ownership interest to a third party, (c) conversion of the joint venture into a third party's solely owned business through sale to the third party, and (d) sale of a JV company to the public through an IPO.[19]

A second way to exit a joint venture is to dissolve and liquidate the JV company.

A third way is for the joint venture to refund the equity contribution paid by a partner. Note that the ability to refund a partner's contribution depends on organizational form. Stock corporations are generally not permitted to refund equity contributions in this manner. Although a share buyback might be used as an exit route from a joint venture organized as a stock corporation, the ability to do so is generally constrained by availability of funds. If a joint venture is organized as a partnership or LLC, an equity contribution refund can be used as a means of exiting the joint venture (*see* Chapter 9).

5.4.2 Methods of Exiting through Sale of Stock

5.4.2.1 First offer/ first refusal
A right of first refusal restrains a JV partner from selling its shares to a third party unless the other partner has refused to purchase the shares on the same terms offered by the third party. A right of first offer obligates a partner wishing to sell its shares to negotiate in good faith with the other partner exclusively before negotiating with any third parties. If the partner has attempted to negotiate sales terms with the other partner but failed to reach an agreement, it may sell its shares to a third party. The right of first offer is thus a right of first negotiation.

A right of first refusal, by contrast, gives the other partner the right to purchase the shares at a given price and terms before the other partner sells them to a third party on the same terms. As such, a right of first refusal is somewhat stronger than a right of first offer and can be conceptualized as a call option.[20]

---

[19] *See* Hewitt, *supra* note 1, at Ch. 13-40–44.
[20] *See id.*, at Ch. 12-6–18.

5.4.2.2 Put/call options

A put option gives a partner wishing to exit a joint venture the right to be bought out by the other partner on demand (exit by compulsory buyout). Likewise, a call option gives a partner the right to buy the other partner's shares in the joint venture on demand (compulsory squeeze-out through buyout).[21]

5.4.2.3 Use of pseudo-auctions

A Texas shootout is a pseudo-auction in which one partner offers to purchase the other partner's shares at a price of its choosing. If the other partner refuses the offer, it must purchase its partner's shares. The purchase price is determined by the fairest sealed bid method.[22] In a sale shootout, one partner offers to sell its shares to the other partner at a price of its choosing. If the other partner rejects the offer, it must offer to sell its shares to its partner at a price lower than the initially offered price. This reverse-bidding process continues at progressively lower prices until one partner agrees to purchase the other's shares.[23]

Russian roulette is a pseudo-auction in which one partner offers to sell its shares to the other partner at a price of its choosing. If the other partner rejects the offer, the first partner gains the right to purchase the other partner's shares at the offered price. Russian roulette is theoretically a reasonable option in certain cases but it is not feasible when (1) ownership percentages differ substantially, (2) the joint venture is an international joint venture and foreign ownership restrictions prohibit conversion to a wholly owned subsidiary of a foreign company,[24] or (3) the joint venture's business model is not conducive to operation as a solely owned business. Russian roulette also poses practical challenges, including the difficulty of predicting which partner will end up owning the JV company. Additionally, if the partners differ in terms of financial strength, Russian roulette is unfair to the financially weaker partner.

5.5 VALUATION OF OWNERSHIP INTERESTS

In joint ventures that are organized as stock corporations, transferability of shares cannot be completely restricted. JV partners therefore have the potential to transfer their shares, but are typically prevented from freely

---

21 *See id.*, at Ch. 13-34–39; Ch. 10-23–24.
22 *See id.*, at Ch. 10-29–30.
23 *See id.*, at Ch. 31.
24 *See id.*, at Ch. 10-25–27.

exiting by transferability restrictions in the joint venture agreement. To provide a means of recovering invested capital, partners must agree in advance on exceptions to transferability restrictions and fix the prices at which shares may be sold.[25]

When a partner exits a joint venture, conditions of exit become a key issue. Of particular importance is determining the disposition of the joint venture's assets (residual property) and liabilities, and the method of valuing any ownership interests to be transferred.[26]

In cases where an existing partner is replaced by a new partner and the joint venture continues to operate, the joint venture's value will vary depending on which partner exits. In such cases, the joint venture's value must be reappraised to factor in related transactions between the partner and joint venture. Additionally, a joint venture's value differs depending on the human capital contributed by the JV partners. Other than differences in the value of the ownership interests of controlling shareholders versus minority shareholders due to the control premium, even the value of 50:50 partners' ownership interests will differ in practice depending on which partner is exiting. This is one important idiosyncrasy of valuing ownership interests in joint ventures.

Sales prices of joint venture ownership interests are sometimes determined by a sale procedure such as Russian roulette, but joint venture agreements usually stipulate that when an ownership interest is transferred through a method that requires valuation of the ownership interest, the discounted cash flow (DCF) method is to be used.

However, even when a pre-existing agreement between partners exists, exiting partners sometimes seek to transfer their ownership interests (shares) in the joint venture to a third party in an exception to the existing agreement. In such cases, the sales price is typically determined by ascertaining the price offered by the third party first, and then using the DCF method to value the ownership interest inclusive of the value of the third party's prospective contributions to the joint venture.

When a partner wishing to exit a joint venture has received a buyout offer from a third party, the highest possible price is generally sought. However, valuation (projected future cash flows) of an ownership interest will differ depending on which partner is exiting.

For example, how much would Toyota's ownership stake in NUMMI be worth if Toyota sold it to GM? When valued in present-value terms,

---

[25] *See id.*, at Ch. 12-1–3. Japanese law (Article 144 of the Companies Act) prohibits stipulation of a buyout price in articles of incorporation. Buyout prices are consequently stipulated contractually in Japan.

[26] *See id.*, at Ch. 12-19–22.

NUMMI's value would presumably differ depending on which partner would be the surviving owner (i.e., whether Toyota remains or exits). Assume that if Toyota were the exiting partner, it would have to sell its equity stake to GM at a discounted price but if GM were the exiting partner, Toyota would have to pay a steep price to buy out GM. Such an outcome would be unfairly advantageous to the partner that contributes less to the joint venture. A reasonable way to rectify this inequity would be to set the sales price at the exiting partner's pro rata share of an arm's-length buyout price not contingent on the joint venture being managed by any specific party, either in an agreement in advance by the partners or pursuant to *ex post* judicial evaluation by a court.[27]

In preparation for one partner potentially exercising a put option to sell its equity stake to the other partner, there should be negotiations in advance for determining the buyout price and the procedure for executing the sale. If the joint venture agreement has a right of first refusal clause, the buyout price is often on parity with the price offered by a prospective third-party purchaser. In such cases, there is no need for the partners to negotiate the buyout price or method of setting the buyout price at the time of the joint venture's inception. Alternatively, the partners will have the JV company appraised or valued by a neutral third party (such as an accounting firm or other specialist) based on fair accounting standards.[28] However, both of these methods pose risks – with the former method, the third-party bid may be speculative or a bluff, and with the latter method, the sales price is not set unequivocally.

When a partner exercises a call or put option in response to an event attributable to the fault of the other partner (e.g., material breach of contract, misappropriation of the JV company's assets, or other such misdeed), the partner may seek damages from the other partner. One way to collect damages is through a contractual provision that incorporates a penalty into the sales price by adding a premium to the put option's exercise price or discounting the call option's exercise price. For example, such a provision could require the at-fault partner to purchase the other partner's ownership interest at a price equivalent to the greater

---

[27] In most actual cases where a partner exits a failed joint venture, the partner's ownership interest is valued at the equivalent of the partner's share of liquidation value. *See Zenichi Shishido, Godo Kaisha no Taishain no Mochibunhyoka [Valuation of Exiting LLC Members' Ownership Interests], in* KIGYOHO NO GENZAI [ENTERPRISE LAW TODAY] 427 (2014).

[28] In such cases, issues to be negotiated include selection of an appraiser (accounting office) to value the JV company's stock, and the scope and method of information disclosure to the appraiser.

of the joint venture's DCF valuation or the market value of its net assets or, conversely, the at-fault partner may be forced to sell its ownership interest at a price equivalent to the lesser of the same two valuations.[29]

When the joint venture agreement stipulates that the going-concern value be used to value the exiting partner's ownership interest upon the exercise of a put option, the following issues come into play. First, a financially weak partner is in danger of being squeezed out because it cannot afford to purchase the other partner's ownership interest at the going-concern value, which is generally higher than the liquidation value. Second, when a joint venture has more going-concern value in the hands of one partner than it does in the hands of the other partner, only the latter partner would benefit from the full value of the put option.

5.6 POST-EXIT ARRANGEMENTS

5.6.1 Strategic Considerations in Designing Post-Exit Arrangements

Exit strategies are important in business. In addition to recovery of contributed capital and disposition of the joint venture's assets and liabilities, JV partners should consider many other post-exit matters, including: employee compensation, use of brand names, utilization of patents and know-how, and assumption of contractual relationships with suppliers and customers. The following discussion highlights points that JV partners should be mindful of when bargaining with each other and drafting agreements associated with establishing a JV company.

Post-exit arrangements will differ depending on a number of factors, such as whether the exiting partner exits completely or partially, whether the joint venture's business will remain in operation as a solely owned business, or whether the business will be discontinued and the JV company dissolved. If the joint venture will be converted to one partner's solely owned business or if the exiting partner does not exit completely and maintains the joint venture to the extent of its residual ownership interest, the following two points should be taken into consideration in drafting agreements.

First, a joint venture comprises a bundle of rights and obligations stemming from multiple agreements between the JV partners and

---

[29]   Kitazume, Masahiko, *M&A to Jointo Bencha no Zeimu* [*M&A and Joint Venture Taxation*], *in* 2 BIZINESU HOMU TAIKEI: M&A JOINTO BENCHA [2 BUSINESS LAWS: M&A AND JOINT VENTURE] 273 (Michiaki Nakano & Zenichi Shishido eds., 2006).

between the partners and the JV company. Some of these contractual rights and obligations cease to exist upon termination of the joint venture. Others (e.g., confidentiality and non-compete duties) continue to exist beyond the joint venture's termination. It is incumbent upon JV partners to distinguish between these two categories of rights and obligations.

Second, the choice of interdependency between or independence of the two contracts is also important, for example whether or not a licensing agreement, which may be an integral resource of the joint venture business, will continue to exist and succeed to the remaining partner upon the termination of the joint venture agreement; or whether the joint venture agreement will continue to exist upon termination of an important ancillary contract, such as a factory lease contract.

5.6.2 Issues Regarding Recovery of Human Capital and Employees

The above discussion pertains mainly to valuation methods with respect to recovery of monetary capital. By comparison, withdrawal of human capital is more difficult to deter or restrict. Human capital, particularly obligations to pay employees' salaries, pensions, and other post-retirement benefits, imposes a heavy burden when an unprofitable joint venture is terminated. When a JV company is dissolved, it must be liquidated, and it can no longer continue to employ its workforce. However, because joint ventures have parent companies involved in management, stricter restrictions on dismissal of employees may exist. Whether a JV company can legally dismiss its entire workforce or only selected employees will differ depending on the labor laws of the country in which it is located.

5.6.3 Recall of Seconded Personnel

When an exiting partner operates a business related to that of the joint venture and the partner has seconded employees to the joint venture, the seconded employees will typically be recalled from the joint venture if they possess special skills essential to the partner's business. The agreements under which they were seconded to the joint venture will terminate upon the joint venture's termination and they will return to the parent company to which they are contractually bound. In cases where one partner exits while the JV company continues to exist, the remaining partner or the exiting partner's third-party successor can prevent the exiting partner from withdrawing human resources through an inter-partner agreement that prohibits recall of employees essential to the joint venture's business (if the employees were seconded to the joint venture, they would become permanent employees of the JV company). However, depending on the labor laws of the joint venture's home country, this kind of prohibition without the consent of the concerned employees may be illegal or unenforceable on the grounds that it violates labor contract law or the employees' freedom to choose their own job (freedom of contract).

5.6.4 Ancillary Contract Termination/ Succession

When a partner contributes human capital to a joint venture in the form of services provided pursuant to an outsourcing agreement, that human capital is withdrawn by the termination of ancillary contracts upon the joint venture's termination. Additionally, a partner can reclaim commercial rights (e.g., access to sales channels) from a joint venture by assuming the joint venture's contractual obligations (taking over customer lists, etc.) related to those commercial rights.

5.6.5 Duty to Not Use Intellectual Property

Intellectual property such as trademarks, invention patents, and especially know-how and other intangible information, cannot be physically repossessed. When a joint venture is terminated, intellectual property licensing agreements between the joint venture and the licensor partner that provided the intellectual property should likewise terminate. Additionally, the licensor partner should impose time-limited confidentiality and non-compete duties on its co-partner with respect to information acquired while the joint venture agreement was in effect, thereby preserving the exclusiveness of intellectual property and making it unavailable to both the other partner(s) and the joint venture.

5.6.6 Taxation Issues

When a JV company organized as a corporation is dissolved and liquidated, tax consequences may arise from asset sales, debt forgiveness, and distribution of the JV company's residual assets to the JV partners. Further, when a partner transfers its ownership interest in a joint venture, issues may arise with respect to the adequacy of the ownership interest appraisal value and the tax treatment of any gain/loss on the transfer.

5.7 CASE ANALYSIS

The following example, involving a JV company that was converted to a solely owned business upon one partner's exit, illustrates key exit-related bargaining points when JV partners are preparing to establish a joint venture.

Two partners, P1 and P2, establish a joint venture as a brand licensee. P1, the licensor partner, owns a trademark, know-how, and patents for operating coffee shops. P1 licenses to the joint venture the rights to use (1) a well-known trade name (trademark), (2) a well-known, distinctive store design (trade dress), and (3) manuals on how to serve customers and operate the shops' equipment (know-how) (the trademark, trade dress, and know-how are collectively referred to below as the "brand").

If the brand license agreement (a type of franchise agreement) between P1 and the joint venture established with P2's capital contribution were to terminate when P1 exits the joint venture, the joint venture would no longer be able to utilize the brand and would consequently face an existential crisis. P2 wants to be able to continue to operate existing coffee shops after P1 exits, but the parties to the brand license agreement are P1 and the JV company (JV), not P2.

First, to ensure that P2 does not lose rights that are essential to operating the coffee shops as a solely owned business in the event of termination of the joint venture, the brand license agreement entered into at the time of the joint venture's inception must be drafted to preclude P1 from exercising a right to cancel the agreement or refusing to extend the agreement upon expiration of its term and to ensure that the license agreement does not automatically terminate upon the joint venture agreement's termination. Alternatively, the license agreement may be drafted to permit P2 to purchase the requisite intellectual property from P1. An example of a case in which a JV partner acquired the trademark from the other partner upon termination of the joint venture is Lion Corporation's acquisition of the trademark for the Bufferin pain reliever brand.[30]

---

[30] Lion Corporation announced on June 29, 2007 that it had acquired commercial rights to the Bufferin pain-reliever brand in Japan, Asia, and Oceana for ¥30.4 billion from major US pharmaceutical maker Bristol-Myers Squibb. At the same time, Lion announced termination of its joint venture agreement with Bristol-Myers Squibb's Japanese subsidiary and dissolution/liquidation of the JV company. The purpose of the acquisition was to launch a solely owned business in the product market that had been the JV company's business domain and to

Second, one way for P2 to hedge its risk is to contractually stipulate that in the event that P1 terminates the brand license agreement or joint venture agreement, P1 must pay P2 a penalty sufficiently large to allow for the redesign of all of the coffee shops.

Third, if it would be senseless to continue to operate the JV's business without the brand license in the event that the license agreement is terminated, P2 could stipulate in the joint venture agreement that it has the right to demand that the joint venture be dissolved. Note, however, that if the joint venture were dissolved, both P1 and P2 would have difficulty recovering their investment capital.

---

implement an independent business strategy utilizing the Bufferin brand. *See* www.lion.co.jp/en/press/html/2007014f.htm.

PART II

Synergies and intellectual property

6. Synergies

In deciding whether to establish a joint venture, each prospective partner should determine the total return it can realize by establishing the joint venture and identify the risks of the joint venture plan. In other words, each partner should individually ascertain the benefits and drawbacks of partnering with another. This chapter discusses those benefits in terms of synergies, while Chapter 2 discusses drawbacks in terms of opposing interests and risks.

Immediately below, synergies are defined as the total return that partners can realize by participating in a joint venture. In the second section, 11 objectives of participating in a joint venture from the standpoint of synergies are discussed. Finally, in the third section, the topic turns to antitrust restrictions that JV partners may run afoul of in their pursuit of synergies. In the fourth section, we look at the basis for establishing a JV company to realize synergies instead of merely forming a contractual alliance.

6.1 DEFINITION OF SYNERGIES

This book uses the term synergies to mean the total return that partner companies are able to realize by establishing and operating a joint venture. While the concept of synergies can have various meanings, it generally refers to economies of scope or, from a macro standpoint, social utility (e.g., benefits to consumers/workers, regional economic development) spawned by a synergistic alliance between two companies. Economies of scope is the value that partners derive by combining their economic resources or assets in excess of the value that they collectively would have derived by operating separate businesses. We choose to define synergies as the total return to each partner company for two reasons. First, each partner company's total return is important from a business-planning standpoint. Additionally, maximization of synergies cannot be discussed in a game-theoretic context without defining synergies as we do herein.

The total return that JV partners can earn from establishing and operating a joint venture can be classified into three types: return on investment, return from transactions, and ancillary return. The sum total of these three constitutes the synergies realized by the partners.[1]

6.1.1   Return on Investment

Return on investment is return on the joint venture's value as a business. It flows to JV partners as shareholders based on respective ownership percentages in the JV company. JV companies are typically valued by discounting their projected future cash flows to present value. As shareholders, the JV partners receive return in the form of profit distributions and/or capital gains. The legal rights through which shareholders realize return on their investment include corporate law-based claims on dividends, claims on residual asset distributions upon the JV company's liquidation, and claims on the proceeds from the sale of their shareholdings in the JV company. Potential return on investment increases as the value of the assets of the JV company increases (capital gains).

6.1.2   Return from Transactions

Return from transactions is return that JV partners directly earn by engaging in transactions with their joint ventures. Partners realize return from transactions through various types of legal claim that they hold as the joint venture's contractual counterparty.

Return from transactions derives from two types of transaction. The first is pro rata self-dealing transactions utilized as a means of sharing return among all partners in proportion to their respective ownership interests. It bears noting that when return is shared in proportion to ownership percentages, it may include what are in essence hidden dividends. In lieu of return in the form of profits distributed as dividends under corporate law, JV partners sometimes earn return from transactions with the joint venture with terms that are advantageous to the partners. Return from pro rata self-dealing transactions is essentially no different from regular dividends in some ways, such as the following. In both cases, the JV partners have the ability to withdraw value from their joint venture in proportion to their ownership percentages, provided that the consideration received by partners from the transactions is allocated

---

[1]   Regarding sharing of the three types of returns, *see supra* Ch. 4.

appropriately, in either unit volume or value terms, in proportion to their respective ownership interests.[2]

The second type of transaction from which partners can earn return is non-pro rata self-dealing transactions with their joint ventures.[3] Return from non-pro rata self-dealing transactions is not shared in proportion to the partners' ownership percentages. Instead, one partner obtains return at the expense of the other partner through the joint venture. However, in cases where one partner contributes a disproportionately large share of the joint venture's human capital,[4] the other partner could conceivably agree, as a result of bargaining in the aim of sharing return in proportion to the partners' de facto contributions to the joint venture, to allow a partner to receive a disproportionately large share of return from transactions as a necessary precondition to establishing the joint venture – incentivizing the other partner to contribute resources in the first place.[5]

Transactions between joint ventures and their owners are included from the outset in the vast majority of joint venture plans. Companies often form joint ventures primarily with the aim of earning return from transactions rather than return on investment.

When a JV partner engages in transactions with its joint venture but could be replaced as the joint venture's transactional counterparty at any time through a contractual arrangement with a third party, the transactions should be fairly priced at arm's length. When this is accomplished, the issue of sharing total return specific to a joint venture theoretically should not come into play. In practice, however, a partner may earn de facto return from these transactions in the following two scenarios. First, even when the joint venture and one partner agree to conduct transactions at arm's length, there is generally some degree of

---

[2] In valuing a JV company, hidden constructive dividends should be included in cash flows. Pro rata self-dealing transactions require research into tax issues.

[3] *See supra* Ch. 4, 4.3.

[4] In a 50:50 joint venture, the partners' contributions of monetary capital may be equal, but their de facto contributions of human capital are never identical. Consequently, if the partner that contributes the more important human capital receives a share of returns identical to that of the other partner, that partner's incentives would be distorted to contribute human capital in the future. Such an inconsistency between partners' ownership percentages and their shares of de facto human capital contributions are referred to herein as an "imbalance."

[5] For example, the partner may allow the other partner to earn returns from a license agreement or production outsourcing agreement. As an essential cost of maintaining the joint venture's existence, such returns should be deducted from cash flows in valuing a JV company.

latitude in setting the price within an arm's-length price range. Profits are consequently transferred from the joint venture to that one partner through the transactions. The second scenario involves stable return arising from long-term, continuous relational contracts.[6]

Joint ventures with the primary objective to generate return on investment are generally designated as profit-centers, while joint ventures whose primary objective is return from transactions are generally designated as cost-centers.[7] A JV company that was originally a cost-center could become a profit-center during its growth stage. Management autonomy typically increases as a joint venture transitions from cost-center to profit-center. The most successful outcome for a profit-center joint venture is an IPO.

6.1.3 Ancillary Return

Ancillary return includes all return earned by JV partners other than return on investment and return from transactions. In other words, this is return specific to the recipient partner, which is neither proportionate to the partners' respective ownership interests nor gained at the expense of the other partner.[8]

Typical examples of ancillary return include knowledge or know-how acquired from a partner, cartel-like benefits obtained from a tacit non-compete agreement between partners, enhancement of brand value, gains on disposal of fixed assets, and expectations of future transactions, among others.

6.1.4 Synergies as Sum Total of Three Types of Return

We define synergies as the sum total of return on investment, return from transactions, and ancillary return gained by each partner. Realizing synergies is the partners' objective in forming a joint venture; the three types of return encompass return (synergies) that is unavailable to the JV partners individually and only able to be realized through partnering with

---

[6] Partners must also be aware of potential tax ramifications if transactions between a partner and a JV company are priced outside of the arm's-length price range under tax law.

[7] *See infra* Ch. 11. This is a theoretical classification. Even profit-center joint ventures sometimes distribute returns from transactions to only one partner.

[8] Because ancillary return accrues exclusively to a specific partner, it should not be factored into the valuation of a JV company as both a positive and negative.

each other. Granted, return on investment and return from transactions also include non-synergistic return that the partners most likely would have realized operating individually; all ancillary return is synergistic.

In previous research on joint ventures, the mainstream approach has been to evaluate joint ventures in isolation from their owners. In contrast, our analysis places particular importance on JV partner return from joint ventures.

From a corporate law standpoint, a joint venture is an individual company separate from its owners. From a substantive standpoint, however, a joint venture is essentially an agreement among its share-holders (partners). Game-theoretic analysis of joint ventures is not possible unless individual JV partner return is taken into consideration. An approach that focuses on the individual return of each partner is valid both at the time a joint venture is established and when the partners renegotiate with each other during the joint venture's operational phase – even upon the decision to dissolve the joint venture.

6.2 CLASSIFICATION OF JOINT VENTURES BY OBJECTIVE

From the standpoint of realizing synergies, joint ventures can be classified into the following 11 types based on the JV partners' objective(s) in forming the joint venture. First, partners may form joint ventures (1) to collaborate instead of compete with each other, (2) to share production capacity or other facilities, or (3) to secure resources. For these three types of joint venture, the objective is to achieve greater efficiencies between incumbent businesses. Partners may also form joint ventures to (4) access sales channels, (5) gain reputational backing, (6) obtain local expertise, (7) ease frictions, (8) introduce a brand, (9) introduce technology, (10) conduct collaborative R&D, and/or (11) share expenses. For these eight types of joint venture, partners have the objective of entering a new business or market.

JV partners often have different and multiple objectives in establishing a joint venture. When the partners' objectives differ, the joint venture becomes a hybrid of two or more of the above types. For example, in the case of a joint venture between a major European candy maker and a mid-size Japanese candy maker, the European company's objective is to gain access to sales channels while the Japanese company's objective is to introduce a brand. The two partners need not realize the same types of synergies from the joint venture. Partners' strategic objectives or operational capabilities may be similar or different. When there are several types of synergies available to a partner, it is important for the partner to determine the main objectives to avoid misunderstandings related to the joint venture's essential nature.[9]

Below, we look at each of the 11 objectives for forming a joint venture.[10]

6.2.1 Collaboration in lieu of Competition

Forming a joint venture as an alternative to competition can also be called alliance-building. If there is one dominant company in a certain market, two lower-ranked companies in the same industry can form a joint venture to expand their combined market share and compete more effectively against the top company. Because joint ventures limit competition between the partners within a certain market, joint ventures between competitors can sometimes have the same effect as cartel-like tacit collusion unless they lead to an intensification of competition with the top-ranked company.

Examples include the joint venture between Toshiba, Hitachi, Sony, and Innovation Network Corporation of Japan in the market for OLED displays for smartphones,[11] as well as the joint venture formed by Softbank, Advantage Partners, a public-private fund, and a joint group of five overseas companies to launch a next-generation PHS business.[12]

---

[9] Determining types of synergy is important in designing a joint venture's structure. Having a clear sense of purpose is the key to devising diverse means. Alliance partners have not to obtain the same advantages from cooperation through joint venture. *See* Jay B. Barney, Gaining and Sustaining Competitive Advantage 369, 372 (4th ed. 2011).

[10] Ian Hewitt, Hewitt on Joint Ventures, Ch. 1-6 (5th ed. 2011) cites the following 10 reasons for forming a joint venture: cost-savings, risk-sharing, access to technology, expansion of customer base, entry into developing economies, entry into new technical markets, pressures of global competition, leverage (consolidated investment issues), creeping sale or acquisition, and catalyst for change. For a more comprehensive listing of specific examples of different types of joint ventures, *see infra* Appendix 2.

[11] *See* Nihon Keizai Shinbun, April 3, 2012, at 11; November 16, 2011, at 11; and June 7, 2011, at 1.

[12] *See* Nihon Keizai Shinbun, December 14, 2010, at 11. On facilitating tacit collusion, Barney, *supra* note 9, at 367 discusses a similar joint venture in the US steel industry.

6.2.2 Facility-sharing

Facility-sharing can also be considered a means of cost-cutting. Facility-sharing joint ventures typically aim to eliminate waste by sharing an underutilized manufacturing plant or other such facility. While sometimes used as a restructuring tactic in declining industries, facility-sharing joint ventures are also used to achieve economies of scale or to utilize a local partner's manufacturing plant when entering a new market. Before forming a facility-sharing joint venture, the prospective partners need to weigh the advantages of a joint venture against alternative options such as the transfer of operating assets, leasing facilities, and entering service agreements.

Facility-sharing joint ventures generally have relatively short lives and become one partner's wholly owned subsidiary upon termination of the joint venture. The reason for this tendency is that facility-sharing joint ventures are often used by one partner as a means of gradually exiting a market while pursuing economies of scale and rationalization through joint utilization of less profitable production facilities.[13] Examples include the joint venture between Sony and Samsung Electronics to jointly manufacture LCD panels by utilizing existing production capacity[14] and the joint venture between Shionogi & Co and Germany's Degussa AG.[15]

6.2.3 Securing Resources

The objective of securing resources can also be called securing uninterrupted supply. Companies engaged in extraction of natural resources in foreign countries are sometimes required to partner with a locally owned company to gain access to the resources. To secure a continuous supply of essential raw materials, such companies form joint ventures with partners that possess mining rights or patents on production technologies.

---

[13] *See* Barney *supra* note 9, at 371 for a discussion of utilizing joint ventures as real options to resolve the "lemon problem" stemming from information asymmetry. Barney also discusses using joint ventures to correctly value assets divested upon the seller's exit from a business by forming a 50:50 joint venture with the seller, directly observing the seller's management resources (including intangible assets), and then buying out the seller's remaining 50% equity stake after determining its intrinsic value.

[14] *See* NIHON KEIZAI SHINBUN, December 27, 2011, at 11; October 30, 2011, at 1; April 26, 2011, at 13. Sony and Samsung terminated their joint venture in 2012.

[15] *See* NIHON KEIZAI SHINBUN, June 25, 2003, at 15.

The same objective can also be accomplished by acquiring an equity stake in, or forming a cross-shareholding relationship with, a local company. Examples include the joint venture between Itochu Corporation and a Brazilian bioethanol producer to secure sugarcane to produce bioethanol[16] and the joint venture between ExxonMobil and Russia's Rosneft to secure petroleum resources in the Arctic Ocean.[17]

6.2.4 Utilization of Sales Channels

When companies enter a new geographic market, they sometimes form a joint venture with a company that already possesses a sales network and local market experience if doing so is more time- and cost-efficient than building a sales network independently. In these cases, the market-entering company must compare the costs and benefits of forming a joint venture against costs to enter the market through distributorship agreements in order to determine which option is most advantageous.

Examples include the joint venture between major Japanese publisher Kadokawa and mail-order marketer Senshukai, which was an operation established to sell the former's books via the latter's network,[18] and the joint venture between Japanese travel agency JTB and Lotte.com, a subsidiary of the Korean conglomerate Lotte established to promote tourism in Korea.[19]

6.2.5 Reputational Backing

Companies that lack name recognition or credibility in a new market sometimes form a joint venture with an incumbent company to enhance reputation in that market through association with the incumbent company.

For example, Aeon, a major Japanese retailer, acquired a stake in Tesco's Japanese supermarket chain and folded it into the Aeon Group

---

[16]   *See* NIHON KEIZAI SHINBUN, September 24, 2008, at 9.
[17]   *See* NIHON KEIZAI SHINBUN evening edition, April 17, 2012, at 3.
[18]   *See* NIHON KEIZAI SHINBUN, April 16, 2009, at 11.
[19]   *See* NIHON KEIZAI SHINBUN, April 25, 2007, at 13. Barney *supra* note 9, at 369–371 discusses low-cost market entry as an objective that is a composite of several of the objectives discussed above, including building a distribution network (access to sales channels), tapping into a local company's cultural knowledge (mentorship), and circumventing political/trade barriers (avoidance of frictions).

with the aim of revitalizing its business.[20] Tesco Japan subsequently began carrying Aeon brand merchandise, becoming a wholly owned subsidiary of Aeon in 2012. Another example is the joint venture between Itochu and Proteome Systems, an Australian biotech company that possesses protein analysis technology used in genomic drug development that was unknown in Japan.[21] The joint venture with Itochu gave Proteome Systems credibility in Japan.

6.2.6 Obtaining Local Expertise

Companies seeking to enter a new geographic market sometimes form joint ventures with local companies with experience in local matters such as consumer preferences and store siting. Companies considering such a joint venture must compare the costs and benefits of a simple consulting contract to determine which is most advantageous.

Mentorship joint ventures have become less prevalent in recent years. Companies that have utilized this structure include Starbucks Coffee, which formed a joint venture with Sazaby League when expanding into the Japanese market because of the need for a local mentor.[22] Another example is the joint venture between Mos Food Services, which operates a premium hamburger chain in Japan, and Korea's Media Will Holdings.[23] Mos Food partnered with Media Will to learn about Korean consumers' preferences and gain a foothold in the Korean market.

6.2.7 Alleviation of Friction

Foreign companies may form joint ventures with local companies to ease the various frictions that often arise in the process of entering a new geographic market. Such frictions may involve legal and/or practical matters. A joint venture is sometimes the only way to enter a country with foreign-ownership restrictions. Even where no such legal restrictions exist, economic frictions may impede market entry. A joint venture may be used to soften one partner's identity as a foreign company.

---

[20] *See* NIHON KEIZAI SHINBUN, June 18, 2012, at 1.

[21] *See* NIHON KEIZAI SHINBUN, May 18, 2002, at 9.

[22] Starbucks International (Starbucks Coffee's international arm and subsidiary) and Sazaby (currently Sazaby League), a Japanese retailer and restaurateur, formed an alliance to jointly operate a chain of stores in Japan and established Starbucks Coffee Japan. www.starbucks.co.jp/company/history/fy 1999.html.

[23] *See* NIHON KEIZAI SHINBUN online edition, September 9, 2011.

For example, Toyota formed its NUMMI joint venture with GM to alleviate trade frictions between Japan and the US.[24] To ease religious and cultural frictions when expanding into Islamic markets, Tokyo Marine & Nichido Fire Insurance formed a joint venture with Saudi Arabia's Alinma Bank and a Saudi government-affiliated institution.[25]

6.2.8 Brand Introduction

Another common reason for forming a joint venture is to utilize a partner's famous brand or brand image. Companies typically use such joint ventures to introduce a foreign company's branded products to their home markets. Companies considering such a joint venture must compare a simple license agreement or distributorship agreement to determine which option is most advantageous.

The other partner's objective in forming such a joint venture is often to gain access to sales channels. In other words, one partner aims to expand its geographic market while the other aims to expand its product line. By forming a joint venture, the partners combine their respective strengths and weaknesses in a complementary fashion.

Examples include Meiji-Borden, which introduced Lady Borden premium ice cream to Japan,[26] and the joint venture between Kikkoman and Taiwan's Uni-President Enterprises to manufacture and sell soy sauce and vinegar in Taiwan under the Kikkoman brand name.[27]

6.2.9 Technology Introduction

When a joint venture is formed to introduce technology, one partner will transfer a patented invention and/or technological know-how to the joint

---

[24] ZENICHI SHISHIDO & ATSUSHI KUSANO, KOKUSAI GOBEN: TOKYOTA-GM JOINTO BENCHA NO KISEKI [INTERNATIONAL JOINT VENTURES: A CASE STUDY OF THE JOINT VENTURE BETWEEN TOYOTA AND GENERAL MOTORS] (1988). *See also* NIHON KEIZAI SHINBUN, April 7, 2010, at 3; September 26, 2009, at 11; June 30, 2009 at 1 and 3; February 16, 2004, at 7; February 12, 2004, at 8. When Toyota Motor and General Motors (GM) formed their New United Motor Manufacturing Inc. (NUMMI) joint venture, GM's main objective was presumably to gain compact-car production know-how and Toyota's main objective was presumably to gain North American market access by easing trade frictions. *See* Barney *supra* note 9, at 365–367.

[25] *See* NIHON KEIZAI SHINBUN, April 1, 2010, at 1.

[26] Regarding Meiji-Borden, *see* www.referenceforbusiness.com/history2/52/Meiji-Dairies-Corporation.html.

[27] *See* NIHON KEIZAI SHINBUN, September 27, 2008, at 15.

venture. The licensor partner's objective in forming such a joint venture is often to enter a new market. In these cases, prospective partners must determine whether a joint venture or simple license agreement is most advantageous. A licensor partner may transfer its technology and/or other intellectual property to the other partner in addition to the JV company, or it may transfer its technology to the JV company only and not to its partner to avoid a "boomerang effect". In the latter case, the partner will indirectly gain access to the technology through the JV company.[28] A joint venture of the former type is generally the best means of acquiring know-how if it is implicit, complex, and/or difficult to replicate and therefore not learnable through a simple license agreement.

Examples include Fuji Xerox, a joint venture formed by Fujifilm and Xerox to introduce Xerox's copier technology to Japan, and the joint venture between Kuraray, a Japanese diversified chemical maker, and China's Zhejiang Hexin to bring Kuraray's industrial waste treatment technologies to China.[29] Another good example is major US electric steelmaker Steel Dynamics' joint venture with Japan's Kobe Steel to gain access to Kobe Steel's technology.[30]

6.2.10 Collaborative R&D

In R&D joint ventures, the partners exchange know-how bilaterally. Such joint ventures may be limited to R&D or they may involve manufacturing as well. Joint R&D activities are generally more effective and efficient because of reduced risk, lower costs, shorter development cycles, and technological compatibilities. Benefits can also yield from expediting technological innovation. However, prospective partners must compare forming a joint venture with other available options, such as a license agreement and/or production outsourcing agreement, to determine which will lead to the best result.

Examples of collaborative R&D joint ventures include the water-treatment joint venture that paired Fuji Electric's measurement and control technologies complementarily with NGK Insulators' sludge incineration facilities.[31] Another example is the joint venture established by

---

[28] *See infra* Ch. 7. For the licensor, licensing is a means of utilizing unused intellectual property; for the licensee, it is a means of low-cost business expansion.

[29] *See* NIHON KEIZAI SHINBUN online edition, May 18, 2002.

[30] *See* NIHON KEIZAI SHINBUN, June 21, 2007, at 1; November 22, 2007, at 13.

[31] *See* NIHON KEIZAI SHINBUN, February 28, 2007.

Idemitsu Kosan, Kanematsu, Tokyo Gas, and eight other companies with the aim of jointly developing environmental technologies to produce methane gas from gases emitted by raw garbage.[32] In the US pharmaceutical industry in particular, R&D joint ventures between Big Pharma and development-stage biotech companies are common.[33]

6.2.11 Cost-sharing

When launching a risky new business or when operating an investment-intensive business, companies sometimes form joint ventures to manage risk and share costs. Typical businesses that utilize this basis include those related to oilfield development and aircraft development.

One example of a cost-sharing joint venture is the consortium of 30 small and mid-sized Japanese confectionery makers that was established to access the Chinese market (an effort to mediate the costs associated with exporting their products to China).[34] Another such example is the joint venture between Mitsui OSK Lines, Itochu, Algeria's Sonatrach, and a Sonatrach subsidiary that was formed to build and maintain a fleet of LNG tankers through a special-purpose company.[35]

6.3 ANTITRUST LAW

By establishing a joint venture, both partners are able to earn synergistic return that would not be available via an independently run business. However, when a joint venture generates synergistic return by restraining competition, it may face the risk of violating anti-cartel and business combination regulations under antitrust law.

For example, in a facility-sharing joint venture between horizontal competitors with large market shares, restrictions on production volumes that are supportive of products' sales prices could constitute an agreement in restraint of competition. Joint ventures established as an alternative to competition or to gain access to sales channels run the risk of becoming an unreasonable restraint of trade in the form of a price cartel.[36]

---

[32] *See* NIHON KEIZAI SHINBUN, January 22, 2008, at 15.
[33] *See infra* Ch. 14, 14.3.
[34] *See* NIHON KEIZAI SHINBUN, November 11, 2010, at 9.
[35] *See* NIHON KEIZAI SHINBUN, June 11, 2004, at 13.
[36] Japan's Antimonopoly Act, Article 3. *See* Japan Fair Trade Commission's advisory decision of December 11, 1975 (*Shinketsushu* vol. 22 at 101).

Additionally, partners in R&D joint ventures must pay close attention to guidelines promulgated by competition authorities relating to joint R&D.[37]

From the preparatory stage preceding a joint venture's establishment, partners must be mindful of antitrust law restrictions when negotiating how they will share control of the joint venture and the total return derived therefrom. Based on guidelines issued by the competition authorities in the country in which their JV company will be established and operate, the partners must look at factors such as the nature of their relationship (whether they will act as competitors), their joint venture's form of organization (company or contractual arrangement), the value-chain segment in which their joint venture will operate (upstream, downstream, or somewhere in between), influential related markets, market share, competitive environment (e.g., market concentration), and the joint venture's business purpose (e.g., reasonable necessity of establishing a joint venture, resultant improvement in consumer welfare). The partners must be prepared to assert and substantiate that any factors with a competition-restraining effect are reasonably necessary for the joint venture's business purpose.

Antitrust law also includes *ex ante* procedural regulations that must be complied with before a joint venture is established. Closing a business combination during the regulatory waiting period is prohibited. In addition to abiding by the waiting period, JV partners must comply with other (e.g., notification) requirements and be careful to refrain from gun-jumping. It is particularly important to check antitrust law restrictions in the case of horizontal joint ventures between competitors whose combined sales, assets, and market shares are substantial because such a joint venture would have market power.[38]

---

[37] For US guidelines, *see* 1988 Antitrust Guide Concerning Research Joint Ventures, National Cooperative Research Act of 1984; for European guidelines, *see* the Treaty on the Functioning of the European Union, Treaty on Joint Research Functions, Block Exemption Regulation on R&D Agreements; for Japanese guidelines, *see* paras 4 and 5(8), 5(9) and 5(10) of Japan Fair Trade Commission, *Guidelines Concerning Joint Research and Development under the Antimonopoly Act* (April 20, 1993; revised January 1, 2010) www.meti.go.jp/policy/kyosofunso/pdf/kyoudou.pdf.

[38] *See* Hewitt, *supra* note 10, at Ch. 16. Regarding the US, *see* 1988 Antitrust Guide Concerning Research Joint Ventures, National Cooperative Research Act of 1984; 1988 Antitrust Enforcement Guidelines for International Operation. Regarding Europe, *see* the Treaty on the Functioning of the European Union, Treaty on Joint Research Functions, Block Exemption Regulation on R&D

6.4 REASONS FOR CREATING A JV COMPANY IN ADDITION TO A CONTRACTUAL ALLIANCE

Most synergies can also be realized through a contractual alliance instead of a joint venture. Conceivable reasons for establishing a JV company (using equity) instead of limiting the partners' relationship to a contractual alliance are discussed below.

First, for the partners, obtaining mutual commitment is highly significant.[39] Once a company has been established, exit costs are higher than they would be in a mere contractual relationship. If the partners were to initially form a contractual relationship with the intention of converting it to a joint venture in the event that the venture succeeded, one might not be able to sufficiently incentivize the other.

Second, from a licensor's standpoint, joint ventures are sometimes used to prevent technology from becoming contaminated by disputable ownership claims. By forming a separate legal entity in the form of a joint venture that serves as an intermediary between the licensor partner and the other partner (licensee partner) instead of contractually licensing technology directly to the licensee, a licensor can prevent the transfer of its technology from the joint venture to the licensee partner. Another advantage is that the licensor has more control over licensed technologies when they are ring-fenced within a joint venture.

More specifically, partners in this second scenario will also enter into the following types of agreement. First, they will agree not to exchange technology between themselves (i.e., failure to exchange technology will not constitute a breach of the licensor partner's obligations) and that personnel seconded to the joint venture are barred from contact with the other partner's technology information (i.e., personnel who deal with technology information would be permanently transferred to the JV company).

Next, the licensor partner and JV company will enter into an agreement concerning information-system access rights (establishment of a firewall) and an agreement prohibiting the joint venture from disclosing information to the other partner. Lastly, the JV company will enter into confidentiality agreements with its personnel.

Third, joint ventures are sometimes used as a vehicle for a licensor to secure ongoing rights to products of the licensed technology's further

---

Agreements, Guidelines on Horizontal Cooperation Agreements, and Block Exemption Regulation on Specialization Agreements.

[39]   *See* COLIN MAYER, FIRM COMMITMENT 117 (2013).

development. In contrast to contracts, which typically have an expiration date, companies generally exist in perpetuity. Specifically, the licensor partner can ensure its ability to utilize related inventions and improvement inventions developed by the joint venture by entering into one of the following types of agreement.[40] Flow-back or assign-back agreements are agreements through which a licensor partner becomes a patentee of improved technologies. This type of agreement may fully transfer the rights to improved technologies to the licensor partner or it may stipulate that such rights are to be co-owned by the licensor partner and joint venture. Alternatively, the joint venture may be the sole patentee and agree to license improved technologies to the licensor partner. This type of arrangement, called a grant-back license, may be an exclusive, sole, or nonexclusive license. An exclusive grant-back license precludes even the joint venture from exploiting the licensed technology. Under a sole grant-back license, by contrast, the joint venture exclusively licenses the technology to the licensor partner but retains the right to exploit the licensed technology itself. A third contractual modality is the option agreement, which obligates the joint venture to notify the licensor partner of any improvements to technologies while giving the licensor partner the right to a grant-back license to such technologies if the licensor partner wishes to license them.[41]

Fourth, from a licensee's standpoint, joint ventures are said to be more conducive to gaining know-how than a simple license agreement because the licensor has an incentive to proactively transfer know-how to a company that it co-owns.

Fifth, using a legal entity separate from the JV partners and granting it autonomy is more conducive to incentivizing key personnel, managing business performance, and diversifying risks.

---

[40] *See* Brian G. Brunsvold, Dennis P. O'Reilley & D. Brian Kacedon, Drafting Patent License Agreements, Form 10.01 "Improvements" (6th ed. 2008).

[41] In Japan, if such an agreement poses a risk of incentive distortion of the licensee to independently conduct R&D (e.g., by not requiring payment of reasonable consideration), it reportedly would likely constitute an unfair trade practice (General Designation No. 13, "trading on restrictive terms") and be illegal (*see* Japan Fair Trade Commission, *Guidelines to Application of the Antimonopoly Act Concerning Review of Business Combinations*, (May 31, 2004; revised June 14, 2011) www.jftc.go.jp/dk/kiketsu/guideline/guidelineshishin 01.htm and *Guidelines for the Use of Intellectual Property under the Antimonopoly Act* (September 28, 2007; revised January 1, 2010) www.jftc.go.jp/dk/guideline/unyoukijun/chitekizaisan.html.

Sixth, a company can obscure its identity by partnering with one or more other companies (e.g., a joint venture can enable a company to expand into a foreign country in which trade frictions exist or, in Japan, enable a company that belongs to a large corporate group, a so-called *keiretsu*, to transact business with unaffiliated companies).

Nevertheless, it is not always more advantageous to establish a separate legal entity for the joint venture than to enter into a contractual business alliance. The obvious advantages of a contractual alliance include expeditiousness and ease of exit.

7. Intellectual property and incentive bargaining

JV partners usually contribute some form of intellectual property (IP) to their joint ventures. The allocation of IP rights to the joint venture and among the partners and definition of the terms under which the IP may be exploited are the legal means of delineating the scope of the partners' and the joint venture's respective businesses. These issues are important matters that influence sharing of control, sharing of total return, and threat of exit.

7.1 PLANNING RELATED TO HUMAN CAPITAL CONTRIBUTIONS TO JOINT VENTURES

7.1.1 Definition of IP and Contributions of Human Capital

The term "intellectual property" means inventions, devices, new varieties of plants, designs, works and other property that is produced through creative activities by human beings (including discovered or solved laws of nature or natural phenomena that are industrially applicable), trademarks, trade names, other marks that are used to indicate goods or services in business activities, and trade secrets and other technical or business information useful in business activities. IP rights include patent rights, utility model rights, plant breeder's rights, design rights, copyrights, trademark rights, other IP-related rights that are stipulated by laws and regulations, and rights pertaining to an interest protected by law. The legal protections that result from conferral of IP rights convert technical or reputational information into assets. In essence, IP rights grant the right to prevent third parties from unauthorized use of human intellectual works such as inventions, or devices and intangibles[1] such as trademarks,

---

[1]   *See* IAN HEWITT, HEWITT ON JOINT VENTURES, Ch. 17 (5th ed. 2011). US Treasury Regulation 26 CFR §1.482-4(b) broadly defines an intangible as an asset that "derives its value not from its physical attributes but from its intellectual content or other intangible properties," such as a license, franchise,

thereby conferring economic benefit through artificially created scarcity. Licensing of IP is one key objective for partners in many joint ventures and technology tie-ups. As such, it is subject to inter-partner bargaining.

In terms of human capital that JV partners contribute to their joint ventures, the partners must take into account, aside from vested IP rights, the actual extent to which legal status required for business operations (e.g., regulatory licenses) and use of know-how and other such information are legally protected. JV partners also must be aware that IP licensing is not only a means to earn monetary return in the form of royalties, but also a key issue that influences sharing of control and threat of exit. Additionally, by protecting the rights of and generating return for partners that have created IP, IP rights incentivize partners to contribute resources to their joint ventures to promote development of the joint venture's business and maintain competitive order between the partners, and between the joint venture and individual partners.

7.1.2   Motivation to Elect to Form a Joint Venture

Partner A and Partner B want to partner with each other to realize synergies through joint development or application of a technology. Partner A owns the technology and Partner B wants to commercially exploit it. Partner A could choose to furnish the technology directly to Partner B through a licensing agreement. Alternatively, the two partners could jointly form a corporation. Licensing agreements and joint ventures are not mutually exclusive alternatives. The question is whether the partners manage their cooperative or adversarial relationship and the licensed technology's mode of exploitation through direct contractual obligations as parties to a license agreement, or whether they indirectly manage these matters by organizing their relationship as a JV company.

7.1.2.1   In-kind contribution or transfer
If the partner that owns the IP (hereinafter referred to as the licensor partner) contributes it to the JV company as an in-kind capital contribution, the licensor partner would be able to acquire an ownership interest in the JV company through a nonmonetary capital contribution. If the licensor partner has no plans to exploit the IP in any of its businesses other than the joint venture, an in-kind capital contribution would enable it to expeditiously monetize the IP with certainty, acquire an ownership

---

customer list, system, or procedure. A licensor partner may also contribute sub-licensable IP rights owned by a third party.

interest in the joint venture,[2] and signal commitment that will incentivize its prospective partner to contribute capital to the joint venture. If the licensor partner plans to operate an existing business in competition with the JV company, it will typically choose to license its IP. Even if the licensor partner does transfer the IP to the joint venture, it will license back the IP for use in its own businesses. However, once the licensor partner transfers its IP, it is at risk of losing its right to manage and dispose of IP in the event that it loses control of the JV company. Bargaining over sharing of control is therefore even more critical than usual in such a scenario.

From the standpoint of the partner that needs the licensor partner's IP to form the joint venture (the licensee partner), an in-kind contribution is preferable. When the licensor partner's human capital contribution to the JV company is converted to financial capital in the form of rights allocated to the JV company, the JV company is able to exercise the IP rights. Whereas in direct licensing agreement scenarios the licensor partner may sometimes skimp on providing IP to the joint venture, in the case of in-kind capital contributions of IP the licensor partner is prevented from partially withholding the IP and the scope for opportunistic behavior is limited.

7.1.2.2 Licensing

From the licensor partner's standpoint, licensing is more advantageous than transferring IP in certain respects even though the licensor partner will incur expenses to preserve its rights. The advantages include that the licensor partner retains the right to manage and dispose of the IP rights, is able to control the terms of the license, and can effectively recover its IP by terminating the license agreement at the joint venture's conclusion.

If the IP is licensed directly to the licensee without creating a joint venture, the licensor is at risk of competing behavior by the licensee. The licensee could potentially master the licensed technology and the licensor could lose its controlling right over the licensee after termination of such license agreement. And then the licensee could become a competitor in the same or similar technological domain as the licensor. However, the licensor partner can control this risk by licensing its IP to the JV company. If the licensor partner is involved in the joint venture's

---

[2] If a licensor partner contributes IP rights to a JV company as an in-kind capital contribution, the licensor partner's share of total returns attributable to the IP rights would be a return on investment. If the licensor partner licenses IP rights to the JV company, its share of total returns attributable to the IP rights would be a return from transactions.

management, it will also be able to participate in decision-making and/or monitoring regarding how the licensed IP rights are exercised by the JV company.

From the licensee partner's standpoint, direct licensing of IP is more advantageous if the licensee partner intends to independently pursue opportunities. While use of a JV company would limit such opportunities, it may work to dispel the licensor partner's reservations, thereby incentivizing the licensor partner to contribute its IP to the joint venture.

If the licensor partner grants a license to a JV company, a joint venture can better enable the exchange of not only documented formal knowledge, but also implicit knowledge through information sharing and human interaction within the JV company. Establishment of a joint venture should therefore facilitate the transfer of knowledge from the partners to the JV company and increase JV synergies.

Situations that warrant particular attention include (a) direct competition between the JV company and a solely owned business of the licensor partner, (b) transfer of the licensed IP rights from the licensor partner to a third party, in some jurisdictions requiring perfection such as registration, resulting in the loss of the JV company's license against the assignee, (c) emergence of a rival company as a result of the licensor partner granting another license to a third party or a leak of know-how through a technology tie-up, and (d) continued payment of royalties on worthless IP in perpetuity.

7.1.3   Opportunities and Threats between Partners: Technology Tie-up Schemes and Avoidance of Potential Competition

If a licensor partner directly licenses the IP to, or enters into a joint development contract with, the other partner, the co-partner may independently gain sufficient knowledge of the IP to become a potential competitor of the licensor partner.[3] However, by licensing IP to a joint venture, the licensor partner can prevent the emergence of a rival if it structures the licensing arrangement as a "black box" designed to preclude use of its know-how by the other partner, accumulates technology and/or reputational assets in the JV company, and retains control of the JV company. Additionally, IP rights are territorial. IP licenses can be limited in scope in non-territorial terms also. Consequently, if a licensor partner and a JV company operate identical businesses, they can

---

[3]   *See* GORDON V. SMITH & RUSSELL L. PARR, INTELLECTUAL PROPERTY: LICENSING AND JOINT VENTURE PROFIT STRATEGIES 359–391 (1993).

divide the market geographically or by product/service segments – subject to the constraints of antitrust law.

When IP rights required to operate a joint venture are licensed, the licensor partner must first decide on the licensee, the license's geographic scope (territory), the objective scope of the licensed product(s) and/or service(s), and the license's duration. The licensor partner must then decide whether to grant the JV company nonexclusive rights or to prohibit the other partner from competing with the JV company by granting exclusive rights to the JV company. Other matters to consider include rights to access or use information regarding the fruits of the joint venture's operations. If the partners want to clearly delineate their respective solely owned businesses from their joint venture's business, they will use an exclusive license.

The IP holder partner may sometimes be concerned about the risk of losing IP through cooperative relationships. Information is inherently susceptible to copying. Once obtained, knowledge cannot be repossessed. JV partners sometimes gain the know-how of the other partner in the course of running their joint ventures and apply that know-how to their solely owned businesses. Partner companies from developed countries that form joint ventures with local partners in developing countries and transfer technology to the joint ventures sometimes face the threat of a "boomerang effect," where the local partner becomes a rival after the JV company's dissolution and encroaches on the developed-country partner's home market.

Since know-how can be used freely if obtained legally, prospective licensor partners must take precautions against the possibility of a breakdown in negotiations before disclosing know-how to a prospective partner. Such precautions include entering into a nondisclosure agreement that imposes a duty of confidentiality and prohibits use of the know-how for unauthorized purposes and/or signing a memorandum of understanding regarding exploitation of IP rights and use of the know-how. Through such means, JV partners can protect their IP, including patents and know-how pertaining to technologies related to the joint venture, even during the preparatory stages of establishing a joint venture. Given that joint ventures may end up being relatively short-lived enterprises, a partner must also be cognizant of the risk of the other partner utilizing know-how in its solely owned businesses and becoming a competitor after the joint venture has been terminated.

7.1.4 Human Capital Contributions and Monitoring

7.1.4.1 Human capital contributions at inception of joint venture

When a JV partner contributes IP rights to a joint venture, a key issue involves the identification and valuation of IP that is essential to the joint venture in light of the joint venture's purpose. Valuation of IP is directly connected with valuation of JV ownership interests and sharing of return on investment in cases where an in-kind capital contribution of IP was made at the joint venture's inception. If a partner definitively and permanently contributes essential resources such as patent rights to a joint venture by assigning them or contributing them as an in-kind capital contribution, the partner's equity ownership interest at the time of the joint venture's inception will increase, but the partner is also giving the other partner an opportunity to earn return on investment from the IP. Conversely, if the partner retains ownership of those resources and furnishes them to the joint venture through a patent license agreement, the partner is able to benefit exclusively from royalty income on an ongoing basis as a return from the patent license.[4]

7.1.4.2 Antitrust implications of license terms and avoidance of competition with JV partners

If a licensor partner operates a solely owned business in parallel with its joint venture in the same market in which the joint venture operates or a market related thereto, the partner and JV company must be mutually prohibited from operating businesses in competition with each other within the scope of the joint venture agreement. Such a prohibition is needed to prevent spillovers, where the JV company expands its operations beyond its geographic territory or product markets or, conversely, the licensor partner expands its solely owned business to encroach upon the scope of the joint venture's business. This prohibition also prevents free-riding on resources contributed by another risk-bearing licensor partner.

For a licensor partner, a duty not to compete has disadvantages as well as advantages. Specifically, the licensor partner loses the freedom to operate a solely owned business in the same business domain as the joint venture if the joint venture's business is not as successful as anticipated. In cases where a less restrictive alternative to a non-compete clause exists, licensor partners must be aware that antitrust issues could arise and that the exchange of market information between partners through

---

4   *See* Hewitt, *supra* note 1, at Ch. 17-21.

monitoring may constitute circumstantial evidence of conspiracy.[5] If JV partners adopt a business strategy of contributing all of their available financial and human capital to the joint venture's business and refraining from operating similar businesses themselves, such a strategy is less problematic except when a partner exits the joint venture. However, if the partners continue to operate solely owned businesses similar to their joint venture's business, they face a conflict of interest.

IP rights are country-specific in accord with the principles of territoriality. Patents granted in different countries for the same invention are independent of each other. IP rights can be restricted to a licensed territory or specific country. By drafting license agreements that limit the scope of licensed products/services and the license's geographic scope pursuant to the principle of territoriality, JV partners can delineate territories between themselves and their joint ventures. Even if a license has a procompetitive effect, it still needs to be assessed to determine if it is substantively illegal by analyzing economic factors and weighing the procompetitive effect against its anticompetitive effect attributable to market partitioning.

Because IP creates market power, license agreements between JV partners and their joint ventures must be vetted with respect to antitrust law issues. For example, such license agreements must be analyzed to determine whether the license constitutes a monopoly or conspiracy prohibited by antitrust law (see Sherman Antitrust Act, 15 U.S.C. §1 and 2, Clayton Act, 15 U.S.C. §7, and Japan's Antimonopoly Act, Article 3). JV partners must also be careful to avoid contractual terms that could constitute unfair trade practices or unfair methods of competition that would substantively restrain competition or unreasonably restrain trade or commerce in the relevant market. Examples of such terms include tying of goods purchases to a patent license or an assignment back of improvement inventions constituting patent misuse.[6]

License agreements and joint ventures are means of realizing similar economic effects through different legal structures.[7] Technology tie-ups and business combinations have commonalities and differences. A JV

---

[5] *See* BRIAN G. BRUNSVOLD, DENNIS P. O'REILLEY, AND D. BRIAN KACEDON, DRAFTING PATENT LICENSE AGREEMENTS, 405–451 (6th ed. 2008).

[6] *See Statutory Provisions and Guidelines of the Antitrust Division*, www.justice.gov/atr/public/divisionmanual/chapter2.pdf.

[7] *See* Japan Fair Trade Commission, *Guidelines to Application of the Antimonopoly Act Concerning Review of Business Combinations* (May 31, 2004; amended June 14, 2011) www.jftc.go.jp/en/legislation_gls/imonopoly_guidelines. files/110713.2.pdf.

company may be exempt from antitrust laws in the context of its parent–subsidiary relationship. Consequently, JV partners may be able to undertake business activities that exploit licensed technologies through shared management control of the JV company. By contrast, license agreement clauses such as restrictions on the sale of licensed products pose a risk of violating antitrust laws. JV partners should accordingly engage in planning based on case law and fair trade authorities' guidelines to minimize antitrust risk while also achieving their joint ventures' intended objectives. Such planning involves reviewing national antitrust authorities' guidelines with respect to IP license agreements.[8]

7.1.4.3 Monitoring

Another issue that ought to be addressed at the time of a joint venture's inception is how to monitor whether the other partner has actually contributed IP rights to a JV company. The answer to this question is obvious when the IP in question is a brand, but when the IP consists of patents or know-how, determining whether the licensor partner has fully contributed technology essential to the joint venture's business can be difficult. Know-how is intrinsically difficult to specify in its entirety before it is disclosed. Proving that the other partner has in fact failed to perform its obligations is likewise difficult. Practical means of addressing such difficulties include: due diligence conducted by experts during preparatory stages, and monitoring. Monitoring can be accomplished through such means as ascertaining the technological composition of the joint venture's products manufactured through exploitation of patented know-how and verifying the product performance attainable through use of that know-how.

Once a joint venture is operational, partners must monitor the opportunistic behavior of the other partner whose solely owned business spills into the joint venture's rightful business domain. Likewise, the JV company's competitive behavior in the rightful business domains of businesses solely owned by partners may also need to be monitored. In

---

[8]   For guidelines regarding IP licensing and antitrust law, *see* national competition authorities' latest guidelines, such as Japan Fair Trade Commission, *Guidelines for the Use of Intellectual Property under the Antimonopoly Act* (September 28, 2007; amended January 1, 2010) www.jftc.go.jp/en/legislation_gls/imonopoly_guidelines.files/070928_IP_Guideline.pdf; US Department of Justice and Federal Trade Commission, *Antitrust Guidelines for Licensing of Intellectual Property*, www.justice.gov/atr/public/guidelines/0558.htm; and *Antitrust Enforcement and Intellectual Property Rights – Promoting Innovation and Competition* (2007) www.justice.gov/atr/public/hearings/ip/222655.pdf.

particular, a JV partner must monitor the other partner's opportunistic behavior by imposing duties with the prior written consent of the partner or through advance notification and after-the-fact reporting with respect to newly consummated license agreements and key R&D agreements between the partners and the JV company. Among transactions of which a JV partner is notified in advance, it is also important for the partner to have veto rights over designated types of transactions or transactions whose value exceeds a specified materiality threshold. Such transactions should also be subject to the approval of the JV company's board of directors. In order to delineate the scope of counterparties in cooperative relationships, it is also important to monitor (1) acts aimed at forming alliances between a licensor partner and third parties other than the other partner within the domain of a licensed technology, and (2) sub-licensing arrangements that could give rise to a potential competitor. Lastly, from the standpoint of deciding how contributed resources will be used through participation in management, a licensor partner should monitor its joint ventures by vetting new-business plans and investment plans to ensure that JV companies do not stray beyond the scope of their businesses even if they stay within their defined physical boundaries.

7.1.4.4 JV companies as licensees

When a JV company is in the process of being established, the content of IP license agreements between a licensor partner and the JV company is negotiated between the JV partners. Once the JV company is operational, however, the value of the licensed IP typically changes over time. Accordingly, the licensee must avoid the risk of continuing to pay unwarranted remuneration for obsolete technology by ensuring that it has the opportunity to periodically review and, if necessary, renegotiate license agreements. When a license agreement is renegotiated while a joint venture is in operation, the legal entity that renegotiates the license agreement with the licensor partner is the licensee – i.e., the JV company – not the other partner. License agreement negotiations between a JV company and a JV partner (Partner A) that owns IP rights essential to the joint venture's business typically take one of two forms. First, a JV company director effectively appointed by Partner B may negotiate on behalf of the JV company. In such cases, the JV company is substantially acting as Partner B's agent and the negotiations are a proxy contest where the JV company's representative negotiates to protect Partner B's interests with respect to the arrangement for sharing total return stipulated in the JV agreement. Second, in cases where the JV company has gained autonomy, it may negotiate with the aim of protecting its own interests.

7.2   ACQUISITION OF CONTROL THROUGH IP RIGHTS

If the terms of a license agreement limit the products and/or services for which the licensed brand or technology can be used, the licensor partner can control the JV company's business domain and product/service offerings. Additionally, if the licensor partner requires the JV company to use a brand name or trademark for products and/or services within a specified business domain, the partner has the means to gain de facto decision-making authority over the joint venture's business by simultaneously licensing the brand name or trademark and imposing a duty to use it.

Another function of brands is to assure the quality of branded products. The licensor partner can order the JV company to engage in specific acts of commission or omission for quality control/maintenance purposes. Licensor partners can also stipulate detailed terms and conditions for use of their brands in advertising. Although a JV company is a jointly owned business, a partner that licenses its product brand/trademark to the JV company can thus gain effective control over the JV company's management decisions in the realm of marketing.

Deciding on the information systems that a JV company will use in its day-to-day operations is an important management issue for JV partners. The partners must decide on detailed specifications for the systems. They can have the JV company use systems identical to or effectively compatible with their own. If a partner is able to access the JV company's information systems, its operations will effectively be partially integrated with the JV company's operations to the extent of its transactional relationship with the joint venture. Such access will also ensure that the partner has an effective means of monitoring the JV company. Additionally, corporate culture and workflows are influenced the specifications of application systems. Accordingly, selecting information systems, designing business forms, and granting partners the right to access the JV company's information are technological means that support sharing of control from behind the scenes. Therefore, negotiating which partner will have authority over such matters and incidental agreements to determine system specifications and access terms becomes important. As a rule, information system issues in a joint venture formed through M&A or formed to operate an existing business are more important than in a joint venture formed to launch a new business.

7.3 IP RIGHTS AS A MEANS OF SHARING TOTAL RETURN

7.3.1 Return on Investment

A JV partner can acquire an equity interest through in-kind contributions of IP in addition to monetary capital contributions. In such cases, the partner contributing IP earns return on its investment in the form of dividends distributed by the JV company.

7.3.2 Return from Transactions

The licensor partner can earn exclusive return from transactions, and do so before distribution of return on investment, by receiving royalties on its IP rights licensed to the joint venture.

In terms of noncash economic benefits, JV partners must address two important issues. First, which partner(s) will own or be licensed IP rights developed by the JV company? Second, will one or both partners have the right to use such IP in solely owned businesses outside the scope of the joint venture's business while the joint venture is in operation and after its termination? JV partners should count their respective shares of this noncash economic value as part of their return from transactions.

7.3.3 Tax Issues

First, in terms of taxation on gifts or gratuitous transactions, key issues include whether the joint venture is exploiting the licensed IP rights and whether it is doing so gratuitously or in exchange for paid consideration. From the tax authorities' standpoint, a JV company paying consideration to one of its owners for IP rights that are not being exploited raises gift tax issues. Conversely, if the JV company is not paying consideration for IP rights that it is exploiting, taxation of income from a gratuitous transaction becomes an issue. Additionally, if a JV company's IP rights are gratuitously granted back to a licensor partner, the parties to the grant-back must demonstrate a value–exchange relationship to avoid taxation of the transaction as a gratuitous transfer of an economic benefit.

Second, a key issue with respect to transfer price taxation of transactions between a partner and a JV company is whether the JV company is a foreign related party.[9] If a corporation engages in a transaction with a foreign related party (generally defined as a foreign corporation that directly or indirectly owns 50 percent or more of the corporation) by, for example, buying or selling an asset or providing a service and the value exchanged for the asset or service is greater or less than its arm's-length price, the transaction is treated for corporate income taxation purposes as having been executed at the arm's-length price (e.g., ¥100) instead of the price actually paid (e.g., ¥120). The ¥20 difference between the price actually paid by the buyer and the arm's-length price is treated as equivalent to a gift, not part of the transaction price. This ¥20 is not deductible as an expense by the buyer; it is taxable income.

Next, if a JV is determined to be a foreign related party effectively controlled by one of its parent companies, it needs to decide on an arm's-length price calculation method. Its options include three basic methods: (a) the comparable uncontrolled price method, whereby arm's-length prices are set within the price range of previous transactions for similar technologies, (b) the resale price method, and (c) the cost-plus method.[10] However, these pricing methods were designed to be used for goods transactions. In the case of IP, there are few comparable arm's-length transactions involving similar intangible assets, similar contractual terms, and a similar technological application. Additionally, the cost of developing IP tends to be difficult to ascertain. Calculating an appropriate royalty rate is even more difficult when the IP in question is a relationship-specific asset that has value only when exploited by a specific company in a specific business.

Consequently, the parties to the transaction end up selecting the most appropriate pricing method based on the nature of the transaction and their roles, after consideration of which party will bear upfront invest-ment risk, which party has borne the costs to date, the balance between

---

⁹ For an example involving the sale of goods in which a joint venture was subject to transfer price taxation, the Osaka Regional Taxation Bureau (ORTB) ruled in 2006 that Takeda Pharmaceutical had underreported profits from the US market on product supply transactions that occurred from April 1999 through March 2005 between itself and TAP Pharmaceutical Products, a 50:50 joint venture between itself and Abbott. The ORTB levied some ¥57 billion of additional taxes and penalties under a transfer price tax assessment, www.takeda.com/news/2013/20130325_5701.html.
¹⁰ In the Adobe case (www.courts.go.jp/app/files/hanrei_jp/584/037584_hanrei.pdf) (Tokyo High Court, October 20, 2008), Adobe Japan used a method equivalent to the resale price method, whereby it determined similarity to comparable transactions based on comparative assessment of the functions of the parties to the transactions and the transactions' risks.

the parties' shares of expected future return and their risk burdens, and the relationship between benefits and the value exchanged for those benefits. When a licensor partner exclusively licenses its solely owned IP to a JV company, another pricing method that may be used is a variant of the (d) transactional net margin method.[11] With this method, the parties to the transaction would focus on the JV company that will pay royalties, calculate an operating profit margin commensurate with the IP's non-unique functions and the level of risk involved, and then estimate the residual profits in excess of the profit margin thus calculated that are unique to the IP. When a licensor partner and the JV company both contribute IP, another alternative is (e) the residual profit split method. Under this method, the two companies tally their combined operating profits regularly earned from non-related parties and share the residual profits earned on the value of their IP. By using one of these two methods, taxpayers can justify the reasonableness of the royalty rates to tax authorities. However, the tax authorities have discretion to select one of the three aforementioned basic pricing methods or any other method equivalent or similar thereto. In practice, running royalties are typically set through negotiation at a certain percentage of revenues derived from the licensed IP, within an arm's-length price range (i.e., between the floor and ceiling of the market transaction price range).

In the case of ordinary license agreements, royalties negotiated between independent parties are generally presumed to be reasonable. However, the fact that royalties were negotiated between JV partners is by itself not sufficient to prove that the royalties are reasonable under tax law.

JV partners must take reasonable steps to document that license royalties are based on arm's-length pricing in order to ensure that the licensing partner and joint venture are held accountable to the interests of the non-licensor partner. Keys factors pointing to the reasonableness of the terms of the licensing agreement include that: (a) the transaction scheme and value–exchange relationship are economically rational; (b) the transaction is structured such that the party that bore the risk of IP development expenses earns income from the IP; (c) relationships

---

[11] In the TDK case, decided by the National Tax Tribunal (NTT) on February 1, 2010, the NTT reduced by ¥14.1 billion a ¥21.3 billion transfer tax assessment levied by the Tokyo Regional Taxation Bureau on transactions between TDK and its overseas subsidiaries. *See* Baker & McKenzie, *Client Alert* (2010) www.bakermckenzie.co.jp/e/material/dl/supportingyourbusiness/newsletter/tax/Client_Alert_tax_20100210.pdf. *See also* www.pwc.com/gx/en/international-transfer-pricing/assets/japan.pdf.

between legal rights and responsibilities are structured in accord with the transaction scheme, agreements have been executed in writing, and internal authorization documents are complete and in order;[12] (d) documents (objective data) required by tax authorities have been prepared; (e) the transactions are being executed as agreed; and (f) the transactions are scheduled to continue for a predetermined duration unless preconditions change.[13] Licensee partners have de facto documentation obligations as taxpayers. Specifically, they must prepare and retain documentation of their transactions with foreign related parties and documentation of the arm's-length pricing that they used. Such documentation is to be submitted to the tax authorities at their request in the event of a transfer price taxation audit. Licensee partners therefore must conduct ongoing document management even after their joint ventures are operational.[14]

7.3.4 Ancillary Return

A licensor partner that licenses a corporate brand or trademark to a JV company may benefit exclusively from ancillary return in the form of enhancement of its brand's value, at the licensee's expense, resulting from the licensee advertising or otherwise promoting the brand. One function of brands is to identify the source of the branded products/ services. Even when a JV company remains in operation as one partner's solely owned business after dissolution of the joint venture, if the licensor partner is able to use a brand established in a market through the JV company's use of the brand, the licensor partner can benefit from the brand's reputation and power to draw customers in that market.

If a licensor partner and its JV company enter into a reciprocal license agreement and/or product supply agreement while also agreeing to develop technologies for separate markets or applications, the partner can, as part of its technology development strategy, benefit from ancillary return in the form of lower R&D investment and manufacturing cost

---

[12] *See* OECD, *White Paper on Transfer Pricing Documentation* (2013) www.oecd.org/ctp/transfer-pricing/white-paper-transfer-pricing-documentation.pdf.

[13] *See id.*; OECD, *Transfer Pricing Guidelines for Multinational Enterprises and Tax Administrations*, www.oecd-ilibrary.org/taxation/oecd-transfer-pricing-guidelines-for-multinational-enterprises-and-tax-administrations-2010_tpg-2010-en; Article 66(4) of Japan's Special Taxation Measures Act, National Tax Agency Commissioner's Directive on Interpretation of the Special Taxation Measures Act, and the NTA's Transfer Pricing Guidelines.

[14] For Japan, *see* Article 22(10) of the Special Taxation Measures Act Enforcement Ordinance (fiscal 2010 tax reform).

savings. This, in turn, leads to improved cost competitiveness within the domain of the partner's solely owned business through an efficient division of labor.

When a JV partner and JV company are linked by a single information system and able to access each other's information, they are effectively pooling their know-how. When one partner has exclusive rights to access and use a JV company's information, that partner alone will benefit from the know-how created during the joint venture's operational phase. Such a situation will affect the partners' assessment of JV synergies in the context of imbalances in ancillary return.

7.4 IP RIGHTS AND EXIT

7.4.1 Threat of Exit

When instead of transferring ownership of solely owned brand- or technology-related IP rights, a JV partner licenses them to the JV company, expiration or termination of the license agreement(s) related to IP rights essential to the joint venture's business creates a threat of exit. The licensor partner can gain a sustained bargaining advantage over the other partner not only prior to the joint venture's inception, but also during any renegotiations while the joint venture is operational. This advantage can influence the sharing of control.

7.4.2 Issues upon the Joint Venture's Termination

Even after a joint venture is terminated by a partner's exit, a licensor partner can, in a sense, recover its human capital by terminating license agreements and thereafter prohibiting use of licensed IP. Such recovery of human capital has an economic function similar to dividing designated residual assets between partners and returning to the contributing partner relationship-specific assets contributed as in-kind capital contributions. The contributing partner will also want assurances that the other partner is contractually prohibited from exploiting the IP rights or bound by a duty of confidentiality with respect to licensed know-how or a duty to refrain from competition through use of the licensed know-how after termination of the joint venture.

Methods of doing so include having the JV company transfer or gratuitously license the IP rights to the licensor partner upon termination of the license agreement(s) between the licensor partner and JV company. In such a scenario, the partners need to enter into an agreement after the joint venture's termination. If the other partner entirely buys out the licensor partner's equity stake in the JV company or a third party takes over the joint venture's business, the licensor partner could seek to exit in stages, while allowing the agreements licensing IP rights essential to the joint venture's business to remain in effect with revised terms.

If a brand license agreement is terminated after a joint venture has long utilized a licensor partner's brand pursuant to a license agreement that was repeatedly renewed, the joint venture loses the commercial rights and competitive advantage conferred by the brand license in the course of its operations. In such cases, if the JV company is then converted to a solely owned business by a non-licensor partner, the JV company or non-licensor partner has to newly launch its own brand and build brand recognition in the market from scratch. Its business will almost certainly be adversely affected by the rebranding.

7.4.3 Bankruptcy of a Partner

If the JV company remains in existence after termination of the joint venture upon the exit of the licensor partner, the JV company's residual IP at the time of the exit, including improvement inventions attributed to the JV company, can be distributed solely to the licensor partner as designated human capital. Once the joint venture has been terminated, the licensor partner is no longer obligated to contribute resources to the joint venture. The licensor partner will likely terminate existing agreements with the JV company, rendering the JV company unable to exploit the licensor partner's IP.[15] The JV company or the non-licensor partner therefore must enter into a separate agreement with the licensor partner if it wishes to continue to exploit or utilize the licensor partner's IP.

Complications arise in the event of the bankruptcy of the licensor partner or licensee JV company. The licensor partner's bankruptcy is generally grounds for termination of the joint venture agreement. It will also extinguish the JV company's license(s) granted by the licensor partner. If the licensee JV company goes bankrupt, the licensor partner faces the risk of information about its technology falling into the hands of third parties.

Under bankruptcy law, license agreements that provide for payment of running royalties are construed as executory contracts because they

---

[15] Termination of the license agreement would render the JV company unable to utilize all IP covered by the license agreement, including third-party IP rights that the licensor partner has the right to sub-license.

permit the licensee to continuously utilize the licensed IP rights.[16] The bankruptcy trustee may assume or reject such license agreements at its discretion. If the trustee rejects a license agreement, the agreement terminates and the licensee has the right to claim damages. However, the licensee can retain its license if the license agreement includes a covenant not to sue (11 U.S.C. §365). In the US, nonexclusive patent licenses are legally binding and enforceable against the licensor's successors when the licensor has assigned or otherwise transferred the patent after the license's effective date.[17] International bankruptcy cases, however, are complicated by the fact that requirements to perfect license rights against successor licensors differ by country.

7.5   LICENSE AGREEMENTS

Brand licensing transactions differ qualitatively from technology licensing transactions. Whereas technology is a creation of human intellectual activity, a brand identifies the source of a product or service in commercial activities and embodies its owner's commercial reputation.

7.5.1   Brand Licenses

A corporate brand license links the licensor and licensee(s) as a single group of affiliated companies that share an external reputation based on the same brand. Co-use of the same brand entails the risk of reputational damage due to a brand licensee's actions, meaning that the licensor and licensee(s) share reputational risk.[18]

---

[16]   Perlman v. Catapult Entertainment, Inc. (*In re* Catapult Entertainment, Inc.), 165 F.3d 747 (9th Cir. 1998) (cert. dismissed); Institute Pasteur v. Cambridge Biotech Corp., 104 F.3d 489 (1st Cir. 1997), cert. denied, 117 S. Ct 2511 (1997). However, a paid-up license with no continuing obligations may not be considered an executory contract. The contracting parties may not terminate the license agreement, and should take a risk of assignment of the license agreement.

[17]   *See* Keystone Type Foundry v. Fastpes Co., 272 F. 242, 245 (2d Cir. 1921). In Japan there are statutory provisions. *See* Article 99 of the Patent Act, Article 19(3) of the Utility Model Act, and Article 28(3) of the Design Act. However, registration perfects a nonexclusive license of a trademark/product brand (Article 31 of the Trademark Act).

[18]   Some companies may also have management policies opposed to forming JV companies as a general rule. Joint ventures in which one partner earns returns only from the other partner's well-known brand offers little benefit to the brand's

From the standpoint of societal reputation, co-use of a corporate brand should ideally be limited to majority-owned subsidiaries of the company that owns the brand trademark. Economically, royalties from brand licenses are perpetual, as long as the brand remains in use. The terms under which a licensor partner permits a JV company to use its brand are therefore an important issue even from a long-term perspective.

Under brand license agreements, the licensor may receive remuneration in the form of (1) corporate brand royalties, (2) product brand royalties, and/or (3) brand management fees (e.g., advertising expenses, service fees). Important matters to be negotiated between the parties to a brand license agreement include the calculation of royalties and prohibition of the brand's use upon termination of the agreement. One concern for licensor partners in particular is ancillary return/losses, such as changes in brand value.[19]

7.5.1.1 Corporate brands

A corporate brand is a name that identifies a business entity in its commercial activities. Corporate brands are a type of IP right with customer drawing power based on brand image and company reputation resulting from customers' perceptions of product and service quality. Corporate brand rights consist of nonexclusive and exclusive corporate brand licenses. They protect against free-riding and brand dilution. Brand owners may enjoin other parties from competing unfairly by wrongfully using a name or corporate brand, which may cause a likelihood of confusion with the name or brand of another company or merchant.

JV partners that own and exclusively use a corporate brand sometimes license the brand to their JV companies, thereby providing the JV company with the benefit of an established brand's customer drawing power and a corporate identity as an affiliated company. JV partners that allow their brand to be used by their JV companies may charge royalties for the privilege.

7.5.1.2 Product brands

A product brand or trademark identifies the product's source by associating the product with a specific merchant. It confers the right to use a

---

owner if the joint venture's objective is brand value. In such cases, the brand owner would typically choose to set up a wholly owned subsidiary instead of a joint venture and should adopt a policy of forming joint ventures only with partners whose brands' societal reputations are at least on a par with its own brand's reputation.

[19] *See* Hewitt, *supra* note 1, at Ch. 17-28.

registered trademark for designated products or services. JV partners with competitive, well-known product brands may nonexclusively license their registered trademarks to their JV companies and charge trademark royalties as consideration for the license.[20]

Product brand/trademark license agreements typically identify the licensed brand, specify whether the license is exclusive or nonexclusive, and contain provisions on royalties, the license's scope, the licensor's rights to manage brand usage, specific instructions on how the brand may be used based on brand use guidelines, restrictions on the JV company's origination and independent use of proprietary brands, actions to be taken in response to brand infringement by a third party, and agreement on termination terms.[21]

7.5.1.3 Trade dress

Trade dress refers to the total look and feel of products and services, including symbols with the power to identify the source of the product or service. Total look and feel is conveyed by maintaining and continuously using a uniform image presented to consumers with respect to nonfunctional attributes (e.g., outward appearance) of the product or service. If the image is inherently distinctive such that it evokes an association with a specific commercial enterprise and acquires secondary meaning, the image may be protected under trademark law against other parties' acts likely to cause confusion. In Japan, trade dress is protected by the Unfair Competition Prevention Law or tort law. In the US, there is an extensive body of case law regarding §43(a) of the Lanham (Trademark) Act (15 U.S.C. §1125).[22]

A classic example of trade dress is a broadly defined presentation of corporate identity (e.g., store design, decor, color) standardized by franchise agreements in a joint venture established to vertically integrate retail distribution channels. Trade dress is one type of commercial know-how. At the same time, it is similar to a trademark in that it

---

[20] *See* J. THOMAS MCCARTHY, MCCARTHY ON TRADEMARKS AND UNFAIR COMPETITION (4th ed. 1998–2013); U.S. Patent & Trademark Office, *U.S. Trademark Law* (2013) www.uspto.gov/trademarks/law/tmlaw.pdf.

[21] For examples of trademark license agreement forms, *see* Hewitt, *supra* note 1, at Precedent 19; ch. 17-30.

[22] Regarding trade dress, *see* McCarthy, *supra* note 20, at §8; WILLIAM E. LEVIN, TRADE DRESS PROTECTION (2d ed. 2008–2012). Uniform external product designs conducive to uniform branding across multiple products constitute corporate identity. User familiarity with how to use a product is a type of brand attribute, which also serves as a barrier to brand switching.

involves product presentation. For example, gas stations, convenience stores, and coffee shops such as Starbucks clearly identify the source of their goods/services and promote their corporate identity to consumers by meticulously standardizing everything from their stores' color schemes to utensil designs and customer service procedures.

For JV companies that manufacture and sell products or provide services, product designs and service businesses' modus operandi (method of operation) and store designs are related to corporate identity. Designs and user interfaces have the power to associate products with their source in the minds of consumers through their total look and feel. To ensure brand competitiveness, it is strategically important for JV companies to expeditiously secure product design rights in the countries in which they operate. To maintain consistency with its corporate identity and enhance its IP's value, the licensor partner typically imposes on the JV company various duties of commission and/or omission with respect to use of designs, corporate brand/trademarks, trade dress, and the like. By doing so, the licensor partner effectively controls the details of the JV company's business.

7.5.1.4 Brand management

The licensor partner must prevent use of the licensed product(s) beyond the scope of the license, to avoid having its trademark/tradename registration rescinded by national authorities, or to prevent everyone from freely using it without restriction as a result of blurring, dilution, or genericism of the mark. Even if it preserves its rights, it must also avoid being rendered unable to exercise them because of its brand name gaining currency among consumers as a common noun under applicable law. The licensor partner accordingly must manage its brands to preserve their value, particularly the distinctiveness of famous marks, and to prevent tarnishing of its brand image. To do so, the licensor partner must, based on its own brand strategy, stipulate the brand management duties to be performed by the JV company and draft detailed guidelines regarding the terms and mode of the brand's use. The licensor partner must also conduct monitoring to ensure that the JV company complies with its guidelines regarding matters such as the licensed brand's mode of use and quality control of products and services that use its trademark/brand name.

7.5.2 Technology Licenses

Technology licenses encompass a wide variety of subject matter, including patents, know-how, trade secrets, and human resources such as seconded personnel. Whether a JV partner needs to license technology to its JV company depends on how the JV company's functions are designed by the partners in the joint venture agreement. License agreements between one partner as licensor and the JV company as licensee typically stipulate (1) how newly developed technologies are to be contributed as management resources essential to execution of the JV company's business and (2) the allocation of rights to enjoin and claim damages for IP infringement by third parties. Other matters often covered by such agreements include the ownership and exploitation of new inventions and/or improvement inventions developed by the JV company, license royalties in the context of inter-partner sharing of return from transactions, and methods by which the licensor partner may monitor the actions of the other partner and the JV company. Technology license agreements between the JV company and one partner require the consent of the other partner.[23]

7.5.2.1 Patent rights and technology license agreements[24]

The main obligations of parties to a technology license agreement, particularly one that grants a license to a patented invention, are the licensor's covenant not to sue and the licensee's duty to pay royalties. Matters that JV partners should ensure are addressed in a technology license agreement include, first, specification of the scope of the licensed patent rights and/or technology. In addition, the agreement should specify whether the license is exclusive or nonexclusive. Other important matters with respect to the license's scope include: the scope of products and/or services to which the licensed technology may be applied, the license's geographic scope, sub-licensing rights or have-made rights (e.g., whether the licensee may outsource production to a third party), the agreement's expiration date, and other relevant time limits. Finally, the agreement must stipulate the terms and conditions of the license fee, including the royalty rate, the method of calculation, reporting duties, and payment terms.

Technology license agreements normally include a duty of confidentiality and provisions for allocating rights to improvement inventions related to the licensee's creations and the terms under which such inventions may be exploited. Other matters typically covered in technology license agreements include duties to provide technical assistance,

---

[23] *See* Hewitt, *supra* note 1, at Ch. 17-23.
[24] See Brunsvold, O'Reilley, and Kacedon, supra note 5; Hewitt, supra note 1, at Precedent 18, Ch. 7. DONALD S. CHISUM, CHISUM ON PATENTS (1978–Present).

cooperation, and/or technical know-how, rights to access technical information, indemnification in the event of infringement of a third party's rights, and, in some cases, performance guarantees if the licensed technology is exploited. With respect to ways of exit, issues specific to a given joint venture sometimes may be incorporated into so-called standard clauses, such as remedies for contractual breaches, agreement cancellation rights, surviving obligations upon termination of the agreement, governing law, jurisdiction and dispute resolution procedures.[25]

If the JV company develops an invention by improving the licensed technology, the JV company typically agrees to transfer or license IP related to the improvement to the licensor partner. Such IP becomes a special asset that originated from management resources contributed by the licensor partner. The licensor partner therefore has the exclusive right to use the IP. The IP is a return on the licensor partner's human capital contribution to the joint venture and not to be shared with the other partner. In other words, for the licensor partner, the contractual terms regarding allocation and exploitation of patent rights related to improvement inventions qualitatively count as return from transactions and constitute part of the consideration for the patent license granted to the JV company. Additionally, when the licensor partner exits the joint venture, such patent rights are residual property preferentially distributed to the licensor partner.

One method used to transfer rights to technologies developed by the JV company with its own ideas and capital is the grant-back, whereby the JV company licenses technology that it developed back to the licensor partner after applying for a patent. Another method is the assign-back, whereby the JV company assigns patent rights to the licensor partner. A third method is the flow-back, whereby the licensor partner has the right to patent technologies developed by the JV company and applies for the patents itself. All three methods are means by which licensor partners reap the fruits of JV companies' technological development efforts.

License agreements between JV partners and their JV companies may also take the form of cross-licenses. When cross-licenses are granted gratuitously or when one party receives more value than it provides to its counterparty, it is sometimes necessary for the parties to exchange balancing payments.

---

[25] *See* Hewitt, *supra* note 1, at Ch. 18.

7.5.2.2 Technological know-how and seconded personnel

When personnel are seconded to a JV company by a partner, the JV company and secondee must enter into an employment agreement regarding ownership and assignment of inventions developed by the secondee in the course of their employment and payment of fair compensation to the inventor for dependent inventions.[26] In addition to license agreements, know-how may be furnished through means such as service agreements or management/technology assistance agreements regarding know-how brought to a JV company by its officers or employees seconded to the JV company by the other partner.[27]

When personnel seconded to a JV company return to the employ of the non-licensor partner that seconded them, the non-licensor partner is able to make self-interested use of IP created within or disclosed to the JV company. Thus, it becomes an issue for the licensor partner as to how to prohibit and monitor the non-licensor partner's unlicensed use of know-how disclosed to the JV company by the licensor partner.[28] One method is to impose on secondees a duty of confidentiality, a duty not to compete, and a prohibition against unauthorized use effected through an agreement between the JV company and the seconded individuals and a secondment agreement between the JV company and the non-licensor partner that seconded the personnel. A second method is to monitor patent applications filed by the non-licensor partner and/or new businesses in technological fields in which the seconded personnel were involved. By monitoring them, the licensor partner can investigate whether the non-licensor partner that seconded personnel to the JV company is engaged in unauthorized use of technology related to know-how disclosed by the licensor partner. Whichever method is used, managing knowledge stored in an individual's memory is practically impossible. There are essentially no effective legal means for restricting the unobservable learning effects of human interaction.

---

[26] *See id.*, at Ch. 18. Under Japanese patent law (Article 35 of the Patent Act), a company may assume the rights to patents of inventions developed by employees and set standards for calculating fair compensation for such rights pursuant to internal regulations instead of employment agreements. In the United States, the "Hired to Invent" doctrine and "Shop Right" may be applicable to assignment of inventions from an employee to their employer. However, an express assignment agreement should be safer for employees. *See* IpVenture, Inc. v. Prostar Computer, Inc., 503 F.3d 1324 (Fed. Cir. 2007).

[27] *See* Hewitt *supra* note 1, at Ch. 18-21.

[28] *See id.*, at Ch. 11-6.

Acquisition of know-how is a learning race that invites moral hazard. Once a JV partner acquires all of the know-how it wants from the other partner through their joint venture, it no longer has any incentive to continue to invest capital in the joint venture. JV partners are accordingly in a race to learn everything they need before the other partner does. Whichever partner is the slower learner is at a disadvantage in that it is at risk of the other partner exiting before it completes its learning objectives. Partners consequently must devise arrangements to restrain the other partner's self-serving and opportunistic behavior.[29]

7.5.2.3 Computer program copyright

During the due diligence stage preceding a joint venture's establishment, it is important for JV partners who plan to contribute copyrights in computer programs and/or manuals, drawings, technological standards, or other written works to be used in the joint venture to verify that they have the legal right to grant the rights to such assets to the JV company and that third parties' rights will not be infringed.[30] In the case of computer programs in particular, partners must verify a complex web of inter-related rights, including but not limited to copyrights in the programs, patent rights to software-related inventions, copyrights in related documentation, trade secrets in the form of source code, availability of maintenance/support services, and license agreements for third-party software embedded in the programs.

With software, duplication of an existing program enables a JV company to produce completely identical software products. In the case of design drawings, if the JV company produces products in accord with the drawings, it can lower its barriers to market entry by dispensing with product design, the second half of the R&D process. If a JV partner discloses and allows the JV company to use technological information, it should consider executing a copyrighted-work license agreement (e.g., for software source code) in addition to any license agreements for patents and/or know-how. In cases where identical products are to be produced in accord with completed drawings, the partner should also consider a cost contribution arrangement to share reasonable expenses in

---

[29] *See* JAY B. BARNEY, GAINING AND SUSTAINING COMPETITIVE ADVANTAGE 365 (4th ed. 2011).

[30] *See* MELVILLE B. NIMMER & DAVID NIMMER, NIMMER ON COPYRIGHT (1985–Present).

proportion to the partners' respective shares of projected future profits to resolve the issue of free-riding on its R&D and/or manufacturing costs.[31,32]

7.5.2.4   Cross-licenses and sharing control

A cross-license is an agreement whereby multiple parties license their proprietary IP to each other. If a cross-license agreement between a JV partner and a third party grants sub-licensing rights to the partner, the partner may license to its JV company the IP rights to which the agreement pertains.

However, if the license's scope is limited to the licensee or recipient of a covenant not to sue and its majority-owned or majority-controlled subsidiaries, a JV company that is less than 51 percent owned by a JV partner will not meet the definition of a subsidiary. In such a case, the JV company will not be eligible to exploit the in-licensed IP rights pursuant to the cross-license agreement. Accordingly, when one partner plans to enter into a license agreement with the JV company, special attention must be given to situations where the partner has in-licensed third-party IP rights for technologies that it can use itself but cannot sublicense to a non-subsidiary joint venture. When bargaining over sharing of control in these cases, the partners must delineate the scope of the joint venture and determine their respective ownership percentages in light of the restrictions on usage of such IP rights.[33] If the licensor partner's ownership interest in the JV company is reduced below 51 percent, the IP rights that the licensor party sub-licensed to the JV company are extinguished. This scenario creates a threat of exit for the non-licensor partner. Consequently, the non-licensor partner is constrained in its ability to bargain for majority control.

---

[31]   Cost-contribution arrangements are agreements that stipulate that the parties to the agreement will share the risks of specified corporate activities and the returns derived from those activities by sharing designated expenses required to conduct such activities in proportion to the parties' respective shares of projected future profits. For example, instead of paying IP license royalties to a partner, a JV company may bear a portion of the expenses incurred to develop the IP. Transfer price taxation's arm's-length principle comes into play in cost-contribution arrangements. 26 C.F.R. §1.482–7 (Title 26 – Internal Revenue, Sharing of Costs).

[32]   *See* Brunsvold, O'Reilley, and Kacedon, *supra* note 5, at 355–378.

[33]   *See* Hewitt, *supra* note 1, at Ch. 17-8.

PART III

Staged bargaining

8. Pre-contract bargaining

8.1 JOINT VENTURE LIFECYCLE: FOUR STAGES

Joint ventures are characterized by a lack of separation between owner-ship and management. Key management matters are therefore determined through bargaining between JV partners. The purpose, form, guiding principles, and practicalities of bargaining differ depending on the stage of a joint venture's lifecycle. Joint venture governance also changes dynamically over a joint venture's life.

The joint venture lifecycle can be broadly divided into four stages. The first stage is the preparatory stage, where prospective JV partners discuss going into business and prepare to establish a joint venture together, ultimately closing a joint venture agreement (Section 8.2). The second stage is the establishment stage, where the partners execute a joint venture agreement giving rise to the joint venture (Section 8.3). The third stage is the operation of the joint venture. During this stage, partners monitor each other to ensure that the other is complying with its contractual obligations. The joint venture agreement is sometimes re-negotiated during the third stage if the operating environment has changed since the joint venture's inception (Chapter 10). And finally, the fourth stage is the transformation or termination of the joint venture (Chapter 12).[1]

---

[1] Although these four stages are not necessarily universal to all joint ventures, we present them as an ideal model. *See* IAN HEWITT, HEWITT ON JOINT VENTURES, Ch. 1-15 (5th ed. 2011). Hewitt's lifecycle comprises six stages: (1) initiation, (2) early partner agreement, (3) learning stage, (4) changes in dependency, (5) buy-out discussions, and (6) termination.

8.2 PREPARATORY STAGE: PRE-CONTRACT BARGAINING

8.2.1 Definition and Activities

During the preparatory stage, JV partners discuss and decide upon the joint venture's business model, the scheme for establishing the joint venture, ways to maximize the three types of return and basic policies regarding the sharing of control and total return. They then prepare to execute the joint venture agreement.

8.2.2 Matters to be Addressed Internally prior to Bargaining

Before beginning negotiations to establish a joint venture, prospective JV partners should first make a fully informed decision as to whether or not a joint venture is the best option for achieving their objectives. It is important for JV partners to understand why they have chosen to establish a JV company instead of a wholly owned subsidiary or contractual business alliance in light of the joint venture's intended purpose and necessary management resources (intended synergies).

Prior to selecting a partner, the joint venture project manager should formulate an effective incentive bargaining strategy, based on a clear understanding of the joint venture's purpose (definition of synergies), financial and human capital requirements, and potential risks and return. In order to do so, the project manager should first seek guidance from top management regarding the 'big-picture' behind and the partner's interest in the joint venture plan. Once the project team has conducted its due diligence and obtained legal advice, it should prepare for the negotiation by formulating a proposed initial bargaining position (contractual terms), the best alternative to a negotiated agreement (BATNA[2]), which would realize a threshold value, and a nonnegotiable bottom-line position that will serve as a benchmark for terminating negotiations. The matter must then be referred to management decision-makers. Bargaining outcomes sometimes deviate from the original plan, but if preparations are adequate, a partner should be able to start bargaining from an advantageous position and seize the initiative in incentive bargaining.

---

[2] On BATNA (best alternative to negotiated agreement), *see* HOWARD RAIFFA, THE ART AND SCIENCE OF NEGOTIATION 45 (1982); HOWARD RAIFFA, JOHN RICHARDSON & DAVID METCALFE, NEGOTIATION ANALYSIS 110 (2007).

Second, a party seeking to form a joint venture must identify partner candidates and evaluate the risks and opportunities associated with each candidate, as well as contemplating the ideal division of roles and responsibilities. The party should also assess its own value from the standpoint of its potential partners, define roles and responsibilities, and distinguish between risks and opportunities. Appropriate partner selection is a key determinant of a joint venture's success or failure.

Third, in the case of an international joint venture, a prospective JV partner must carefully research the investment environment of the country in which the JV company is to be established. Such research should be broad in scope, encompassing the country's politics, economy, ethnic composition, culture, infrastructure, taxation, environmental regulations, antitrust laws with implications for partners' ownership percentages, and other relevant laws (e.g., corporate law, labor law).[3] Liability for failure to comply with local laws or other local social responsibilities cannot be avoided contractually. Inadvertent illegalities could even lead to a joint venture's failure.

Another important consideration is the country's political climate: where there is a high risk of anti-government revolt or government expropriation of the JV company, it is advisable to consider establishing the joint venture in a third-party country. The party should consider whether the intended country is a member of the ICSID (International Centre for Settlement of Investment Disputes) Convention, in case of a dispute with the country's government.

8.2.3 Typical Process

The core inter-partner bargaining takes place during the preparatory stage. During this stage, it is important for prospective JV partners to assess synergies (the sum total of the three types of return) and analyze risks.

At this stage the partners must decide on the joint venture's business model, strategies for maximizing return (non-zero-sum bargaining aiming to maximize the size of the pie), and basic policies regarding the sharing of return (zero-sum bargaining to determine how the pie will be divided). In the initial preparatory stage, conflicting interests often come to a head when the partners attempt to specifically determine their respective rights and obligations (particularly how the pie will be divided). Partners are sometimes able to reach an agreement more quickly by first seeking to

---

[3] *See* Hewitt, *supra* note 1, at Ch. 2-21.

maximize the size of the pie and deferring negotiations with respect to dividing the pie until the final stage of the bargaining process.

The process of joint venture negotiations between large companies generally unfolds as follows. First, the partners individually formulate bargaining strategies and plans for the joint venture. They also conduct feasibility studies, which involve due diligence regarding the other partner, investigating the investment environment in the country in which the JV company is to be established, identifying resources that will be required by the joint venture, and assessing expected synergies.

Next, the partners engage in pre-contract bargaining and prepare to launch the joint venture's operations. After signing a letter of intent (LOI) and confidentiality agreement,[4] the partners can conduct further feasibility studies and due diligence. This is when the parties begin negotiating the joint venture agreement in preparation for establishing the joint venture.[5] The corporate staff of each potential JV partner must formulate a bargaining strategy in advance. In doing so, uncertainties can be eliminated to the maximum extent possible by drafting a big-picture vision of the joint venture, confirming the joint venture's initial status and goals, formulating a roadmap that specifies how and by whom the goals will be achieved, and defining all planned actions and roles.[6]

Joint venture bargaining is a group effort. A working group or other team of relatively low-level personnel typically handles preliminary negotiations on behalf of each partner. Progressively higher-level personnel on both sides subsequently get involved in hammering out an

---

[4] Confidentiality agreements typically stipulate: (a) the purpose for which disclosed information may be used, (b) definition and exclusions of confidential information, (c) obligations of receiving party to restrict access to the information and prohibit its use for other purposes, (d) requirement for both parties to preserve confidentiality and prohibit unauthorized disclosure to a third party, (e) return or destruction of exchanged information if negotiations break down (f) the duration of obligations, and (g) general provisions. A letter of intent or memorandum of understandings may provide additional clauses that authorize the parties to conduct due diligence on each other, prohibit similar or competing negotiations with third parties, and set a deadline for deciding whether to proceed with the joint venture plan.

[5] *See* Hewitt, *supra* note 1, at Ch. 2. Regarding confidentiality agreements in the context of information exchange, *see id.*, at Precedent 1; International Trade Centre, *Model Contracts for Small Firms: Legal Guidance for Doing International Business* (2010) www.intracen.org/uploadedFiles/intracenorg/Content/Exporters/Exporting_Better/Templates_of_contracts/2%20International%20Corporate%20Joint%20Venture.pdf.

[6] *See* Hewitt, *supra* note 1, at Ch. 2-3; Ch. 2-5.

agreement. The final round of bargaining typically involves the partners' respective chief executives. Typically, the outcomes of bargaining conducted at the lower levels of the partners' organizations are recorded in documents but have little if any legally binding force (e.g., minutes of meetings). Once the bargaining reaches certain milestones, the partners enter into an LOI or memorandum of understanding (MOU). When a final agreement is reached between the partners' chief executives, a joint venture agreement is drafted and executed upon formal approval by both partners.

The joint venture agreement is an important document that serves as the basis for resolving disputes between partners and sets the starting point for future renegotiation. It is a basic contract that stipulates the fundamentals of respective rights and obligations in terms of operating the joint venture. The specifics of these rights and obligations and the terms of ancillary transactions are often stipulated in separate agreements.

The biggest threat in the preparatory stage is the risk of a breakdown in negotiations. As preliminary negotiations progress, costs and manpower requirements increase in tandem with an expansion in the scope of the due diligence research. Manpower requirements for negotiating points of contention also increase. The prospective JV partners bear this cost burden.

There are a number of factors that could derail negotiations. If one party has gained the upper hand in the negotiations, the other party may feel aggrieved, or, alternatively, one party may be disappointed by a feasibility study assessment of the joint venture's economics. The bargaining environment often becomes tense when it appears that negotiations might break down. In such an environment, the party most threatened by the risk of a breakdown (e.g., the party that is too committed to the deal to back out or is staking its survival on the joint venture) will tend to make bigger concessions. However, both parties are threatened by the risk of a breakdown in negotiations to some extent. As a consequence of this, there is a tendency for both parties to seek compromise through mutual concessions.[7]

---

[7] One party will have a bargaining advantage over the other if it possesses accurate information on the other party's interests and disinterests. For example, if one party knows that the other party is staking its survival on the joint venture, bargaining between the parties will likely be one-sided. In actuality, however, both parties' information about each other is asymmetric. Even a party with an objectively advantageous bargaining position will tend to be overly apprehensive about the outcome of negotiations. Additionally, even if one party has multiple

8.2.4   Employment of Agents

In the case of an international joint venture located in a country with laws and business practices that are unfamiliar to the JV partners, outside experts (e.g., attorneys, accountants, consultants) and/or trustworthy local consultants should be hired on an as-needed basis during the due diligence stage. However, when hiring outsiders, it is important to keep in mind the risk of information leaks, betrayal, and front-running.

A foreign company that engages in activities on the basis of building relationships of trust with local power brokers is at risk of being criminally prosecuted for bribery if any of the parties with which it is seeking to ingratiate itself is a politician or civil servant.[8] A JV partner can even be held liable for the acts of its local agent or local partner when the agent pays money to a foreign government official or politician as a consulting fee, rebate, facilitation fee, or other similar remuneration. JV partners should be aware of foreign countries' anti-bribery laws, such as Japan's Unfair Competition Prevention Law, the US's Foreign Corrupt Practices Act, and the UK's Bribery Act. JV partners that are concerned about the risk of funds being used to bribe foreign governments should appoint compliance officers, prohibit bribery by personnel on assignment overseas, and incorporate ethical standards into purchasing management regulations. If payments are made, accurate accounting records should be prepared and retained for internal control.[9]

8.2.5   Subject Matter of Bargaining

Bargaining during the preparatory stage tends to be focused on the basics of establishing and operating the joint venture, including a clear definition of the joint venture's purpose, sharing of control, sharing of total return, exit rights, and setting the respective partners' legal obligations to

---

potential joint-venture partners, it will effectively become locked into one prospective partner as the negotiations progress, limiting its ability to select another partner.

   [8] For example, in January 2012 the US Department of Justice fined Marubeni Corporation $54.6 million for its involvement in a conspiracy to bribe Nigerian officials in violation of the US Foreign Corrupt Practices Act. *See* www.mofo.jp/topics/legal-updates/tlcb/20120210.html#E.

   [9] *See* Hewitt, *supra* note 1, at Ch. 2-15. *See also* Japanese Ministry of Economy, Trade and Industry, *Guidelines to Prevent Bribery of Foreign Public Officials* (May 26, 2004) www.meti.go.jp/english/information/downloadfiles/briberye2.pdf; the UK's Bribery Act 2010, www.legislation.gov.uk/ukpga/2010/23/pdfs/ukpga_20100023_en.pdf.

contribute valuable monetary and human capital essential to the joint venture (incentive design).

Other matters on which JV partners should reach an agreement during the preparatory stage include their respective ownership percentages in the context of sharing control, organizational form and basic governance design (including controls over the JV company's senior management team), financial capital contribution methods (e.g., monetary contribution, in-kind contribution, assignment of business operations, absorption of split-off business operations), the number and percentage of directors that each partner may appoint, the appointment of the chief executive officer or other executives, veto rights over important matters, how the JV company is to be financed, ancillary agreements to be entered into, and methods of evaluating the joint venture's performance.[10] If the JV company is to finance its working-capital requirements with a bank loan in addition to equity capital, the JV partners should also confer on the selection of a lead bank and acceptable loan terms, including the formulation of a business plan and loan repayment schedule and deciding which partner(s) will guarantee the loan.

8.2.6   Balance of Power between Partners

8.2.6.1   Commitment risk

During negotiations in the preparatory stage, prospective JV partners worry that their prospective co-partner will withhold resources from the joint venture, engage in opportunistic behavior, or withdraw from negotiations at a late stage. While it is generally best to keep one's weaknesses concealed, one JV partner generally has a bargaining advantage over the other by virtue of information asymmetry. Additionally, the partner that would be worse off if negotiations were to break down (e.g., a partner that is unable to survive without the joint venture) is at a disadvantage in the negotiations because it has no choice but to participate in the joint venture and will suffer a detriment if the parties are unable to reach an agreement.

Additionally, sometimes one partner must make an upfront investment during the preparatory stage in order to expedite the launch of the JV company's operations post establishment. Because this requires the partner to commit to the joint venture before the other partner, the resources that it contributed in advance to the joint venture may be held "hostage" during negotiations. As it is obvious to both sides that the

---

[10]   *See* Hewitt, *supra* note 1, at F-1.

partner, having already invested, would be worse off if negotiations were to break down, that partner would be unable to mount a credible threat of exit and would therefore be forced to make concessions.

8.2.6.2   Internal issues within a partner

Relative bargaining power is also affected by the internal politics of each partner company. Partner companies may suffer from agency problems, where the negotiators' decisions can be influenced by self-interest or where the negotiators can cover their mistakes through ratification from elsewhere within the corporate bureaucracy.[11] For example, negotiators may agree to terms that are disadvantageous to their company if they can shield themselves from blame by obtaining the CEO's approval. As a means of protection, a company involved in joint venture negotiations must craft incentives so that the negotiators' interests are aligned with those of the company. Additionally, it must make sure that negotiators do not overstep their discretionary authority and commit potentially fatal negotiating errors after splitting up authority among multiple negotiators. As negotiation teams do not always exhibit uniform solidarity, the decision-making process should include prior consultations with the stakeholders of each partner, such as the CEO and executive officers who manage important resources related to the joint venture, banks who will undertake project finance, labor unions, and key personnel to be seconded to the joint venture.

8.2.7   Letter of Intent or Memorandum of Understanding

The content of agreements negotiated by JV partners are recorded in a written agreement corresponding with each stage of the negotiation process. At each stage, the negotiations lead to more detailed and feasible agreements. JV partners carry out initial joint venture negotiations while relying on mutual trust without entering into a formal, legally binding agreement. Accordingly, in addition to entering into a confidentiality agreement, the partners typically enter into an interim agreement in the form of an LOI or MOU with limited legally binding force during the preparatory stage.[12]

---

[11]   Negotiation teams do not always exhibit uniform solidarity. Factional strife within a partner's organization could cause skewed business judgments. For example, a negotiator who is to be seconded to a joint venture can use his/her authority and arrange advantageous transactions for the joint venture or for his/her own benefit instead of the partner's best interest.

[12]   *See* Hewitt, *supra* note 1, at Ch. 4-8.

Subsequent negotiations between the partners proceed based on the content of the LOI or MOU. Whenever the negotiating team subcommittees agree on a matter, minutes of the associated meeting(s) are prepared. These step-by-step agreements are ultimately adjusted and revised based on a holistic view of the agreement, and then included in the joint venture agreement's draft or term sheet. Through this negotiation process, the agreement's terms and conditions become increasingly detailed and finalized.

LOIs and MOUs are used interchangeably. These two types of legal documents normally contain provisions on the following matters:[13]

(a) purpose of joint venture, including the scope of cooperation between partners;
(b) bargaining procedures, actions to be undertaken by the partners toward JV company establishment, and an associated schedule;
(c) information-provision and accountability duties; due diligence;
(d) contingency clauses (e.g., those that require the JV company to be established subject to both partners' internal approval, third party approvals, or other express conditions precedent or subsequent);
(e) basic principles for sharing control of the joint venture (e.g., capital contributions and ownership percentages; director appointment rights; allocation of representative director, CEO and CFO positions in connection with the sharing of executive authority);
(f) basic principles for sharing total return from the joint venture;
(g) duty of confidentiality or duty of disclosure per stock exchange regulations;
(h) duty to refrain from unusual transactions in business domains related to the joint venture;
(i) duty to bargain in good faith and duty to bargain exclusively for a certain period of time;
(j) sharing of bargaining and preparatory costs;
(k) regulatory compliance procedures (e.g., antitrust law filings related to business combinations, preparations for applying for business licenses);
(l) governing law (the governing-law or choice-of-law clause specifies that the laws of a mutually agreed-upon jurisdiction will govern the interpretation and enforcement of the terms of the contract);
(m) contract rescission rights and a review clause for use in the event that unanticipated facts are discovered before the joint venture is

---

[13] *See id.*, at Ch. 4-7; Precedent 2; International Trade Centre, *supra* note 5.

established (note: freedom to exit rights (e.g., dissolution rights) are not needed where the partners have not yet contributed capital to the joint venture, but a partner generally may terminate the LOI/MOU if the other partner goes bankrupt or otherwise becomes incapacitated as a JV partner);

(n) limitations on the agreement's binding force and liability for damages (e.g., exemption from liability for reliance damages);

(o) other standard clauses.

8.2.8 Due Diligence

Partners forming joint ventures sometimes misrepresent their ability to contribute promised resources to the joint venture. Before entering into a joint venture agreement, partners should conduct an appropriate level of due diligence to verify the other partner's internal resources as well as sufficient research on the market in which the joint venture will operate. Due diligence is generally conducted by a team of external attorneys assisted by external accountants and internal staff from specialized organizational units related to the joint venture.

JV partners conduct due diligence, directing inquiries to the prospective partner's staff, requesting disclosure of and analyzing related documents, ascertaining the current status of resources slated to be contributed to the JV company, and making decisions on matters that will affect the JV company's establishment and influence the success of its operations.[14] The matters investigated during the due diligence process vary depending on the joint venture's purpose, nature, and attributes, but the major focal points of due diligence generally include the following:

(a) operational matters (e.g., nature of business, products, markets, customers, suppliers, distributors, information systems);

(b) financial matters (e.g., profitability, liquidity, cost-sharing among affiliated companies);

(c) legal matters (e.g., registration requirements, minutes of directors' meetings, title to and security interests in assets to be contributed to the joint venture, important contracts, material legal disputes, permits and licenses, contingent liabilities (if any), legal compliance status);

---

[14] *See* Hewitt, *supra* note 1, at Ch. 2-10–22; Precedent 3. *See also* NISHIMURA SOGO ED., M&A-HO TAIZEN [PERSPECTIVE OF M&A LAW] 693–727 (2001).

(d)   technology (e.g., technical documentation, R&D resources, IP, license agreements);
(e)   operational assets (e.g., land, buildings, production/other facilities);
(f)   environment and safety (e.g., environmental and product-safety laws and regulations);
(g)   human resources (e.g., employment contracts, employee regulations, salary levels, employee benefits);
(h)   taxation (e.g., explanation of taxes which will/may be applicable to the joint venture).

Once the prospective JV partners determine that the joint venture is viable based on thorough preliminary research, including mutual due diligence, they conclude the bargaining process. If both partners make a final decision to invest in the joint venture through their respective internal corporate approval processes (e.g., deliberation by the board of directors of each), their respective project managers will then compile and retain legal documents (e.g., permits/licenses) and records of the negotiations to date. After following up to ensure that all preconditions are fully satisfied, the JV partners sign a joint venture agreement.

8.2.9   Conclusion of Joint Venture Agreement

The preparatory stage culminates in the signing of the joint venture agreement.[15] At the time the joint venture agreement is signed, the JV partners must also select the type of business entity,[16] draft the JV company's articles of incorporation, and finalize the content of important ancillary agreements related to specific transactions that are necessary for operations after establishment.[17] The partners may also enter into a shareholder agreement that stipulates matters not included in the articles of incorporation (e.g., shareholder voting agreements). If multiple classes of stock are to be issued, the partners must decide on the rights associated with each class.[18] Other tasks to be completed at this stage include formulation of a business plan for the joint venture, approval criteria for investments to be funded by the JV company, rules regarding

---

[15]   For sample joint venture agreement forms, *see* Hewitt, *supra* note 1, at Precedent 6; Precedent 8; Precedent 9; F-2; International Trade Centre, *supra* note 5.
[16]   *See* Hewitt, *supra* note 1, at Ch. 3. *See also infra* Ch. 9.
[17]   *See* Hewitt, *supra* note 1, at Precedent 11. *See* also *infra* Ch. 9.
[18]   *See* Hewitt, *supra* note 1, at Precedent 12.

financing activities (e.g., equity capital increases, material debt financing, debt guarantees by parent company), and the JV company's dividend policy.

As the partners weigh the advantages and disadvantages of the joint venture based on the results of their feasibility studies, they may decide to form a contractual business alliance[19] instead of a JV company. Alternative options may be a joint R&D agreement,[20] license agreement, or other form of cooperative relationship that does not require a separate entity to execute business. The partners could also opt for a business combination such as a merger or a sale of business operations from one to the other.

8.3 ESTABLISHMENT STAGE

8.3.1 Definition of and Activities during Establishment Stage

During the establishment stage, the partners follow the steps laid out in the joint venture agreement that were negotiated and formalized. The establishment stage includes formal establishment of the company; transfer of assets required by the joint venture, through in-kind capital contributions or other means; and finalization and execution of ancillary agreements essential to the joint venture's operations.

After execution of the joint venture agreement, which finalizes the results of negotiations, the partners establish the joint venture as a legal entity by fulfilling all legal requirements, such as obtaining necessary permits or licenses; drafting articles of incorporation; contributing capital in exchange for stock; appointing officers; and complying with any other corporate law formalities, such as convening an organizational meeting of shareholders and registering the JV company's establishment. The partners then inject human capital (e.g., seconded personnel) into the JV company and do whatever else is required to render it operable.[21]

During this stage, there is not usually much room for further bargaining. Instead, the partners simply perform the agreements negotiated during the preparatory stage. For example, if the partners have entered

---

[19] For a sample of a strategic alliance agreement form, *see id.*, at Precedent 4.

[20] For a sample of an R&D collaboration agreement form, *see id.*, at Precedent 5; J. McIntyre Machinery, Ltd. v. Nicastro, 564 U.S., 131 S. Ct. 2780, 180 L. Ed. 2d 765 (2011) www.supremecourt.gov/opinions/10pdf/09-1343.pdf.

[21] *See* Hewitt *supra* note 1, at Ch. 2.

into ancillary agreements such as a license agreement, a secondment agreement, an asset transfer agreement, and/or a financing agreement, the bulk of the bargaining for these transactions should already be completed. In actuality, however, joint venture agreements sometimes fail to anticipate certain matters while others may be omitted for a number of reasons. Consequently, bargaining between partners often continues during the establishment stage in order to rectify omissions or deficiencies in existing agreements.

8.3.2 Subject Matter of Bargaining and Balance of Power

The establishment stage occurs during a time frame in which the JV partners perform the agreements negotiated during the preparatory stage. There are typically only a few matters that require further bargaining. However, the joint venture agreement executed by the partners is not all-inclusive. Drafting a contract that comprehensively covers all acts required to establish a JV company is impossible in practice. As a result, the partners generally continue to negotiate the specifics of any matters not adequately addressed by the joint venture agreement.

As the joint venture agreement is performed during the establishment stage during which specific conflicting interests are at a minimum, the balance of bargaining power between the partners is more or less equal. However, the extent to which the agreement draws a line between what is renegotiable and what is absolutely nonnegotiable will influence the balance of power between partners in future negotiations.

Further, the post-signing attitudes of the partners can complicate the negotiation environment. Once the joint venture agreement has been formally signed, the partners are no longer at risk of a breakdown in negotiations. At this point, the partners have the opportunity to consider whether the negotiations to date have been a success from the standpoint of their respective interests and expected return. A partner that is dissatisfied with the outcome of the negotiations to date should regard further bargaining as an opportunity to redress perceived inequities. A disgruntled partner may pose a threat of opportunistic behavior and revert to an adversarial bargaining posture, particularly if there is only weak commitment to respecting the relational and/or implicit contracts that constitute the joint venture's principal framework as of the execution of the joint venture agreement.[22]

---

[22] *See id.*, at F-2.

8.3.3   Performance of Joint Venture Agreement

Upon establishment, the partners perform all obligations related to monetary and human capital and the closing of the joint venture agreement.[23] Monetary capital contributions take the form of cash or specific assets. Partners need to monitor performance and to assess the fair value of any in-kind investments to protect their own interests.

Human capital is a qualitative resource that is ordinarily contributed by the partners on a continual basis during the operational stage. However, human capital is sometimes contributed at the time of a joint venture's establishment as well. Such human capital contributions may take the form of know-how or manuals in addition to the secondment of key personnel. Although in most jurisdictions stock corporations are not permitted to issue stock in exchange for labor, human capital contributions are actually imperative for joint ventures. Joint ventures must therefore secure human capital contributions through means such as entering into secondment agreements immediately after the establishment of the venture. Partners can efficiently assign personnel to their JV companies by making sure to clearly determine internal organization and the roles, authority, and responsibilities of key staff.

8.3.4   Steps Involved in Establishing a Joint Venture Company

The establishment stage involves compliance with corporate law requirements such as convening a shareholder meeting, registering the company's establishment, and filing various notifications in compliance with labor and tax laws. The JV company must also obtain any required government licenses or permits for the businesses it will operate. JV partners should also notify and obtain any necessary consents from third parties with whom they have preexisting joint venture-related contracts.

In terms of regulatory requirements, partners must be aware that antitrust restrictions are a potential showstopper. The partners need to check antitrust law provisions with respect to matters including acquisition of the JV company's stock, appointment of interlocking officers, changes in the ownership of business operations, contractual restrictions on business operations, and international cartels. When establishing a JV company, partners must be aware of *ex ante* regulation of business combinations.

---

[23]   *See id.*, at Ch. 7.

In Japan, parties to business combinations that could effectively restrain competition have a duty to notify the Japan Fair Trade Commission in advance of the joint venture's establishment (Antimonopoly Act, Article 10(2)). In the US, §7A of the Clayton Act (Hart-Scott-Rodino Antitrust Improvement Act of 1976) requires premerger notification of regulatory authorities and prohibits business combinations during the waiting period if a pending purchase or sale of stock or assets could effectively restrain competition. It also provides that the Department of Justice or Federal Trade Commission may issue injunctions against mergers.[24] The European Union has similar regulations concerning business alliances that would have a restraining effect on competition. JV partners should exercise care to ensure that they do not violate applicable business-combination regulations, including notification and waiting-period requirements, by adjusting their establishment-stage schedules and carrying out any requisite antitrust preparations, prior to the closing of their joint venture agreement.[25] For example, one method of establishing an international joint venture that accounts for the risk of antitrust enforcement involves the local partner establishing a wholly owned subsidiary in its home country then selling an equity stake in the subsidiary to its overseas partner while also granting the overseas partner a put option that becomes exercisable in the event of antitrust law precluding formation of the joint venture.

8.3.5 Conclusion of Ancillary Agreements

As an entity with the legal capacity to possess rights and assume obligations, the JV partners and JV company enter into ancillary agreements required to operate the joint venture, contribute resources to the

---

[24] *See* §1 of the Sherman Act (prohibition against contracts, combinations and conspiracies in restraint of trade or commerce) and US Antitrust Guidelines for Collaborations among Competitors (2000). With regard to business alliances tantamount to a merger in terms of their impact on competition, *see* §7 of the Clayton Act (restrictions on business combinations) and the US Fair Trade Commission's Horizontal Merger Guidelines.

[25] *See* Article 101 of the Treaty on the Functioning of the European Union (prohibition against agreements and concerted practices restrictive of competition). If a joint venture is a full-function joint venture possessing all functions of an autonomous business entity on a long-term basis, the EU Merger Regulation and Horizontal Merger Guideline will apply to the joint venture if it constitutes a "concentration." *See* Commission Notice on the Concept of Full-Function Joint Ventures under Council Regulation (EEC) No. 4064/89 on the Control of Concentrations between Undertakings, OJ C66, 02.03.1998, p. 1.

joint venture, and share total return.[26] Such agreements are often important transactional contracts essential to running the joint venture's operations. These may include asset assignment agreements, IP license agreements, management consultation agreements, secondment agreements, supply agreements, factory lease agreements, product purchase agreements, and/or IT system usage agreements.

The design of the joint venture agreement and ancillary agreements is one determinant of a joint venture's long-term success or failure. Whether the transactions and/or cooperative relationships contained in the ancillary agreements proceed as planned may significantly impact return from transactions. IP rights and ancillary agreements can also affect the sharing of control, as they can be used to exert influence on the JV company.

Failure to execute ancillary agreements could cause major problems for a partner that has already contributed capital to the JV company. In practice, ancillary agreements are usually integrated into the joint venture agreement or the joint venture agreement is entered into contingent upon the execution of certain ancillary agreements.

8.3.6   Joint Venture Employees

The JV company's personnel at the time of its establishment are particularly important.[27] After a JV company has been established, motivating newly seconded or transferred employees is a human capital issue with important implications for day-to-day management. Providing required human capital resources to the JV company is no doubt crucial to future operations. Partners should also obtain buy-in from personnel before they are seconded or transferred, by providing them with information about their salaries, benefits, job titles, the scope of their discretionary authority, personnel evaluation systems, secondment conditions (including insurance and pension plan arrangements), HR regulations, and other such matters.

There may be other factors that increase the cost of secondment that partners should be aware of. In the case of a foreign JV company, obtaining visas and/or work permits for seconded personnel is sometimes surprisingly time-consuming. Additionally, if the JV partners guarantee that the personnel they second to the joint venture will possess a certain

---

[26]   *See* Hewitt, *supra* note 1, at Ch. 6.
[27]   *See id.*, at Ch. 18.

minimum skill level and assume responsibility for training and dispatching personnel, they may incur additional costs every time one of their seconded employees leaves the JV company. Another point that JV partners cannot forget is that workers are also wage creditors with a preferential claim against their employer.

9. Legal measures for finalizing bargains

Having discussed in detail the rationale behind JV partners' incentive bargaining with each other (Chapters 2 and 6) and the subject matter thereof (Chapters 3–5 and 7), we now look at how partners legally finalize the results of their incentive bargaining. This is ultimately done in the form of a joint venture agreement between shareholders – an agreement which is negotiated through a step-by-step process (see Chapter 8 for details).

A joint venture agreement's content encompasses both (1) transactional agreements involving the joint venture's business and (2) governance processes that constitute the JV company's organizational management framework.[1] Portions of the joint venture agreement are finalized and given legally binding effect and enforceability by the JV company's charter/articles of incorporation, ancillary agreements, and laws that apply to the joint venture's business organization form.

9.1 JOINT VENTURE AGREEMENT

When finalizing the details of the joint venture agreement, the parties should be aware of: (a) contract culture and draftsmanship, (b) incomplete contracts and relational contracts, and (c) binding effect and enforceability. We briefly summarize these issues below.

---

[1] Prior to establishing a JV company, the partners negotiate and, in the joint venture agreement, stipulate the general terms of ancillary agreements between the JV company and themselves, then craft the binding ancillary agreements after the joint venture agreement has been executed. These terms are included to ensure that the terms are fair and reasonable and deter partners from opportunistic behavior regarding return from transactions.

9.1.1 Issues Related to Contract Culture and Draftsmanship

Differences in contract culture and draftsmanship between Asian and Western companies can become an issue when Asian companies form business alliances with European and American companies. For example, if a European or American company, accustomed to the culture of private autonomy based on self-responsibility and *ex post* judicial regulation, expertly drafts a comprehensive contract that encompasses all rights and obligations and submits it to a prospective Asian partner that lacks expertise in that kind of contractual draftsmanship, the Asian partner will not only be at a linguistic disadvantage, it will also be in a disadvantageous bargaining position due to its lack of proficiency in contractual draftsmanship and the contract-culture gap between the two parties. Conversely, a European or American company would likely consider a protectionist developing country's government regulation of and intervention in contractual terms and conditions to be overly constraining on the joint venture agreement.

9.1.2 Issues Related to Incomplete Contracts and Relational Contracts

When establishing a joint venture, both partners endeavor to: stipulate fundamental matters in their joint venture agreement and transactional agreements incidental to the joint venture's business; finalize their respective rights and obligations; and agree in advance on how to deal with future variables to the extent they are foreseeable. However, it is impossible to draft a joint venture agreement that fully anticipates all future events in sufficiently concrete detail. Consequently, joint venture agreements can be categorized as incomplete contracts.

Instead of attempting to stipulate rights, duties, and responsibilities with respect to unpredictable future events, JV partners often choose to draft their joint venture agreement in the form of a relational contract that prescribes only a minimal basic framework for their relationship. This framework includes general principles regarding the joint venture's purpose and goals, the method of equitable sharing of total return, decision-making standards for dealing with unforeseen circumstances, and inter-partner dispute resolution mechanisms.[2] When a joint venture

---

[2] Regarding relational contracts, *see* PAUL MILGROM & JOHN ROBERTS, ECONOMICS, ORGANIZATION AND MANAGEMENT 131–132 (1992). Regarding joint venture agreements as relational contracts, *see* JOHN ROBERTS, THE MODERN FIRM 104 (1992).

agreement is drafted as a relational contract, matters unanticipated by the partners when the agreement was executed are determined by renegotiation between the partners in accord with the agreed-upon dispute resolution framework.

9.1.3   Issues Related to Binding Effect and Enforceability

A joint venture agreement is a contract between both partners. The JV company is not a party to the agreement and is therefore not directly legally bound by it. In other words, a joint venture agreement is a private agreement between the partner-shareholders. Partners can bring legally binding force to bear on their joint venture only indirectly, by exercising their voting rights under company law pursuant to their agreement with each other. This makes crafting a workable method of enforcing the joint venture agreement an important issue for both partners.

9.2   ANCILLARY AGREEMENTS CONCERNING TRANSACTIONS WITH THE JOINT VENTURE

Transactional agreements regarding the joint venture's operations become binding and enforceable once ancillary agreements have been executed after the joint venture's establishment. Ancillary agreements include transactional agreements between the joint venture and its owners and between the joint venture and third parties. Transactional agreements between the joint venture and its owners are particularly integral to the basic design of the joint venture agreement. Such agreements affect how the partners share control and the total return of their joint venture.[3]

Additionally, ancillary agreements are often essential to the joint venture's operations. Such agreements include contracts regarding

---

[3]   For example, a partner that licenses important technology or a famous brand to its joint venture could gain de facto control of the joint venture through its IP.

technology transfer, secondment of personnel, raw material supplies, leasing of production facilities, product sales, and information systems.[4]

9.3 AGREEMENT REGARDING JOINT VENTURE GOVERNANCE AND ORGANIZATIONAL LAW

9.3.1 Joint Venture Agreements and Organization

Joint ventures are classified into three types: (a) corporate joint ventures, (b) non-equity contractual alliances, and (c) cooperative contractual alliances.[5]

With a corporate joint venture, the partners jointly establish a separate corporation. Non-equity contractual alliances take the form of a partnership (e.g., the BP–Mobil joint venture) or a consortium (e.g., general contractors jointly bidding on a project) that operates the joint business and allocates profits and losses among the partners. Cooperative contractual alliances are collaborative relationships (e.g., R&D collaboration agreements) whereby the partners jointly operate a business based solely on mutual contract obligations without legally forming a partnership or consortium.[6] Beyond these common examples, partners may choose to organize their joint venture as a separate entity using the alternative business organization forms (e.g., LLCs) that are available in many jurisdictions. Partners must choose the most suitable form of business organization for both the joint venture's needs and partner interests.

In selecting the form of their joint venture, partners must identify the respective advantages and disadvantages of various alternatives, comparing attributes such as: whether the form constitutes a separate legal entity, tax implications, the extent of the partners' external liability, company

---

[4] Such ancillary agreements include agreements regarding partners' human capital contributions, particularly contributions of relationship-specific assets. The content of ancillary agreements related to management of business functions, such as procurement of raw materials, manufacturing, sales, and R&D, are stipulated in the joint venture agreement. After a JV company has been established, the partners and the JV company make formal contracts regarding those matters stipulated in the joint venture agreement.

[5] On corporate joint ventures, *see* IAN HEWITT, HEWITT ON JOINT VENTURES, (5th ed. 2011) Ch. 3-28–43; Ch. 5. On partnership, *see id.*, at Ch. 3-9–27. On contractual alliance, *see id.*, at Ch. 3-5–8; Ch. 4.

[6] *See id.*, at Ch. 4-2; Ch. 3-18.

organization expenses, administrative and operating costs, operational flexibility, and the ease of exit.

Stock corporations are legal entities separate from their owners that can confer limited external liability on all of their shareholders. On the other hand, corporations are subject to corporate taxation and, relative to other forms of business organization, are more costly to establish and operate while also being less flexible in terms of organizational management. Because withdrawal is not permitted and shareholders' ability to exit is limited, capital contributions have a commitment effect.

Partnerships are subject to pass-through taxation, are inexpensive to establish and operate, and afford a high degree of flexibility in terms of organizational management. However, partnerships are not separate legal entities and partners have unlimited external liability. Withdrawal is permitted, enabling partners an easy exit. The flipside of this ease of exit is that partnerships are fragile organizations.

In the U.S., LLCs have been gaining prevalence rapidly in recent years, as a form of organization that is a separate legal entity which confers limited liability on its members, and is subject to pass-through taxation. Exit rules differ from state to state.[7] Japanese LLCs are separate legal entities that confer limited liability on members and flexibility in terms of organizational management, but pass-through taxation does not apply. Further, Japanese LLC members' freedom to exit their LLCs is mandatory under law.

The joint venture agreement must finalize the organizational form that was bargained for in light of the planned joint venture's strategic objectives, the nature of its business, and the mandatory and default rules that apply due to their choice of organizational form.

9.3.2   Impact of Organizational Law on Bargaining

Selection of the form in which a joint venture will be organized is the first subject of bargaining between partners because it determines the default rules that will apply to the joint venture. As the default rules constitute a starting point for bargaining, they have a major impact on all subsequent bargaining. The partners bargain over changes to the default rules in the second stage of bargaining.[8]

---

[7]   *See infra* note 14.

[8]   Default rules are non-mandatory rules to which the parties are deemed to have consented unless the JV company's charter expressly stipulates otherwise. If there are judicial precedents regarding the type of agreement deemed to exist in the absence of an explicit agreement between the parties, such precedents are

To illustrate, when a business is organized as a partnership or LLC, the general rule is that decisions on major matters require unanimous approval of the partners/members and regular operational decisions require majority approval. In contrast, in stock corporations, decisions are generally made by majority rule based on ownership percentages. While JV partners can bargain to modify the default rules, the extent (the scope of charter autonomy) differs depending on the joint venture's organizational form. Additionally, the degree to which the default rules may be modified influences bargaining between the partners.

9.3.3 Durability of Agreements between Partners

The selection of a joint venture's organizational form has two main effects on the durability of negotiated agreements. The first involves the agreements' legal stability: if the partners select a certain organizational form, will the results of bargaining be legally finalized as an agreement between shareholders or in the JV company's charter? The second focal point is the *ex post*, de facto binding force of the inter-partner bargaining given the selection of organizational form. That is, how easily can a partner exit at renegotiation junctures?

9.3.3.1 Freedom of charter

If the partners choose to establish a joint venture that differs from the default rules, express provisions in either the JV company's charter or an agreement between shareholders is necessary. When these are included in the charter, the modifications are binding on the JV company and future shareholders. Modifications to default rules that are incorporated into the charter are generally more legally stable than equivalent modifications merely stipulated in an agreement between shareholders.[9]

Key issues in terms of mandatory rules' relationship with the results of bargaining between JV partners include determination of ownership

---

also incorporated into the default rules. Changing the default rules entails bargaining costs. *See* Zenichi Shishido, *Goben Godo Kaisha* [*Joint Venture LLCs*] *in* KIGYO-HO KINYU-HO NO SHINCHORYU [NEW TREND OF CORPORATE LAWS AND FINANCE LAWS] 213, 216 (Koide et al. eds., 2013).

[9] Legal effects of incorporating shareholders' agreement into the charter are different depending on jurisdictions.

percentages,[10] governance design options,[11] modifiability of management's duties of care and loyalty,[12] and exit options.[13]

---

[10] In joint ventures, it is necessary to rectify imbalances between partners' ownership percentages and their respective human capital contributions lest a partner's incentives be distorted to contribute human capital that is disproportionately important to the joint venture relative to the partner's ownership percentage based on its monetary capital contribution (*see* Ch. 2, 2.1). Partnerships and LLCs generally afford more flexibility than stock corporations in terms of allowing ownership percentages to be disproportionate to partners' respective shares of monetary capital contributed. However, even if a joint venture is organized as a stock corporation, the JV partners have considerable flexibility to rectify imbalances by issuing multiple shares of stock. This difference between stock corporations and partnerships/LLCs under organizational law is consequently not very important. However, partners must beware of tax-law restrictions on rectifying such imbalances by adjusting ownership percentages.

[11] Corporations are characterized by a separation of ownership and management, with mandatory rules requiring the corporation to be managed by third parties (directors) or a third-party body (board of directors) separate from the shareholders. In contrast, partnerships and LLCs are generally managed by their partners/members and do not require establishment of a management body.

[12] With respect to freedom of contract, in most US jurisdictions the duty of care in stock corporations can be contracted around, but the duty of loyalty cannot. However, in 2000, the Delaware General Corporation Law was amended to allow stock corporations to renounce any interest of the corporation in any business opportunities that are presented to the corporation's officers or directors, thereby avoiding liability for breach of the duty of loyalty. (8 Del. Code §122 (17)). In Delaware LLCs, both the duty of care and the duty of loyalty can be contracted around, and can even be totally eliminated by charter; only the duty ("covenant") of good faith and fair dealing is mandatory in all situations (Del. Code Ann. Tit 6, §§17-1101(d); 18-1101(c)). In Japan, the fiduciary duty (without distinction between the duty of care and the duty of loyalty) cannot be contracted around in either stock companies [*Kabushiki-kaisha*] or LLCs [*Godokaisha*]. In LLCs, however, exculpation is possible through amendment of the charter. In stock companies, outside directors can limit, by charter, *ex ante* damages from breach of their fiduciary duties to two years of compensation. Officers and executive directors can only limit such possible damages *ex post*, either by shareholder resolution or resolution of the board of directors, to four to six years of compensation (depending on rank). *See* Zenichi Shishido, *Legislative Policy of Alternative Forms of Business Organization: The Case of Japanese LLCs*, in RESEARCH HANDBOOK ON PARTNERSHIPS, LLCs AND ALTERNATIVE FORMS OF BUSINESS ORGANIZATIONS, Ch. 22 (Robert W. Hillman & Mark J. Loewenstein eds., 2015).

[13] *See infra* note 14.

The scope of matters that can be included in a JV company's charter is generally discussed in terms of charter autonomy, but it actually encompasses two issues. The first is the extent to which mandatory rules prevail, rendering any agreements that differ from the mandatory rules invalid. The second is the extent to which valid contractual agreements between shareholders can be written into the charter.

9.3.3.2 Exit rights

If a joint venture is organized as a partnership or LLC,[14] the partners can withdraw their contributed capital more easily than if the joint venture were organized as a stock corporation in the following two respects. In other words, in joint ventures organized as a partnership or LLC, capital contributions do not constitute much of a commitment and the results of inter-partner bargaining have a low degree of de facto binding force.

First, a JV partner can unilaterally withdraw its share of monetary capital from the partnership or LLC's jointly owned property. On the other hand, if the joint venture were organized as a stock corporation, withdrawal of monetary capital from the joint venture would require a resolution or decision to dissolve the JV company.

Second, partners can repossess in-kind capital contributions by giving themselves the advance right to do so in their JV company's charter. If the in-kind capital is a relationship-specific asset in particular,[15] granting a right to repossess it acts as an incentive for the partner to participate in the joint venture in the first place. At the same time, this places the joint venture in a precarious position, as the partner's exit would likely terminate the joint venture itself.

In contrast, if the joint venture is organized as a stock corporation, capital contributions are generally not refundable, making it difficult for partners to exit. Consequently, capital contributions to joint ventures organized as stock corporations constitute more of a commitment.

---

[14] U.S. state laws regarding exit options from an LLC can be categorized into three types. The first type of legislation gives members mandatory withdrawal rights, which cannot be abandoned (e.g., California Corporations Code §17706.01(a)). The second type of legislation gives members default withdrawal rights, which can be modified by charter (e.g., Uniform Limited Liability Company Act (2006) §§601, 602(1), 110). The third type of legislation does not stipulate anything about withdrawal rights, although it does allow members to create a withdrawal right in their charters (e.g., 6 Del. Code §18-603). Japan's LLC law resembles the first type (Companies Act Article 606). *See* Shishido, *supra* note 12.

[15] Examples of relationship-specific assets include a production plant that requires special equipment.

Results of inter-partner bargaining also have more of a de facto binding force, albeit at the expense of increasing the risk of a squeeze-out.

9.4 JOINT VENTURE'S CHARTER/ARTICLES OF INCORPORATION

When a joint venture is organized as a corporation, partners incorporate the joint venture agreement's provisions in the articles of incorporation in order to strengthen the legal binding force, as corporate law provides additional methods of enforcing articles of incorporation. The ability to limit the joint venture's legal capacity to the scope of the business purpose stated in its charter is particularly important. If the joint venture's management commits an act beyond this, shareholders can seek to invalidate the act.[16] It bears noting, however, that even acts outside the corporation's explicit business purpose may be treated as valid to protect external counterparties that have entered into transactions with the joint venture.

9.4.1 Issues Related to Charter Autonomy

Charter autonomy means the freedom for business owners to organize their company through drafting of the company's charter in an agreed-upon form that fulfills their objectives, irrespective of the provisions of organizational law.

A joint venture agreement stipulates basic matters concerning the joint venture's business purpose, form of organization, governance framework, and business model. Ideally, such provisions can be accurately reflected in the charter, giving them validity under corporate law as well. Additionally, the joint venture agreement and charter are ideally drafted with identical language to avoid interpretation disputes stemming from differences in wording.[17] Broad charter autonomy is needed to achieve these tasks.

---

[16] *See* 8 Del. Code §124 (Effect of lack of corporate capacity or power; ultra vires). E.g. Southeastern Pennsylvania Transportation Authority v. Volgenau, C.A. No. 6354-VCN, 2012 BL 225637 (Del. Ch. Aug. 31, 2012) http://courts. state.de.us/opinions/download.aspx?ID=193080. Partners may also be able to claim damages based on directors' breach of their fiduciary duties.

[17] Joint venture agreement clauses not directly related to the JV company's organization or operation (e.g., clauses pertaining to business plans or transactional agreements) are rarely included in the charter. Matters absolutely required

However, in jurisdictions that limit charter autonomy,[18] parties seeking to establish a company generally use a model charter drafted to coincide with the wording of applicable company law provisions. In such jurisdictions, there tends to be a strong reluctance to draft charters that differ from the default rules, unless charter provisions expressly permit differences.

9.4.2 Relationship between Charter and Joint Venture Agreement

The ability to incorporate the joint venture agreement into the charter is a deterrent against breaches of the joint venture agreement. If the joint venture agreement's content is replicated in the JV company's charter, partners can seek to invalidate opportunistic acts by the other partner or an appointee that has violated the charter.

On the other hand, in jurisdictions in which company law imposes some sort of restriction on charter autonomy, the charter may cut against the enforcement of the joint venture agreement. The joint venture agreement's provisions often differ from the JV company's charter, and the charter may effectively bar/invalidate/dismiss provisions in the joint venture agreement under company law. In such a scenario, there is a risk of one partner or the JV company failing to abide by the joint venture agreement. A partner that is focused on this risk may be reluctant to

---

or advisable to be included in the charter are routinely contained in the charter even if omitted from the joint venture agreement.

[18] In Japan, a continental-law country, corporate law provisions, which used to be a part of the Commercial Code, were generally mandatory rules until the Companies Act of 2005 was established. The Companies Act shifted away from mandatory rules in favor of charter autonomy as a general rule. However, in Japan, a notary must examine a company's original charter and certify that it does not violate the Companies Act. Only charters thus certified may be used to register a newly established company. Because little information is publicly available on how notaries conduct such certification examinations, when U.S. or U.K. companies, whose home countries grant broad charter autonomy, establish joint-venture companies in Japan, the unpredictability of the Japanese notary examination requirement is a source of apprehension. Additionally, if the charter does not pass the examination, one or both partners may end up dissatisfied as a result of being forced to revise the charter or otherwise negotiate a compromise. In this respect, LLCs effectively have broader charter autonomy than stock corporations because their original charters are not required to be examined by a notary.

contribute capital upon the joint venture's establishment. Additionally, once the joint venture has been established and is operational, the partner may incur excessive costs to monitor opportunistic behavior by its partner, detracting from the value of the joint venture's synergies.

To alleviate this risk, both partners should endeavor to maximally incorporate the joint venture agreement provisions into the JV company charter[19] while devising ways to ensure the enforceability of the joint venture agreement provisions that exceed the bounds of charter autonomy. For example, as a safeguard against the other partner-appointed directors passing a resolution in breach of the joint venture agreement, the joint venture agreement may impose a duty to comply with agreements that restrict appointed directors' voting rights in accordance with the joint venture agreement, thereby enabling the partners to bring claims for damages against each other on the grounds of direct breach of the joint venture agreement.[20]

However, damages clauses are rarely used for breaches of joint venture agreements. The reason is that joint ventures entail a risk of unforeseen circumstances, making it practically impossible to estimate in advance damages sufficient to compensate a company with large cash flows for a contractual breach or charter violation that poses a business continuity risk to the company. Moreover, when prospective JV partners bargain regarding the establishment of a joint venture, too much focus on the amount of damages payable in the event of a contractual breach may lead to an overall bargaining tenor tainted with adversarial prudence, with

---

[19]   However, joint venture agreements include provisions that deal solely with matters regarding both partners' conduct, business plans, ancillary agreements' content, and inter-partner dispute resolution procedures. These provisions are not directly related to the joint venture's organization or operation under company law. As such, they are typically not included in the charter. Accordingly, there is no sense in attempting to incorporate the joint venture agreement in its entirety into the charter.

[20]   It is advisable to restrict directors appointed by partners from engaging in acts that pose conflicts of interest by charging partners with an explicit duty to provide instructions to their appointed directors pursuant to the joint venture agreement. In the absence of such a contractual clause, partners would have difficulty claiming damages against the other partner based on liability for breach of contract and would have to consider other means of directly pursuing tort liability against the other partner.

enough potency to prevent the partners from reaching a reasonable agreement.[21]

---

[21] When bargaining to establish a joint venture, neither partner can predict which, if either, will commit breach of contract in the future. Additionally, the business environment could change drastically, making it impossible for either partner to fulfill its contractual obligations. Both partners therefore tend to be reluctant to agree to punitive contractual provisions such as a liquidated damages clause.

10. Post-contract bargaining

Post-contract bargaining includes monitoring and renegotiation by and between partners.

10.1 MONITORING DURING THE OPERATIONAL STAGE

After a joint venture has been established, each partner monitors whether the other partner has contributed resources to the joint venture as promised. If one partner discovers a material fact contrary to the other partner's representations or warranties, that partner may claim damages against the other partner.

During the operational stage, JV partners should utilize prior notification duties, consent rights, after-the-fact reporting duties, and audit rights to monitor the performance of the other partner and the joint venture. Using these tools, partners can acquire the information necessary to effectively exercise their veto rights.

In order to implement the joint venture agreement, the JV partners create various internal regulations for the JV company, such as standards for setting directors' meeting agendas, corporate decision-making and approval rules, rules regarding when policy matters require a parent company's prior consent or notification, and employment contracts.

When JV partners appoint officers to their JV company, they typically also enter into a voting agreement with shareholders to ensure that the control-sharing arrangements contained in the joint venture agreement are not at odds with corporate law requirements for institutional decision-making processes.

10.2 NEED FOR RENEGOTIATION BETWEEN PARTNERS

10.2.1 Types of Renegotiation: Supplemental and Revisionary

Even after entering into a joint venture agreement, JV partners need to engage in two types of renegotiation. The first type is supplemental renegotiation,[1] where the partners flesh out the specifics of the joint venture's business in accordance with the general ideas laid out in the joint venture agreement. This process is integral to performing a joint venture agreement in the course of the joint venture's day-to-day operations. The second type is revisionary renegotiation,[2] whereby the partners change the joint venture agreement's basic rules in response to changes in the joint venture's internal or external environment.

If supplemental renegotiation fails, the resultant lack of contractual specificity would tend to impede the joint venture's business. If revisionary renegotiation fails, the existing joint venture agreement would superficially remain in effect but the joint venture would be unable to adequately respond to major changes in its internal or external environment. Moreover, when a partner refuses to engage in either type of renegotiation in good faith, serious secondary problems, such as an adversarial relationship between the partners, could arise.

10.2.2 Seeds of Renegotiation in the Preliminary Bargaining Stage

When partners establish a joint venture, they enter into a joint venture agreement and transactional agreements related to the joint venture's operations that stipulate their respective rights and obligations and, to the extent possible, other basic matters necessary to operate the joint venture's business. Meanwhile, they endeavor to agree in advance on how to deal with future variables to the extent foreseeable. However, the partners are incapable of anticipating every detail of all future events

---

[1] For example, negotiation of a transactional agreement's specific terms is a form of supplemental renegotiation.

[2] Examples of types of revisionary renegotiation include issuing equity to a third party to be admitted as a new JV partner and revising the partners' ownership percentages. Both entail revision of the joint venture agreement and materially change how control and/or total return are shared by the partners.

(i.e., they are subject to bounded rationality). Additionally, their bargaining is subject to cost and time constraints. Consequently, JV partners invariably end up with incomplete contracts.[3]

In practice, JV partners often elect to draft their joint venture agreement as a relational contract that serves as a basic framework for their future relationship. Leaving certain future matters (e.g., specific action plans or responses to contingencies) for future renegotiation between the partners, such agreements typically stipulate the joint venture's business purpose, quantitative management targets, general rules for the equitable sharing of total return from the joint venture, standards for dealing with unforeseen circumstances, the scope of the partners' responsibilities to take action in response to such circumstances, the partners' decision-making authority, and dispute resolution procedures.

10.2.3   Causes of Renegotiation Difficulties

The environment in which JV partners renegotiate is not necessarily as cooperative as the bargaining environment when the partners first establish their joint venture. Difficulties often arise, stemming from conflicts between the partners. Causes of such difficulties include the following three factors.

10.2.3.1   Change in partners' relationship of trust

As noted above, joint venture agreements are incomplete contracts and, as a practical workaround, are therefore usually drafted as relational contracts. Such relational contracts are implicitly predicated on the expectation that renegotiation between the partners will proceed smoothly and rationally by virtue of a relationship of mutual trust and that the partners will be able to agree on a course of action that serves their common interests. However, mutual trust between partners may change over time. The environment in which the partners renegotiate may not be as cooperative as they expected when they entered into their joint venture agreement, particularly with respect to matters that pose conflicts of interest.

---

[3]   Once bargaining to establish a joint venture has progressed beyond the phase gate that breaking the deal would be too costly, finalizing the joint venture agreement and moving toward establishing the joint-venture company become the prospective partners' priority. At this stage, to avoid running out of time, the partners often expedite the bargaining process by leaving room for future renegotiation, rather than drafting detailed contractual provisions.

10.2.3.2 Relationship-specific assets

A joint venture's assets usually consist of equipment, technology, and production facilities specific to its business purpose. These assets can be characterized as "relationship-specific assets,"[4] in that their value is maximized if they are used for the joint venture's business purpose. If used for any other purpose, the assets lose much of their value.

Relationship-specific assets sometimes impede renegotiation between partners. This situation typically arises in one of two scenarios. The first is when the partners are negotiating a change in the joint venture's business model that would entail disposal of relationship-specific assets and the resultant loss would be borne disproportionately by one partner.[5] The second scenario is when one partner wishes to exit the joint venture,

---

[4] The assets acquired to conduct specific transactions are called "relationship-specific assets." The specific investments have value in a limited range of economic activities. Additionally, the cost of transforming these specialized investments into alternative uses must be high. See JAY B. BARNEY, GAINING AND SUSTAINING COMPETITIVE ADVANTAGE 57 (4th ed. 2011). Relationship-specific assets cannot easily be used for other transactions, typically due to the following reasons:

(a) locational specificity (e.g., production facilities constructed adjacent to each other); or

(b) application-specific products' specifications (e.g., products customized to be technologically highly specialized to a contractual counterparty's products); or

(c) non-substitutable special-purpose assets; or

(d) production equipment for manufacturing the partner's patented products; or

(e) special know-how.

In many cases, joint ventures' relationship-specific assets can be of value only in the context of the joint venture's relationship with one JV partner. When the partner exits from the joint venture, the joint venture's business operations should discontinue upon the partner's exit. And then the relationship-specific assets should immediately lose their value. Therefore, generally speaking, the liquidation value of a relationship-specific asset tends to be substantially less than its going-concern value.

[5] If relationship-specific assets lent to the joint venture by one partner are returned to the partner, that partner alone would incur a loss when disposing of the assets. Similarly, when most of a joint venture's workforce was seconded to the joint venture by one partner, that partner would incur a de facto loss when those potentially redundant workers return to its employ. In such scenarios, there would be a strong sense of inequity regarding how the losses are shared. In contrast, if relationship-specific assets are owned by the joint venture, the joint venture would bear the entire loss on disposition of the assets. If both partners have agreed to share asset impairment losses in proportion to their respective

bring in a third party as a replacement, and withdraw important relationship-specific assets that it originally contributed to the joint venture. In that situation, the joint venture would not be able to remain in operation unless the incoming third party were able to contribute assets that were an adequate substitute for the relationship-specific assets to be withdrawn by the exiting partner. If such a third party cannot readily be found[6] or if the partner's exit otherwise materially jeopardizes the joint venture's continued viability, the remaining partner may bear ill will toward the exiting partner. In such an event, the partners would face difficulty in reaching an agreement through renegotiation.

10.2.3.3 Opportunistic behavior by partners

Another major impediment to renegotiation is post-contractual opportunism by one or both partners. Because future events generally cannot be all-inclusively and specifically anticipated in the joint venture agreement, agreed-upon procedures for resolving potential problems are sometimes inadequate and/or inequitable to one partner's interests.[7] The other partner may attempt to take advantage of such a loophole in the joint venture agreement at the expense of its partner. We refer to such self-interested behavior as "post-contractual opportunism."

Opportunistic behavior impedes partners from reaching an agreement by poisoning the renegotiation environment. When one partner engages in opportunistic behavior, the other partner may respond self-defensively by completely refusing to cooperate, even at the risk of breaching the joint venture agreement. In such an event, the joint venture may end up in a deadlock. A joint venture unable to make decisions could be forced to shut down its operations or may even be driven into bankruptcy if it is unable to respond to crises in a sufficiently timely manner.

---

ownership percentages, there would be no sense of inequity and both partners would be more likely to agree to renegotiate.

  6 Due to the difficulty of finding a third party to replace an existing JV partner, joint venture agreements sometimes impose a duty to find a replacement on the exiting partner and grant veto rights to the remaining partner.

  7 For example, joint venture agreements sometimes grant discretionary decision-making authority over designated matters exclusively to one partner or to a corporate officer appointed by one partner. In such cases, the partner that possesses such authority could have an advantage over the other partner by virtue of being able to maintain its vested rights by merely refusing to renegotiate with the other partner.

10.2.4 Pre-liquidation Renegotiation and Turnaround Renegotiation

Joint venture agreements typically contain provisions regarding liquidation in the event that the joint venture is no longer able to operate under its existing business model due to circumstances such as one partner's exit. In such cases, the relationship-specific assets and, as a result, the joint venture may be devalued from going-concern value to liquidation value. The partners would need to renegotiate regarding how to allocate the loss arising from the disposal of these assets.

On the other hand, partners facing potential liquidation could instead renegotiate to somehow turn around the joint venture's business with the aim of profiting from the continued use of its assets.[8] If such renegotiation succeeds, the joint venture would be able to maintain its going-concern value, to the benefit of both partners. In turnaround renegotiations, both partners must negotiate creatively in a cooperative bargaining. Additionally, if the joint venture agreement contains a liquidation clause establishing grounds for dissolution or gives the partners veto rights to maintain the status quo, both partners must refrain from resorting to these options until the renegotiation process has run its course.[9]

If turnaround renegotiations prove unsuccessful, partners typically transit to pre-liquidation renegotiation in accord with their joint venture agreement's provisions.

10.3 RENEGOTIATION DURING THE OPERATIONAL STAGE

10.3.1 Types of Renegotiation during the Operational Stage

The subject matter of renegotiation differs by the stage of the joint venture's life cycle as described below.

---

[8] If a major problem arises that makes a joint venture's status quo unsustainable, both partners must agree to radical measures, such as additional capital contributions, major operational changes, replacement of a partner, a change in the nature of the joint venture's business, or a change in the relationship between the partners.

[9] Typical scenarios in which engaging in turnaround renegotiation would be preferable to exercising veto rights or initiating dissolution of the joint-venture company pursuant to the joint venture agreement include when one partner wishes to continue the joint venture or expand its operations on a solo basis or when a partner wishing to exit can be replaced with a sufficiently capable and committed third party.

10.3.1.1   Renegotiation regarding the joint venture's establishment

JV partners sometimes renegotiate immediately before[10] or soon after establishing their joint venture in response to a drastic change in the operating environment, failure to satisfy a closing condition, or other such circumstances. In such cases, the partners conduct revisionary renegotiations regarding whether to modify or abandon their joint venture plan.

10.3.1.2   Supplemental renegotiation of specific operational matters

During a joint venture's operational stage, the partners confer about matters not stipulated in their joint venture agreement and conduct supplemental renegotiation to mutually decide upon the details that arise during the routine running of the joint venture's business. If both partners renegotiate these supplemental matters in accord with the joint venture agreement's intent, they can reach a reasonable agreement on specific terms.

10.3.1.3   Revisionary renegotiation in response to major operational issues

While joint venture agreements generally provide a framework for renegotiation in the event that a major problem arises or the joint venture's operating environment changes during the operational stage, they seldom stipulate specific procedures for resolving such matters. Consequently, when such issues arise, the partners conduct revisionary renegotiation to modify the joint venture's business plan and/or the joint venture agreement's provisions or rules.

10.3.2   Subject Matters of Renegotiation during the Operational Stage

10.3.2.1   Specific subject matters of revisionary renegotiation

First, partners may engage in revisionary renegotiation when there are major changes in a joint venture's operating environment that imperil the venture's continued viability. Examples include changes in industry structure, chronic shrinkage in target markets or business domains, loss of competitiveness vis-à-vis rivals' new products, inability to procure, or increased cost of procuring raw materials or parts, failure to achieve operational profitability, loss of a business license, damage or losses that

---

[10]   Although, strictly speaking, the renegotiation takes place immediately before the partners sign their joint venture agreement, it can be characterized as revisionary renegotiation in that it revises the basic agreement initially tentatively reached between the partners.

threaten business continuity, lawsuits claiming major damages, adverse changes in industrial policies (e.g., subsidies, tax breaks) or non-adoption of favorable industrial policies, or changes in country risk in the venture's domicile country.[11] When partners renegotiate in response to such circumstances, the negotiations mainly revolve around whether to attempt a turnaround or liquidate the joint venture.

Second, partners may engage in revisionary renegotiation when there are major changes in one or both of the partners' internal situations. Examples include one partner's loss of interest in continuing the joint venture; one partner's discontinuation of its own operations involved with the joint venture; a change in one partner company that gives rise to concerns about financial viability, bankruptcy, or suitability to support or operate another business (caused by, e.g., a major change in a partner's shareholder structure, a change in management, failure to obtain formal approval of a partner's shareholders or board of directors, or departure of a senior executive that possesses core technology or business know-how), the joint venture's failure to meet partners' expectations, partners' concern with inequitable sharing of profits and losses, distrust between partners, a major disagreement between partners regarding the venture's future (e.g., business expansion), or a dispute between partners regarding a matter unrelated to the joint venture's business. In such cases, the partners must renegotiate regarding radical changes to their joint venture, such as a change in the nature of the joint venture's business, replacement of one partner, revision of the partners' ownership percentages, or transfer of the joint venture to one partner through a buyout of the other partner.

10.3.2.2   One-sided vested interests in revisionary renegotiation

From the standpoint of incentive bargaining, renegotiation that merely changes how existing return is shared (zero-sum bargaining) tends to be rejected by whichever partner would be disadvantaged by the change. Consequently, renegotiation is generally not successful unless it expands the size of the pie by adding value to the joint venture (non-zero-sum bargaining).

When one partner has a vested interest according to the terms of the joint venture agreement, that partner has an advantage over the other partner in that it can easily preserve its vested interest by simply refusing

---

[11]   One example of a joint venture in which country risk came into play is Sakhalin 2. *See* The Corner House Friends of the Earth (England, Wales and Northern Ireland) WWF UK, *Sakhalin II (Phase 2) Compliance Review* (2006) www.thecornerhouse.org.uk/sites/thecornerhouse.org.uk/files/Sakhalin.pdf.

the other partner's request to engage in revisionary renegotiation or by vetoing any of the other partner's proposed revisions. The partner wishing to renegotiate therefore must engage in incentive bargaining to induce the other partner to renegotiate. One approach is to convince the other partner that the status quo is materially detrimental to the other partner's vested interests (e.g., the status quo would result in the joint venture's bankruptcy). Another approach is to offer the other partner a sufficient incentive (e.g., an increase in its share of return due to additional profits expected to be derived from a new business model) that outweighs the other partner's vested interests and renegotiation costs.[12]

10.3.2.3   Forums for renegotiation

Forums for direct bargaining between partners after a joint venture's establishment include the joint venture's management committee, operating committee, or steering committee. Such committees are more aptly regarded as external forums for bargaining between both partners than decision-making bodies internal to the joint venture.[13]

Once established, a JV company is an independent legal entity, which must comply with corporate law rules regarding institutional decision-making procedures. Joint venture agreements therefore often include a stipulation that the partners will endeavor to the best of their abilities to ensure that the JV company's board of directors ratifies agreements negotiated by the partners.

A JV company's directors' meetings sometimes serve as a forum for direct bargaining between the JV partners. When corporate officers appointed by the partners negotiate among themselves or when one partner and the JV company negotiate transaction terms, the JV company is sometimes represented by a corporate officer appointed by the other partner in order to ensure fairness. In such cases, the representative negotiates on behalf of the other partner's interests.

---

[12]   If partner X pursues a strategy of incentive bargaining whereby X offers a portion of its share of returns to Y to incentivize Y to renegotiate and contribute additional resources to the JV company, such a strategy actually makes X worse off. In this situation, Y will have obtained an advantageous return allocation, and will have no incentive to give up this advantage in future renegotiation, and thus X will have no incentive to pursue such disadvantageous renegotiation.

[13]   Operating committees make decisions on material matters only. Although under corporation law, such matters should be decided by the board of directors, statutory authority for management decision-making authority can be delegated to the operating committee with the unanimous consent of shareholders.

In joint ventures that have been granted autonomy, typically profit-center joint ventures,[14] bargaining may take place between the JV company's corporate officers and the partners in addition to bargaining between the partners. In other words, tripartite bargaining may become necessary.

10.3.2.4 Duty to renegotiate

JV partners renegotiate with each other of their own volition. They are under no obligation to accede to the other partner's requests to renegotiate. Joint venture agreements therefore hardly ever impose a duty to renegotiate. However, even absent such a duty, JV partners usually agree to renegotiate at the other partner's request.[15] First, partners may rationally decide that renegotiation is in their best interests based on an economic comparison between the current, status quo return and the expected return obtainable through renegotiation. Second, a partner may choose to renegotiate in order to maintain an amicable relationship and ensure the other partner's continued cooperation, as one partner's withdrawal of cooperation poses a secondary risk of management deadlock in which the partners are unable to reach any future agreements with each other.

10.4 RENEGOTIATION AT THE TERMINATION STAGE

10.4.1 Renegotiation to Continue Joint Venture despite Grounds for Termination

Grounds for termination of joint venture agreements typically include the following:[16]

---

[14] *See infra* Ch. 11.

[15] In the scheme of joint venture agreements, partners may choose to resolve future issues as they arise through renegotiation. In other words, joint venture agreements can be characterized as a relational contract that provides renegotiation procedures to resolve unforeseen future issues.

[16] *See infra* Ch. 12. *See* also IAN HEWITT, HEWITT ON JOINT VENTURES, Ch. 13; Ch. 11 (5th ed. 2011). Other grounds for termination include bankruptcy of the joint venture and compulsory termination pursuant to a decision to dissolve the joint venture.

(a)   grounds for termination stipulated in the joint venture's charter (e.g., achievement of or failure to achieve the joint venture's purpose);
(b)   expiration of the joint venture's fixed term, agreed upon at the time of its establishment, or a mutual decision to discontinue operations at a predetermined interim milestone;
(c)   change in a partner's business strategy (e.g., conversion of joint venture to one partner's solely owned business, decision to exit business);
(d)   a partner's bankruptcy or change of control;
(e)   a partner's material breach of the joint venture agreement or an ancillary agreement.

However, a successful turnaround renegotiation typically yields a much larger payoff than pre-liquidation renegotiation as discussed above. Consequently, even when grounds for terminating the joint venture agreement exist, partners generally voluntarily refrain from initiating the termination procedures stipulated in the agreement until they have made an effort to renegotiate to continue the joint venture.

Such turnaround renegotiation can be realized in two scenarios. One scenario is when the balance of rights and obligations between the partners would be lost, if one of the partners were to initiate the process of exiting from and winding up the joint venture pursuant to the joint venture agreement.[17] The other scenario is when one partner has an interest in keeping the joint venture's business alive.

10.4.2   Renegotiation in Connection with Joint Venture Termination Procedures

If both partners agree to terminate the joint venture in accord with their joint venture agreement, supplemental renegotiation is typically required to agree or decide upon certain details of the termination procedures on an ex-post basis. If both partners agree to a turnaround and modify their joint venture agreement, their renegotiation could be considered revisionary. For further discussion of termination of joint ventures, see Chapter 12.

---

[17]   When a partner allows its joint venture to use a portion of its manufacturing plant or has seconded personnel comprising most of the joint venture's manufacturing workforce, the partner may end up saddled with redundant workers or production capacity upon dissolution of the joint venture.

10.5   JOINT VENTURE FUNDING METHODS AND RENEGOTIATION

Raising additional capital for a joint venture is another context that requires renegotiation between partners. Because there are various well-established methods of raising capital, renegotiation concerning the specifics of such methods seldom poses problems. The most common points of contention are the amount of capital to be raised and how it will be used. Renegotiation objectives and issues that often arise during renegotiations to raise additional capital are summarized below for each of the major methods of raising capital for joint ventures.

10.5.1   Equity Offering to Existing Shareholders

In renegotiations regarding an equity offering to existing shareholders, both partners' objectives are preventing dilution of the partners' existing ownership interests (eliminating the risk of being squeezed out), assessing the rationality of their obligations to contribute additional equity capital, and reaching an agreement regarding their rights to subscribe to the equity offering.[18] If a JV company raises equity capital through a pro rata rights issue to its existing shareholders, both partners are able to retain their existing ownership percentages. This approach thus poses no risk of dilution.

10.5.2   Equity Offering to a Third Party

Raising capital through an equity offering to a third party not only changes the JV partners' existing ownership percentages, it can also radically change the existing co-management relationship and/or bargaining environment between the partners by giving a third party voting rights in the JV company. Partners can avoid such changes by issuing nonvoting preferred stock to the third party. However, to provide an

---

[18]   The subject matter of such renegotiation may include: (1) the need for and uses of over-budget funding, (2) causes of and responsibility for the joint venture's funding deficit, (3) future vision and business plans for the joint venture, (4) exercise of veto rights if one partner is unable or unwilling to contribute additional capital, and (5) method of contributing additional capital in the form of in-kind contributions of relationship-specific assets or existing business operations.

incentive for the third party to contribute capital under such terms, the partners will likely need to offer a guaranteed dividend on the non-voting stock.

10.5.3 Debt Financing

Debt financing does not change the partners' existing ownership ratios and therefore poses few, if any, dilution concerns. The joint venture, however, would incur interest and repayment obligations, resulting in an increase in its non-operating expenses.

Joint ventures are generally not granted credit lines by banks because they do not independently qualify for credit. Given the difficulty of independently obtaining bank financing, JV companies often borrow from a parent company or an affiliate thereof, or utilize bank financing guaranteed by a parent company. In such cases, indemnification and credit guarantee fees are issues for inter-partner bargaining.[19]

In practice, differences in the partners' ability to raise capital and the financing terms available to them influence the sharing of control. In financing-related renegotiations between partners, the partners' relative bargaining power is determined solely by their financial strength. The partner that contributes the larger share of additional capital will increase its de facto say in the joint venture's business in proportion to its monetary contribution. Financing a joint venture therefore involves indirectly vying for control of the joint venture in addition to sharing finance risk (i.e., the risk of default due to failure of the joint venture).

10.5.4 Retained Earnings

Retained earnings are an internal source of funding for a JV company. Internally generated funding poses no risk of dilution for the JV partners. For the JV company, dividends are the effective cost of capital, but retained earnings are equity, which entails no interest or repayment

---

[19] Parent companies tend to be hesitant to guarantee their joint ventures' liabilities. Joint ventures therefore sometimes pursue project finance, but banks often demand a parent-company guarantee or charge over contract for transactions between the joint venture and its parent companies (partners). *See* Hewitt, *supra* note 16, at Ch. 7-28–29. Joint venture agreements sometimes contain provisions regarding partners' additional financing obligations, parent-company financing, proration of debt-guarantee liability, and the guarantor partner's right to claim reimbursement from the other partner.

obligations, unlike debt financing. However, the partners' dividend policies may constrain the internal retention of profits. Additionally, use of reserves or retained earnings may be subject to restrictions under corporate law.

10.5.5 Change in Prices of Transactions with Partners

JV partners sometimes help improve their JV company's cash flow by repricing transactions between themselves and the joint venture in a manner advantageous to the joint venture. Such repricing poses little problem if the revised price is within an arm's-length price range, but profit transfers to a joint venture that lack economic rationality may have adverse tax ramifications. For example, they may be subject to gift taxation in the case of domestic transactions or transfer price taxation in the case of transactions with a foreign related party.

10.5.6 Conversion of Joint Venture to a Profit-Center

Converting a joint venture to a profit-center[20] is a method of obtaining funding from third parties through commercial transactions. Through this approach, a joint venture may increase its capital by earning business profits from third parties. To convert a joint venture into a profit-center, the partners must grant autonomy to the joint venture. Doing so reduces the partners' control over the joint venture in relative terms. Commencement of transactions with third parties is a transformation of the joint venture's business model that both partners must consent to through revisionary renegotiation.

10.5.7 Initial Public Offering (IPO)

One method of raising capital from public capital markets is an initial public offering (IPO) of a joint venture. Given that an IPO's effectiveness as a means of raising capital depends largely on equity market conditions, even if an IPO is not contemplated in a joint venture's original medium/long-term plan, it is generally presented as one option for raising capital. The partners would decide whether to actually proceed with the IPO by renegotiating with each other during the joint venture's operational stage.

---

[20]   *See infra* Ch. 11, 11.1.

11. Cost-centers, profit-centers, and human capital provider autonomy

11.1 COST-CENTER VERSUS PROFIT-CENTER

11.1.1 Definitions and Significance of the Distinction

Joint ventures are classified as either cost-centers or profit-centers. Cost-center joint ventures are typically organized to serve a cost-cutting or risk-aversion role through cost control in a segment of at least one of the partners' value-chain functions. Merely reducing or minimizing partners' operating costs may serve the partners' objective to maximize profits. In contrast, profit-center joint ventures are organized with the aim of earning profits from third parties and sharing those profits between the JV partners. Profit-center joint ventures aim to increase profitability for both partners. Cost-centers' and profit-centers' key performance indicators are expenses and profits, respectively.

JV partners use very different means of controlling these two types of joint venture to ensure effective fulfillment of the respective functions and purposes. For example, in cost-center joint ventures, control mainly revolves around relatively simple cost-cutting pressures. In profit-center joint ventures, in contrast, incentives such as autonomy granted to the joint venture's management team are typically a key means of control.

During the business-planning process, both partners should distinguish between cost-centers and profit-centers.

11.1.2 Characteristics of Cost-Center Joint Ventures

In cost-center joint ventures, managers are generally only given responsibility and authority for cost control; profits are beyond the purview of their authority. Thus, the primary management objectives are cutting costs, establishing cost-control systems, and subsequently conducting required operations at minimal cost. Autonomy and incentives are generally not required in this setup.

11.1.2.1 Two types of cost-center joint venture

There are two types of cost-center joint venture. The first type is a typical cost-sharing (i.e., facility-sharing) joint venture[1] where both partners reduce costs by spinning out and combining certain cost-center functions previously performed in-house (e.g., production, delivery, procurement of materials). Upon establishment of a cost-center joint venture, both partners simply transfer internal cost-centers to the joint venture. This type of joint venture typically starts out using the same management methods used previously by the partners individually. As the partners' ultimate objective is for the joint venture to become the lowest-cost supplier, instead of giving the joint venture special treatment as an investment target, the partners typically treat it no differently than a subcontractor supplying the same type of goods or services. They also often escalate demands for cost savings, promote efficiency through competition, and transact business with the joint venture using the same standard contract forms that they use in their dealings with unrelated subcontractors. There is little if any need to grant such joint ventures autonomy as an incentive.

The second type of cost-center joint venture is a new breed where the partners jointly establish a cost-intensive business function that was not previously performed in-house. This type of joint venture is often used in businesses that rely on capital-intensive infrastructure(s) or other assets. One example is a joint venture established by five telecom carriers to build and operate a PHS mobile telecom infrastructure.[2] All five partners are able to access the joint venture's service infrastructure at cost. Other examples include joint ventures formed by seaborne shipping lines and major oil companies or oil-producing countries to build, own and operate extremely costly LNG tankers.

In general, cost-sharing joint ventures are most promising when used to share costs greater than either partner could shoulder individually in the development of a new product or cultivation of a new market. Examples include joint development of drugs or new high-tech products,

---

[1] *See supra* Ch. 6, 6.2 (11).

[2] For example, with infrastructure becoming increasingly expensive to construct/install and maintain in recent years, the resultant cost burden is often too heavy for even large corporations to bear individually. It is rational for companies in the same or related industries to jointly own infrastructure and share the cost of ownership. *See e.g.*, Nihon Keizai Shinbun, December 14, 2010, at 11. Five overseas telecom equipment manufacturers acquired equity stakes in Softbank's next-generation PHS business and supplied telecom equipment to it.

fulfillment of a mandate to install a telecommunications or IT infrastructure, and joint execution of large-scale public works projects.[3]

Management of such joint ventures sometimes necessitates hiring
outside managers, whose skills extend beyond that of the partners'
internal resources. This recruiting requires careful planning of managerial
autonomy and incentives.[4]

11.1.2.2 Control of cost-center joint ventures

The benchmark for assessing the efficiency of cost-center joint ventures
is the cost comparison with that of outsourcing to a third party.[5] An
existing cost-center joint venture that fails this economic rationality test
loses its raison d'être. In such an event, the joint venture should be
reassessed and modified or even dissolved.

Due to cost pressures, cost-center joint ventures typically require direct
governance and rigorous monitoring by both partners. In most cases, the
JV partners directly manage the cost-center joint venture through an
operating committee instead of granting decision-making authority
(autonomy) to the joint venture's management team. Cost-center joint
ventures are often integrated into the partners' value chains and are not
permitted to engage in transactions with third parties, and therefore there
is no need for independence and discretion to contract with and pursue
profits from third parties.

Initially, cost-center joint ventures are staffed with personnel seconded
by the partners. Because such personnel's compensation is an expense of
the joint venture, rather than an expense for the respective partners, both
partners have an incentive to engage in opportunistic cost-shifting
behavior by seconding more personnel to the joint venture than the other
partner.

---

[3] When two or more companies partner to jointly operate a cost-intensive
business, they must be careful not to run afoul of antitrust law. Under antitrust
law, joint ventures are often regulated as one form of business combination.

[4] Given such joint ventures' purpose of sharing large costs, they require
more sophisticated mutual restraint and monitoring systems. At the same time, it
is also especially important to avoid excessive mutual distrust between partners.

[5] To efficiently reduce costs, a cost-center joint venture must (a) be
integrated into the JV partners' supply chains, (b) conduct only cost-basis
transactions with the two partners, (c) minimize the cost of administrative
functions transferred to it by the partners, and (d) pursue cost savings by
scrapping unneeded duplicative assets.

11.1.3   Characteristics of Profit-Center Joint Ventures

The main objective of establishing a profit-center joint venture is to create a new business entity able to earn profits from third parties, instead of merely combining and minimizing the cost of assets spun out by the partners.[6]

Profit-center management techniques are complex. Profit-centers require management capabilities that balance cost control and profit control. Given the high level of skills required, the senior management of a profit-center joint venture should be given strong incentives in the form of compensation, responsibility, and authority.

In particular, because profit-center joint ventures are expected to earn profits from third parties, they must be granted broader authority to engage in transactions with third parties. They must also be permitted to include profit elements in their transactions with both JV partners instead of merely conducting cost-based transactions for the partners. Accordingly, this structure necessitates broad independence and decision-making authority to engage in transactions with third parties.

Although a profit-center joint venture may initially maintain some degree of dependency and remain a part of the value chains of one or both parent companies, once it has successfully launched its operations, it may need independent decision-making authority (autonomy) in regard to internally retaining profits or independently borrowing funds to expand its operations. At this stage, the operating committee, staffed by senior executives of both partners, recedes into an advisory role or is dissolved, and the joint venture is thereafter indirectly governed by the partner-appointed directors.

Subsequent to this, corporate officers are typically assigned to the joint venture on a permanent, full-time basis and compensated based on the joint venture's operating performance. Other seconded personnel are also

---

[6]   Both partners expect the joint venture to supply goods and/or provide services at lower prices than available from third-party suppliers. Thus, at least initially, a profit-center joint venture may resemble a cost-center joint venture. However, as described below, such ventures become more profit-center focused as they become more established. Ultimately, when both partners spin out their own businesses to form a joint venture and engage in business planning to preclude their intervention in the joint venture (e.g., by agreeing to a non-compete clause), dividend distributions from the joint venture become their expected return.

formally transferred to the joint venture as permanent employees. Additionally, the joint venture may start hiring new employees as it commences business activities. As a result, the joint venture establishes itself as a permanent, independent company in the minds of its workforce. At this stage, return on equity would become the benchmark for evaluating the joint venture's operating performance.

Ultimately, the partners should be able to maintain an appropriate level of monitoring over the joint venture by exercising their voting rights as shareholders. They may also consider bringing in external capital or even floating an IPO, changing the joint venture's structure.

11.1.4   Comparative Analysis

Cost-center joint ventures are integrated into both partners' value chains and totally controlled by the JV partners. As such, they are not independent entities from a bargaining standpoint. Additionally, in a cost-center joint venture, appointed corporate officers and seconded personnel loyalty lies with the partner that dispatched them to the joint venture. In effect, bargaining is still conducted between the partners. Additionally, many conflicts and opportunities for opportunistic behavior tend to arise for both partners, given their incentive to try to shift more costs to the joint venture than the other partner does. Moreover, the cost-cutting effects tend to be relatively short-lived because at some point costs cannot be reduced any further. Considering these facts, cost-center joint ventures are not easily sustained over long timeframes. In many cases, cost-center joint ventures end up being terminated and their operations outsourced.[7]

Profit-center joint ventures are, by nature, enterprises that exceed the partners' individual capabilities. This causes the partners to need each other's active involvement and/or investment in the endeavor. Bargaining to establish a profit-center joint venture consequently consists mainly of incentive bargaining to induce one's prospective partner to contribute more capital. During the post-establishment operational phase, the partners typically grant an appropriate degree of autonomy to a profit-center

---

[7]   Another option is to adopt a basic policy of converting a cost-center joint venture to a profit-center joint venture, shifting the joint venture's focus to providing the JV company's goods and/or services to third parties and strengthening the JV company's senior management's sense of commitment to the joint venture by granting them autonomy. JV partners therefore sometimes agree in the joint venture agreement to convert their joint venture from a cost-center to a profit-center as a medium/long-term business plan.

joint venture's management team and workforce, giving them a sense of commitment to the joint venture. Incentive bargaining that involves the joint venture as an independent negotiator is conducive to earning greater profits. In such cases, both partners' control rights are, in general, limited to ordinary shareholder rights.

11.2 MONITORING AND THE AUTONOMY OF HUMAN CAPITAL PROVIDERS

11.2.1 Autonomy[8]

As mentioned previously, joint venture management teams are usually comprised of personnel seconded by both JV partners. If they possess any autonomy, it is at the will of the partners. In determining the scope of management's autonomous authority, partners should consider the following points.

First, the scope of autonomy typically changes as a joint venture grows. During the startup stage immediately following a joint venture's establishment, the joint venture is unable to survive unless its parent companies shoulder many or all of its costs (i.e., resembling a cost-center). At this stage, autonomy granted to seconded management personnel is typically very limited. Management autonomy increases once the joint venture starts generating enough profits to survive independently (i.e., it has become a profit-center).

Second, the scope of autonomy will differ depending on management policies held by the parent companies with respect to the joint venture. If the parent companies treat the joint venture as part of their own operations, they will typically want to limit the venture to a cost-center role. When parent companies grant more autonomy, costs associated with internal bargaining and the reconciliation of interests arise. Such costs act as a disincentive against granting autonomy for cost-center joint ventures. In contrast, if the parent companies intend to develop their joint venture into a business that independently earns profits from third parties, the parents would likely accept these costs and grant broad autonomy to incentivize seconded management personnel.

---

[8] As used herein, "autonomy" means independence from both JV partners. More specifically, it means the extent to which personnel seconded to the joint venture are able to make decisions independently of the partner that seconded them, particularly the managing partner.

Third, the relationship between the parent companies may also affect the amount of autonomy granted to the joint venture's management. For example, if the relationship between parent companies is not amicable, the corporate officers and other seconded personnel may exclusively pursue the interests of their parent company of origin, potentially resulting in a sort of proxy war. This would render management dysfunctional due to a lack of commitment to the joint venture's common interests. Granting autonomy in this scenario would be extremely ill-advised. JV partners cannot grant autonomy to their joint venture unless the partners can agree on basic management policies and they trust each other to refrain from opportunistic behavior.

Fourth, a joint venture's major suppliers or creditors[9] may pressure the parent companies to grant independence to the joint venture's management team and increase its autonomy, in order to mitigate the fear of the parent companies' exercise of excessive control or covert siphoning of profits from the joint venture to themselves. Conversely, a joint venture's autonomy may be reduced if a major supplier seeks a credit guarantee from the parent companies or requires the parent companies to keep the joint venture business under their control so that they are considered sustainable and creditworthy.

11.2.2 Incentive Bargaining between Monetary Capital Providers and Human Capital Providers

The individuals who actually run a joint venture are the personnel seconded by the parent companies. The parent companies must strike a balance between authority to monitor the joint venture as monetary capital providers and the autonomy granted to the seconded personnel as human capital providers. If the parent companies monitor too invasively or grant too little autonomy to seconded personnel, there will be a disincentive for personnel in regard to contributing human capital to diligently run the joint venture's operations. The parent companies must therefore make some sort of commitment that ensures a certain degree of management autonomy. Conversely, if the parent companies grant too much autonomy to the seconded personnel, the personnel could undermine the parent companies' interests by recklessly pursuing the joint venture's interests above all else. Parent companies are sometimes so worried about such an outcome that they treat the joint venture's

---

[9] In Japan, a main bank (primary financial bank) plays a role of delegated monitor and uses its opinion to influence management decisions in its debtor companies.

management personnel as mere figureheads, thereby discouraging them from contributing human capital. Considering this, parent companies should therefore be sensitive to the necessity of striking a balance between these two extremes.

In fact, parent companies and their joint ventures often have opposing interests. Personnel seconded to a joint venture inherently face a conflict of interest in terms of whether to prioritize the interests of the joint venture or their parent company of origin.[10] Broadly speaking, there are three types of conflict of interest: conflicts related to (1) transactions, (2) allocation of corporate opportunities, and (3) information disclosure. Conflicts of interest with respect to information disclosure can be a particularly sensitive issue related to sharing control of a joint venture.[11] For example, personnel seconded to the joint venture who have knowledge of their parent company's profit structure could use that information to attempt to negotiate exploitative transaction terms, such as demanding a cut of the parent company's profit margin.[12]

11.2.3 How Autonomy is Granted

Partners typically adjust the scope of management authority using the internal corporate approval regulations to define the power and authority of the JV company's board of directors as well as the CEO's decision-making. The scope of autonomy is broadened by expanding the chief executives' decision-making authority while limiting the subject matter of directors' resolutions to material matters. In order to limit the power and authority of a chief executive, the partners can limit the chief executive's decision-making authority and require a directors' resolution or the shareholders' advance approval for even minor matters. In joint ventures with minimal autonomy, all material matters are decided by an operating committee comprised of senior executives of both parent companies (see Appendix 1: Measures for Balancing Autonomy and Monitoring).

One way of expanding autonomy is to alter rules applicable to the board of directors. A primary method is to grant discretionary authority to the joint venture's chief executive and limit matters requiring a directors' resolution. However, even without changing the rules regarding matters requiring a directors' resolution, parent companies can grant

---

[10]   *See* Zenichi Shishido, *Conflicts of Interest and Fiduciary Duties in the Operation of a Joint Venture*, 39 Hast L. J. 63 (1987).

[11]   *See id.*, at 80, 112.

[12]   On the corporate law problem of seconded directors' duty of loyalty, *see supra* Ch. 2, 2.1.

greater autonomy to their appointee directors by modifying the voting instructions given to the directors. For example, they could allow their appointee directors to vote in the joint venture's best interests on a limited range of matters instead of requiring directors to vote as instructed by their parent companies. Finally, another way to expand autonomy is to narrow down the list of matters requiring shareholders' advance approval (one type of veto right often held by JV partners). Even upon making these concessions of authority, partners can still indirectly monitor the directors' execution of important business by requiring that the JV company prepare detailed minutes of its directors' meetings.

Additionally, parent companies sometimes take action to signal the joint venture's autonomy to seconded personnel, thereby strengthening personnel incentives and directly alleviating autonomy concerns. Examples include abolishing an existing operating committee; bringing in a third-party shareholder (e.g., a bank); hiring permanent employees to staff the JV company; and permanently transferring seconded personnel to the JV company.

Profit-center joint ventures are sometimes granted independent management decision-making authority because without it they would lack credibility with banks, suppliers, and other non-partner stakeholders. If suppliers perceive a joint venture to be a puppet of its parent companies, they will likely seek a credit guarantee or comfort letter[13] from one or both parent companies. If the joint venture possesses independent authority, suppliers will likely respect that status and deal with the joint venture as an independent business entity. The most extreme approach to granting autonomy to a joint venture by bringing in third-party shareholders is an IPO.

One impediment to granting autonomy to a joint venture is the existence of conflicting interests where the joint venture is operationally integrated into one of its parent company's operations. This impediment is eliminated if the parent company discontinues operations that involve the joint venture, thereby fully transferring the associated management resources to the JV company and ending the conflicting interests relationship.

---

[13]   A comfort letter, or keep-well letter is an instrument whereby a sponsor assures a lender that it will appropriately guide and oversee a project company and ensure that the company remains in business. If, contrary to this assurance, the project company defaults, the sponsor is not obligated as a guarantor but it may be liable for damages.

11.2.4 Methods of Monitoring

Even when seconded management personnel have been granted broad autonomy, parent companies must monitor their joint ventures. JV partners should, as shareholders, at least check the JV company's directors' meeting agendas and related documents in advance in addition to reviewing the meetings' minutes afterwards.

Generally speaking, parent companies are in a continuous state of monitoring joint venture operating performance and issuing instructions to the joint ventures on matters that require the parent company's approval. If directors seconded to a joint venture fail to comply with the parent company's instructions, dismissal from their position and reassignment to the parent company is possible.[14] Additionally, parent companies may employ a contingent governance framework, where they withhold advance approval of proposed shareholder resolutions and/or veto director appointments or management compensation resolutions when the joint venture performs poorly.

11.2.5 Operating Committees

An operating committee is a committee that is comprised of senior executives of both parent companies and independent of the JV company. Operating committees are authorized to make important management decisions on behalf of the joint venture within the scope of the decision-making authority delegated to it (this type of committee may have various other names, e.g., management committee, steering committee). The key defining factor of such a committee is that rather than being an internal decision-making body within the joint venture, such committees are more of an external body that serves as a forum for bargaining between the partners. In other words, such committees are a venue for reaching unanimous decisions among all shareholders, making them

---

[14] If a joint venture's chief executive appointed by a parent company faithfully follows the parent company's instructions, such an arrangement would enable the parent company to control the joint venture. Further, if the chief executive's interests are aligned with a parent company, specific instructions may not even be necessary, and the parent company can grant the joint venture autonomy with a heightened degree of confidence. Appointment of the joint venture's chief executive is particularly important in the case of overseas joint ventures, given the difficulty of a parent company effectively controlling an overseas joint venture.

effectively equivalent to shareholder general meetings in terms of authority. In the event of a deadlock, partners sometimes form ad hoc
committees in hopes of reaching an agreement before having to resort to
arbitration. Because operating committees, in effect, enable shareholders
to directly manage a JV company, they also dilute the joint venture's
independence.

12. Termination of the joint venture

The final stage of post-contract bargaining is termination of the joint venture, in other words, exit of at least one partner.

12.1 TERMINATION BY AGREEMENT

Broadly speaking, termination provisions in a joint venture agreement generally fall into one of two categories. First, one or both partners may exit the joint venture while keeping the JV company in operation, preserving its value. Second, the partners may dissolve the JV company. The first of these categories has four variations: (a) conversion of the joint venture into one partner's solely owned business, usually through a buyout of the other partner's stock;[1] (b) replacement of one partner through sale of its equity stake to a third party; (c) conversion of the joint venture into a third party's solely owned business through M&A; and (d) sale of the JV company to the public through an IPO.

12.2 TERMINATION WITHOUT AGREEMENT

12.2.1 Buyout/Sellout[2]

When JV partners' decisively conflicting interests prevent them from reaching an agreement, the joint venture may be terminated through

---

[1] For example, Ajinomoto and Unilever entered into a share sale agreement on February 18, 2003, in conjunction with termination of their joint ventures in six Asian countries/regions, as the two companies wanted to pursue their own independent business strategies in Asia. Under the share sale agreement, Ajinomoto sold its entire shareholdings in seven JV companies to Unilever Group companies in two installments. *See* www.ajinomoto.co.jp/ajinomoto/press/2003_02_18_1.htm. Key issues in terms of execution of this option are (1) timing, (2) price (valuation standards and procedures), and (3) funds required to buy out the exiting partner. Regarding share sale agreements, *See* IAN HEWITT, HEWITT ON JOINT VENTURES, Precedent 14 (5th ed. 2011).

[2] See id., at Ch. 12.

compulsory exit by one of the partners. Potential means of compulsory exit include (a) one partner's exercise of a put or call option granted as an exit right at the time of the JV company's establishment, (b) one partner's de facto put option via a threat to exacerbate the losses on the other partner that would be incurred if the joint venture were dissolved by a court order, and (c) rescission of the joint venture agreement due to material breach of joint venture agreement by the other partner.

When JV partners are unable to reach an agreement and the exit mechanisms designed at the time of the joint venture's establishment do not work, other options include arbitration, voluntary dissolution of the JV company, termination of the JV company due to business failure, and litigative dissolution, where the JV partners square off in an adversarial relationship and terminate the JV company through bankruptcy proceedings. When a JV company's largest creditor is its parent company, the parent company may seize control of the JV company through corporate reorganization proceedings and squeeze out the other partner through a capital reduction, thereby converting the joint venture into its own solely owned business.

12.2.2 Arbitration

Joint venture agreements often include clauses that require partners to submit to alternative dispute resolution,[3] particularly arbitration, when they are involved in a dispute and unable to reach an agreement between themselves. However, by the time JV partners agree to go to arbitration, the joint venture's survival is often in doubt. In such cases, rather than proceeding on the unrealistic assumption that the joint venture will continue, the arbitration often ends up determining the terms of the joint venture's termination.

One advantage of arbitration is that disputes can be resolved more expeditiously and less expensively than if the matter were decided by protracted judicial proceedings in a three-tiered court system. Arbitration cases can be resolved by a specialized arbitrator in a single round of proceedings, enabling greater procedural flexibility.

A second advantage is that arbitration can resolve disputes more flexibly than the courts, particularly in continental-law countries like Japan.[4] Arbitral awards can also be based on conventions other than a

---

³ *See id.*, at Ch. 14.

⁴ In civil litigation in continental-law countries such as Japan, judicial decisions are based on the elements and burden of proof required with respect to a specified cause of action.

country's positive law. Unlike the courts, arbitrators can, even without rights under positive law, comprehensively reconcile the disputants' interests, including altering relationships outside the purview of the cause of action.

Third, it is possible to have arbitral awards based on specialized knowledge because, unlike the generalist judges found in traditional court systems, the parties can agree on an arbitrator with specialized knowledge pertinent to their dispute.

Fourth, arbitration is a particularly popular dispute resolution procedure in cases in which one or both partners have little trust in or familiarity with the court system of the country in which the JV company was established. If a dispute involves an international joint venture, the JV partners can transcend national sovereignty by having their dispute arbitrated in a third-party country. In developing countries where trust in the national judicial system is low, arbitration may yield a more fair resolution than the courts, especially when parties are disadvantaged in terms of retaining competent legal counsel due to unfamiliarity with the local language, legal system, or legal procedures. When a dispute pertains to the joint venture agreement or an ancillary agreement between partners, the partners can avoid the disadvantage of arguing their cases in an unfamiliar local language and court system if they enter into an international commercial arbitration agreement.

Fifth, arbitral hearings and awards can be kept confidential, unlike court decisions, which generally become public knowledge.

Arbitration's disadvantages include, first, that disputants must agree in advance to submit to arbitration.[5] Second, the disputants may not be able to agree on the appointment of an arbitrator. Third, parties to arbitration cannot be compelled to submit documents, so the refusal of one party could obstruct discovery. Fourth, arbitration is generally infeasible when a large number of disputants are involved; it is best utilized as a method of resolving one-to-one disputes. Fifth, compulsory enforcement of an arbitral award requires a separate enforcement order.

12.2.2.1 Arbitration rules and arbitral bodies

It is important for JV partners to specify their agreed arbitration rules and arbitral body in the joint venture agreement. The most prominent

---

[5] For a sample arbitration agreement form, *see* Hewitt, *supra* note 1, at Precedent 21. Joint venture agreements generally contain an arbitration clause, but the clause may not be drafted in sufficient detail to be enforceable. Consequently, when partners renegotiate once a dispute has arisen, one partner may refuse to sign an arbitration petition.

arbitration regulations are the United Nations Commission on International Trade Law's (UNCITRAL) New York Convention (United Nations Convention on the Recognition and Enforcement of Foreign Arbitral Awards).[6] UNCITRAL Arbitration Rules and the UNCITRAL Model Law on International Commercial Arbitration are commonly used as ad hoc arbitration rules.[7] Other important rules include the International Bar Association's Rules on the Taking of Evidence in International Arbitration.[8] The International Centre for Settlement of Investment Disputes (ICSID) is an important institution for joint ventures involving the governments of developing countries.[9]

12.2.2.2 Governing law and arbitral forum
In terms of governing law and arbitral forum selection, it is advisable for JV partners to choose a neutral, third-party country that is neither partner's home country.

12.2.2.3 Arbitrators
Arbitrators may be selected and challenged by the disputants, an arbitral body, or a court. JV partners should stipulate arbitrator selection criteria in advance to avoid being unable to appoint arbitrators when a dispute occurs. Disputes involving joint ventures are typically arbitrated by a panel comprising three arbitrators, with both partners and a neutral third party (e.g., an arbitral body) each appointing one of the arbitrators.

12.2.2.4 Arbitral awards' binding force and enforcement
Arbitral awards have formal legal force (i.e., they are equivalent in legal effect to a final judicial judgment). To enforce an arbitral award, one must petition a national court for compulsory enforcement. In Japan, enforcement is guaranteed by the Convention on the Recognition and Enforcement of Foreign Arbitral Awards. In Japan it is easier for a party to petition for and receive compulsory enforcement of a foreign arbitral award than a foreign court judgment, without having to re-litigate the matter. JV partners should be aware that foreign arbitral awards may be unenforceable if they contravene local law.

---

6 www.uncitral.org/uncitral/en/uncitral_texts/arbitration/NYConvention. html.
7 www.uncitral.org/uncitral/uncitral_texts/arbitration.html.
8 www.ibanet.org/.
9 https://icsid.worldbank.org/ICSID/Index.jsp.

12.2.3 Judicial Dissolution

The availability of and procedures for judicial dissolution vary widely by jurisdiction. In Japan, for example, a minority shareholder may petition the courts for judicial dissolution of a corporation in the event of a deadlock or other such irresolvable management impasses (Companies Act Article 833). Similarly, under UK law, companies may be compulsorily dissolved pursuant to the Insolvency Act §122(1)(g).[10] Delaware General Corporation Law § 273 provides a mechanism for the judicial dissolution of a joint venture corporation having only two stockholders, each of whom owns 50 percent of the stock therein.[11] Aside from this specific situation, Delaware corporate law does not allow shareholders to petition a court for the compulsory winding-up or judicial dissolution of a JV corporation.[12] Under Delaware's LLC Act (§18-802), however, the court may appoint a liquidating trustee to wind up an LLC's affairs.[13] New York Business Corporation Law provides judicial dissolution not only for deadlock cases (§1104), but also in cases of oppression (§1104-a).[14]

---

[10]   *See* Hewitt, *supra* note 1, at Ch. 13-50; Ch. 11-42. Additionally, upon a showing of unfairly prejudicial conduct, such as oppression of minority shareholders, a court may make a wide range of orders including a buyout of the complainant's share. *See* U.K. Companies Act, 2006, §§994, 996.

[11]   *See e.g.*, In the Matter of Bermo Inc., C.A. 8401-VCL (Del. Ch. Feb. 9, 2015) http://courts.state.de.us/opinions/download.aspx?ID=219060.

[12]   Only one case seems to have granted the remedy of dissolution on the ground of persistent breach of fiduciary duty owed to the minority shareholder. *See* Carlson v. Hallinan, 925 A.2d 506 (Del. Ch., 2006). Also, Delaware General Corporation Law §226 provides for the appointment of a custodian in cases of deadlock, either at the shareholder or director level.

[13]   *See* Spellman v. Katz (In re KSA, L.L.C.), C.A. No. 1838-VCN, 2009 WL 418302 (Del. Ch. Feb. 6, 2009); Lola Cars International Limited v. Krohn Racing, LLC, et al., C.A. No. 4479-VCN (Del. Ch. Nov. 12, 2009) http://www.nybusinessdivorce.com/uploads/file/Lola.pdf. In this case, the Delaware Court of Chancery refused to dismiss dissolution claims arising out of a deadlocked joint venture structured as a limited liability company.

[14]   *See* Matter of Kushner (Smiles Candy Corp.) www.nybusinessdivorce.com/uploads/file/KushnerOrder. *See also* Model Bus. Corp. Act §14.30(2) (2005).

12.2.4 Termination Due to Bankruptcy

12.2.4.1 Bankruptcy of JV company

JV companies are generally resistant to bankruptcy because their parent companies tend to assume responsibility for their obligations before they become insolvent. However, the rare case of a JV company's bankruptcy due to unprofitable operations generally involves one of two scenarios. In one scenario, the JV company files for bankruptcy or corporate reorganization at the direction of the parent company from which its chief executive was appointed.[15] In the second scenario, one partner petitions to initiate bankruptcy or reorganization proceedings as a result of a dispute with the other partner.

12.2.4.2 Bankruptcy of a partner

Joint ventures run their businesses with the reputational backing of the JV partners. If a partner goes bankrupt, the subsequent loss of ongoing access to human capital renders the joint venture dysfunctional. Additionally, the JV company may lose the confidence of creditors and other financiers. The bankruptcy of a partner involved in a joint venture's operations consequently tends to lead to failure of the joint venture's business and is therefore generally grounds for rescission of the joint venture agreement.

12.3 PRACTICAL ISSUES RELATING TO JOINT VENTURE TERMINATION

12.3.1 Inter-Partner Agreements and Corporate Law Procedures

Shareholder general meeting resolutions under corporate law are a matter separate from the joint venture agreement. Therefore, even if the joint venture agreement is rescindable, dissolution of the JV company requires separate legal procedures (e.g., a special resolution at a general meeting

---

[15] For example, Spansion Japan, a Japanese JV company co-owned by Fujitsu and major US semiconductor maker AMD, filed for corporate reorganization at the Tokyo District Court on February 10, 2009. Its total liabilities at the time were ¥74.1 billion. *See* http://investor.spansion.com/phoenix.zhtml?c=189782&p=irol-newsArticle&id=1405135.

of shareholders that requires both partners' consent to convene).[16] However, if grounds for dissolution are stipulated in the articles of incorporation, one partner can commence dissolution proceedings under corporate law without the other partner's consent upon occurrence of any of the stipulated grounds for dissolution.[17]

12.3.2 External Barriers to Exit

Even after a JV company has been dissolved, numerous issues remain, including political issues in developing countries, distribution of residual assets or allocation of residual losses, dismissal of employees, handoff of suppliers and customers, assumption of financial claims and liabilities, and allocation and utilization of patents and know-how. Joint ventures tend to involve complexly intertwined ancillary agreements such as license agreements and continuous supply agreements. Termination of a joint venture thus usually entails more than just settlement of the partners' ownership interests. The following is an overview of matters requiring action by the partners upon dissolution of the joint venture.[18]

12.3.2.1 Succession of licenses

Special care is required in countries that require government approval to dissolve a JV company or transfer stock in a local company to a foreign company. Depending on the country's government regulations on international joint ventures, government authorities' approval may also be required for actions such as buyouts that convert the JV company to a wholly owned subsidiary of a foreign partner or dissolutions of JV companies. Even when a foreign partner is permitted to completely buy out its local partner, it may not necessarily be able to assume the business licenses or permits that were granted to the JV company by virtue of the local partner.

---

[16] *See* 8 Del. Code §275. In Japan, without a written record of the shareholder general meeting's special resolution that dissolved the JV company, a stock corporation's dissolution cannot be recorded in the public registry and the corporation cannot be liquidated (Companies Act Article 926; Commercial Registration Act Article 72).

[17] Regarding judicial dissolutions, *see supra* 12.2.3.

[18] *See* Hewitt, *supra* note 1, at Ch. 13-20–33; Ch. 20-21. In the case of international joint ventures in developing counties, foreign partners could assume a potential risk of change in regulations by local government that impose a special liability on the foreign investor.

12.3.2.2 Handoff of suppliers and customers

When one partner takes over a joint venture's business following the dissolution and liquidation of the JV company, taking over or terminating relationships with suppliers and customers can be a difficult task in practice. One difficulty is determining which party will bear the cost of maintaining business relationships that cannot be terminated. Continuous supply agreements, for example, are difficult to unilaterally terminate. If a JV company has business relationships that cannot or should not be terminated, the partners will have to decide which one of them will take over the JV company's obligations. In doing so, they should consider which one of them (a) has more of a competitive advantage by virtue of similarity (in terms of, e.g., business model, technology, geographic proximity, experience) between its own operations and the JV company's business, (b) is more motivated to diligently run the business, and (c) is more committed to maintaining relationships with suppliers and customers because it stands to gain from doing so even after assuming the liabilities and responsibilities of the JV company's business. Based on these factors, the partner for whom it is more economically rational typically takes over the JV company's business, subject to any constraints on its capacity to assume risks as the ultimate loss-bearer. If either partner assumes a duty to avoid operating a business in competition with the joint venture, it must be careful to comply to the extent that it remains bound by this duty after the JV company's dissolution.

12.3.2.3 Succession and dismissal of employees

When a JV company is dissolved and liquidated, any secondment agreements between the partner and JV company cease to be enforceable. Typically, some or all of the seconded personnel return to the employment of the JV partner from which they were seconded. Employees hired by the JV company itself, however, must be dismissed because their employment contracts terminate once the JV company ceases to exist, though they may be rehired by one of the partners, one of the partner's affiliates, or a supplier of the former JV company. However, while management has the right to discontinue operations, it may not necessarily have the freedom to dismiss workers. In international joint ventures in particular, JV partners must beware of local legal restrictions on the dismissal of employees.

12.3.2.4 Return of in-kind contributions and IP rights

When a JV company is dissolved and liquidated, monetary capital is first returned to the JV partners through distribution of the company's residual assets. Second, the cancellation of ancillary agreements may result in further assets that can be returned to the partners. For example, upon cancellation of a lease agreement, a partner may demand the return of specific property and restoration of the leased premises to their original condition. Another example is that a partner may take possession of the JV company's inventory pursuant to cancellation of a product sales agreement or execution of a sales agreement between a partner and the joint venture to transfer the title of tangible assets owned by the joint venture to the partner. Human capital in the joint venture's possession as of the time of its termination pursuant to cancellation of ancillary agreements is also distributed to the partners. For example, when a secondment agreement is terminated, skilled employees could be returned to a partner.

Further, a JV company's residual economic value is not limited to its residual assets booked, according to generally accepted accounting principles and corporate law, on the balance sheet of the joint venture. Tangible and/or intangible assets not recorded in the books may include, for example, the JV company's rights to patent inventions for which a patent application is pending or not yet filed, R&D processes' interim deliverables (e.g., drawings, specifications, and prototypes), computer programs, and databases. JV partners sometimes take possession of such assets and utilize them in their solely owned businesses.

Transfers of certain types of assets or rights (e.g., mining rights) require the permission of government authorities. JV partners need to be aware that such rights may not be transferable from the JV company to a partner in some cases.

12.3.2.5   Warranties to successors
If a third party wholly or partially takes over a joint venture's operations, the third party and JV partners must reach an agreement on which of them assumes liability in the event of a patent infringement dispute or product liability problem stemming from a defect in products already sold.

12.3.2.6   Partners' duties of confidentiality and noncompetition after the joint venture's termination
In joint venture agreements, the partner that is to take over the joint venture's operations after its termination sometimes imposes duties on the other partner to shield itself from any adverse repercussions of the other partner's actions. Such duties may include a duty of confidentiality, a prohibition against using information for unauthorized purposes, and/or a duty to refrain from competition for a specified time frame after the joint venture's termination. A duty to refrain from competition limits the

duty-bound partner's freedom to conduct future business activities. The partner must therefore carefully scrutinize the terms of such an agreement, including its operational scope, geographic scope, and time frame. Additionally, in the case of a joint venture between competitors, the partners must exercise care so that a duty to refrain from competition is not found to constitute a cartel in violation of antitrust laws.

12.3.2.7 Long-term tort liability

Even after exiting, JV partners sometimes remain legally liable for the past actions of the joint venture. For example, if a now-defunct JV company had polluted the environment while it was in existence, the JV partners may be forced to assume the JV company's tort liability. In one case, a joint venture contaminated the soil surrounding a chemical manufacturing plant with polychlorinated biphenyls (PCBs), which are dioxin-like compounds. A company formed through a merger with the parent company upon dissolution of the joint venture was subsequently ordered to bear some of the site remediation costs. The order was upheld by the Tokyo High Court.[19]

12.3.2.8 Sharing of joint venture losses

12.3.2.8.1 The principle of shareholder limited liability and the sharing of joint venture losses   JV partners are in effect unable to benefit from shareholder limited liability in some cases. In practice, it is difficult for partners to escape from a joint venture when the JV company is in default on its obligations. When the partners have entered into an agreement to guarantee the performance of the joint venture or undertake its liability to a third party with respect to their JV company's transactions with unrelated parties, the partners must perform the JV company's obligations if they guaranteed the obligations.[20]

Additionally, even if the partners have not guaranteed the JV company's obligations, compulsory government regulations may require partners to share the JV company's losses by withdrawing personnel seconded to the JV company, arranging for the rest of the JV company's workforce to be rehired by affiliated companies, fully repaying the JV

---

[19]   *See* in re Mitsubishi Gas Chemical, 1309 Hanrei Taimuzu 137 (Tokyo High Ct., Aug. 20, 2006).

[20]   This situation is similar to a general partnership, in which partners are allocated shares of losses of the joint venture. In Japan, the partners may be liable for damages pursuant to a comfort letter, which is often required by a lender.

company's creditors, and taking over business operations essential to suppliers and/or customers.

12.3.2.8.2 Assumption of JV company's debts Joint venture agreements sometimes contain a debt assumption clause (also known as a "basket clause") stipulating that the parent companies will assume the JV company's debts in the event of the JV company's dissolution or liquidation. For example, Company A may agree to assume accounts-payable obligations that arise in the course of the JV company's operations while Company B agrees to fulfill the JV company's lease obligations. Legal liquidation (e.g., a bankruptcy filing) is an option of last resort to allow the partners to exit from the joint venture without assuming all of the JV company's liabilities. When the JV partners have not agreed in advance to assume their JV company's liabilities, the partners must renegotiate and agree on how to share losses before they can liquidate the JV company.

Even if JV partners have entered into a loss-sharing agreement in advance, they may not be able to liquidate their JV company in accord with their agreement. In such cases, one or both partners may end up bearing losses in excess of their legal liability under corporate law or the joint venture agreement. For example, even if the partners fulfill their own contractual responsibilities in accordance with the joint venture agreement, they may still face the risk of damage to their external reputations. Such reputational damage may take the form of being shunned by prospective customers and/or perceived as unreliable by prospective alliance partners. The partner that faces the most reputational risk and would incur more costs is therefore likely to be at a disadvantage in renegotiating loss sharing with the other partner. Other examples include joint ventures that need governmental license such as electric power companies, where the partners are at risk of revocation of their licenses upon dissolution of the JV company. In such a situation the partner that is most committed to maintaining its license would be at a disadvantage in renegotiations.

12.3.2.8.3 Partners' liability for joint venture's conduct A parent corporation is not liable for the contracts or tortious acts of its subsidiary. However, a parent company could be jointly and severally liable for its subsidiary's debts based on the principle of piercing the corporate veil, apparent or ostensible agency, or *alter ego*/unity of interest doctrine, as these legal theories may be applied to joint ventures. In addition, when joint ventures are engaged in high-risk businesses (e.g., resource extraction) or involved with a national government, the JV partners are less likely to be able to assert limited liability. For example, concerning compliance with environmental regulations adopted to resource extraction business, partners in the resource extraction business should be careful about complying with environmental regulations, as parent companies are held liable for environmental incidents or damage done by the joint venture.[21] They accordingly entail an additional element of risk, which partners should account for in both the operational and termination phases of a joint venture.

12.3.2.8.4 Risk of shareholder derivative actions Although a company's acts and liabilities are not attributed to its shareholders in most jurisdictions, when a JV company has failed, it may not be socially permissible for its parent companies to renounce liability. Thus, when JV companies are dissolved, the JV partners sometimes lend funds to the JV company for the purpose of fully repaying its debts and then discharge the loan. If the directors of a JV partner are subsequently sued by its shareholders for forgiving a loan to the joint venture, the directors' liability would likely be decided based on the business judgment rule.[22] The court would presumably rule that the partner's directors did not violate their fiduciary duty of care if (a) the factual basis of their decision was free from material errors, (b) their decision was reasonable in terms of both its process and content, and (c) they did not overstep their discretionary authority.

---

[21] For example, MOEX Offshore agreed to a $90 million partial settlement of liability in the *Deepwater Horizon* oil spill, which occurred in the Gulf oil exploration project. A subsidiary of Mitsui Oil Exploration Corporation, MOEX Offshore, invested a minority stake in the joint venture that operated the oil exploration project. *See* Department of Justice, Office of Public Affairs (February 17, 2012) www.justice.gov/opa/pr/moex-offshore-agrees-90-million-partial-settlement-liability-deepwater-horizon-oil-spill. On the subject of the other parent company's liability in the environmental field, *see* Comprehensive Environmental Response, Compensation and Liability Act (CERCLA) 42 U.S.C. §1906 et seq. and other state statutes.

[22] Although the standard varies by jurisdiction, in general, to survive the business judgment rule, directors should (a) be free of personal interest or self-dealing, (b) be in good faith, (c) make an informed decision, which reflects a reasonable effort, (d) act in a manner that they reasonably believe to be in the best interests of the corporation, and (e) act with the care that an ordinarily prudent person would reasonably be expected to exercise in a like position and under similar circumstances.

12.3.2.8.5 Tax treatment of losses If JV partners bear their JV company's losses, they must be aware of the tax ramifications (e.g., gift taxation) of doing so. A partner should consult with tax experts about the losses' tax-deductibility when (1) the partner assumes the joint venture's debts, bears its losses, or discharges loans to the venture in conjunction with the venture's dissolution or transfer of control, and (2) its decision to do so is justifiable on the grounds that the partner would incur larger losses in the future if it had not done so.

PART IV

The success and future of joint ventures

13. Successful joint ventures: avoiding common joint venture pitfalls

13.1 TYPES OF JOINT VENTURE FAILURE

In this book, we define a successful joint venture as one that sees success in terms of both organizational and operational management. Successful organizational management means that the JV partners have incentivized each other to contribute resources to their joint venture, avoided moral hazard, maintained a cooperative relationship in terms of controlling and operating their joint venture, and reciprocally contributed necessary capital to the joint venture as promised. Successful operational management means that the sum total of the three types of return from the joint venture (i.e., return on investment, return from transactions, and ancillary return) has met or exceeded the partner expectations. While these two types of success are related, they must be logically distinguished from each other.

Conversely, joint ventures can fail due to both organizational management failure and operational management failure. This chapter will distinguish these two types of failure, consider possible causes of organizational management failure, and introduce methods of preventing and resolving any failures.

13.1.1 Organizational Management Failure

The first type of joint venture failure is organizational management failure, which is a failure by the partners to incentivize each other to contribute resources to, cooperatively manage, and share control of their joint venture. An example of organizational management failure is when insufficient incentives to contribute capital in the establishment stage result in the failure of the joint venture business's ability to actually coalesce. Another example is when a joint venture fails due to inequitable sharing of total return, which distorts the incentives of one partner to contribute resources to the joint venture in subsequent rounds of bargaining.

Organizational management failure sometimes stems from opportunistic or self-serving behavior by one or both partners. If, for example, JV partners disagree on a financial strategy or management policies (e.g., sales strategies), inter-partner conflicts tend to emerge once the joint venture reaches a certain level of profit or loss.

Even if JV partners shared the same objectives upon the establishment of the JV company, future intentions may subsequently diverge over time as circumstances and their respective objectives for contributing capital to the joint venture change. This is exemplified when two partners co-operate in operating a joint venture within an explicitly limited business domain and one partner seeks to thwart the joint venture's growth if a competitive relationship develops between one partner's solely owned business and the joint venture. Such a joint venture is highly susceptible to failure.[1]

13.1.2 Operational Management Failure

A second type of failure is operational management failure. Even if the JV partners have a cooperative relationship, their joint venture will not necessarily grow. The success or failure of a joint venture's business hinges on both macro-environmental factors such as political, economic, sociological, and technological (PEST) factors and micro-environmental factors such as Porter's five forces.[2] If a joint venture fails operationally as a result of events that were unanticipated at the time of its establishment, the partners may choose to wind it up.[3] Examples of miscalculations at the

---

[1] In resource development joint ventures in developing countries with a high country risk, inter-partner conflicts regarding resource concessions tend to intensify if the joint venture is more successful than expected (e.g., resource extraction exceeds expectations). In such cases, strong-arm tactics sometimes come into play, such as the local partner's seizing control of the joint venture with the backing of the country's government, abduction or murder of local employees of a partner that will not consent to *ex post* revision of terms regarding the sharing of total return, increased taxation, import/export restrictions, and/or foreign currency remittance restrictions.

[2] On the five forces, *see* Michael E. Porter, *The Five Competitive Forces that Shape Strategy*, HARVARD BUS. REV. 86–104 (January 2008). The five forces are: (1) existing competitive rivalry between suppliers, (2) the threat of new market entrants, (3) the bargaining power of buyers, (4) the power of suppliers, and (5) the threat of substitute products (including changes in technology).

[3] Kao and Novartis Consumer Health dissolved their JV company because it was unlikely to achieve its initial earnings forecast (March 2002). *See* www.novartis.co.jp/pdf/p020326.pdf.

time of a JV company's establishment include overestimation of a partner's capabilities or a problem originating from the joint venture's business itself.

If the business operated by a JV company fails, the JV partners must decide whether to exit or attempt to turn around the unprofitable business. Upon choosing the latter, potential solutions on the renegotiating table would include modification of existing control-sharing arrangements, partner investment of additional capital in the joint venture, and even the replacement or complete buyout of one partner.[4] When partners successfully incentivized each other to contribute the monetary and human capital that was necessary and sufficient at the time the joint venture was established but the business nonetheless fails due to subsequent circumstances, the partners typically exit the insufficiently synergistic joint venture, either immediately or in stages. If the partners choose to exit, a decision must be made in regard to divesting unprofitable operations while keeping the JV company in existence or complete liquidation.

13.2 CAUSES OF ORGANIZATIONAL MANAGEMENT FAILURE

13.2.1 Dissatisfaction with Share of Total Return

Even when the establishment-stage incentives are sufficient, the joint venture's business succeeds, and the total return derived from the joint venture is shared in accordance with the joint venture agreement, one partner may sometimes become dissatisfied with its share of the return. If the joint venture is a single-round game, the other partner has no reason to renegotiate the sharing of total return, even if its partner becomes dissatisfied. However, the need for cooperative bargaining in a joint venture does not end after the first round. The partners' initial contribution of capital commences the joint venture's business activities. Once the fiscal year ends, the partners receive pro rata shares of the joint venture's total return. They then formulate investment and joint venture management plans for the next round; this sequence is repeated every year.

---

[4] Legal liquidation is also an option (*see* Ch. 12). Additionally, assistance from a government-affiliated entity such as the Innovation Network Corporation of Japan could potentially be utilized to reorganize a JV company.

When one partner is dissatisfied with its share of total return under the initial joint venture agreement, the other partner may have to agree to renegotiation if it wants the joint venture's business to succeed.[5] If the satisfied partner is unwilling to change the rules, the dissatisfied partner may refuse to contribute sufficient resources to the joint venture in the next round. If the partners do renegotiate but fail to reach an agreement, the joint venture may have to be wound up.

When a joint venture fails because one partner becomes dissatisfied with its share of total return as a result of the joint venture achieving unexpectedly high profitability, the joint venture's failure could be classified as an incentive failure stemming from a miscalculation (e.g., erroneous assumptions) at the time of establishment.[6]

In terms of sharing return on investment, partners may have conflicting interests with respect to dividend policies. For example, the partners in an overseas JV company may disagree over whether to retain profits locally on a long-term basis or distribute short-term dividends to overseas partners. Japanese companies generally tend to pursue long-term profits and growth of the joint venture by allowing it to retain most of the profits while distributing only a small amount in dividends. European and US companies, by contrast, tend to favor rapid recoupment of JV investments through high dividend payout ratios.[7] Thus, JV partners from different countries may come into conflict regarding dividend policy.

If return from transactions is shared unevenly, the partner with the smaller share is often dissatisfied. For example, one partner may receive all return from transactions while the other partner's total return is limited to dividends.[8] Another scenario that could cause one partner to become

---

[5] *See* ZENICHI SHISHIDO, DOKIZUKE NO SHIKUMI TOSHITENO KIGYO: INSEN-TIBU SHISUTEMU NO HOSEIDORON [THE FIRM AS AN INCENTIVE MECHANISM: THE ROLE OF LEGAL INSTITUTIONS] 180 (2006).

[6] Failure to expand the size of the overall pie is largely a business-environment or market issue. Dissatisfaction with how the pie is allocated is attributable to organizational management failure.

[7] This preference may be a function of whether the company is the local partner or foreign partner instead of whether it is a Japanese or Western company.

[8] Causes of this type of failure may include not only inadequate planning at the time of the joint venture's establishment but also problems with the monitoring or autonomy of the JV company's management team. JV companies' senior management personnel tend to make decisions in light of the interests of the partner that appointed them. If the other partner fails to monitor senior management's decision-making, it may receive a disproportionately small share of return from transactions relative to its ownership percentage.

disgruntled is when a joint venture has licensed technology from the other partner and continues to pay royalties to that licensor partner even after the licensed technology's economic value has diminished. In such cases, the disgruntled partner would generally be better off terminating the joint venture and launching its own business using a substitute technology.

Miscalculations can also occur with respect to ancillary return. For example, a JV partner in a developing country seeking to acquire technology or know-how from a partner based in a developed country is deprived of this ancillary return if only relatively unsophisticated technologies are disclosed to the JV company and there is no transfer of technology to the partner.

13.2.2 Domination by One Partner

There are sometimes factors that increase the probability of failure from the time of the joint venture's inception. Organizational management failure may occur when control of the JV company is not shared in accordance with the original joint venture agreement due to one partner's excessively strong bargaining power.

The following are three examples. First, in a joint venture dependent on production facilities located at one partner's plant, the partner that controls the plant has excessively strong bargaining power which may lead to de facto decision-making power over the JV company, irrespective of ownership percentages. Second, if one partner is unable to adequately monitor the joint venture, such as where the joint venture is housed at the other partner's plant, that partner is unable to identify and restrain potentially opportunistic behavior. Third, in the case of a joint venture between a supplier and a buyer, when there is sufficient bargaining power held by the buyer, power over the terms of transactions between the supplier partner and JV company may shift, resulting in a sharing of return from transactions disproportionate to the ownership interests. In any of these cases, even if the partners agree to have veto rights, one partner may have so much bargaining power that the veto rights are effectively nullified, leading to autocratic control by one partner.

13.3 PREVENTING AND RESOLVING ORGANIZATIONAL MANAGEMENT FAILURES

In practice, JV partners try to predict possible organizational management failures and then implement methods to prevent or resolve these disputes in the joint venture agreement. This section will introduce commonly used methods.

13.3.1 Prevention Methods

The first type is the preventive method, which seeks to preemptively eliminate potential sources of unnecessary conflict. Joint venture agreements often contain provisions to prevent and/or resolve disputes, particularly deadlocks.

13.3.1.1 Preemptive division of decision-making responsibility
Joint venture agreements sometimes designate specific matters where one partner may have sole discretion to make management decisions. Examples of such matters might include one partner's provision of working-capital loans to the joint venture, as needed. By granting unilateral decision-making authority over such matters, the joint venture agreement aims to avoid a potential source of renegotiation breakdowns that lead to management failure.[9]

This method of granting sole discretion to one partner should be carefully designed, and its usefulness should be limited to (a) day-to-day operational issues, which are not highly important for either partner; or (b) sole risk operations by one partner. Day-to-day management authority (broad discretionary authority) over the joint venture may be granted to one partner or its seconded directors, but this should only occur if that partner possesses management resources that are more compatible with certain aspects of the joint venture's operations. For example, in the case of a sales joint venture, the partner that provides sales channels would likely have primary decision-making authority over marketing strategy.

13.3.1.2 Internal regulation of veto rights
Deadlocks are sometimes caused by an abuse of veto rights. One effective means of preventing veto rights from being exercised abusively or arbitrarily is to set detailed regulations for their use on important matters at the earlier stages of bargaining, so neither partner has a chance to veto at a later date. Such matters may include rules regarding the JV company's general shareholder meetings and directors' meetings, directors' executive authority, directors' decision-making authority, and resolutions to assign executive responsibilities to directors. Because these

---

[9]   *See* IAN HEWITT, HEWITT ON JOINT VENTURES Ch. 10-5 (5th ed. 2011).

internal regulations must be relatively detailed to be effective, they should be carefully tailored to the JV company's actual situation.

13.3.1.3 Partner committee

A rational method of resolving board-of-director deadlocks in a joint venture is for the JV partners, the true parties to the dispute behind the deadlock, to engage in direct renegotiation to reconcile their conflicting interests. One specific approach is to establish a dispute-resolution escalation system where full authority to resolve deadlocks is delegated to an inter-partner steering committee or operating committee that serves as an arbitration board.[10] This method generally saves time, cost, and effort, as the partners do not need to act through intermediaries. Further, the true cause of a deadlock may be not only rational, but also emotional (e.g., a partner's dissatisfaction or loss of motivation to manage the joint venture). A pre-designed management committee is therefore the most effective forum for candid renegotiation and resolution of interpersonal issues between disputants.

13.3.2 Termination Methods

Second, joint venture agreements sometimes stipulate in advance particular means of resolving deadlocks that result in the termination of the joint venture. Examples of such means include a call-option clause, a compulsory buyout clause, dissolution of the JV company, and nullification of partner consent requirements for stock transfers when a deadlock occurs.[11]

13.3.3 Mediation Methods

Third, a joint venture agreement may provide methods for deadlocked partners to resolve conflicts, allowing the joint venture to continue to exist. Examples include a cooling-off mechanism, a dispute review panel, escalation of disputes to the executive level,[12] an independent director's swing vote, and alternative dispute resolution methods such as mediation

---

[10] Legally, this prevention method is considered as the delegation of management.

[11] *See* Hewitt, *supra* note 9, at Ch. 10-18–31.

[12] *See id.*, at Ch. 14-2.

or arbitration.[13] Partners may also grant particular alliance managers or "gatekeepers" the authority to solve a particular issue.[14]

Additionally, the parties may choose to avail themselves of the legal tools provided by the joint venture's home jurisdiction. For example, under Delaware's General Corporation Law, a shareholder may petition a court to appoint a custodian or receiver to execute business in place of the company's board of directors in order to maintain the company's status quo.[15] A court may also appoint a provisional director to the board of directors whose role is to cast the deciding vote if the shareholders are unable to elect directors, the company is at risk of irreparable injury due to a management dispute, or the company has abandoned its business without dissolving, liquidating, or distributing its residual assets.[16]

13.4 THE BOTTOM LINE: CREATING A SUSTAINABLE JOINT VENTURE

From a bargaining power perspective, a joint venture only resembles a repeated, rather than single-round, game as long as both partners continue to pose a threat of exit which supports bargaining power. Perpetuation of the threat of exit is therefore an important factor in sustaining a joint venture, allowing both partners to realize synergies through equitable sharing of total return. If the partners consider each other's management resources to be essential to the joint venture's business, compromise will be required to gain the partner's consent, regardless of whether they are a majority or minority owner of the joint venture.

Successful joint ventures resolve problems through cooperative dialogue and agreement between partners, building a rich interpersonal relationship of trust. In successful joint ventures, the partners do not stipulate a complete set of detailed terms and conditions in the agreements associated with the joint venture's establishment. Instead, the content of these agreements is limited to certain important matters, such as their legal relationship and the joint venture's economic framework.[17]

---

[13] *See id.*, at Ch. 10-8–17.
[14] *See id.*, at Ch. 14-02.
[15] 8 Del. Code §226.
[16] 8 Del. Code §353.
[17] Such relational contracts help to reduce the threat of cheating. *See* JAY B. BARNEY, GAINING AND SUSTAINING COMPETITIVE ADVANTAGE 384 (4th ed. 2011).

As long as the partners are in agreement on the joint venture's purpose and strategic vision, there should remain potential for them to reach an agreement on any disputes that may arise.

14. New trend: hybridization of joint venture agreements and venture capital investment agreements

14.1 CONTRACTUAL ORGANIZATIONS

Joint venture agreements and venture capital investment agreements are both means of contractual organization. Contractual organization refers to a relationship among a relatively small number of contractual parties (investors) that wish to incentivize each other to contribute capital through shared ownership and shareholder agreements.[1] However, joint venture agreements and venture capital investment agreements differ substantially in terms of how they are used in practice. They have consequently been perceived as fundamentally completely separate from each other. Even as research subjects, they have been treated as belonging to different fields.[2] However, the changing business climate of technological innovation has given rise to the need for large corporations to deepen their relationships with start-up companies. As a result, contracts that are a cross between a joint venture agreement and venture capital investment agreement are gaining prevalence through trial and error. The two types of agreements are converging with each other.

Broadly speaking, this trial-and-error approach may take two forms. The first is a joint venture between a start-up company and large corporation that strategically partner with each other to work on a specific project. The second is a venture capital arrangement where the large corporation acquires an equity stake in the start-up company.

---

[1] *See* Zenichi Shishido, Dokizuke no Shikumi toshiteno Kigyo: Insentibu Shisutemu no Hoseidoron [The Firm as an Incentive Mechanism: The Role of Legal Institutions] (2006) 125.

[2] For examples of research on joint venture agreements, *see* Ian Hewitt, Joint Ventures (5th ed. 2011); for examples of research on venture capital investment agreements, *see* Michael J. Halloran, et al., Venture Capital and Public Offering Negotiation (3rd ed. 2000); Paul A. Gompers & Josh Lerner, The Venture Capital Cycle (2d ed. 2004).

Recently, these hybrid contractual organizations that combine attributes of both approaches have been emerging as a prominent trend.

14.2 COMPARISON BETWEEN JOINT VENTURE AGREEMENTS AND VENTURE CAPITAL INVESTMENT AGREEMENTS

Joint ventures are business entities formed by two or more mutually independent companies, called parent companies or JV partners.[3] The partners contribute monetary capital to and participate in the management of their joint ventures. The relationship is governed by a joint venture agreement, which is a matrix of rights and duties between the partners, formed through shared ownership and shareholder agreements. In contrast, a venture capital investment is a form of private equity financing for development-stage companies. Venture capital investment fulfills the role of connecting investors with entrepreneurs.[4] We define a venture capital investment agreement as a matrix of rights and duties between venture capitalists and entrepreneurs, formed through shared ownership and shareholder agreements.

Both types of agreement are means of contractual organization involving a relatively small number of contractual parties that wish to incentivize each other to contribute capital through shared ownership and shareholder agreements. With both types of agreements, the parties engage in incentive bargaining that deals with the sharing of total return separate from the sharing of control.[5]

One difference between typical joint venture agreements and venture capital investment agreements is that the former must reconcile imbalances between monetary capital contributions and human capital contributions while the latter does not. Because joint ventures are a joint business, each partner typically contributes both monetary capital and human capital (non-separation of ownership and management). Discrepancies consequently arise between a partner's share of total return as a monetary capital contributor and the partner's contribution as a human capital contributor. If not rectified, such imbalances can distort the incentive of the partner with more important human capital (*see* Chapter 2). In contrast, with a venture capital investment, venture capitalists often

---

[3] Shishido, *supra* note 1, at 70.
[4] *Id.*, at 94.
[5] *Id.*, at 125–126.

serve on their investee companies' boards of directors as hands-on investors, but the investment target companies themselves are managed exclusively by their founders. Because the human capital contributors (entrepreneurs) and monetary capital providers (venture capitalists) are separate from each other, there is no need to rectify imbalances as in a joint venture.[6]

The second difference is that joint ventures typically involve self-dealing transactions while venture capital investments do not. In a joint venture, all partners contribute capital in pursuit of their respective business objectives. Self-dealing transactions between the partners and their joint venture are part of the joint venture plan from the outset. Additionally, such self-dealing transactions are often used as a means of reconciling the imbalances discussed above. Venture capital investment agreements, by contrast, generally leave little if any scope for self-dealing transactions between the venture capitalist and portfolio companies.[7]

A third difference is that venture capitalists often fund their investments with staged financing schemes whereas JV partners do not. In venture capital investment agreements, venture capitalists, as monetary capital providers, often impose milestones (operational targets) on the portfolio company's founders, the human capital providers. After making an initial investment, a venture capitalist withholds the next stage's investment until the next milestone has been achieved. Venture capitalists use such staged financing as a means of effectively gaining control over portfolio companies. By contrast, it would be senseless to impose milestones in a joint venture. While partners may renegotiate regarding the contribution of additional financial capital to their joint venture, such renegotiation is not the same as staged financing.[8]

A fourth difference relates to whether the parties intend to exit the venture. Whereas venture capitalists aim to exit through an IPO or M&A deal, JV partners usually bargain based on the assumption that they will continue to jointly operate their joint venture as an unlisted company. While joint venture agreements often include exit clauses (e.g., a put option), such clauses are intended as a precaution against future disputes, not a means of exit for an investor.[9]

Lastly, a fifth difference is the importance of reputation. Reputation is often cited as one factor behind the success of the Silicon Valley model.

---

[6]   *Id.*, at 127.
[7]   *Id.*, at 127.
[8]   *Id.*, at 135.
[9]   *Id.*, at 127.

Because venture capitalists typically invest repeatedly in similar start-up companies within a specific region, they have a strong incentive to maintain a good reputation. In contrast, most joint ventures are one-off agreements. JV partners are therefore said to not have much incentive to maintain a good reputation in each other's eyes.[10]

In sum, joint venture agreements and venture capital investment agreements both share the fundamental attribute of serving as a framework for incentive bargaining, but their actual content has historically differed completely due to differences in how the two types of agreements were typically used. In recent years, however, this traditional distinction between joint venture agreements and venture capital investment agreements has been blurred by changes in large corporations' involvement with technologically innovative start-up companies.

14.3 STRATEGIC ALLIANCES IN PURSUIT OF TECHNOLOGICAL INNOVATION

The form of the optimal relationship, including the optimal organizational structure and financing methods, between a large corporation and start-up company depends on the nature of the technology at issue because a technology's attributes affect information asymmetry and transaction costs.[11] For example, in the biotechnology and pharmaceutical industries, the differences between large corporations and start-up companies, in terms of their proprietary technologies and incentive structures for their researchers and engineers involved in developing their technologies, are larger than in IT industries.[12] As a result, in the biotechnology and pharmaceutical industries, it is reportedly more

---

[10] *Id.*, at 128.

[11] *See* Ronald J. Gilson, *Locating Innovation: The Endogeneity of Technology, Organizational Structure, and Financial Contracting* 110 Colum L. Rev. 885, 888, 890 (2010).

[12] Due to large cultural gaps between major pharmaceutical companies and development-stage biotech companies, the strategy of acquiring development-stage companies has not worked well in the biotech industry, unlike Cisco Systems' successful acquisition strategy in the IT industry. When Eli Lilly, a major pharmaceutical company, acquired Hybritech, a biotech company, many of Hybritech's researchers and other scientists left the company in response to differences in employee incentive structures between the two companies. *See id.*, at 912, 913.

difficult for the personnel of a large corporation and a start-up company to collaborate on R&D.

14.3.1 Dealing with Uncertainty

Strategic alliances between major pharmaceutical makers and development-stage biotech companies for the purpose of developing new drugs ("drug-development joint ventures"[13]) are common in the US and Europe. When viewed as contractual organizations, drug-development joint ventures are distinguished as a means of mitigating the risk of unpredictable business uncertainties[14] rather than the risk of the other partner's predictable opportunistic behavior.[15]

---

[13]   Joint ventures generally take the form of a new company jointly established by the JV partners but, broadly defined, they also include joint ventures organized as partnerships and contractual joint ventures based solely on a contractual relationship (*see supra* Ch. 8). The drug-development joint ventures discussed herein are broadly defined joint ventures in the form of broad collaborative agreements that include narrowly defined joint ventures, license agreements, and joint development agreements. *See* Ronald J. Gilson, Charles F. Sabel & Robert E. Scott, *Contracting for Innovation: Vertical Disintegration and Interfirm Collaboration* 109 COLUM. L. REV. 431, 467 (2009). Large corporations may acquire an equity stake in start-up companies or they may provide R&D funding on a contractual basis. In the former case, the two companies conduct a joint venture by means of an equity investment in an existing company instead of establishing a new company. The latter case is a type of contractual joint venture. Empirical research has found that the amounts invested in joint ventures that do not involve equity investment tend to be considerably smaller than investments in joint ventures that do involve equity investment. *See* David T. Robinson & Toby E. Stuart, *Financial Contracting in Biotech Strategic Alliances* 50 J. L. & ECON. 559, 564, 572 (2007).

[14]   *See* Gilson, Sabel, & Scott, *supra* note 13, at 435.

[15]   Historically, the main challenge in designing contractual organizations was dealing with hold-up, where one partner is hesitant to contribute resources in light of the risk of the other partner engaging in opportunistic, albeit economically rational, behavior (moral hazard). *See* David T. Robinson & Toby E. Stuart, *Network Effects in the Governance of Strategic Alliance*, 23 J. L. ECON. & ORG. 242 (2006). Even in drug-development joint ventures, both parties are aware of moral hazard problems and frequently include best-efforts clauses in their agreements, but they do not necessarily attempt to resolve such issues with explicit agreements. In particular, implicit agreements often suffice when reputational incentives are expected to constrain opportunistic behavior. *See* Robinson & Stuart (2007), *supra* note 13, at 579–581.

Drug development is extremely costly, requires a long development period,[16] and has a low success rate.[17] Strategic alliances are one means of diversifying these risks and mitigating uncertainties. Strategic alliances are particularly effective when the cost of inter-partner cooperation is low.[18]

In drug-development joint ventures between a biotech start-up company and Mega Pharma company, the cost of collaboration is relatively low. First, drug-development joint ventures are not horizontal joint ventures between competitors but vertical joint ventures that aim to develop products to be supplied by the biotech company to the pharmaceutical company.[19] Conflicts of interest related to corporate opportunities or competition between partners are consequently a relatively minor issue, though drug-development joint ventures do involve self-dealing transactions. Second, with pharmaceutical companies repeatedly engaging in many similar strategic alliances,[20] the pharmaceutical industry is a rare sector in which reputation comes into play, even in joint ventures. Moral hazard problems are therefore relatively minor.[21] Third, the contractual organizations can be structured to reduce the costs of collaboration. In drug-development joint ventures, the attributes of the new drugs to be developed and the development program's rate of progress cannot be specified in advance. Accordingly, the joint venture agreement typically stipulates that the R&D program's direction is to be

---

[16] On average, human clinical trials to obtain US FDA marketing approval for a new drug cost $80 billion and take over 12 years based on pre-2004 data. Drug development is therefore too expensive and too time-consuming for venture capital investment. *See* Gilson, *supra* note 11, at 910, 914; Robinson & Stuart (2007), *supra* note 13, at 563.

[17] *See* Robinson & Stuart (2007), *supra* note 13, at 563; Gilson, *supra* note 11, at 910.

[18] *See* Raghuram G. Rajan, *Presidential Address: The Corporation in Finance,* 67 J. FIN. 1173, 1211 (2012).

[19] *See* Robinson & Stuart (2007), *supra* note 13, at 564.

[20] In Japan, such strategic alliances have been rare. Recently, however, they have been gaining prevalence even in Japan. Rohto Pharmaceutical and SEEMS Inc. have jointly commenced somatic stem cell research. Similarly, Dainippon Sumitomo Pharma acquired a ¥1.5 billion equity stake in Retina Institute Japan and formed an alliance to commercialize induced pluripotent stem cell technology (NIHON KEIZAI SHINBUN, May 17, 2013, at 11). Additionally, Amgen, the world's largest biopharmaceutical maker, and Astellas Pharma announced plans to establish a joint venture to conduct clinical trials on new drug candidates (NIHON KEIZAI SHINBUN, May 30, 2013, at 13).

[21] *See* Gilson, *supra* note 11, at 914.

determined by stipulated governance procedures, such as a joint committee comprised of representatives of both partners.[22] Additionally, drug-
development joint ventures are often structured as a stepwise investment
arrangement where the Mega Pharma partner has the right to decide
whether to continue or withdraw from the joint venture at specified
junctures. Such arrangements offer optionality to the Mega Pharma
partner.[23] Moreover, the Mega Pharma partner often has the sole right to
unilaterally terminate the joint venture agreement, mainly as another
means of mitigating uncertainty.[24]

14.3.2 Mega Pharma Partners' Multiple Roles

Drug-development joint ventures agreements are a cross between a
typical joint venture agreement and a typical venture capital investment
agreement.[25]

As in a typical joint venture, drug-development JV partners contribute
human capital and monetary capital, but their respective shares of the
contributed capital usually differ substantially. The start-up biotech
partner contributes the vast majority of the human capital while the Mega
Pharma partner contributes the vast majority of the monetary capital, at
least in the drug-development program's initial stages. Drug-development
joint ventures resemble relationships between entrepreneurs and venture
capitalists in this respect. In fact, Mega Pharma companies often acquire
an equity stake in the biotech start-up companies with which they partner.
Unlike venture capitalists, however, pharmaceutical companies acquire an
equity stake, not for the purpose of selling their stake after increasing the
start-up company's value but to ensure the success of their collaboration
with the start-up company. The relationship between the two companies
is thus in essence a joint venture.

---

[22] *See* Gilson, Sabel, & Scott, *supra* note 13, at 435; Gilson, *supra* note 11,
at 913. Leaving certain future decisions to be determined through predetermined
governance procedures is a characteristic of contractual organizations.

[23] *See* Robinson & Stuart (2007), *supra* note 13, at 572.

[24] *See id.*, at 584. A statistically significant inverse correlation has been
observed between the size of equity investments and unilateral termination rights.
This correlation reflects the substitutability of the sharing of control based on
ownership rights and contractually based sharing of control. *See id.*, at 584–585.

[25] Both venture capital investment agreements and joint venture agreements
vary widely in terms of the degree of separation between the human capital
provider and monetary capital provider. In other words, even outside of drug-
development joint ventures, there are venture-capitalistic joint ventures and
joint-venturistic venture capital arrangements.

Once a drug-development joint venture progresses from the development stage to the clinical-trial stage, the Mega Pharma partner plays a bigger role in terms of providing human capital. As the drug development progresses to the stage where commercialization is a realistic prospect, the Mega Pharma partner will assume the role of purchaser of the drug patent. This purchase constitutes a self-dealing transaction between the joint venture and one partner. At this point, the Mega Pharma partner's interests would conflict with the biotech partner's, with respect to the purchase price and other transaction terms. In anticipation of such a conflict, drug-development JV partners often agree in advance to set royalties at a predetermined percentage of the drug's prospective sales.[26] The Mega Pharma partner may even acquire the biotech company itself, not merely its technology. However, due to differences in corporate culture, such post-acquisition R&D programs are seldom successful.[27] Senior executives of biotech start-up companies that form strategic alliances with Mega Pharma companies are generally wary of the pharmaceutical company acquiring control of their company, and often set a limit on the maximum ownership stake that the Mega Pharma partner can acquire.[28]

In sum, one distinguishing characteristic of drug-development joint venture agreements is that as the development program progresses, the Mega Pharma partner's role as a collaborator evolves from investor to co-developer, to purchaser of the newly developed drug(s).

14.3.3 Stage-by-Stage Design of Contractual Organizations

As noted above, drug-development joint ventures are distinguished by a changing relationship between the partners, particularly in terms of the Mega Pharma partner's role, as the development program progresses from one stage to the next. Drug-development joint ventures' contractual organization is also designed to change in response to progress from one stage to the next.

First, drug-development joint ventures are similar to venture capital investment agreements in that the Mega Pharma partner contributes financial capital in installments based on achievement of milestones.[29] For example, an alliance agreement between Warner-Lambert (Mega

---

[26] *See* Gilson, Sabel, & Scott, *supra* note 13, at 471.
[27] *See* Gilson, *supra* note 11, at 913.
[28] *See* Robinson & Stuart (2007), *supra* note 13, at 574.
[29] *See id.*, at 561. As noted above, joint ventures rarely involve milestone investments.

Pharma partner) and Ligand Pharmaceuticals (biotech start-up partner) stipulated a number of specific milestones. The partners agreed that Ligand would receive an additional payment upon achievement of each milestone and would be entitled to sales-based royalties if a marketable new drug was ultimately developed to be sold in the market.[30]

Second, another similarity between drug-development joint ventures and venture capital investment agreements is that sharing of control changes as the venture advances through the stages of the standardization process. Venture capital investment agreements grant ample autonomy and control to the investment target company's founders during the company's initial development stage with the aim of encouraging technological innovation or differentiation.[31] As the company matures, however, the venture capitalist seeks standardization from the company's founders[32] and uses milestones to chart a course toward such standardization.[33] Similarly, in drug-development joint ventures, the biotech start-up partner plays the lead role in the differentiation stage (discovery of seeds of new drugs through biotech research) while the Mega Pharma partner plays the lead role in the standardization stage (clinical trials to obtain regulatory approval and commercialization).[34] Control of the joint venture is shared in accord with the partners' shifting roles.[35] The Mega Pharma partner also often acquires an equity stake in the biotech partner as a means of sharing control but, unlike venture capitalists, it rarely appoints any directors to the biotech company's board. Instead, the Mega Pharma partner seeks to gain monitoring and decision-making authority over a specific project through its equity stake.[36]

Third, inter-partner incentive bargaining in a drug-development joint venture is governed by a combination of explicit agreements (legally

---

[30] *See* Gilson, Sabel, & Scott, *supra* note 13, at 471.

[31] *See* Rajan, *supra* note 18, at 1175.

[32] *See id.*, at 1192, 1197.

[33] *See id.*, at 1200.

[34] *See* Gilson, *supra* note 11, at 912.

[35] In the drug-candidate development stage, the start-up biotech partner is granted broad discretion, but once the new drug candidate progresses to the clinical-trial and commercialization stages, decision-making authority largely shifts to the Mega Pharma partner. *See* Josh Lerner & Robert P. Merges, *The Control of Technology Alliances: An Empirical Analysis of the Biotechnology Industry* 46 J. INDUS. ECON. 125, 136 (1998); Gilson, Sabel, & Scott, *supra* note 13, at 469.

[36] *See* Robinson & Stuart (2007), *supra* note 13, at 578.

enforceable agreements based on verifiable facts) and implicit agreements (legally unenforceable agreements based on observable facts).[37] The composition of this combination differs depending on the stage of the development program. In the initial development stage, the partners use a combination of implicit agreements and governance arrangements, such as a joint management committee,[38] to learn about each other's capabilities and reliability.[39] The final stage, however, is governed by an explicit option agreement in case a new drug candidate is identified.[40] In a conventional joint venture, bargaining between the partners is rarely predicated on one partner's exit[41] from the outset. In this respect,

---

[37] *See* Gilson, Sabel, & Scott, *supra* note 13, at 435; Robinson & Stuart (2007), *supra* note 13, at 561.

[38] Such joint committees set R&D policies and resolve disputes without a legally enforceable explicit agreement. *See* Gilson, *supra* note 11, at 913; Robinson & Stuart (2007), *supra* note 13, at 578. Such arrangements are a distinctive characteristic of contractual organizations. However, Big Pharma partners often have the option of unilaterally terminating projects, as in the aforementioned alliance agreement between Warner-Lambert (Big Pharma partner) and Ligand Pharmaceuticals (biotech partner). *See* Gilson, Sabel, & Scott, *supra* note 13, at 469; and Robinson & Stuart (2007), *supra* note 13, at 578. As a safeguard against opportunistic termination by the Big Pharma partner, such alliance agreements typically have noncompete clauses that require the Big Pharma partner to pay royalties to the biotech partner if it independently continues the development program and files a new drug application within a certain period after terminating the joint project. *See* Gilson, Sabel, & Scott, *supra* note 13, at 470.

[39] *See* Gilson, *supra* note 11, at 913. The more that a partner invests in enhancing its reputation of competence and reliability as a development collaborator, the less likely it is to engage in opportunistic behavior. *See* Gilson, Sabel, & Scott, *supra* note 13, at 436. In conventional co-development joint ventures, partners tend to face a prisoner's dilemma regarding information disclosure. *See* Shishido, *supra* note 1, at 78.

[40] Option agreements contain explicit stipulations regarding entitlement to IP rights in new drug technologies. For example, if a new drug candidate has been identified, the Big Pharma partner may have the option of conducting clinical trials on the drug candidate at its own expense. If it exercises its option and successfully brings a new drug to market, the biotech partner would have the right to receive royalties. If it elects not to exercise this option, the biotech partner would be able to regain ownership of the developed technology (new drug candidate). *See* Gilson, *supra* note 11, at 913–914. *See also* Robinson & Stuart (2007), *supra* note 13, at 585.

[41] We use "exit" here in a broad sense. A venture capital exit means the sale of the equity stake in the investee company in the case of a successful venture capital investment. For the Big Pharma partner, however, exit means withdrawing

drug-development joint ventures are similar to venture capital investment agreements.

14.4   STRATEGIC ALLIANCES BETWEEN VENTURE CAPITALISTS AND LARGE CORPORATIONS ACTING AS STRATEGIC INVESTORS

14.4.1   Joint Venture Capital

Aside from joint ventures, large corporations' involvement with start-up companies includes venture capital investments also. While joint ventures between large corporations and start-up companies are project-based collaborations, venture capital investments are equity investments by the large corporation with the aim of helping the start-up company grow.[42]

In contrast to regular venture capital investments, large corporations engage in venture capital investment not to increase their return on investment but to benefit their own businesses by gathering information on new technologies. In this sense, large corporations act as strategic investors, not financial investors.

Some large manufacturers have long administered corporate venture capital funds whose mission is to discover promising start-up companies and help them grow by investing monetary and human capital. Recently, however, large corporations are increasingly forming strategic alliances with specialized venture capitalists instead of running venture capital funds on their own. Given that such alliances are joint ventures in the venture capital business, this trend has given rise to the new concept of joint venture capital.[43]

Joint venture capital's distinguishing characteristic is that a large corporation forms a strategic alliance with a venture capitalist in connection with setting up a venture capital fund. Joint venture capital can be joint venture based or venture capital based. In the former case, a large

---

from the joint project by deciding whether to exercise its option to acquire the new drug technology developed through the project.

[42]   *See* Robinson & Stuart (2007), *supra* note 13, at 562. Even in drug-development joint ventures, the Mega Pharma partner may acquire an equity stake in the biotech partner, but it does so from the standpoint of sharing control to ensure the success of a specific drug-development project.

[43]   *See* Joseph A. McCahery & Erik P.M. Vermeulen, *Conservatism and Innovation in Venture Capital Contracting,* 2 TOPICS IN CORP. L. & ECON. 16, 20 (2013).

corporation and incumbent venture capitalist jointly establish a venture capital fund.[44] In the latter case, a large corporation invests as a strategic limited partner in a venture capital fund established by an incumbent venture capitalist.[45] In either case, joint venture capital differs from the drug-development joint ventures discussed above in that the large corporation takes an indirect approach in its involvement with the start-up companies, exercising very limited control only through its venture capitalist partner.

14.4.2 Synergies

As strategic investors, large corporations contribute much more than capital to the venture capital funds in which they invest. First, a venture capital fund can attract other investors by virtue of the reputational benefit of having a famous large corporation as an investor. Second, the large corporation can tap into its experience and industry knowledge to help conduct due diligence on potential portfolio companies and to advise portfolio companies on technology and marketing. Third, the large corporation can help the venture capital fund recoup invested capital by acquiring the fund's portfolio companies that would be of value to its own business. Fourth, the fund can take advantage of opportunities to invest in companies spun off by the large corporation.[46]

Meanwhile, by participating in a joint venture capital arrangement, the large corporation can obtain information about the types of technologies

---

[44] One example of such a fund is the Shell Technology Venture Fund 1, formed by Royal Dutch Shell with two other investors (Coller Capital and Abu Dhabi Investment Authority) and Kenda Capital as the fund manager. *See* Yuliya Chernova, *Shell Looks for Startups, Tech Partnerships Now More than Ever*, WALL STREET JOURNAL, March 22, 2013 (blogs.wsj.com/venturecapital/2013/03/22/shell-looks-for-startup-tech-partnerships-now-more-than-ever/tab/print/).
Another example is a partnership formed by venture capitalist Index Ventures and rival pharmaceutical companies GlaxoSmithKline and Johnson & Johnson. *See* McCahery & Vermeulen, *supra* note 43, at 23.

[45] For example, Royal Dutch Shell has invested in Chrysalix Energy Venture Capital as a limited partner. *See* Chernova, *supra* note 44.

[46] *See* McCahery & Vermeulen, *supra* note 43, at 20–21. However, because a venture capitalist's job differs substantially from a large corporation's manager or engineer's job, some take the view that it is more efficient for a large corporation to limit its role to that of an investor in a venture capital fund and focus exclusively on gaining access to information as a major limited partner (interview with Nobuo Matsuki, founder of MKS Partners and professor at Tokyo Institute of Technology, May 14, 2013).

being developed by start-up companies and gain opportunities to acquire the venture capital fund's portfolio companies ahead of its rivals.

In sum, joint venture capital is a promising strategic alliance for both venture capitalists[47] and large corporations.[48] Within such synergistic potential, however, lie joint venture capital's problems.

14.4.3   Conflicts in Joint Venture Capital Arrangements

The main reason that corporate venture capital funds run by large corporations have not achieved much success is the high potential for conflicting interests. As mentioned above, large corporations' primary objective in engaging in venture capital investment is to acquire technologies useful to their own businesses. This objective is not aligned with a portfolio company's other shareholders' objective of increasing the portfolio company's value: the large corporation investor will want to acquire these technologies at the lowest possible cost, while other shareholders will want to maximize the sale price. This is also likely to conflict with the interests of the portfolio company's founders, who typically aim to remain independent and eventually float an IPO.

When a large corporation invests in a start-up company through a joint venture capital arrangement, the large corporation does not directly acquire an equity stake in the start-up company. Joint venture capital therefore likely alleviates the aforementioned conflicts between the large corporation and the portfolio company's founders. In place of this conflict, however, another conflict arises between the large corporation and the fund's other investors.[49]

Three incentive bargaining relationships exist in joint venture capital arrangements. The first is the relationship between the venture capital fund and the large corporation as a strategic investor. The second is between the venture capital fund and its other financial and strategic

---

[47]   If defined as payoffs that partners gain by participating in a joint venture, joint venture synergies can be classified into 11 categories. *See* Ch. 6, 6.2. Synergies for venture capitalists that are partners in joint venture capital arrangements include cost-sharing, reputational backing, mentorship, and access to sales channels.

[48]   For the large companies in joint venture capital arrangements, synergies include technology introduction and access resources.

[49]   Conventional venture capital investment agreements rarely give rise to conflict-of-interest problems. However, venture capital investments are not entirely free of conflicts of interest (e.g., technical information obtained from one portfolio company may be used to benefit other portfolio companies). *See* Gilson, *supra* note 11, at 897.

investors. The third is between the major corporation and other investors in the venture capital fund.[50]

As noted previously, venture capitalists can reap various non-financial synergies from major corporations acting as strategic investors.[51] However, financial investors aware of the conflicts of interest discussed above will likely pressure the venture capitalist to impose prohibitory covenants and/or transactional restrictions on the strategic investor's participation in the fund. However, such covenants and restrictions will limit the venture capitalist's ability to benefit from knowledge, management resources, and/or investment opportunities provided by the strategic investor.[52]

Venture capitalists have the option of restricting participation in their funds to strategic investors without seeking investments from financial investors. If they do so, however, the strategic investors will have too much influence, likely leading to reemergence of the aforementioned conflicts between corporate venture capital funds and the portfolio companies' founders. Additionally, if several strategic investors invest in the same fund, conflicts of interest analogous to a regular joint venture's inter-partner conflicts of interest regarding return from transactions would likely arise.[53]

---

[50]   *See* McCahery & Vermeulen, *supra* note 43, at 21.

[51]   In return for such synergies, the venture capitalists may use side letters to give strategic investors more advantageous terms than other investors. *See id.*, at 22. In this respect, joint venture capital arrangements are similar to joint ventures in that they both involve the reconciliation of imbalances between partners/investors' contributions and return.

[52]   *See id.*, at 21.

[53]   The venture capitalist Index Ventures' joint venture capital fund with strategic investors GlaxoSmithKline and Johnson & Johnson as strategic investors avoids conflict-of-interest problems by requiring the strategic investors to openly bid against each other if either one is interested in acquiring one of the fund's portfolio companies or technology developed by a portfolio company. *Id.*, at 23.

Appendix 1

Table A1.1 shows practical measures for balancing autonomy of joint venture management and monitoring by JV partners, which relates to Chapter 3 (Sharing control), Chapter 10 (Post-contract bargaining), and Chapter 11 (Autonomy of human capital providers).

JV partners will decide "Important policy matters" by themselves because they are matters of agreement between partners. According to default corporate laws, at least, "Fundamental changes, election of directors" must be decided by shareholder meeting, and among "Important business matters," some are decided by shareholder meeting and others are decided by the board of directors according to local corporate law rules or the joint venture agreement. "Operational matters" can be decided by the joint venture management.

In most joint ventures, however, JV partners typically decide matters either by shareholder meeting or by the board of directors themselves, usually via an operating committee, because (1) JV partners would like to keep direct control of the joint venture business, rather than via their agents, and (2) JV partners can monitor each other via the operating committee. As a result, joint venture management autonomy will be limited. In non-autonomy model joint ventures, such as cost-center joint ventures, the operating committee will decide a wider range of decision matters, even operational matters. If it is preferable to give joint venture management more autonomy, as in the case of profit-center joint ventures, JV partners may choose autonomy model joint ventures that adopt default corporate laws concerning decision-making of JV companies.

Table A1.1   Measures for balancing autonomy and monitoring

	Important policy matters	Fundamental changes, election of directors	Important business matters	Operational matters	
				Non-routine matters	Routine matters
Examples of items/ matters for decision-making or approval	* Fundamental changes of joint venture business * Exit of either partner * Dispute between co-partners	* Amendment of articles of association * Election of director, statutory auditor candidate * Approval/change of remuneration ceiling * Transfer/take over of business, merger, corporate divestiture	* Business report, financial statements, * Disposal / dividend of retained earnings * Appointment/removal of representative directors, executive directors * Compensation for directors/auditors * Authority and seniority of directors * Establishment, change, abolishment of division, branch, business office, plant, factory, etc. * Quarterly and annual financial closing * Transfer/take over of business, merger, corporate divestiture, share exchange, equity transfer, other executive office reorganization, dissolution * Issuing of new shares and warrants, stock split, decrease of capital, capital reserve * Conclusion or amendment of important contract * Business development and commercialization of new business * Acquisition of assets (including lease) * Annual/mid-term business plan * Borrowing of large amount	* New issue and important non-routine operational matters (re: manufacturing, sales activities, R&D, logistics, cash management etc.) * Operational matters of large amount	* Minor routine operational matters * Operational matters of medium/low amount

Table A1.1 (continued)

	Important policy matters	Fundamental changes, election of directors	Important business matters	Operational matters	
				Non-routine matters	Routine matters
			* Important matters of JV company's subsidiary companies (incl. establishment of new subsidiary corporation) * R&D policy (incl. license agreement) * IT matters * All other high level business issues and matters		
1 Autonomy model (default corporate laws)	Agreement between co-partners	Resolution/approval of GM of shareholders or BM of directors in accordance with classification of default rules under the corporate law[1]		Approval by a director or an executive officer in charge	
2 Typical JV model	Agreement between co-partners	Prior consent of co-partners or resolution/approval of the operating committee and formality of resolution/approval of GM of shareholders or BM of directors in accordance with classification of default rules under the corporate law		Resolution or approval of BM of directors	Approval by a director or an executive officer in charge
3 Non-autonomy model	Agreement between co-partners	Prior consent of co-partners or resolution/approval of the operating committee and formality of resolution/approval of GM of shareholders or BM of directors in accordance with classification of default rules under the corporate law		Approval by a director or an executive officer in charge	

Note: [1] The precise classification of authority given to GM of shareholders and BM of directors may vary according to the jurisdiction of corporate laws, where the JV company is incorporated.

Appendix 2

Table A2.1   Joint ventures reported in press over the past 15 years

Type of synergy	Date of article	News-paper	JV partners	Notes
• Utilization of Sales Channels • Alleviation of Friction	September 1, 2014	Nikkei page 1	Ryohin Keikaku Co., Ltd. 51%, Indian local retail companies remaining (no detailed reference about shareholding ratio)	Ryohin Keikaku intends to advance into Indian general merchandise market
• Technology Introduction • Cost Sharing	August 30, 2014	Nikkei page 13	Mitsubishi Heavy Industries, Ltd. 89%, the Development Bank of Japan Inc. 10%, IHI 1%	Development of commercial aircraft engine
• Facility Sharing • Utilization of Sales Channels	August 29, 2014	Nikkei page 15	China subsidiary of Minebea Co., Ltd. 75%, China bearing manufacturer Cixi New MeiPeiL in Precision Bearing Co., Ltd 25%	Minebea Co., Ltd. to advance into Chinese bearing market
• Facility Sharing • Cost Sharing	August 25, 2014	Nikkei page 17	Sony, Panasonic Corporation, etc. major electronics seven companies (no detailed reference about shareholding ratio)	Co-management company of 4K&8K TV patents
• Securing Resources • Facility Sharing • Cost Sharing • Utilization of Sales Channels	August 12, 2014	Nikkei page 15	Mitsui & Co., Ltd. 49.9%, Brazil grain production company SLC Agricola 50.1%	Soybean, production and export of corn
• Collaborative R&D • Facility Sharing • Cost Sharing • Utilization of Sales Channels	August 6, 2014	Nikkei page 12	Innovation Network Corporation of Japan (INCJ) 75%, Japan Display Inc. 15%, Sony 5%, Panasonic Corporation 5%	Integrated new company re Organic EL panel
• Collaborative R&D • Facility Sharing • Cost Sharing	August 4, 2014	Nikkei page 1	Nissan Motor Co., Ltd 50%, Mitsubishi Motors Corporation 50%	New electric vehicle (EV) development

Type of synergy	Date of article	News-paper	JV partners	Notes
• Collaborative R&D • Facility Sharing • Cost Sharing • Utilization of Sales Channels	August 1, 2014	Nikkei page 12	Innovation Network Corporation of Japan (INCJ) 75%, Japan Display Inc. 15%, Sony 5%, Panasonic Corporation 5%	Integrated new company re Organic EL panel
• Technology Introduction • Utilization of Sales Channels	July 26, 2014	Nikkei page 12	Hitachi 35%, Germany Reinhausen GmbH 65%	German power transmission and distribution equipment leading manufacturer to advance into Japan
• Cost Sharing • Utilization of Sales Channels	July 21, 2014	Nikkei page 3	Development Bank of Japan Inc. 50%, Thailand conglomerate Charoen Pokapan 50%	Japanese companies Asia foray support fund (40 billion yen)
• Utilization of Sales Channels	July 17, 2014	Nikkei page 13	Sumitomo Electric Industries, Ltd. 25% →0%, US 3M 75% →100%	JV partnership to be broken off, a wholly owned subsidiary of US 3M
• Utilization of Sales Channels • Alleviation of Friction	July 2, 2014	Nikkei page 15	Independent investment fund octave Japan 28.2%, Rakuten, Inc. 18%, Noevir Holdings 13.4%, Alpen Co., Ltd. 7.4%, Malaysia LCC major company AirAsia 33%	AirAsia to advance into Japanese LCC business
• Technology Introduction • Facility Sharing • Utilization of Sales Channels • Brand Introduction	June 28, 2014	Nikkei page 12	Nissan Motor Co., Ltd 50%, Germany Daimler, Inc. 50%	Stepping forward by luxury brand car Mexico
• Utilization of Sales Channels	June 27, 2014	Nikkei page 9	China Hareon Solar Technology Co., Ltd., South Africa local companies (no detailed reference about shareholding ratio)	Hareon Solar Technology Co., Ltd. to advance into South Africa Solar market
• Utilization of Sales Channels • Alleviation of Friction	June 27, 2014	Nikkei page 13	Rakuten, Inc., Malaysia LCC major company AirAsia 33%, etc. (no detailed reference about shareholding ratio)	AirAsia to advance into Japanese LCC business
• Securing Resources • Cost Sharing	June 27, 2014	Nikkei page 15	Mitsubishi Rayon Co., Ltd. 50%, Saudi Basic Industries Corporation (SABIC) 50%	Mitsubishi in order to secure the acrylic resin raw material investment 50 billion yen

Type of synergy	Date of article	News- paper	JV partners	Notes
• Utilization of Sales Channels • Technology Introduction	June 24, 2014	Nikkei page 12	Convenience store Ministop 39%→0%, Logistics major Senko Co., Ltd.10%→0%, Kazakhstan Lancaster Group 51%→100%	Japan urges withdrawal from Kazakhstan. JV partnership to be broken off, a wholly owned subsidiary
• Utilization of Sales Channels	June 24, 2014	Nikkei page 9	Singapore LCC major company Scoot, Inc. 49%, Thailand LCC major company Nok Air 49%, CEO of Nok Air 2%	To advance into LCC international lines in Thailand
• Securing Resources • Cost Sharing	June 19, 2014	Nikkei page 7	Mitsubishi Corporation, Mitsui & Co., Ltd., Royal Dutch Shell, Russia National Oil Company Gazprom majority (no detailed reference about shareholding ratio)	Sakhalin 2 Follow-up story about existing JV's business
• Facility Sharing	June 19, 2014	Nikkei page 12	Cosmo Oil Co., Ltd., Tonen General Sekiyu K. K. (no detailed reference about shareholding ratio)	Refinery integration
• Utilization of Sales Channels	June 19, 2014	Nikkei page 12	Family restaurant major company Royal Holdings Co., Ltd. 49%, Taiwan distribution leading group Uni-President Enterprises Corporation 51%	Withdrawal from Shanghai, reduced only to Taiwan
• Technology Introduction • Utilization of Sales Channels	June 8, 2014	Nikkei page 1	Daihatsu Motor Co., Ltd., China First Automobile Works Group (no detailed reference about shareholding ratio)	Daihatsu to advance into China small car market
• Facility Sharing	June 7, 2014	Nikkei page 1	Cosmo Oil Co., Ltd., Tonen General Sekiyu K. K. (no detailed reference about shareholding ratio)	Refinery integration
• Facility Sharing	May 29, 2014	Nikkei page 14	Cyber Laser Inc., Taiwan machine tools leading company Tongtai Machine & Tool Co., Ltd. (no detailed reference about shareholding ratio)	Razor equipment production

Type of synergy	Date of article	News-paper	JV partners	Notes
• Utilization of Sales Channels • Technology Introduction	May 27, 2014	Nikkei page 12	Maeda Corporation 50%, Turkey construction leading company Garanti Koza İnşaat Sanayi ve Ticaret A.Ş. 50%	Orders taking from Japanese companies in Turkey
• Collaborative R&D • Facility Sharing	May 26, 2014	Nikkei page 11	Innovation Network Corporation of Japan (INCJ) est. 35%, Japan Display Inc. 20%–30%, Sony est. 10%, Panasonic Corporation est.10%	Organic EL development for tablet
• Technology Introduction • Utilization of Sales Channels	May 26, 2014	Nikkei page 11	Sony 70%, Shanghai companies 30%, and Sony 49%, Shanghai companies 51%	Sales game machine "play station" (PS) in China
• Technology Introduction • Utilization of Sales Channels	May 19, 2014	Nikkei page 1	Nomura Holdings, Inc. 60%, Shanghai Lujiazui Development (Group) Company Ltd. 40%	Securities business for wealthy in China
• Facility Sharing	May 15, 2014	Nikkei page 12	Nippon Steel & Sumitomo Metal Corporation, China International Marine Containers (CIMC), Baosteel Group Corporation (no detailed reference about shareholding ratio)	Offshore oil base for steel processing JV in China
• Technology Introduction • Utilization of Sales Channels	May 10, 2014	Nikkei page 13	Kawasaki Heavy Industries, Ltd. 50%, Anhui local companies 50%	Construction of garbage incineration facility in China
• Technology Introduction • Utilization of Sales Channels	May 8, 2014	Nikkei page 13	Mitsubishi Chemical Holdings Corporation 60%, China Corp. 40%	Pesticide-free vegetables automatic cultivation system factory in China
• Securing Resources • Cost Sharing	May 1, 2014	Nikkei page 14	Royal Dutch Shell 50%, China National Petroleum Corporation (CNPC) 20%, Mitsubishi Corporation 15%, Korea Gas Corporation 15%	Canada LNG business
• Facility Sharing	April 26, 2014	Nikkei page 3	Mazda Motor Corporation 50% →0%, Ford Motor Company 50%→100%	JV partnership to be broken off, a wholly owned subsidiary to sell manufacturing JV to Ford Motor Company

Type of synergy	Date of article	News-paper	JV partners	Notes
• Technology Introduction • Utilization of Sales Channels	April 25, 2014	Nikkei page 12	Oji Holdings Corporation., Indonesian Conglomerate Salim Group (no detailed reference about shareholding ratio)	Diapers production and sales in Indonesia
• Obtaining Local Expertise • Utilization of Sales Channels	April 24, 2014	Nikkei page 13	Mitsubishi Corporation 49%, India Tata Group 51%	India Tata Group to advance into Japan IT industry in Mitsubishi help
• Technology Introduction • Alleviation of Friction	April 23, 2014	Nikkei page 1	Sumitomo Corporation, Mitsubishi Corporation, Marubeni Corporation, JICA total 49%, Myanmar government 51%, (no detailed reference about shareholding ratio)	Investment in industrial construction
• Obtaining Local Expertise • Utilization of Sales Channels	April 21, 2014	Nikkei page 1	Mitsubishi Corporation 49%, IT company of Tata Group 51%	India Tata Group to advance into Japan IT industry in Mitsubishi help
• Technology Introduction • Utilization of Sales Channels	April 18, 2014	Nikkei page 14	Fujio Food System 40%, Indonesia Major restaurant Prima Ltd. 60%	To provide Japanese set meal, noodles in Indonesia
• Collaborative R&D • Facility Sharing	April 15, 2014	Nikkei page 14	Fujitsu Ltd. 40%, Panasonic Corporation 20%, the Development Bank of Japan Inc. 40%	Semiconductor design and development
• Collaborative R&D • Facility Sharing	April 15, 2014	Nikkei page 3	Fujitsu Ltd. 40%, Panasonic Corporation 20%, the Development Bank of Japan Inc. 40%	LSI (large-scale integrated circuit) design and development
• Cost Sharing • Facility Sharing	April 12, 2014	Nikkei page 1	Toyota Motor Corporation 25%, Nissan Motor Co., Ltd 25%, Mitsubishi Motors Corporation 25%, Honda Motor Co., Ltd. 25%	To develop a charging facility infrastructure for PHV plug-in hybrid vehicles
• Technology Introduction • Utilization of Sales Channels	April 10, 2014	Nikkei page 12	Tokyu Livable, Inc. 80%, Taiwan Hands Tailung 20%	Residential brokerage for rich in Taiwan

Type of synergy	Date of article	News-paper	JV partners	Notes
• Collaborative R&D • Facility Sharing	April 15, 2014	Nikkei page 14	Renesas Electronics Corporation 55%, Sharp Corporation 25%, Taiwan semiconductor manufacturers Powerchip Technology Corporation 20%	Apple Acquires smartphone core technology semiconductor JV
• Technology Introduction • Cost Sharing • Utilization of Sales Channels	February 18, 2014	Nikkei page 3	Mitsui & Co., Ltd., US investment bank The Goldman Sachs Group, Inc. (GS) (no detailed reference about shareholding ratio)	Manufacture and sale of food in India
• Securing Resources • Cost Sharing	February 15, 2014	Nikkei page 3	The Government of Japan, UAE government (no detailed reference about shareholding ratio)	Basic agreement on the infrastructure to build aluminum and steel pipe line production
• Facility Sharing • Utilization of Sales Channels • Brand Introduction	February 14, 2014	Nikkei page 1	Sumitomo Rubber Industries, Ltd., The Goodyear Tire & Rubber Company (no detailed reference about shareholding ratio)	Sumitomo Rubber Industries, Ltd., and The Goodyear Tire & Rubber Company agree to eliminate 6 JV companies
• Technology Introduction • Cost Sharing • Utilization of Sales Channels	February 6, 2014	Nikkei page 1	KDDI, Sumitomo Corporation, Myanmar Posts and Telecommunications (MPT) (no detailed reference about shareholding ratio)	Mobile phone JV study started
• Technology Introduction • Utilization of Sales Channels	January 28, 2014	Nikkei page 12	Hitachi 70%→100%, China local companies 30%→0%	JV partnership to be broken off, a wholly owned subsidiary of Hitachi
• Collaborative R&D • Facility Sharing	January 27, 2014	Nikkei page 3	Sony 10%, Hazuki International 35%, Indian Patent application business services company Evalueserve Japanese subsidiary 55%	Patent application business services company
• Utilization of Sales Channels • Facility Sharing	January 24, 2014	Nikkei page 13	An aluminum rolling company 49%, European leading aluminum rolling company Constellium N.V. 51%	Automotive aluminum plate production in US

Type of synergy	Date of article	News-paper	JV partners	Notes
• Securing Resources • Cost Sharing	December 28, 2013	Nikkei page 11	Marubeni Corporation 49.9%→24.95%, the Development Bank of Japan Inc. 0%→24.95%, Denmark wind power world's checkmate Dong Energy A/S51%	Ceding of offshore wind power generation interests in Gunfleet Sands in UK
• Utilization of Sales Channels	December 25, 2013	Nikkei page 12	Showa Shell Sekiyu K.K., Cosmo Oil Co., Ltd., Tonen General Sekiyu K. K., Sumitomo Corporation (no detailed reference about shareholding ratio)	LPG business integration
• Cost Sharing	December 24, 2013	Nikkei page 9	Toshiba 0%→50%, leading power company of Spain IBE.MC 50%→0%, French energy GDF Suez 50%	Acquisition of UK nuclear power interests
• Utilization of Sales Channels	December 21, 2013	Nikkei page 1	Showa Shell Sekiyu K.K., Cosmo Oil Co., Ltd., Tonen General Sekiyu K. K., Sumitomo Corporation (no detailed reference about shareholding ratio)	LPG business integration
• Utilization of Sales Channels	December 21, 2013	Nikkei page 9	Mitsubishi Corporation 25%, China Zhejiang Dayang 75%	Selling tuna, Japanese seafood in China
• Facility Sharing • Utilization of Sales Channels	December 19, 2013	Nikkei page 9	Ajinomoto Company, Incorporated 49%, Toyo Suisan Kaisha, Ltd. 51%, in Indian JV, Ajinomoto Company, Inc. 51%, Toyo Suisan Kaisha, Ltd. 49%, in Nigerian JV	Manufacturing and sales of instant noodles in India and Nigeria
• Facility Sharing • Utilization of Sales Channels	December 13, 2013	Nikkei page 13	Mitsubishi Heavy Industries, Ltd. 65%, Hitachi 35%,	Integration of thermal power generation business
• Utilization of Sales Channels	December 6, 2013	Nikkei page 13	Daikin Industries, Ltd. 75%, Saudi Arabia investment company 25%	The air conditioning sales company in Saudi Arabia
• Utilization of Sales Channels • Technology Introduction	December 5, 2013	Nikkei page 11	Mitsubishi Corporation15% ,Indonesia PT. Pan Brothers Tbk 85%	Clothing production in Indonesia

Type of synergy	Date of article	News-paper	JV partners	Notes
• Technology Introduction • Utilization of Sales Channels • Alleviation of Friction	December 5, 2013	Nikkei page 3	JFE Holdings, Inc., Myanmar local companies (no detailed reference about shareholding ratio)	Subsidiary for Myanmar infrastructure orders taking
• Cost Sharing • Utilization of Sales Channels	November 21, 2013	Nikkei page 3	Nomura Holdings, Inc. 50%, UK Intermediate Capital Group (ICG) 50%	M&A funds
• Facility Sharing • Utilization of Sales Channels	November 21, 2013	Nikkei page 13	Nisshinbo Holdings Inc. 70%, Continental AG's Chinese subsidiary 30%	Auto parts production in China
• Utilization of Sales Channels	November 1, 2013	Nikkei page 5	Mitsubishi UFJ Lease & Finance Group 75%, Indonesia Racketeering 25%	Automobile leasing in Indonesia
• Utilization of Sales Channels • Technology Introduction	October 31, 2013	Nikkei page 1	Mitsubishi UFJ Financial Group, Inc., JPMorgan Chase & Co. (no detailed reference about shareholding ratio)	Asset management services for wealthy class
• Utilization of Sales Channels • Brand Introduction	October 30, 2013	Nikkei page 13	Shiseido Co., Ltd. 65%, IndonesiaSinar Mas Group 35%	Cosmetics market development in Indonesia
• Utilization of Sales Channels • Technology Introduction	October 22, 2013	Nikkei page 1	Fuji Electric Co., Ltd., NGK Insulators, Ltd. (no detailed reference about shareholding ratio)	Water infrastructure management in big data
• Technology Introduction • Utilization of Sales Channels	October 21, 2013	Nikkei page 7	Tata Group 51%, Singapore Airlines 49%	LCC business international expansion
• Utilization of Sales Channels • Technology Introduction	October 10, 2013	Nikkei page 11	Nissin Foods Holdings Co., Ltd. 50%, Turkey food Yildiz Holdinga.S. 50%	Instant pasta sales in Turkey
• Collaborative R&D	October 4, 2013	Nikkei page 15	Nissha Printing Co., Ltd. 25%, Taiwan TPK 65%, Cambrios Technologies US 10%	Flexible touch panel development
• Utilization of Sales Channels	October 2, 2013	Nikkei page 13	Mitsui & Co., Ltd. 30%, US engineering Floor 70%	Construction equipment leasing business in Columbia

Type of synergy	Date of article	News-paper	JV partners	Notes
• Utilization of Sales Channels • Technology Introduction	October 2, 2013	Nikkei page 13	Nisshin Steel Holdings Co., Ltd. 55%, ITOCHU/Marubeni Steel 35%, US special steel Worthington Industries, Inc. 10%	Special steel production for automobiles in China
• Utilization of Sales Channels • Technology Introduction	October 2, 2013	Nikkei page 13	Marubeni Corporation 33.3%, Belgium chemical Solvay SA 33.3%, French CDC 33.3%	Cogeneration business for European companies
• Cost Sharing • Utilization of Sales Channels	October 2, 2013	Nikkei page 13	Net marketing major company IMJ, US venture capital (no detailed reference about shareholding ratio)	Fund to support the Japanese venture business
• Utilization of Sales Channels • Technology Introduction	September 17, 2013	Nikkei page 9	ISE Foods. Inc., China local companies (no detailed reference about shareholding ratio)	The largest poultry farm in the Japanese technology in China
• Cost Sharing • Facility Sharing	September 13, 2013	Nikkei page 1	Sony 10%, Toshiba 10%, Hitachi 10%, Innovation Network Corporation of Japan (INCJ) 70%	Japan Display Inc. to obtain 200 billion yen funding
• Cost Sharing • Facility Sharing	September 3, 2013	Nikkei page 7	US communications Verizon Communications Inc. 55%→100%, UK Vodafone Group Plc 45%→0%	JV partnership to be broken off, a wholly owned subsidiary of Verizon
• Alleviation of Friction • Technology Introduction	September 3, 2013	Nikkei page 9	Toyota, China Hunan Corun New Energy (no detailed reference about shareholding ratio)	Development of nickel-metal batteries for hydride cars
• Cost Sharing • Facility Sharing	August 30, 2013	Nikkei page 7	US communications Verizon Communications Inc. 55%→100%, UK Vodafone Group Plc 45%→0%	JV partnership to be broken off, a wholly owned subsidiary of Verizon
• Utilization of Sales Channels • Facility Sharing	August 16, 2013	Nikkei page 13	Meiji Holdings Co Ltd, Thailand Charoen Pokphand Group Company Ltd. (no detailed reference about shareholding ratio)	Production and sales of yogurt in Thailand
• Utilization of Sales Channels • Facility Sharing	August 13, 2013	Nikkei page 13	Konishi Co., Ltd. 40%→75%, Vietnam local companies 60%→25%	Production/sales company of adhesive in Vietnam, Konishi strengthen control

Type of synergy	Date of article	News-paper	JV partners	Notes
• Alleviation of Friction • Technology Introduction	August 10, 2013	Nikkei page 1	JFE Holdings, Inc. 60%, Myanmar government Ministry of Construction 40%	Myanmar infrastructure construction
• Technology Introduction • Utilization of Sales Channels	August 9, 2013	Nikkei page 1	IHI 49%, South Korea Hyundai Group 51%	IHI provides turbo engine charger technology
• Cost Sharing • Utilization of Sales Channels	August 9, 2013	Nikkei page 11	J-Power 50%→100%, Mitsubishi Diamond Power 50%→0%	Thermal power generation JV partnership to be broken off, a wholly owned subsidiary of J-Power
• Utilization of Sales Channels • Facility Sharing	August 6, 2013	Nikkei page 1	Toshiba, US SanDisk Corporation (no detailed reference about shareholding ratio)	Co-operation of new semiconductor plant
• Securing Resources • Cost Sharing • Technology Introduction	July 24, 2013	Nikkei page 7	Argentina's state-owned oil Company YPF, US oil Chevron (no detailed reference about shareholding ratio)	Argentina shale gas
• Utilization of Sales Channels • Technology Introduction	July 22, 2013	Nikkei page 7	Automotive supplies Autobacs Group 49%, Indonesia Salim Group 51%	Automotive supplies in Indonesia by know-how transfer
• Utilization of Sales Channels • Collaborative R&D	July 18, 2013	Nikkei page 10	JVC Kenwood Corporation 49%, VC ZMP 51%	Automobile traffic control system development
• Utilization of Sales Channels • Collaborative R&D	July 18, 2013	Nikkei page 3	SoftBank Corp. 50%, US Environmental system VC Bloom Energy 50%	Industrial fuel cell development
• Collaborative R&D	July 18, 2013	Nikkei page 2	Tokyo Electric Power Company, Incorporated (TEPCO), French Areva SA (no detailed reference about shareholding ratio)	Nuclear power plant decommissioning technology development
• Utilization of Sales Channels • Cost Sharing	July 11, 2013	Nikkei page 9	Nissan Motor Co., Ltd, IndiaAshok Leyland (no detailed reference about shareholding ratio)	Commercial vehicles production new plant in India
• Utilization of Sales Channels • Cost Sharing	July 10, 2013	Nikkei page 3	Italy Fiat 50%, PSA Peugeot Citroën S.A. 50%	Commercial vehicles production new plant expansion in Europe (90 billion yen investment)
• Utilization of Sales Channels	July 2, 2013	Nikkei page 15	Sumitomo Forestry Co., Ltd. 50%, US Bloomfield 50%	Housing sales in US

Type of synergy	Date of article	News-paper	JV partners	Notes
• Technology Introduction • Cost Sharing • Utilization of Sales Channels	June 28, 2013	Nikkei page 11	Sharp Corporation 8%, China Electronics Corporation (CEC) 92%	Energy-saving LCD panel "IGZO" production
• Technology Introduction • Cost Sharing • Utilization of Sales Channels	June 26, 2013	Nikkei page 11	Sharp Corporation 8%, China Electronics Corporation (CEC) 92%	Energy-saving LCD panel "IGZO" production
• Facility Sharing • Utilization of Sales Channels	June 26, 2013	Nikkei page 9	ANA, Malaysia LCC leading Company AirAsia (no detailed reference about shareholding ratio)	LCCJV partnership to be broken off, a wholly owned subsidiary of ANA
• Technology Introduction • Cost Sharing • Utilization of Sales Channels	June 26, 2013	Nikkei page 1	Sharp Corporation, China Electronics Corporation (CEC) (no detailed reference about shareholding ratio)	Energy-saving LCD panel "IGZO" production
• Utilization of Sales Channels • Technology Introduction	June 26, 2013	Nikkei page 11	Sumitomo Corporation 49%, South Korea CJCJ 51%	Milling & Instant noodles production in Vietnam
• Utilization of Sales Channels • Technology Introduction	June 23, 2013	Nikkei page 7	Portal site management Excite Japan Co., Ltd. 50%, Indonesia Sinarmas group 50%	Portal site management in Indonesia
• Securing Resources • Cost Sharing • Utilization of Sales Channels	June 22, 2013	Nikkei page 1 evening edition	Itochu Corporation, Marubeni Corporation, Japan Petroleum Exploration Co., Ltd. (JAPEX) less than 49%, Russia National Oil Company Gazprom over 51% (no detailed reference about shareholding ratio)	Russian LNG joint marketing for Far East
• Collaborative R&D	June 18, 2013	Nikkei page 5	Tokyo Electric Power Company, Incorporated (TEPCO), French Areva SA (no detailed reference about shareholding ratio)	Nuclear power plant decommissioning technology development
• Technology Introduction	June 17, 2013	Nikkei page 13	Server lending Future Spirits Co., Ltd. 60%, Thailand in Homestead Group 40%	The remote operates a Thai server
• Facility Sharing • Utilization of Sales Channels	June 12, 2013	Nikkei page 11	ANA, Malaysia LCC leading company AirAsia (no detailed reference about shareholding ratio)	LCC JV partnership to be broken off, a wholly owned subsidiary of ANA

Type of synergy	Date of article	News-paper	JV partners	Notes
● Facility Sharing ● Utilization of Sales Channels	June 10, 2013	Nikkei page 1	ANA 51%→100%, Malaysia LCC leading company AirAsia 49%→0%	JV partnership to be broken off, a wholly owned subsidiary of ANA
● Facility Sharing ● Utilization of Sales Channels	June 6, 2013	Nikkei page 13	J-Oil 26%, Toyota Tsusho Corporation 23%, India Ruchi Soya Industries Ltd. 51%	Low-fat oil production in India
● Technology Introduction ● Utilization of Sales Channels	June 5, 2013	Nikkei page 13	JTB 60%, Myanmar Pole Star Travel&Tour 40%	Travel, business trip agency
● Collaborative R&D	June 4, 2013	Nikkei page 12	FUJIFILM Corporation, India Generic drug Dr. Reddy's Laboratories Ltd (no detailed reference about shareholding ratio)	JV partnership to be broken off,
● Collaborative R&D	May 29, 2013	Nikkei page 29	Astellas Pharma Inc. 49%, US biopharmaceutical Amgen inc. 51%	Anti-cancer agents joint development
● Technology Introduction ● Utilization of Sales Channels	May 18, 2013	Nikkei page 11	Terrada Warehouse Co. 70%, VB Hoop Partners 30%	Share house for entrepreneurs
● Facility Sharing ● Utilization of Sales Channels	May 16, 2013	Nikkei page 10	KYB 75%, Marubeni Corporation 25%	Construction machinery parts production in Indonesia
● Cost Sharing ● Utilization of Sales Channels	May 16, 2013	Nikkei page 10	Mitsubishi Corporation majority, four construction equipment rental companies equally sharing rest of shares (no detailed reference about shareholding ratio)	To reduce rental construction machinery equipment purchase cost
● Securing Resources ● Utilization of Sales Channels ● Technology Introduction	May 16, 2013	Nikkei page 9	Mitsui & Co., Ltd. 50%, US chemical Company Celanese Corporation 50%	Methanol production in US (40 billion yen investment)
● Securing Resources ● Utilization of Sales Channels ● Technology Introduction	May 15, 2013	Nikkei page 9	Marubeni Corporation Nippon Meat Packers, Inc. 49%, Myanmar medium-sized trading companies 51%	Meat for chicken breeding processing Myanmar

Type of synergy	Date of article	News-paper	JV partners	Notes
● Utilization of Sales Channels	May 13, 2013	Nikkei page 11	Toyo Engineering Corporation 50%, Brazil engineering major company SOG 50%	To take offshore oil equipment orders from Petroleo Brasileiro S.A.
● Cost Sharing ● Utilization of Sales Channels	May 12, 2013	Nikkei page 1	Itochu Corporation over10%. Turkey national power company (EUAS) up to 49%, Japan Bank for International Cooperation (JBIC) etc. balance (no detailed reference about shareholding ratio)	Nuclear power sales in Turkey. Itochu Corporation invests 70 billion yen
● Utilization of Sales Channels	May 10, 2013	Nikkei page 11	Toyota Boshoku Corporation, Pakistan local company (no detailed reference about shareholding ratio)	Car parts production in Pakistan
● Utilization of Sales Channels	April 25, 2013	Nikkei page 13	Chiyoda Corporation, European construction CCC (no detailed reference about shareholding ratio)	The JV in UAE. To aim to strengthen the order-taking network in the Middle East through partnership with CCC, which is strong in the Middle East
● Utilization of Sales Channels	April 24, 2013	Nikkei page 13	IRIS Ohyama Inc. 51%, K.K. Butai Farm 49%	Rice wholesale in Sendai District in Japan
● Collaborative R&D	April 17, 2013	Nikkei page 13	Sony 51%, Olympus Corporation 49%	Endoscope technology development for surgery
● Utilization of Sales Channels ● Technology Introduction ● Brand Introduction	April 11, 2013	Nikkei page 9	Japan Circle K Sunkus Co., Ltd. 50%, US Circle K Sunkus Co., Ltd. 50%	Asian headquarters
● Securing Resources ● Technology Introduction	April 13, 2013	Nikkei page 3	Royal Dutch Shell, Russia National Oil Company Gazprom majority (no detailed reference about shareholding ratio)	Resources search company in Siberia and Arctic
● Utilization of Sales Channels ● Technology Introduction	April 4, 2013	Nikkei page 13	Nichirei Corporation 49%, Thailand logistics major company The Siam Cement Public Company Ltd. 51%	Logistics of refrigerated food in Thailand and Southeast Asia

Type of synergy	Date of article	News-paper	JV partners	Notes
• Utilization of Sales Channels • Collaborative R&D	March 31, 2013	Nikkei page 7	Hitachi over 80%, Tokyo Electric Power Company, Incorporated (TEPCO) below 20%, (no detailed reference about shareholding ratio)	Delivery power system consulting
• Utilization of Sales Channels • Technology Introduction	March 22, 2013	Nikkei page 10	The Fuji Media Holdings Group 50%, Itochu Corporation 50%	Strengthening content business in Asia
• Utilization of Sales Channels • Technology Introduction	March 13, 2013	Nikkei page 13	Ube Industries, Ltd. 40%, Mitsubishi Corporation 10%, South Korea Lotte Chemical 40%, Lotte Chemical subsidiary 10%	Synthetic rubber production for tires in Malaysia
• Utilization of Sales Channels • Technology Introduction	March 7, 2013	Nikkei page 13	Kosé Corporation 60%, India Elder Pharmaceuticals Ltd. 40%	Cosmetics production and sales in India
• Utilization of Sales Channels • Technology Introduction	March 7, 2013	Nikkei page 15	Sumitomo Corporation 81%, Brazil Major cosmetic pharmaceutical company Cosmotec Especialidadesquímicas Ltda. 19%	Cosmetics production and sales in Brazil
• Utilization of Sales Channels	March 3, 2013	Nikkei page 7	Panasonic Corporation 80.4%, Mitsui & Co., Ltd. 19.6%	Panasonic Corporation aims "Power Assist Suit" robot technology market sales channel development
• Facility Sharing • Utilization of Sales Channels	February 22, 2013	Nikkei page 11	Sekisui Chemical Co., Ltd. 51%, US Lubrizol Corporation subsidiary 49%	Vinyl resin pipe production in Thailand
• Utilization of Sales Channels • Technology Introduction	February 19, 2013	Nikkei page 13	Sumitomo Corporation 50%, Yoyogi Seminar 50%,	Schoolchildren infant English education and childcare
• Cost Sharing • Technology Introduction	February 16, 20	Nikkei page 11	Mitsui & Co., Ltd. 47.6%, other 6 companies rest of shares (no detailed reference about shareholding ratio)	Tohoku Reconstruction Project. Established aquarium in Sendai district

Type of synergy	Date of article	News-paper	JV partners	Notes
● Cost Sharing ● Technology Introduction	February 15, 2013	Nikkei page 11	Daiichi Sankyo Co., Ltd., Innovation Network Corporation of Japan (INCJ), Mitsubishi UFJ Financial Group, Inc. (no detailed reference about shareholding ratio)	Muscular dystrophy drug development costs support
● Cost Sharing ● Utilization of Sales Channels	February 6, 2013	Nikkei page 11	Marubeni Corporation 49%, US Gas pipeline technology major company Williams JV Partners 51%	Gulf of Mexico oil field development, SPAR offshore facility construction project (90 billion yen investment)
● Utilization of Sales Channels	February 4, 2013	Nikkei page 11	Teijin Ltd. 34%, South Korea Chemistry major company SK Chemicals 66%	Manufacture and sale of PPS resin in South Korea
● Securing Resources ● Utilization of Sales Channels ● Cost Sharing	January 30, 2013	Nikkei page 13	Idemitsu Kosan Co., Ltd. 50%, CanadaGas infrastructure major company AltaGas Ltd. 50%	The procurement of LNG from Canada
● Securing Resources ● Utilization of Sales Channels ● Cost Sharing	January 29, 2013	Nikkei page 3	US Pipeline leading company Kinder Morgan, Inc. 51%, Royal Dutch Shell 49%	Royal Dutch Shell decides to make investment in Georgia LNG facility, in order to secure the LNG source
● Collaborative R&D ● Facility Sharing	January 29, 2013	Nikkei page 11	Toshiba, GE (no detailed reference about shareholding ratio)	Technology development JV of thermal power generation (i.e. gas combined cycle (GTCC))
● Collaborative R&D ● Facility Sharing	January 29, 2013	Nikkei page 1	Toshiba, GE (no detailed reference about shareholding ratio)	Technology development JV of thermal power generation (i.e. gas combined cycle (GTCC))
● Utilization of Sales Channels ● Technology Introduction	January 29, 2013	Nikkei page 7	Capital Medica Co., Ltd. 35%, Vietnam Hapaco Group 65%	Japanese-style hospital management know-how transfer into Vietnam
● Facility Sharing ● Utilization of Sales Channels ● Collaborative R&D ● Brand Introduction	January 17, 2013	Nikkei pages 1, 13	Sharp Corporation 50%, Lenovo Corporation 50%	For comprehensive business alliance of LCD TV business between two, to form development, sales JV company and to sell manufacturing company to Lenovo Corporation
● Utilization of Sales Channels ● Cost Sharing ● Technology Introduction	January 17, 2013	Nikkei page 11	Cosmo Oil Co., Ltd. 35%, Showa Shell Sekiyu K.K. 35%, Development Bank of Japan Inc. 30%	Mega Solar joint operation to enjoy Solar Power Feed In Tariff Assistance

Type of synergy	Date of article	News-paper	JV partners	Notes
• Collaborative R&D • Facility Sharing	January 17, 2013	Nikkei page 10	IHI 51%→100%, Germany Daimler Benz 49%→0%	European turbo engine technology development JV. JV partnership to be broken off, a wholly owned subsidiary of IHI
• Securing Resources • Utilization of Sales Channels • Cost Sharing	January 16, 2013	Nikkei page 9	Idemitsu Kosan Co., Ltd. 35.1%, Kuwait National Petroleum Company International 35.1%, Vietnam Petrovietnam 25.1%, Mitsui Chemicals, Incorporated 4.7%	Secure e.g. petroleum and petrochemical products Vietnam refinery
• Utilization of Sales Channels • Cost Sharing • Technology Introduction • Brand Introduction	January 15, 2013	Nikkei page 3	Sanyo Electric Co., Ltd. 47%→0%, TaiwanAbico Group 53%→100%	SANYO Electric Co., Ltd. decides to withdraw its brand from Taiwan. JV partnership to be broken off, a wholly owned subsidiary
• Securing Resources • Cost Sharing • Utilization of Sales Channels	January 9, 2013	Nikkei page 3	Mitsubishi Corporation, Royal Dutch Shell, Iraq National Oil Company (INOC) (no detailed reference about shareholding ratio)	Gas processing JV company in Iraq
• Utilization of Sales Channels • Collaborative R&D	January 9, 2013	Nikkei page 11	Mitsubishi Corporation 50%, Showa Denko K.K. 50%	Joint development and production of nano-carbon-based material
• Utilization of Sales Channels	January 5, 2013	Nikkei page 11	Sega Sammy Holdings Inc. 45%, South Korea Local companies balance (no detailed reference about shareholding ratio)	To advance into integrated resort facility business in South Korea
• Cost Sharing • Utilization of Sales Channels	January 5, 2013	Nikkei page 11	Mitsubishi Corporation 50%, EDF: Electricité de France 50%	Solar power plant project in Europe
• Utilization of Sales Channels • Collaborative R&D	January 9, 2012	Nikkei page 11	Local pharmaceutical product manufacturer K.K. Yoshindo 51%, Ajinomoto Pharmaceuticals Co., Ltd. 49%	Production and joint development of dialysis agent
• Securing Resources • Cost Sharing • Utilization of Sales Channels	December 23, 2012	Nikkei page	Mitsubishi Chemical Holdings Corporation, US Dow Chemical Company (no detailed reference about shareholding ratio)	Shale gas utilization complex business partnership

Type of synergy	Date of article	News-paper	JV partners	Notes
• Facility Sharing	December 22, 2012	Nikkei page 10	Mitsubishi Materials Corporation, US raw concrete manufacturers (no detailed reference about shareholding ratio)	JV partnership to be broken off, to be a wholly owned subsidiary of Mitsubishi Materials Corporation
• Facility Sharing • Technology Introduction	December 21, 2012	Nikkei page 13	Sumitomo Corporation 40%, Daiichi Seminar Group 60%	Online education business
• Facility Sharing • Technology Introduction • Brand Introduction	December 20, 2012	Nikkei page 13	Aeon Group 50% →100%, US Warner Bros. Entertainment, Inc. 50%→0%	JV partnership to be broken off, to be a wholly owned subsidiary of Aeon Group
• Technology Introduction	December 20, 2012	Nikkei page 11	Hitachi Transport System, Ltd. subsidiary 55%, Myanmar Investment firm 45%	By apparel logistics know-how of Hitachi, JV supports Japanese makers to advance into Myanmar business
• Utilization of Sales Channels • Technology Introduction	December 18, 2012	Nikkei page 45	SoftBank Corp. subsidiary 40%, USFOX subsidiary 60%	Professional baseball TV program network
• Utilization of Sales Channels • Technology Introduction	December 4, 2012	Nikkei page 1	Convenience store Lawson, Inc. 51%, Yahoo Japan Corporation 49%	Internet home delivery service
• Utilization of Sales Channels	December 1, 2012	Nikkei page 12	Tokyo Electron Ltd. 51%, Sharp Corporation 49%	Liquidation of solar cell device manufacturing business
• Facility Sharing	December 1, 2012	Nikkei page 13	Mitsubishi Heavy Industries, Ltd. 65%, Hitachi 35%	Integration of thermal power generation infrastructure business of two
• Facility Sharing	November 30, 2012	Nikkei page 3, 13	Mitsubishi Heavy Industries, Ltd. 65%, Hitachi35%	Integration of thermal power generation infrastructure business of two
• Utilization of Sales Channels • Facility Sharing	November 30, 2012	Nikkei page 11	JX Nippon Oil & Energy Corporation 60%–70%, Suzuyo & Co., Ltd. balance (no detailed reference about shareholding ratio)	JX takes over the Suzuyo's gas station network
• Utilization of Sales Channels	November 21, 2012	Nikkei page 13	Kanematsu Corporation Group 60%, Indonesia Cimory Group 40%	Lunch food processing for Japanese companies in Indonesia
• Utilization of Sales Channels	November 16, 2012	Nikkei page 17	Circle K Sunkus Co., Ltd. 30%, Malaysia Kumpulan Mofaz Sdn Bhd 70%	Convenience store business in Malaysia

Type of synergy	Date of article	News-paper	JV partners	Notes
● Facility Sharing	November 14, 2012	Nikkei page 11	Sekisui Chemical Company, Ltd. 51%, Indonesia Local plastic manufacturers 49%	Automotive plastic member production in Indonesia
● Facility Sharing ● Technology Introduction ● Brand Introduction	November 13, 2012	Nikkei page 3	Nissin Foods Holdings Co., Ltd., Ajinomoto Company, Incorporated (no detailed reference about shareholding ratio)	Instant noodles manufacturing sales in Brazil
● Facility Sharing	November 4, 2012	Nikkei page 7	Nissan Motor Co., Ltd 50%, Mitsubishi Motors Corporation 50%	JV succeeded light car manufacturing cost 30%, reduction. Follow-up story about existing JV's business
● Utilization of Sales Channels	October 26, 2012	Nikkei page 13	Yoshinoya Co., Ltd. 50%, Thailand Charoen Pokphand Group Company Ltd. 50%	Beef bowl market foothold in Thailand
● Utilization of Sales Channels ● Technology Introduction	October 26, 2012	Nikkei page 13	Oji Holdings Corporation 60%, Marubeni Corporation 20%, India Major paper companies 20%	Cardboard manufacturing JV in India
● Collaboration in lieu of Competition ● Facility Sharing	October 25, 2012	Nikkei page 9	Sumitomo Corporation $(40.5\% \rightarrow 50\%)$, KDDI $(31.1\% \rightarrow 50\%)$	Past management conflict resolved. CATV mail order, mobile video provides through CATV.
● Reputational Backing	October 22, 2012	Nikkei page 5	JP Morgan Chase & Co., Mitsubishi UFJ Financial Group, Inc. (no detailed reference about shareholding ratio)	JV's M&A consultancy business is favorable. Follow-up story about existing JV's business
● Facility Sharing ● Collaborative R&D	October 16, 2012	Nikkei page 11	Sumitomo Corporation 47.5%, Sumitomo Chemical Company, Ltd. 47.5%, CO_2 separation membrane technology venture business Renesas Energy Research (RER) 5%	Cost reduction using a CO_2 separation membrane technology VB
● Securing Resources	October 10, 2012	Nikkei page 1	Private 11 companies and government form Cooperative Union (no detailed reference about shareholding ratio)	De China. Rare metals mining JV start with magnet ore
● Facility Sharing ● Cost Sharing	October 2, 2012	Nikkei page 1	Hitachi/Toshiba/Sony Integrated company, Japan Display Inc. (no detailed reference about shareholding ratio)	Organic EL mass production to pursuit Samsung

Type of synergy	Date of article	News-paper	JV partners	Notes
• Facility Sharing • Reputational Backing • Collaboration in lieu of Competition	October 1, 2012	Nikkei page 11	Local small and medium-sized mega solar construction companies (no detailed reference about shareholding ratio)	Joint construction company JV united front to get orders
• Technology Introduction	September 29, 2012	Nikkei page 11	Taiyo Nippon Sanso Corporation, German Evonik group (no detailed reference about shareholding ratio)	Specialty gas, Monosilane, contract manufacturing JV. Taiyo Nippon Sanso has been obliged to buy a certain volume of gas. It is decided to liquidate JV due to unprofitable result. Extraordinary loss 23.3 billion yen
• Utilization of Sales Channels • Technology Introduction	September 29, 2012	Nikkei page 3	Sony 51%, Olympus Corporation 49%	Sony aims to get endoscopic surgical technology of Olympus Corporation
• Utilization of Sales Channels • Technology Introduction	September 28, 2012	Nikkei page 1	Sony 51%, Olympus Corporation 49%	Sony aims to get endoscopic surgical technology of Olympus Corporation
• Facility Sharing • Cost Sharing	September 25, 2012	Nikkei page 15	Furukawa Electric Co., Ltd. 50%, Fujikura Ltd. 50%	The transmission line factory in India. Foothold into India
• Utilization of Sales Channels • Alleviation of Friction	September 12, 2012	Nikkei page 3 evening edition	Indonesia LCC largest Lion Group 49%, Malaysia Aircraft maintenance company 51%	To advance into Malaysian LCC business
• Utilization of Sales Channels • Alleviation of Friction	September 4, 2012	Nikkei page 9	Honda Motor Co., Ltd. approx. 90%→100%, India Usha approx. 10%→0%	JV partnership to be broken off, to be a wholly owned subsidiary
• Facility Sharing • Reputational Backing • Cost Sharing	September 4, 2012	Nikkei page 2 evening edition	Hitachi Zosen Corporation, JFE Steel Corporation, Toshiba, etc. 6 firms (no detailed reference about shareholding ratio)	Offshore wind power generation SPCO JV establishment to get funding
• Utilization of Sales Channels • Alleviation of Friction	September 1, 2012	Nikkei page 10	Honda Motor Co., Ltd., Bangladesh two-wheeled local companies (no detailed reference about shareholding ratio)	Two-wheeled market in Bangladesh
• Collaborative R&D	September 1, 2012	Nikkei page 10	Mitsubishi Tanabe Pharma Corporation 51%→1ts%, Medical equipment Nipro Corporation 49%→9%	Nipro withdraws from JV. JV partnership to be broken off, to be a wholly owned subsidiary of Mitsubishi Tanabe
• Facility Sharing • Technology Introduction	September 1, 2012	Nikkei page 10	Denso Corporation 26%, Pakistan Atlas Group 74%	Technical assistance in parts supply to Honda Motor Co., Ltd. in Pakistan

Type of synergy	Date of article	News-paper	JV partners	Notes
• Utilization of Sales Channels • Alleviation of Friction • Technology Introduction • Brand Introduction	August 28, 2012	Nikkei page 9	MAZDA Motor Corporation 50%, China Changan Automobile 50%	MAZDA Motor Corporation aims to advance into Chinese Automotive Market. Chinese original brand vehicles development is intended
• Securing Resources	August 25, 2012	Nikkei page 10	Chile Anglo American Steel (AAS) 50.1%, Mitsubishi Corporation 20.14%, the JV company between Mitsui & Co., Ltd. & Corporacion Nacional del Cobre de Chile 29.5%	To form the JV in accordance with provisions in the amicable agreement in litigation over the copper mine interests among the parties concerned
• Collaborative R&D	August 22, 2012	Nikkei page 10	JX Nippon Oil & Energy Corporation 50%, Sanyo Electric Co., Ltd. 50%	Liquidation of Solar battery JV company established in 2009
• Technology Introduction	August 20, 2012	Nikkei page 11	Thailand Singha Group majority, Japanese food business venture Shinsen-Gumi-Honbu K.K. partial participation (no detailed reference about shareholding ratio)	Start rice production in Thailand
• Facility Sharing • Collaborative R&D	August 18, 2012	Nikkei page 11	Mitsui Engineering & Shipbuilding Co., Ltd. 50%, JFE Engineering Corporation 50%	The recovered methane gas by waste treatment to use power generating in China
• Utilization of Sales Channels • Facility Sharing	August 15, 2012	Nikkei page 11	Sumitomo Corporation 40%, India Special steel major company Special steel major company Mukand Ltd. 60%	Sumitomo Corporation starts processing of automotive special steel in India
• Securing Resources • Facility Sharing • Utilization of Sales Channels	August 14, 2012	Nikkei page 9	Mitsui & Co., Ltd. 49%, Chile afforestation leading company Industrial Bosques Cautin S.A. 51%	Producing papermaking materials, wood chip sales in Chile
• Facility Sharing • Technology Introduction	August 8, 2012	Nikkei page 11	Isuzu Motors Ltd. 50%, China Jiangling Motors Co., Ltd 50%	Automobile engine production in China

Type of synergy	Date of article	News-paper	JV partners	Notes
• Utilization of Sales Channels • Facility Sharing • Technology Introduction	August 3, 2012	Nikkei page 11	Sumitomo Corporation 40%, Thailand Retail Central Group 30%, Makeup, clothing major local company Saha Group 30%	Sumitomo Corporation introduces TV mail-order business in Thailand
• Facility Sharing	August 2, 2012	Nikkei page 11	Fujitsu Ltd., NTT Docomo, Inc., NEC (no detailed reference about shareholding ratio)	Smartphone for semiconductor production JV
• Utilization of Sales Channels	July 14, 2012	Nikkei page 10	Philippine Toyota car dealer Metro bank group 60%, Mitsui & Co., Ltd. 40%	To advance into Philippine car sales market with Toyota cars
• Utilization of Sales Channels • Technology Introduction	July 10, 2012	Nikkei page 11	Asahi Group Holdings, Ltd. (majority), Indofood Jakarta (balance) (no detailed reference about shareholding ratio)	To penetrate Indonesian soft drink market (production & sales)
• Facility Sharing	July 10, 2012	Nikkei page 11	Idemitsu Kosan Co., Ltd. 50%, Taiwan Formosa Plastics Group 50%	To manufacture bonding adhesive in Taiwan
• Collaborative R&D	July 5, 2012	Nikkei page 9	NEC, Lenovo Corporation (no detailed reference about shareholding ratio)	Follow-up story about existing JV's business: joint R&D re tablet PC
• Facility Sharing • Cost Sharing	July 4, 2012	Nikkei page 9	Renesas Electronics Corporation (no detailed reference about shareholding ratio)	Follow-up story about existing JV's business
• Facility Sharing	June 29, 2012	Nikkei page 11	Sharp 37.6%, Taiwan Foxconn Technology Group 37.6%, Dai Nippon Printing Co., Ltd. 9%, others (balance)	Sharp accepts JV investment from Foxconn to reform Sharp's Sakai plant
• Facility Sharing • Cost Sharing	June 23, 2012	Nikkei page 9	Renesas Electronics Corporation (no detailed reference about shareholding ratio)	Follow-up story about existing JV's business
• Securing Resources	June 20, 2012	Nikkei page 12	Australia MGC 56%, Mitsubishi Corporation 24%, Farmers in Tasmania state (balance) (no detailed reference about shareholding ratio)	JV to process milk in Tasmania state in Australia to secure stable supply for export to Japan

Type of synergy	Date of article	News-paper	JV partners	Notes
• Securing Resources	June 20, 2012	Nikkei page 12	Sojitsu Corporation, Sabindo Indonesia (no detailed reference about shareholding ratio)	Culturing prawn in Indonesia, to secure stable export supply to Japan
• Facility Sharing • Reputational Backing • Brand Introduction	June 18, 2012	Nikkei page 1	AEON group of companies 50%, Tesco plc 50%	The AEON group of companies made an investment to rebuild the Tesco network in Japan, to integrate it into the AEON network, and to introduce a private brand.
• Utilization of Sales Channels • Technology Introduction	June 16, 2012	Nikkei page 9	Kenko Mayonnaise Co., Ltd. 49%, Indonesian Jaffa Co. 51%	Produce mayonnaise in Indonesia, follow-up story about existing JV's business
• Facility Sharing • Cost Sharing	June 16, 2012	Nikkei page 9	Renesas Electronics Corporation (no detailed reference about shareholding ratio)	Follow-up story about existing JV's business
• Securing Resources	June 16, 2012	Nikkei page 6	UK BP 50%, Russian Investors Group AAR 50%	BP withdraws from Russian E&P JV, which is securing of resource type, follow-up story about existing JV's business
• Utilization of Sales Channels • Technology Introduction	June 13, 2012	Nikkei page 11	Hisamitsu Pharmaceutical Co., Inc. 49%, Sanofi Group (France) 51%	Introduction of Sanofi pollen allergy medicine into Japan
• Utilization of Sales Channels • Alleviation of Friction • Technology Introduction	June 2, 2012	Nikkei page 13	Isuzu Motors Ltd. increases its shares from 29% to 45%, Russian Sollers group decreases its shares from 71% to 55%	Isuzu Motors Ltd. increased its holding due to its strategy to expand Russian motor sales
• Facility Sharing • Cost Sharing	June 2, 2012	Nikkei page 9	Renesas Electronics Corporation (no detailed reference about shareholding ratio)	Follow-up story about existing JV's business
• Securing Resources	June 2, 2012	Nikkei page 6	UK BP 50%, Russian Investors Group AAR 50%	BP withdraws from Russian E&P JV, which is securing of resource type, follow-up story about existing JV's business
• Securing Resources	June 1, 2012	Nikkei page 11	Inpex Corporation 40%, Russia LUKoil 60%	To acquire petroleum E&P reserve right in Russia through consortium
• Securing Resources	May 26, 2012	Nikkei page 11	Sumitomo Chemical Company, Ltd. 37.5%, Saudi Aramco 37.5%, Saudi Arabian investors 25%	To invest in the petrochemical Plant in Saudi Arabia to secure petrochemical materials

Type of synergy	Date of article	News-paper	JV partners	Notes
• Reputational Backing	May 25, 2012	Nikkei page 13	Sojitsu Corporation, Meidensha Corporation (no detailed reference about shareholding ratio)	To get purchase order of railway equipment and facility in Hong Kong through consortium
• Facility Sharing • Collaborative R&D	May 18, 2012	Nikkei page 11	NEC 49%, Lenovo Corporation 51%	To manufacture PC/joint R&D re tablet PC
• Securing Resources • Cost Sharing	May 16, 2012	Nikkei page 1	Nippon Yusen Kabushiki Kaisha 10%, Mitsubishi Corporation 40%, Japan Oil, Gas and Metals National Corporation 42%, Tokyo Electric Power Company 8%	To acquire 10% of an Australian gas field reserve right for 300 billion yen
• Securing Resources • Cost Sharing	May 16, 2012	Nikkei page 9	Mitsubishi Corporation 20%, Shell 40%, South Korea National Gas Company 20%, China National Oil and Natural Gas Company 20%	To acquire Canadian LNG reserve right jointly
• Utilization of Sales Channels • Alleviation of Friction • Technology Introduction	May 5, 2012	Nikkei page 1	Kawasaki Heavy Industries, Ltd. 30%, Brazil General Contractors Consortium (balance) (no detailed reference about shareholding ratio)	Building of natural resource mining ship, technical support
• Facility Sharing • Utilization of Sales Channels	April 27, 2012	Nikkei page 4	Sumitomo Mitsui Banking Corporation 51%, Orix Group 49%	To liquidate credit-card loan JV project. Orix Group will acquire 100% ownership of the JV
• Securing Resources	April 27, 2012	Nikkei page 9	TDK, Showa Denko K.K (no detailed reference about shareholding ratio)	Local production of magnet, rare earth in China to secure resources
• Utilization of Sales Channels • Alleviation of Friction • Technology Introduction	April 26, 2012	Nikkei page 13	Isuzu Motors Ltd. 50%, RussiaSollers 50%	Isuzu Motors Ltd. will start manufacturing cars in Russia with its own brand
• Utilization of Sales Channels • Cost Sharing	April 25, 2012	Nikkei page 4	Sumitomo Mitsui Banking Corporation, NEC (no detailed reference about shareholding ratio)	Consortium to form a venture investment fund
• Facility Sharing	April 19, 2012	Nikkei page 11	Kasai Kogy o Co., Ltd. 50%, Mexico Grupo Mexico SA de CV 50%	Automotive parts production for Japanese automobile manufacturers in Mexico

Type of synergy	Date of article	News-paper	JV partners	Notes
• Securing Resources • Cost Sharing • Collaborative R&D	April 17, 2012	Nikkei page 3 evening edition	Russian Rosneft Oil Company 66.7%, Exxon 33.3%	Arctic oil development JV (20 trillion yen)
• Utilization of Sales Channels	April 16, 2012	Nikkei page 9	Unipres Corporation 70%, Marubeni Corp. 20%, Indian investment firm 10%	Auto parts production in Indonesia
• Securing Resources • Cost Sharing	April 12, 2012	Nikkei page 1	Mitsubishi Corporation 20%, Shell 40%, South Korea National Gas Company 20%, China National Oil and Natural Gas Company 20%	To acquire Canadian LNG reserve right jointly for 1 trillion yen
• Collaboration in lieu of Competition • Facility Sharing • Collaborative R&D	April 3, 2012	Nikkei page 11	Toshiba, Hitachi, Sony, other public and private fund (no detailed reference about shareholding ratio)	All Japanese firms alliance for organic EL panel development for smartphone use
• Facility Sharing • Collaborative R&D	April 3, 2012	Nikkei page 11	Fujitsu Ltd. 80%, Toshiba 20%	JV partnership to be broken off, to be a wholly owned subsidiary of Fujitsu Ltd.
• Facility Sharing	February 21, 2012	Nikkei page 11	Asahi Kasei Group 50%, the DAISO group 50%	Chlorine joint manufacturing JV. JV partnership to be broken off, to close JV plant.
• Utilization of Sales Channels • Technology Introduction	February 8, 2012	Nikkei page 10	Nippon Gas Co., Ltd. 50%, Australia Clean TeQ Holdings, Ltd. 50%	Design and construction of contaminated water treatment equipment
• Collaborative R&D	February 8, 2012	Nikkei page 11	Suzuki Motor Corp. 50%, UK IEH 50%	Fuel cell system development
• Cost Sharing	February 7, 2012	Nikkei page 5	Japanese government, private firms (Kagome Co., Ltd., Kikkoman Corporation etc.) (no detailed reference about shareholding ratio)	The agriculture strengthening fund plan by the JV government and private firms
• Utilization of Sales Channels	February 7, 2012	Nikkei page 10	Toyota Tsusho Corporation 49%, Sapporo Breweries Ltd. 51%	Production and sales of soft drinks in US
• Facility Sharing	January 21, 2012	Nikkei page 11	Toray Industries, Inc. 50%, Tonen General Sekiyu K. K. 50%	Lithium-ion battery JV partnership to be broken off, to be a wholly owned subsidiary of Toray
• Facility Sharing	January 11, 2012	Nikkei page 10	Sumitomo Chemical Company, Ltd. 40%, Denki Kagaku Kogyo Kabushiki Kaisha 60%	Resin material joint manufacturing JV partnership to be broken off, to be a wholly owned subsidiary of Denki Kagaku Kogyo

Type of synergy	Date of article	News-paper	JV partners	Notes
• Facility Sharing	December 27, 2011	Nikkei page 11	Sony approx. 50%, South Korea Samsung 50% + 1 share	Liquid crystal panel joint manufacturing JV partnership to be broken off, to be a wholly owned subsidiary of Samsung
• Facility Sharing • Utilization of Sales Channels • Cost Sharing	December 7, 2011	Nikkei page 9	Mitsui O.S.K. Lines, Ltd., Mitsui O.S.K. Lines, Ltd. subsidiary, Denmark shipping company, two Singapore shipping companies (no detailed reference about shareholding ratio)	Co-ownership and co-operation of around 35 to 50 vessels, large tanker
• Facility Sharing • Utilization of Sales Channels	December 3, 2011	Nikkei page 12	Mitsui Chemicals, Incorporated, China Petrochemical Corporation (no detailed reference about shareholding ratio)	Additional investment decision to the high-performance resin raw materials factory. Follow-up story about existing JV's business
• Cost Sharing	December 2, 2011	Nikkei page 9	Inpex Corporation 76%, French Total 24%	Australia Northwest offshore LNG. Mining interests co-ownership consortium
• Collaboration in lieu of Competition • Facility Sharing • Collaborative R&D • Cost Sharing	November 30, 2011	Nikkei page 13	NTT Docomo, Inc. 60.45%, commercial broadcasting companies 21.96%, Dentsu Inc. 7.7%, Sharp approx. 10%	Establishment plan announced. Content delivery business JV for smartphone, which is in market saturation
• Utilization of Sales Channels	November 30, 2011	Nikkei page 11	Marubeni Corp. 60%, Japan Communications Inc. 40%	Low price data communications business for business use
• Collaboration in lieu of Competition • Facility Sharing • Collaborative R&D • Cost Sharing	November 29, 2011	Nikkei page 9	Hitachi Construction Machinery Co., Ltd., Nissan (no detailed reference about shareholding ratio)	Innovation Network Corporation of Japan (INCJ) will make majority investment in the integration JV company between Hitachi Construction Machinery Co., Ltd. and Nissan, supporting organizational reform relating to the consolidation of the lagging forklift industry
• Utilization of Sales Channels • Alleviation of Friction • Technology Introduction	November 27, 2011	Nikkei page 7	Mazda Motor Corporation, Russia Major car maker Sollers (no detailed reference about shareholding ratio)	The JV for automobile production plant in Russia
• Facility Sharing	November 22, 2011	Nikkei page 11	Tokai Carbon Co., Ltd. 40%, South Korea Posco 60%	Production base of high-performance graphite for solar cells in South Korea to reduce processing cost there

Type of synergy	Date of article	News-paper	JV partners	Notes
• Facility Sharing • Collaborative R&D	November 17, 2011	Nikkei page 9	Fujifilm Corporation 50%, Kyowa Hakko Kirin Company, Ltd. 50%	R&D and production of bio-generic drugs
• Collaboration in lieu of Competition • Facility Sharing • Collaborative R&D	November 16, 2011	Nikkei page 11	Toshiba, Hitachi, Sony public and private fund (no detailed reference about shareholding ratio)	To manufacture organic EL panel
• Facility Sharing • Brand Introduction • Technology Introduction	November 16, 2011	Nikkei page 1	Nissan, Daimler-Benz AG, Renault (no detailed reference about shareholding ratio)	Co-operation of the production plants of each company's brand car
• Facility Sharing	October 30, 2011	Nikkei page 1	Sony approx. 50%, South Korea Samsung 50% + 1 share	Samsung starts talks planning present liquid crystal panel joint manufacturing JV to be a wholly owned subsidiary of Samsung
• Facility Sharing • Collaborative R&D	October 20, 2011	Nikkei page 13	Kowa Company, Ltd. 50%, Teva Pharmaceutical Industries, Ltd. (Israel) 50%	R&D and production of generic drugs JV partnership to be broken off, to be a wholly owned subsidiary of Teva Pharmaceutical Industries Ltd. (Israel)
• Utilization of Sales Channels	October 13, 2011	Nikkei page 9	Hitachi, Brazil IESA (no detailed reference about shareholding ratio)	Production of monorail vehicle in Brazil
• Utilization of Sales Channels	October 7, 2011	Nikkei page 1	Sony, Ericsson (no detailed reference about shareholding ratio)	Mobile phone JV partnership to be broken off, to be a wholly owned subsidiary of Sony
• Utilization of Sales Channels • Technology Introduction	October 5, 2011	Nikkei page 9	Itochu Corp. 50%, India I&P 50%	Storage and delivery know-how of Itochu to be introduced into India to establish foothold in India
• Technology Introduction	October 5, 2011	Nikkei page 4	Hanoi Water Authority, Vietnam General Contractors (majority), Tokyo Metropolitan Government, Metawater Co., Ltd. (balance)	Introduction of advanced large water purification plant technology of Tokyo Metropolitan Government to Hanoi
• Facility Sharing • Collaborative R&D	September 27, 2011	Nikkei page 13	Kowa Company, Ltd. 50%, Teva Pharmaceutical Industries, Ltd. (Israel) 50%	R&D and production of generic drugs JV partnership to be broken off, to be a wholly owned subsidiary of Teva Pharmaceutical Industries Ltd. (Israel)
• Utilization of Sales Channels • Facility Sharing • Technology Introduction	September 22, 2011	Nikkei page 9	House Foods Corporation 60%, Thailand Osotspa. Co., Ltd 40%	Japanese health drinks, food production and sales in Thailand

Type of synergy	Date of article	News-paper	JV partners	Notes
• Utilization of Sales Channels • Obtaining Local Expertise • Facility Sharing	September 22, 2011	Nikkei page 1	Lawson, Inc. 49%, India Future Group 51%	Lawson-style convenience stores in India
• Utilization of Sales Channels • Obtaining Local Expertise • Facility Sharing	September 9, 2011	Nikkei page 11	MOS Food Services, Inc. 30%, South Korea Media Will HD 70%	MOS burger brand advance into South Korea, consultant function to local firm to explore the preferences of local consumers
• Facility Sharing	August 24, 2011	Nikkei page 11	Aeon group of companies 50%, Daiwa House Industry Company, Ltd. 50%	Management of small shopping center JV partnership to be broken off, to be a wholly owned subsidiary of AEON
• Technology Introduction	August 24, 2011	Nikkei page 13	Kuraray Co., Ltd. 51%, China Hexin Group 49%	Introduction of industrial wastewater advanced treatment technology of Kuraray into China
• Utilization of Sales Channels • Facility Sharing	August 17, 2011	Nikkei page 9	Japan Airlines Co., Ltd., Mitsubishi Corporation, Qantas Airways Ltd. 1/3 each	To introduce LCC business know-how of Qantas Airways Ltd.
• Utilization of Sales Channels • Facility Sharing	July 30, 2011	Nikkei page 11	NEC 60%, Singapore STEE 40%	NEC aims to advance into cloud computing management business in Southeast Asia
• Utilization of Sales Channels • Facility Sharing	July 30, 2011	Nikkei page 13	Hitachi 50%, Fuji Electric Co., Ltd. 30%, Meidensha Corporation 20%	Follow-up story about existing JV's business. Three companies have established JV aiming to integrate the unprofitable substation business, and were unsuccessful. It is agreed that JV will be terminated and they will respectively run the business
• Utilization of Sales Channels • Obtaining Local Expertise • Facility Sharing	July 29, 2011	Nikkei page 10	FamilyMart Co., Ltd ., Vietnam counter party is not decided (no detailed reference about shareholding ratio)	FamilyMart Co., Ltd. has been operating convenience stores business in Vietnam, now will seek appropriate local partners there.
• Utilization of Sales Channels • Technology Introduction	July 28, 2011	Nikkei page 1	Fujifilm Corporation 51%, India DRL 49%	R&D and production of generic drugs
• Utilization of Sales Channels • Facility Sharing • Collaborative R&D	July 21, 2011	Nikkei page 10	All Nippon Airways 67%, Malaysia AirAsia 33%	To introduce LCC business know-how of AirAsia
• Utilization of Sales Channels • Facility Sharing	July 16, 2011	Nikkei page 9	Sharp 50%, Taiwan Foxconn Technology Group 50%	For rationalization of Sharp Sakai Plant, Sharp seeks sales destination in Taiwan

Type of synergy	Date of article	News-paper	JV partners	Notes
• Technology Introduction	July 16, 2011	Nikkei page 1	Mitsui & Co., Ltd. 50%, The Dow Chemical Company (US) 50%	Factory was established in Brazil to produce plant-based plastic from sugar cane, for sales to North America
• Utilization of Sales Channels • Facility Sharing • Collaborative R&D	July 10, 2011	Nikkei page 1	South Korea LG Electronics Incorporated (majority), Hitachi (balance) (no detailed reference about shareholding ratio)	Water and sewerage construction management business in South Korea using seawater desalination technology of Hitachi
• Utilization of Sales Channels • Collaborative R&D	July 9, 2011	Nikkei page 11	Asatsu-DK Inc. (ADK) 51%, Dentsu Digital Holdings 49%	Joint development of the internet market
• Technology Introduction	July 9, 2011	Nikkei page 10	Sharp, Italy Enel SpA, Switzerland STM (no detailed reference about shareholding ratio)	Construction and operation of solar cell manufacturing plant in Italy
• Utilization of Sales Channels • Collaborative R&D	July 7, 2011	Nikkei page 9	Ube Industries, Ltd. 50%, US Dow Chemical Company 50%	Manufacturing of lithium battery in US, for sale to Japanese firms in North America
• Technology Introduction	June 24, 2011	Nikkei page 11	Marubeni Corp. 80%, Hitachi Construction Machinery Co., Ltd. 20%	Marubeni Corp. plans to expand its large construction equipment lease business into Australia and to enter other markets by obtaining Hitachi's know-how relating to large construction equipment
• Cost Sharing	June 14, 20	Nikkei page 9	Marubeni Corp. 50%, Chubu Electric Power Company, Inc. 30%, Qatar Electricity & Water Company 15%, Others	Large gas power plant construction in Oman and 15 years management
• Utilization of Sales Channels • Facility Sharing	June 10, 2011	Nikkei page 13	Kureha Corp. 70%, Itochu Corp. 30%	Manufacture and sale of lithium-ion batteries in US
• Collaboration in lieu of Competition • Facility Sharing • Collaborative R&D	June 7, 2011	Nikkei page 1	Toshiba, Hitachi, Sony, public and private fund firms (no detailed reference about shareholding ratio)	Japanese organic EL panel for smartphone manufacturers' alliance
• Facility Sharing	June 4, 2011	Nikkei page 13	Mazda Motor Corporation, Ford Motor Company (no detailed reference about shareholding ratio)	Production base JV in US, Mazda decided to withdraw from JV relationship
• Collaborative R&D	May 27, 2011	Nikkei page 13	T.RAD Co., Ltd. 50%, Tata Motors, Ltd. 50%	Automobile air conditioner parts joint R&D

Type of synergy	Date of article	News-paper	JV partners	Notes
• Utilization of Sales Channels • Brand Introduction	May 24, 2011	Nikkei page 13	Samantha Thavasa Japan, Ltd. 49.99%, a president of Samantha Thavasa privately holds balance, South Korea Lotte Co., Ltd. 49.99%	Samantha Thavasa aiming to advance into South Korea
• Utilization of Sales Channels • Collaborative R&D	May 24, 2011	Nikkei page 9	Hitachi, Mayekawa Mfg. Co., Ltd. (no detailed reference about shareholding ratio)	Using Mayekawa sales channel in Brazil, Hitachi aims to enter the equipment sales market for plant
• Utilization of Sales Channels • Brand Introduction	May 20, 2011	Nikkei page 13	Welcia Holdings Co., Ltd. of Aeon group of companies less than 40%, China Bailian Group more than 60%	Japanese-style drugstore business in China
• Utilization of Sales Channels • Brand Introduction	May 19, 2011	Nikkei page 3 evening edition	Meiji Holdings Co., Ltd., Thailand Charoen Pokphand Group (no detailed reference about shareholding ratio)	Expansion of sales of milk processed by Meiji hygiene management method in Thailand
• Securing Resources	May 18, 2011	Nikkei page 8	UK BP 50%, Russian Investors Group AAR 50%	BP withdraws from Russian E&P JV. Follow-up story about existing JV's business
• Utilization of Sales Channels • Brand Introduction	May 10, 2011	Nikkei page 3	Calbee, Inc. 50%, South Korea Haitai 50%	Manufactures and sells potato snack confectionery of Calbee in South Korea
• Securing Resources	May 10, 2011	Nikkei page 11	Mitsubishi Gas Chemical/Sojitsu Corporationtotal 37%, Saudi Arabia Sahara Petrochemical Company 48%, other local firms 15%	Paint raw materials cheaper production, export sales in Saudi Arabia
• Cost Sharing	April 28, 2011	Nikkei page 15	Itochu Corp. 20%, UK Suez, Australia Construction companies 80%	Construction and operation of waste treatment power generation facilities in UK
• Securing Resources	April 27, 2011	Nikkei page 1	Asahi Kasei Group 50%, Saudi Arabia SABIC 50%	Resin raw materials cheaper production, export sales in Saudi Arabia
• Facility Sharing	April 26, 2011	Nikkei page 13	Sony 50%, South Korea Samsung 50%	Liquid crystal panel production and supply to Sony. JV marked profit. Follow-up story about existing JV's business

Type of synergy	Date of article	News-paper	JV partners	Notes
• Securing Resources • Cost Sharing	April 26, 2011	Nikkei page 11	Itochu Corp. 32.5%, Japan Petroleum Exploration Co., Ltd. 32.5%, Marubeni Corp. 20%, Inpex Corporation 10%, Itochu Corp. subsidiary 5%	Russia/Far East LNG development
• Collaborative R&D	April 20, 2011	Nikkei page 13	The Fuji Media Holdings Group. subsidiary 71%, Japan IBM 19%, Nishinippon Computer Co., Ltd. 10%	Broadcasting industry cloud computing (For earthquake measures)
• Technology Introduction	April 20, 2011	Nikkei page 1	Toshiba 12%, US NRG 88%	Nuclear-related JV, Expansion plan truncation at the impact of the big earthquake
• Technology Introduction	April 19, 2011	Nikkei page 11	Taiwan TPV Technology Ltd. 70%, Netherlands Royal Philips 30%	Established JV for transfer of TV business of Royal Philips, Royal Philips may withdraw from this business
• Technology Introduction	April 19, 2011	Nikkei page 1	DMG Mori Seiki Co., Ltd., Germany Gildemeister AG, China Shenyang Machine Tool (Group) Co., Ltd., 1/3 each	Small machine tool production and sales in China
• Collaborative R&D	April 15, 2011	Nikkei page 10	Sharp 50%, Lixil 50%	Development of housing equipment, production, sale
• Collaborative R&D	April 14, 2011	Nikkei page 1	Sharp 50%, Lixil 50%	Development of housing equipment, production, sale
• Collaboration in lieu of Competition	April 11, 2011	Nikkei page 15	Mitsui Engineering & Shipbuilding Co., Ltd., JFE, JGC Corporation, Yokogawa Electric Corporation etc. Solar thermal power generation plant-related 10 companies (no detailed reference about shareholding ratio)	To form a consortium with the aim of co-order takings for solar thermal power generation construction
• Cost Sharing	April 8, 2011	Nikkei page 13	Nippon Yusen Kabushiki Kaisha 50%, Thailand Petroleum Corporation and companies under the umbrella 50%	Nippon Yusen to purchase tankers and enter a charter contract for 10 years
• Technology Introduction • Cost Sharing	April 5, 2011	Nikkei page 12	Mitsui & Co., Ltd. max. 30%, Malaysia SDP and TNB (balance) (no detailed reference about shareholding ratio)	Mitsui & Co., Ltd. provides technology introduction and financial support for the biogas power generation business in Malaysia

Type of synergy	Date of article	News-paper	JV partners	Notes
• Collaboration in lieu of Competition	February 23, 2011	Nikkei page 13	Kodansha Ltd., two medium-sized bookstore companies (no detailed reference about shareholding ratio)	Business partnership of stability purchase of selling books
• Technology Introduction • Cost Sharing	February 19, 2011	Nikkei page 12	Aluminum-related firms and Japanese government 59%, Indonesia government 41%	Aluminum smelting plant and power plant in Indonesia
• Securing Resources • Technology Introduction	February 4, 2011	Nikkei page 11	Mitsui & Co., Ltd. 15%, Mitsubishi Rayon Co., Ltd. 5%, Saudi Arabia Saudi Arabian Basic Industries Corporation 50%	Cheap stable production source secure acrylic resin raw materials at Saudi Arabia petro-chemical plant
• Facility Sharing • Collaborative R&D	January 30, 2011	Nikkei page 7	NEC 49%, Lenovo Corporation 51%	PC contract manufacturing, tablet joint R&D
• Utilization of Sales Channels	January 28, 2011	Nikkei page 7	Tokio Marine & Nichido Fire Insurance Co., Ltd. 35%, Malaysia Hong Leong Bank 65%	Islamic finance business. Tokio Marine & Nichido Fire Insurance Co., Ltd. sells its shares to Mitsui Sumitomo Insurance Co., Ltd. and withdraws from the JV relationship.
• Facility Sharing • Collaborative R&D	January 28, 2011	Nikkei page 3	NEC 49%, Lenovo Corporation 51%	PC contract manufacturing, tablet joint R&D
• Facility Sharing • Collaborative R&D	January 26, 2011	Nikkei page 10	NEC 49%, Lenovo Corporation 51%	PC contract manufacturing, tablet joint R&D
• Utilization of Sales Channels • Collaborative R&D	January 25, 2011	Nikkei page 11	Kirin Holdings Company, Ltd. 40%, China Resource Enterprise, Ltd. 60%	Soft drink joint R&D, manufacturing and sales in China
• Collaborative R&D	January 25, 2011	Nikkei page 11	Toray Industries, Inc. 50.1%, Daimler-Benz AG 44.9%, local carbon-related firms 5%	Manufacturing and sales of carbon fiber auto parts in Germany
• Utilization of Sales Channels • Collaborative R&D	January 24, 2011	Nikkei page 1	Kirin Holdings Company, Ltd., China Resource Enterprise, Ltd. (no detailed reference about shareholding ratio)	Soft drink joint R&D, manufacturing and sales in China
• Securing Resources	January 22, 2011	Nikkei page 1	Mitsubishi Corporation 75%, South Korea KOGAS (Korea Gas Corporation 25%	LNG production in Indonesia. Purpose is stable procurement
• Facility Sharing • Collaborative R&D	January 21, 2011	Nikkei pages 1, 9	NEC 49%, Lenovo Corporation 51%	PC contract manufacturing, tablet joint R&D under negotiation

Type of synergy	Date of article	News-paper	JV partners	Notes
• Utilization of Sales Channels	January 18, 2011	Nikkei page 13	Idemitsu Kosan Co., Ltd. 60%, Tokai Bussan Co., Ltd 40%	Joint marketing of pesticide materials
• Utilization of Sales Channels	December 23, 2010	Nikkei page 12	Fujitsu Ltd. 80%, Toshiba 20%	Mobile phone handset sales JV partnership to be broken off, to be a wholly owned subsidiary of Fujitsu Ltd.
• Utilization of Sales Channels • Facility Sharing	December 22, 2010	Nikkei page 9	Toppan Printing Co., Ltd. 51%, Taiwan AU Optronics Corp. 49%	Liquid crystal filter production
• Utilization of Sales Channels	December 22, 2010	Nikkei page 11	Hitachi Metals, Ltd (majority), US rare earth mining company Molycorp (balance) (no detailed reference about shareholding ratio)	The production of magnet alloy from rare earth produced by US Molycorp
• Cost Sharing	December 20, 2010	Nikkei page 1	Itochu Corp. 30%, Italy Abengoa Solar 70%	Solar thermal power plant construction, operation in southern Spain
• Utilization of Sales Channels • Technology Introduction	December 17, 2010	Nikkei page 13	Honda Group 26%, India Hero Group and others (balance) (no detailed reference about shareholding ratio)	Motorcycle production and sales JV in India. Honda will withdraw from the JV relationship to sell its shares to Indian partners. Follow-up story about existing JV's business
• Utilization of Sales Channels	December 17, 2010	Nikkei page 15	Thailand JV Co. (Sumitomo Electric Industries, Ltd. 70%, South Korea Hyosung Corp. 30%), Chinese JV Co. (Sumitomo Electric Industries, Ltd. 30%, South Korea Hyosung Corp. 70%)	Supply of tire reinforcement JVs in Thailand and China
• Collaboration in lieu of Competition • Cost Sharing	December 14, 2010	Nikkei page 11	SoftBank Corp., AP and the five overseas companies union 1/3 each	Next-generation PHS business (total investment 100 billion yen)
• Collaborative R&D	December 14, 2010	Nikkei page 1	Nissan Motor Corp., Mitsubishi Motors Corporation (no detailed reference about shareholding ratio)	Joint R&D of light car technology
• Utilization of Sales Channels	December 1, 2010	Nikkei page 13	Amada Co,. Ltd. 60%, Aida Engineering, Ltd. 40%	Joint sales of small and medium-sized press
• Utilization of Sales Channels • Cost Sharing	November 30, 2010	Nikkei page 1	Mazda Motor Corporation, Sumitomo Corporation (no detailed reference about shareholding ratio)	JV for passenger car plant construction in Mexico, to leave Ford Motor Company strategy

Type of synergy	Date of article	News-paper	JV partners	Notes
• Collaborative R&D	November 26, 2010	Nikkei page 11	Showa Denko K.K. 51%, Air Water Inc. 49%	Special gas production, technology development
• Cost Sharing	November 25, 2010	Nikkei page 11	Sumitomo Corporation 49.9%, French local firms 50.1%	Construction and operation of solar power plant (14 billion yen) in southern France
• Cost Sharing	November 11, 2010	Nikkei page 9	30 Japanese small and medium-sized confectionery-making companies	30 Japanese small and medium-sized confectionery-making companies jointly advance into China to export Japanese confectionary to China. Mutual Aid Society consortium
• Collaborative R&D	October 26, 2010	Nikkei page 11	NSK Ltd. 51%, Toshiba 49%	Joint R&D of electric power steering
• Securing Resources	October 8, 2010	Nikkei page 13	Toyota Tsusho Corporation 50%, Taiwan Fiber Manufacturers 50%	Production of bio-polyester and securing the supply of automotive parts to Toyota
• Utilization of Sales Channels	October 5, 2010	Nikkei page 1	CCC Co., Ltd. 51%, Sharp 49%	Multi-function terminal content delivery
• Utilization of Sales Channels • Technology Introduction	September 30, 2010	Nikkei page 1	Shin Nippon Steel 49%, India Tata Group 51%	Production of automotive cold-rolled steel sheet in India
• Utilization of Sales Channels • Facility Sharing	July 16, 2010	Nikkei page 9	Kureha Corporation (majority), Itochu Corp. (balance) (no detailed reference about shareholding ratio)	Manufacture and sale of lithium-ion batteries in US
• Utilization of Sales Channels	July 14, 2010	Nikkei page 9	Ministop Co., Ltd. 51%, CFS Corporation 30%, Takiya Co., Ltd. 19%	Store that combines convenience and drug stores
• Utilization of Sales Channels	July 2, 2010	Nikkei page 11	Mitsui & Co., Ltd. 50%, US Dow Chemical Company 50%	To differentiate salt to produce chemical raw materials in US
• Technology Introduction	July 2, 2010	Nikkei page 4	Sumitomo Mitsui Banking Corporation 50.1%, UK Barclays PLC subsidiary 49.9%	Introduction of Barclays' business tool for wealthy class of Barclays
• Technology Introduction	June 30, 2010	Nikkei page 1	JX Group, Vietnam state-owned energy company (no detailed reference about shareholding ratio)	JX's technology licensing to Thailand
• Utilization of Sales Channels	June 18, 2010	Nikkei page 12	Furukawa Electric Co., Ltd. 80%→100%, US Lear Corporation 20%→0%	JV partnership to be broken off, to be a wholly owned subsidiary of Furukawa.

Type of synergy	Date of article	News-paper	JV partners	Notes
• Utilization of Sales Channels	June 17, 2010	Nikkei page 9	Fujitsu Ltd. (majority), Toshiba (balance) (no detailed reference about shareholding ratio)	Mobile phone business integration
• Technology Introduction	June 14, 2010	Nikkei page 3	South Korea Hyundai Heavy Industries 80%, China Datang Shandong Power Generation Co., Ltd. 20%	Production of wind turbines in China
• Utilization of Sales Channels	June 12, 2010	Nikkei page 11	Fujitsu Ltd. (majority), Toshiba (balance) (no detailed reference about shareholding ratio)	Mobile phone business integration
• Utilization of Sales Channels	June 12, 2010	Nikkei page 12	Sanyo Electric Co., Ltd. 50%, Nippon Oil Corporation 50%	Manufacturing of thin film photovoltaic. However, commercial production postponed from profitability. Follow-up story about existing JV's business
• Utilization of Sales Channels	June 11, 2010	Nikkei page 9	Fujitsu Ltd. (majority), Toshiba (balance) (no detailed reference about shareholding ratio)	Mobile phone business integration
• Cost Sharing	May 29, 2010	Nikkei page 11	Daikyo Incorporated, J Will Partners (no detailed reference about shareholding ratio)	Fund LLC for Anabuki construction relief
• Utilization of Sales Channels	May 27, 2010	Nikkei page 1	Nichi-Iko Pharmaceutical Company, Ltd. 49%, French Pharmaceutical company Sanofi Group 51%	Leveraged by the sales channels of Nichi-Iko, sales of generic drugs in Japan
• Facility Sharing	May 25, 2010	Nikkei page 3	Onkyo Corporation, Taiwan Inventec Corporation (no detailed reference about shareholding ratio)	The construction and operation of speaker production plant in Tianjin China
• Utilization of Sales Channels	May 18, 2010	Nikkei page 3	Shin Nippon Steel, Luxembourg Ternium (no detailed reference about shareholding ratio)	Production of automotive steel sheets in Mexico
• Collaborative R&D	May 14, 2010	Nikkei page 1	Organo Corporation 50%, US Graver Water Systems, LLC 50%	Technology joint R&D and manufacturer of water treatment systems in US

Type of synergy	Date of article	News-paper	JV partners	Notes
• Utilization of Sales Channels	May 7, 2010	Nikkei page 7	French Peugeot, China Changan Automobile (no detailed reference about shareholding ratio)	Manufacture and sale of passenger cars and light commercial vehicles in China
• Collaborative R&D	April 28, 2010	Nikkei page 1	Toray Industries, Inc., Daimler-Benz AG, (no detailed reference about shareholding ratio) to be negotiated in due course	R&D of carbon fiber auto parts
• Collaborative R&D	April 26, 2010	Nikkei page 1	Toshiba, IHI (no detailed reference about shareholding ratio)	Production technology development of nuclear power plant equipment (large turbine)
• Utilization of Sales Channels	April 19, 2010	Nikkei page 3	NTN, China Luoyang LYC Bearing Co., Ltd. (no detailed reference about shareholding ratio)	Manufacture and sale of automotive parts (bearings) in China
• Alleviation of Friction	April 7, 2010	Nikkei page 3	NUMMI (Toyota 50%, GM 50%)	NUMMI eliminate negotiations. Follow-up story about existing JV's business
• Securing Resources	April 7, 2010	Nikkei page 3	Qatar Petroleum, Cosmo Oil Co., Ltd., Idemitsu Kosan Co., Ltd. other 4 Japanese firms, US firm , French firm (no detailed reference about shareholding ratio)	Refinery in oil plant features in Qatar
• Alleviation of Friction • Utilization of Sales Channels	April 1, 2010	Nikkei page 1	Tokio Marine & Nichido Fire Insurance Co., Ltd. 28.75%, Saudi Arabia Alinma Bank 28.75%, local government agencies (balance)	Sale of Islamic insurance (Takaful)
• Utilization of Sales Channels	March 30, 2010	Nikkei page 1	Hitachi Construction Machinery Co., Ltd. 40%→60%, Tata Motors Ltd. 60% →40%	Production and sales of construction machinery (hydraulic excavator) in India
• Collaborative R&D	March 30, 2010	Nikkei page 13	Toyota 60%→80.5%, Panasonic 40% →19.5%	Battery production for hybrid vehicles
• Securing Resources	March 25, 2010	Nikkei page 9	Toshiba 60%, UK Westinghouse 40%	Uranium sales
• Collaborative R&D	February 25, 2010	Nikkei page 1	Fuji Electric Co., Ltd. (majority), GE (balance) (no detailed reference about shareholding ratio)	Next-generation power grid (smart grid) development, production

Type of synergy	Date of article	News-paper	JV partners	Notes
• Technology Introduction	February 22, 2010	Nikkei page 16	Daikin Industries, Ltd., China Zhu hai Gree Corporation (no detailed reference about shareholding ratio)	Air conditioning of key parts production plant in China
• Utilization of Sales Channels • Cost Sharing	February 19, 2010	Nikkei page 9	Sojitsu Corporation 21.6%, Sao Paulo ETH, Inc. and other firms (balance) (no detailed reference about shareholding ratio)	Production plant construction and operation of sugar cane-derived bio-ethanol
• Collaborative R&D	February 4, 2010	Nikkei page 1	Mitsubishi Corporation, Ebara Corporation, JGC Corporation 1/3each	Integrated business such as construction of water facilities, operations, seawater desalination plant to management
• Utilization of Sales Channels • Technology Introduction	January 29, 2010	Nikkei page 13	Shin Nippon Steel 49%, India Tata Group 51%	Production of automotive cold-rolled steel sheet in India
• Collaborative R&D • Utilization of Sales Channels	January 29, 2010	Nikkei page 1	Aeon group of companies, Mitsubishi Corporation (no detailed reference about shareholding ratio)	Joint R&D of private brand pharmaceutical products, management of drugstore chain
• Brand Introduction • Technology Introduction	January 28, 2010	Nikkei page 13	Rakuten, Inc. 51%, China Baidu, Inc. 49%	E-commerce business in China
• Utilization of Sales Channels	December 16, 2009	Nikkei page 11	KDDI 34%, Olympus Corporation subsidiary 15%, Vietnam FIS 51%	IT management contractor of Japanese firms in Vietnam
• Utilization of Sales Channels	December 5, 2009	Nikkei page 11	GM 50%, China Shanghai Automotive Industry Corporation 50%	Production base to backup of business of GM in India, using sales channels of GM
• Utilization of Sales Channels	December 1, 2009	Nikkei page 3	GE 80%, French Media VIV.PA 20%	Withdrawal resolved by selling JV Co NBCU in US to Comcast Corporation
• Alleviation of Friction • Utilization of Sales Channels	November 20, 2009	Nikkei page 1	Tokio Marine & Nichido Fire Insurance Co., Ltd. 26% (Foreign Investors' upper limit), India Edelweiss Financial Services Ltd 74%	Foray into life insurance market in India
• Collaborative R&D	October 16, 2009	Nikkei page 13	NEC 44%→50%, Panasonic 44%→50%, US semiconductor TI 12%→0%	Semiconductor development for mobile phones. TI withdraws from JV

Type of synergy	Date of article	News-paper	JV partners	Notes
• Brand Introduction	October 1, 2009	Nikkei page 9	China Hangzhou Wahaha Group Co., Ltd. 49%,→100%, French Groupe Danone 51%→0%	The Danone brand products sales JV in China. Since Wahaha was arbitrarily using the Wahaha brand instead of Danone, Danone decided on withdrawal from JV
• Alleviation of Friction	September 26, 2009	Nikkei page 11	NUMMI (Toyota 50%, GM 50%)	NUMMI eliminate negotiations. Follow-up story about existing JV's business
• Utilization of Sales Channels	July 18, 2009	Nikkei page 13	Yamada-Denki Company, Ltd., Housing improvement West Holdings Corporation (no detailed reference about shareholding ratio)	Solar power, design and construction, all-electric construction
• Securing Resources	July 2, 2009	Nikkei page 13	Sapporo Breweries Ltd. 90%, Nagano Ikeda municipality 10%	Agricultural production corporation, Production of domestic grapes for stable supply to local winery
• Collaborative R&D • Cost Sharing	July 2, 2009	Nikkei page 13	Astellas Pharma Inc.17%, US pharmaceutical Maxygen, Inc. 83%	Joint R&D of new drugs by protein improvement
• Alleviation of Friction	June 30, 2009	Nikkei pages 1, 3	NUMMI (Toyota 50%, GM 50%)	NUMMI eliminate negotiations. Follow-up story about existing JV's business
• Technology Introduction	June 24, 2009	Nikkei pages 1, 11	Showa Shell Sekiyu K.K., Saudi Aramco (no detailed reference about shareholding ratio)	To build many small-scale solar power plants and to operate in Saudi Arabia
• Facility Sharing	June 22, 2009	Nikkei page 1	IHI 50%, JFE 50%	JV for the shield excavator business integration
• Cost Sharing	June 19, 2009	Nikkei page 1	JTB, Kinki Nippon Tourist Co., Ltd., Nippon Travel Agency Co., Ltd. etc. LLP (no detailed reference about shareholding ratio)	Joint charter flights operated abroad
• Securing Resources	June 13, 2009	Nikkei page 9	Japan Tobacco Inc., UK leaf tobacco supplier Tribac Leaf (no detailed reference about shareholding ratio)	Secure raw materials procurement for leaf tobacco
• Utilization of Sales Channels	May 7, 2009	Nikkei page 1	Cosmo Oil Co., Ltd. 50%, South Korea Hyundai Oilbank 50%	Petrochemical manufacturing and sales in China

Type of synergy	Date of article	News-paper	JV partners	Notes
• Facility Sharing	April 29, 2009	Nikkei page 11	Toshiba, J-Devices Corporation, US Amkor Technology Inc. (no detailed reference about shareholding ratio)	Consignment of the second process of manufacturing of large-scale integrated circuit
• Utilization of Sales Channels	April 23, 2009	Nikkei page 9	Furukawa Electric Co., Ltd. 20%→80%, US Lear Corporation 80%→20%	Manufacture and sale of automotive parts harness. Furukawa increases share ratio in JV to make it its subsidiary
• Technology Introduction	April 17, 2009	Nikkei page 9	Furukawa Electric Co., Ltd. 45%, India Universal Cables Ltd. 55%	Production and sales of optical fiber
• Utilization of Sales Channels	April 16, 2009	Nikkei page 11	Kadokawa Group Holdings, Inc. 51%, Senshukai Co., Ltd. 49%	Mail order sales of Kadokawa commodity through network of Senshukai
• Securing Resources	April 14, 2009	Nikkei page 1	Sumitomo Metal Industries, Ltd. 30% →40%, India Medium-sized steel makers (majority)	Blast furnace steel plant (200 billion yen to 300 billion yen investment)
• Collaborative R&D	April 11, 2009	Nikkei page 9	Teijin Ltd. 50%, US Cargill, Inc. 50%	Plant-material-resin production plants
• Securing Resources	April 10, 2009	Nikkei page 9	Indonesia metal mining company PT Antam (majority), Showa Denko K.K, Marubeni Corp. (balance) (no detailed reference about shareholding ratio)	Alumina and other ore raw materials production
• Facility Sharing	March 28, 2009	Nikkei page 1	Toshiba, Panasonic (no detailed reference about shareholding ratio)	Small and medium-sized liquid crystal display business JV partnership to be broken off, to be a wholly owned subsidiary of Toshiba
• Facility Sharing	March 28, 2009	Nikkei page 1	Toshiba, Fujifilm Corporation (no detailed reference about shareholding ratio)	Endoscope business JV partnership to be broken off, to be a wholly owned subsidiary of Fujifilm Corporation. Toshiba withdraws from JV
• Facility Sharing • Collaborative R&D	February 11, 2009	Nikkei page 11	Kowa Company, Ltd. 50%, Teva Pharmaceutical Industries Ltd. (Israel) 50%	R&D and production of generic drugs
• Facility Sharing	January 30, 2009	Nikkei page 11	Yokogawa Bridge Corporation 60%, Sumitomo Metal Industries, Ltd. 40%	Bridge business integration

Type of synergy	Date of article	News-paper	JV partners	Notes
● Facility Sharing	January 30, 2009	Nikkei page 11	Sharp 66%, Sony 34%	Liquid crystal panel business JV to be established one year postponement. Follow-up story about existing JV's business
● Utilization of Sales Channels	January 24, 2009	Nikkei page 12	Sanyo Electric Co., Ltd. 50%, Nippon Oil Corporation 50%	Manufacturing of thin film photovoltaic. However, commercial production postponed from profitability. Follow-up story about existing JV's business
● Utilization of Sales Channels	January 15, 2009	Nikkei page 11	Sanyo Electric Co., Ltd. 50%, Nippon Oil Corporation 50%	Manufacturing of thin film photovoltaic
● Utilization of Sales Channels	December 5, 2008	Nikkei page 13	Toyota Boshoku Corporation, US Lear Corporation (no detailed reference about shareholding ratio)	Manufacture and sale of car seat in North America. JV partnership to be broken off, to be a wholly owned subsidiary of Toyota
● Facility Sharing	November 28, 2008	Nikkei page 11	Elpida Memory (Micron) 48.8% →52%, Taiwan Powerchip Technology Corp. (balance)	The production of DRAM at a low-cost JV partnership to be broken off, to be a wholly owned subsidiary of Elpida Memory
● Securing Resources	November 28, 2008	Nikkei page 3	JFE approx. 40%, Middle East government-owned Investment firm subsidiary Foulath (balance)	To secure procurement route in Middle East, other than major iron ore resources supplier
● Technology Introduction	November 27, 2008	Nikkei page 1	Sharp, Italy Enel SpA, European machinery manufacturers (no detailed reference about shareholding ratio)	Construction and operation of solar cell manufacturing plant in Italy
● Technology Introduction	November 19, 2008	Nikkei page 13	Sojitsu Corporation 50%, Dubai ETA Star Group 50%	The line maintenance of business aircraft in Dubai and Middle East area, using the know-how of Sojitsu Corporation
● Brand Introduction	October 21, 2008	Nikkei page 15	Masuya Co., Ltd. 70%, Orix Group subsidiary in Singapore 20%, MOS Food Services, Inc. 10%	Mos Burger store development in Indonesia, aiming also into neighboring countries
● Utilization of Sales Channels ● Brand Introduction	October 3, 2008	Nikkei page 12	Asahi Breweries, Ltd. 50%, Taiwan general trading company Mercuries & Associates, Ltd. 50%	Soft drink and beer manufacturing sales in Taiwan
● Utilization of Sales Channels	October 1, 2008	Nikkei page 11	Sanyo Electric Co., Ltd. 50%, Nippon Oil Corporation 50%	Manufacturing of thin film photovoltaic

Type of synergy	Date of article	News-paper	JV partners	Notes
● Collaborative R&D ● Cost Sharing	October 1, 2008	Nikkei page 11	Showa Denko K.K. 75%, Hoya Corporation 25%	Hard disk business integration
● Utilization of Sales Channels ● Brand Introduction	September 27, 2008	Nikkei page 15	Kikkoman Corporation 45%, Taiwan Uni-President Enterprises Corporation 45%, Others 10%	The production and sales of soy sauce and vinegar under Kikkoman brand
● Utilization of Sales Channels	September 24, 2008	Nikkei page 1	Fujitsu Ltd. 50% →100%, Germany Siemens AG 50%→0%	PC server business in Europe JV partnership to be broken off, to be a wholly owned subsidiary of Fujitsu Ltd.
● Securing Resources	September 24, 2008	Nikkei page 9	Itochu Corp. 20%, Brazil bioethanol companies 80%	Production and sales of bioethanol as gasoline alternative energy, securing bioethanol resources for Japan, Europe and US
● Facility Sharing ● Collaborative R&D	September 23, 2008	Nikkei page 1	Kowa Company, Ltd. 50%, Teva Pharmaceutical Industries Ltd. (Israel) 50%	R&D and production of generic drugs
● Facility Sharing ● Collaborative R&D	July 30, 2008	Nikkei page 15	Pekker-Seiko K.K. 25%, Gifutadaseiki Co., Ltd. 25%, K.K. Seiko Mold 25%, Nihon Choken Kogyo Co., Ltd. 25%	Share of order information, joint purchasing of tools, plant operating conditions, production in consideration of the holdings technology plan, joint R&D
● Utilization of Sales Channels	July 29, 2008	Nikkei page 1	Sony 50%→100%, Germany music software company Bertelsmann AG 50%→0%	Music software JV partnership to be broken off, to be a wholly owned subsidiary of Sony
● Utilization of Sales Channels	July 26, 2008	Nikkei page 4	Mitsubishi UFJ Financial Group, Inc. 50%→51%, US Merrill Lynch & Co., Inc. 50%→49%	Securities company for wealthy class, the JV to be consolidated subsidiary of Mitsubishi UFJ
● Cost Sharing	July 8, 2008	Nikkei page 13	Itochu Corp. 25%, Sony 25%, Tohoku News K.K. 25%, US News Corporation 25%	Stars Channel (CATV) business
● Alleviation of Friction ● Utilization of Sales Channels	July 4, 2008	Nikkei page 1	Sumitomo Corporation 40%, Sekisui Chemical Company, Ltd. 30%, Russia Sewer construction company VKS 30%	Water pipe infrastructure construction in Russia, using Sekisui know-how
● Collaborative R&D	June 21, 2008	Nikkei page 11	NEC Electronics, Elpida Memory (Micron) (no detailed reference about shareholding ratio)	IC drive development and sales

Type of synergy	Date of article	News-paper	JV partners	Notes
• Utilization of Sales Channels • Brand Introduction	May 29, 2008	Nikkei page 15	Otsuka Pharmaceutical Co., Ltd. 49%, French Investment firm 51%	Capital participation in the French drinks company to make it JV company, aiming to enter into European drinks market
• Utilization of Sales Channels	May 29, 2008	Nikkei page 15	M3, Inc. 30%, Germany local firms (balance)	Drug information service on Web to pharmaceutical manufacturers and physicians to support their sales activities in Germany
• Utilization of Sales Channels • Brand Introduction	May 28, 2008	Nikkei page 15	Otsuka Pharmaceutical Co., Ltd. 49%, French investment firm 51%	Capital participation in the French drinks company to make it JV company, aiming to enter into European drinks market
• Collaborative R&D	May 28, 2008	Nikkei page 13	Toyota 60%, Panasonic 40%	Hybrid car battery R&D
• Securing Resources • Cost Sharing	May 6, 2008	Nikkei page 1	Qatar Petroleum, Cosmo Oil Co., Ltd., Idemitsu Kosan Co., Ltd., 4 other Japanese firms, US firm, French firm (no detailed reference about shareholding ratio)	Refineries, oil plant features in Qatar
• Utilization of Sales Channels	April 17, 2008	Nikkei page 11	Shin Nippon Steel 50%, Luxembourg Arcelor Mittal 50%	Production of iron plate for cars for Japanese automotive factories in North America such as Toyota Nissan
• Collaboration in lieu of Competition • Collaborative R&D	April 1, 2008	Nikkei page 18	8 medium-sized audit firms LLC (no detailed reference about shareholding ratio)	Joint research in the audit system, creating tools and their sales promotion
• Utilization of Sales Channels	April 1, 2008	Nikkei page 15	Sumitomo Forestry Co., Ltd. 50%, Australia Housing construction firms 50%	Australia housing construction business
• Utilization of Sales Channels	February 26, 2008	Nikkei page 1	Nippon Sheet Glass Company, Ltd. 50%, Hoya Corporation 50%	Manufacture and sale of plate glass for liquid crystal television in US. The acquisition plan of this JV (more than 100 billion yen) by the Carlyle Group is announced
• Technology Introduction	February 19, 2008	Nikkei page 12	Asahi Breweries, Ltd. 30%, Marubeni Corp. 30%, China Regal Wine Co. 40%	Wine production and sales. Asahi offer of wine production technology and marketing know-how
• Technology Introduction	February 16, 2008	Nikkei page 11	Nippon Oil Corporation 49%, UAE urban development company Al Qudra Holdings 51%	Manufacturing a concrete alternative product by using the petroleum products, and sold as building material in water and sewerage port facilities
• Utilization of Sales Channels	February 5, 2008	Nikkei page 12	Asatsu-DK Inc. 50%, UK advertising WPP 50%	Advertising service for Japanese firms in India

Type of synergy	Date of article	News-paper	JV partners	Notes
• Technology Introduction	January 26, 2008	Nikkei page 11	Sanyo Electric Co., Ltd. 81%, Taiwan Quanta Computer Inc. 19%	Development and manufacture of liquid crystal TV in Taiwan
• Facility Sharing	January 23, 2008	Nikkei page 1	Netherlands Koninklijke Philips N.V. 19.9%, South Korea LG Electronics Inc. 80.1%	Production of liquid crystal panel for its own TV production. Secure cheap stable procurement raw materials. Philips will withdraw from JV by selling its shares
• Utilization of Sales Channels	January 22, 2008	Nikkei page 1	Dentsu Inc. 67%, Hong Kong Focus Media (China) Holding 33%	Internet advertising business in China
• Collaborative R&D	January 22, 2008	Nikkei page 15	Idemitsu Kosan Co., Ltd., Kanematsu Corporation, total 11 companies (no detailed reference about shareholding ratio)	Production of gas with methane main component from gas generated from plant sludge, garbage.
• Utilization of Sales Channels	January 12, 2008	Nikkei page 9	Nissan 25%, Renault 25%, India mid-sized automobile manufacturers Mahindra & Mahindra Ltd. 50%	Passenger car production and sales in India. Dueto Mahindra intends to withdraw from JV, it will be JV between Nissan and Renault
• Collaborative R&D	January 12, 2008	Nikkei page 4	Tokyo Stock Exchange, Inc., London Stock Exchange (no detailed reference about shareholding ratio)	Establishment of professional stock exchange
• Utilization of Sales Channels • Cost Sharing	December 27, 2007	Nikkei page 9	Taiyo Nippon Sanso Corporation 51%, Air Water Inc. 49%	Production and sales of industrial gases that are indispensable to liquid crystal panel production
• Brand Introduction	December 21, 2007	Nikkei page 14	Tomy Company, Ltd. 55%, Toyo Shinyaku Co., Ltd. 45%	Health food sales Tomy to license the characters in these goods
• Facility Sharing	December 21, 2007	Nikkei page 1	Toshiba 15%→0%, Panasonic Group 30% →increase, Hitachi Displays, Ltd. 50%	Manufacturing of liquid crystal display for its own TV manufacturing plant. Toshiba is to withdraw from JV, and to enter business alliance with competitor maker Sharp
• Facility Sharing	December 21, 2007	Nikkei page 1	Toshiba 16%, Panasonic Group 32% →increase, Hitachi Displays, Ltd. 50%	Manufacturing of liquid crystal display for its own TV manufacturing plant
• Facility Sharing	November 27, 2007	Nikkei page 11	Japan Tobacco Inc. 51%, Nissin Food Products Co., Ltd. 49%	To leverage frozen food business by takeover Katokichi Foods K.K. to be a JV
• Technology Introduction	November 22, 2007	Nikkei page 13	Kobe Steel, Ltd. 19.05%, US Electric furnace Steel Dynamics, Inc. (SDI) 80.95%	Construction management of ironworks to implement technology of Kobe Steel to produce high-quality steel in low-grade raw materials

Type of synergy	Date of article	News-paper	JV partners	Notes
• Facility Sharing	November 20, 2007	Nikkei page 1	Japan Tobacco Inc. 51%, Nissin Food Products Co., Ltd. 49%	To leverage frozen food business by takeover Katokichi Foods K.K. to be a JV
• Utilization of Sales Channels	November 15, 2007	Nikkei page 11	Japan Post Holdings Co., Ltd. 51%, Nippon Express Co., Ltd. 49%	Door-to-door logistics service
• Collaborative R&D • Utilization of Sales Channels	November 15, 2007	Nikkei page 11	Sony 50%, Netherlands NXP 50%	Non-contact IC business for mobile phones. Compatibility expansion in Europe
• Utilization of Sales Channels • Technology Introduction	November 14, 2007	Nikkei page 11	Shin Nippon Steel (minority), India Tata Group (majority) (no detailed reference about shareholding ratio)	Production of automotive cold-rolled steel sheet in India
• Securing Resources	October 18, 2007	Nikkei page 11	Taiyo Nippon Sanso Corporation 50%, US Air Products and Chemicals, Inc. 50%	Establishment of purification and liquefaction plant of helium gas, production and sales. Taiyo Nippon Sanso aims to have its own production base as stable source
• Utilization of Sales Channels	October 17, 2007	Nikkei page 12	Electronics stores Best Denki Co., Ltd. (majority), Vietnam of consumer electronics wholesale and retailers Bonday-Benthanh (no detailed reference about shareholding ratio)	By Best's operational know-how transfer, aiming at store network expansion in Vietnam
• Brand Introduction	June 30, 2007	Nikkei page 9	Lion Corporation 49% →100%, US Trademark "Bufferin" owner Pharmaceutical BMS 51%→0%	As Lion Corporation has bought trademark "Bufferin" from the owner BMS, becomes unnecessary to maintain JV
• Technology Introduction	June 21, 2007	Nikkei page 11	Kobe Steel, Ltd., US iron ore big Co. Cleveland-Cliffs, Inc. (no detailed reference about shareholding ratio)	Construction management of ironworks to implement technology of Kobe Steel to produce high-quality steel in low-grade raw materials
• Technology Introduction	June 21, 2007	Nikkei page 1	Mitsubishi Heavy Industries, Ltd. 50% →33.4%, US Caterpillar Inc. 50% →66.6%	Mitsubishi will concentrate management assets into the prime mover business
• Technology Introduction	May 17, 2007	Nikkei page 9	Hitachi 80.01%, US GE 19.99%	Nuclear power business sector integration
• Utilization of Sales Channels	April 25, 2007	Nikkei page 13	JTB 50%, South Korea Lotte Co., Ltd. subsidiary Lotte.com. 50%	JTB is to advance into South Korean travel business

Type of synergy	Date of article	News-paper	JV partners	Notes
● Technology Introduction	February 28, 2007	Nikkei page 9	China Petroleum and Chemical Corporation Sinopec 50%, Saudi Aramco 25%, Exxon Mobil Corporation 25%	Production of ethylene and paraxylene, performance up of refineries
● Collaborative R&D ● Utilization of Sales Channels	February 23, 2007	Nikkei page 13	Fuji Electric Co., Ltd. 50%, NGK Insulators, Ltd. 50%	Fuji Electric has know-how in measurement control in the water treatment business, and NGK has know-how in sewage sludge incineration facilities and machinery and equipment
● Utilization of Sales Channels	January 26, 2007	Nikkei page 7	Sony Life Insurance Co., Ltd. 50%, Netherlands Aegon Levensverzekering N.V. 50%	Development of insurance package
● Cost Sharing	January 17, 2007	Nikkei page 3	Nomura Holdings, Inc. 50%, the Development Bank of Japan Inc. 50%	Joint real estate investment (capital maximum 500 billion yen)
● Collaboration in lieu of Competition	December 23, 2006	Nikkei page 11	French Air Liquide 55%→100%, Germany Linden 45%→4%	As requested by European FTC, JV partnership to be broken off, to be a wholly owned subsidiary of Air Liquide
● Securing Resources	December 22, 2006	Nikkei page 13	Mitsubishi Gas Chemical 24%, Mitsubishi Corporation 24%, Venezuela petrochemical corporation Pequiven approx. 37%, others balance (no detailed reference about shareholding ratio)	New production plant of methanol production capacity world first class (47 billion yen investment)
● Securing Resources	December 22, 2006	Nikkei pages 1, 3	Shell 55%→20% approx., Mitsui & Co., Ltd. 25%→ 15% approx., Mitsubishi Corporation 20% →10% approx. (Sakhalin 2 Project) (no detailed reference about shareholding ratio)	Follow-up story about existing JV's business. Russian government petroleum company Gazprom proposes conditions to the 3 companies of Sakhalin 2 Project for transfer of majority shares in JV
● Collaborative R&D	December 21, 2006	Nikkei pages 1, 15	Nissan below 50%, NEC majority (no detailed reference about shareholding ratio)	Joint R&D of battery for environment-friendly vehicles

Type of synergy	Date of article	News-paper	JV partners	Notes
● Facility Sharing	December 19, 2006	Nikkei page 13	Hitachi Construction Machinery Co., Ltd. China subsidiary TCM 77.5%, Hitachi Construction Machinery Co., Ltd. 10%, Shinkou Imono K.K. 10%, other local firms	Forklift and other construction equipment production and sales in China
● Securing Resources	December 18, 2006	Nikkei page 1	Shell 55%, Mitsui & Co., Ltd. 25%, Mitsubishi Corporation 20% (Sakhalin 2 Project)	Follow-up story about existing JV's business. Russian government petroleum company Gazprom proposes conditions to the 3 companies of Sakhalin 2 Project for transfer of majority shares in JV
● Securing Resources	December 16, 2006	Nikkei page 11	Shell 55%, Mitsui & Co., Ltd. 25%, Mitsubishi Corporation 20% (Sakhalin 2 Project)	Follow-up story about existing JV's business. Russian government petroleum company Gazprom proposes conditions to the 3 companies of Sakhalin 2 Project for transfer of majority shares in JV
● Brand Introduction	December 15, 2006	Nikkei page 9	Italy Fiat S.p.A. 50%, Tata Motors Ltd. 50%	Automobile production and sales in India
● Utilization of Sales Channels	December 15, 2006	Nikkei page 7	Nikko Asset management Co., Ltd. 74.9%, India Ambit Investment Advisors Private Ltd. 25.1%	Asset management company for individual investors in India
● Technology Introduction	December 14, 2006	Nikkei page 1	Mitsui & Co., Ltd., India a government-based metal resources corporation approx. 50%, each (no detailed reference about shareholding ratio)	Special economic zone infrastructure development projects in India
● Facility Sharing	December 14, 2006	Nikkei page 11	Sanyo Electric Co., Ltd. 45%→0%, Seiko Epson Corporation 55%→100%	Sanyo to withdraw from JV. JV partnership to be broken off, to be a wholly owned subsidiary of Seiko Epson
● Facility Sharing	December 13, 2006	Nikkei page 13	Sojitsu Corporation 49%, Beijing Sanyuan Group 51%	Food wholesale distribution delivery network strengthening in China
● Securing Resources	December 13, 2006	Nikkei page 9	Shell 55%, Mitsui & Co., Ltd. 25%, Mitsubishi Corporation 20% (Sakhalin 2 Project)	Follow-up story about existing JV's business. Russian government petroleum company Gazprom proposes conditions to the 3 companies of Sakhalin 2 Project for transfer of majority shares in JV

Type of synergy	Date of article	News-paper	JV partners	Notes
• Cost Sharing	December 12, 2006	Nikkei page 15	Fujiya Co., Ltd. 35.4%, Mizuho 100%, subsidiary fund Basic Capital Management, Inc. 64.6%	The fund-led business transfer of restaurant business of Fujiya to new JV company for reconstruction
• Securing Resources	December 12, 2006	Nikkei pages 1, 11	Shell 55%, Mitsui & Co., Ltd. 25%, Mitsubishi Corporation 20% (Sakhalin 2 Project)	Follow-up story about existing JV's business. Russian government petroleum company Gazprom proposes conditions to the 3 companies of Sakhalin 2 Project for transfer of majority shares in JV
• Facility Sharing	December 9, 2006	Nikkei page 13	Coil leading co. Toko Inc, 49%, Electronic components Elec Kitakami Co., Ltd. 51%	Coil mold, metal terminal production in China
• Facility Sharing	December 9, 2006	Nikkei page 13	KDDI 49%, Tokyo Electric Power Company 51%	Line construction of optical fiber
• Cost Sharing • Facility Sharing	December 8, 2006	Nikkei page 9	Elpida Memory (Micron) 50%, Taiwan Powerchip Technology Corp. 50%	Construction of DRAM semiconductor new plant (800 billion yen–1 trillion yen) to chase Samsung
• Cost Sharing • Collaborative R&D	December 8, 2006	Nikkei page 13	Sony 36.5%, K.K. Techgate Investment 63.5%	Next-generation panel "FED" technology development
• Cost Sharing • Facility Sharing	December 7, 2006	Nikkei pages 1, 11	Elpida Memory (Micron), Taiwan Powerchip Technology Corp. (no detailed reference about shareholding ratio)	Construction of DRAM semiconductor new plant (800 billion yen–1 trillion yen) to chase Samsung
• Cost Sharing	December 7, 2006	Nikkei page 13	SBI HD 50%, China Tsinghua University 50%	Fund to invest in VB in China
• Utilization of Sales Channels	December 7, 2006	Nikkei page 15	Kobelco Construction Machinery Co., Ltd. 30%, Itochu Corp. 70%	Production and sales of construction machinery (hydraulic excavator) in India
• Cost Sharing	December 5, 2006	Nikkei page 13	Mitsubishi Corporation 50%, the Development Bank of Japan Inc. 50%	VC investment fund, investment in technology development VB
• Collaborative R&D • Utilization of Sales Channels	December 3, 2006	Nikkei page 1	Itochu Corp. 19.2%, US VC MPM Capital 80.8%	Validate business, the safety or effectiveness of the material candidates such as cancer treatment, aiming mainly at Japanese market sales channel promotion

Type of synergy	Date of article	News-paper	JV partners	Notes
• Facility Sharing	December 2, 2006	Nikkei page 9	Shin Nippon Steel, Mittal Steel Company, China Baoshan Iron & Steel Co., Ltd. (no detailed reference about shareholding ratio)	Crude iron production JV (China Shanghai)
• Collaborative R&D	December 2, 2006	Nikkei page 7	UK Lucent Technologies, French ALCATEL (no detailed reference about shareholding ratio)	Internet protocol, communication equipment innovation
• Facility Sharing	November 30, 2006	Nikkei pages 1, 13	Shin Nippon Steel, Mittal Steel Company, China Baoshan Iron & Steel Co., Ltd. (no detailed reference about shareholding ratio)	Crude iron production JV (China Shanghai)
• Collaborative R&D • Utilization of Sales Channels • Cost Sharing	November 30, 2006	Nikkei page 13	NTT Docomo, Inc., Fuji Television Network, Inc., Nippon Broadcasting System Incorporated, Sky Perfect Communications Inc., Itochu Corp. 5 companies 20%, each LLC	Five major companies union in mobile phones broadcasting
• Alleviation of Friction • Utilization of Sales Channels	November 29, 2006	Nikkei page 4	Nippon Life Insurance Company 50%, China electronics manufacturers 50%	Life insurance business sales start in Shanghai
• Collaborative R&D • Utilization of Sales Channels • Cost Sharing	November 29, 2006	Nikkei pages 1, 11	NTT Docomo, Inc., Fuji Television Network, Inc., Nippon Broadcasting System Incorporated, Sky Perfect Communications Inc., Itochu Corp. 5 companies LLC (no detailed reference about shareholding ratio)	Five major companies union in mobile phones broadcasting
• Securing Resources	November 24, 2006	Nikkei page 7	UK BP 49%, Russia national oil company Rosneft 51% (Sakhalin 5)	$700 million oil and natural gas development project of Sakhalin
• Utilization of Sales Channels	November 21, 2006	Nikkei page 13	Mitsui & Co., Ltd. 50%, US Advertising.com 50%	To buy the ad frame from publishers, to subdivide resale as Internet advertising frame

Type of synergy	Date of article	News-paper	JV partners	Notes
• Collaborative R&D	November 21, 2006	Nikkei page 11	Sony, Netherlands Koninklijke Philips N.V. (no detailed reference about shareholding ratio)	Non-contact IC development, such as wallet mobile in Europe and Japan
• Facility Sharing	November 17, 2006	Nikkei page 9	Japan Airlines Co., Ltd. 9.9%, Cathay Pacific Airways 9.9%, Cathay's maintenance co. subsidiary Haeco 50.2%, maintenance co. Taeco 12.0%, others (balance)	Aircraft landing gear maintenance business in Xiamen City, China
• Collaborative R&D • Utilization of Sales Channels	November 16, 2006	Nikkei page 11	Teijin Ltd. 25%, Netherlands Econcern 35%, other Netherlands investment 2 firms (balance)	Joint R&D of European bio-fuel (diesel alternative fuel), production and sales
• Utilization of Sales Channels	November 15, 2006	Nikkei page 15	Itochu Corp. 80%, US gas production companies 20%	ITOCHU to get sales network and natural gas source in US
• Collaborative R&D	November 15, 2006	Nikkei page 15	Mitsubishi Corporation 50%→28%, Mitsubishi Chemical Corporation 50%, universities (balance)	Nanotechnology new materials, joint R&D
• Facility Sharing	November 14, 2006	Nikkei page 11	Hitachi Zosen Corporation 50% →0%, JFE 50% →100%	Follow-up story about existing JV's business. Shipbuilding sector JV partnership to be broken off, to be a wholly owned subsidiary of JFE
• Technology Introduction	November 14, 2006	Nikkei pages 1, 13	Hitachi approx. 80%, US GE approx. 20%	Nuclear power business sector integration
• Facility Sharing	November 12, 2006	Nikkei page 7	Hitachi Zosen Corporation 50% →0%, JFE 50% →100%	Follow-up story about existing JV's business. Shipbuilding sector JV partnership to be broken off, to be a wholly owned subsidiary of JFE
• Facility Sharing	November 11, 2006	Nikkei pages 1, 11	Hitachi Zosen Corporation 50% →0%, JFE 50% →100%	Follow-up story about existing JV's business. Shipbuilding sector JV partnership to be broken off, to be a wholly owned subsidiary of JFE
• Utilization of Sales Channels • Brand Introduction	November 10, 2006	Nikkei page 11	French Renault 49%, India Mahindra & Mahindra Ltd. 51%	Manufacture and sale of Renault brand of passenger cars in India
• Cost Sharing	November 9, 2006	Nikkei page 1	Japan Bank for International Cooperation, Export-Import Banks of Asia countries (no detailed reference about shareholding ratio)	Established a special purpose company (SPC), to issue Export-Import Bank bonds and funding for Asian import and export promotion assistance

Type of synergy	Date of article	News-paper	JV partners	Notes
• Utilization of Sales Channels	November 6, 2006	Nikkei pages 1, 9	SoftBank Corp. 50%, US News Corporation 50%	Provider service to share SNS exchange site in Japanese version
• Securing Resources	November 3, 2006	Nikkei page 9	Indian Oil Corporation 49%, Russia 2 national petroleum corporations 51%	Securing resources of oil and natural gas
• Facility Sharing	October 27, 2006	Nikkei page 12	ShinMaywa Industries, Ltd. 45%, China Chongqing Endurance Industry Stock Co., Ltd. 55%	Manufacture and sale of garbage transport system in Chongqing
• Collaborative R&D • Utilization of Sales Channels	October 27, 2006	Nikkei page 13	Denso Corporation 50%, Germany Robert Bosch GmbH 50%	Development, manufacture and sale of diesel engine exhaust gas purification filter
• Cost Sharing	October 26, 2006	Nikkei page 9	French Groupe Danone, Bangladesh Grameen Bank (no detailed reference about shareholding ratio)	To establish a food aid fund NPO in Bangladesh
• Securing Resources	October 26, 2006	Nikkei page 11	Shell, Mitsui & Co., Ltd., Mitsubishi Corporation (Sakhalin 2 Project) (no detailed reference about shareholding ratio)	Russian government is to seek payment of environmental added tax under the equity ratio to 3 companies of Sakhalin 2 project
• Technology Introduction • Brand Introduction	October 24, 2006	Nikkei page 9	All Nippon Airways 25%, UK InterContinental Hotels Group PLC 74%, JV co. between two 1%	ANA decided to ask the InterContinental Group to strengthen its hotel business using their know-how
• Securing Resources	October 18, 2006	Nikkei page 7	China National Petroleum Corporation 49%, Russia national oil company Rosneft 51%	Oil and natural gas development project
• Technology Introduction • Utilization of Sales Channels	October 17, 2006	Nikkei page 13	Shin Nippon Steel 36.3%→44.7%, Thailand Siam Cement Public Company Ltd 63.7%→55.3%	Plywood manufacturing in Thailand. The effective control by Shin Nippon Steel through its technology.
• Technology Introduction	October 16, 2006	Nikkei page 11	Mitsui & Co., Ltd. 45%, US Clear Channel Communications (CCCO) 55%	Outdoor advertising business by utilizing the know-how of CCCO
• Cost Sharing	October 16, 2006	Nikkei page 9	Marubeni Corp. 40%, Qatar Electricity & Water Company 40%, Qatar Petroleum 20%	Thermal power generation business JV in Qatar
• Utilization of Sales Channels	October 14, 2006	Nikkei page 11	Sony 50%, UK Ericsson 50%	Mobile phone manufacturing and sales

Type of synergy	Date of article	News-paper	JV partners	Notes
• Facility Sharing	October 14, 2006	Nikkei page 11	Tokyo Electric Power Company, Incorporated (TEPCO) 91%, Steam user companies Nippon Shokubai Co., Ltd., Asahi Chemicals Co., Ltd. (balance)	Surplus steam supply business generated by the thermal power plant
• Technology Introduction • Utilization of Sales Channels	October 12, 2006	Nikkei page 13	Mitsui & Co., Ltd. 50%, Israel Aerospace Industries (IAI) 50%	The remodeled Boeing aircraft to cargo planes to enter global sales. IAI has a remodeling technology, Mitsui has a market
• Utilization of Sales Channels	October 9, 2006	Nikkei page 1	Toshiba 0%→20%, South Korea, LG Electronics Inc. and Koninklijke Philips N.V. 100%→80%	LG/Philips 100%, subsidiary in Poland to be a JV by accepting the equity participation of Toshiba. The production and sales of liquid crystal panel in Europe
• Collaborative R&D • Cost Sharing	October 5, 2006	Nikkei page 13	6 Companies (Nippon Oil Corporation, Inpex Corporation, Japan Petroleum Exploration Co., Ltd., Cosmo Oil Co., Ltd., Nippon Steel & Sumikin Engineering, Chiyoda Corporation), Japan Oil, Gas and Metals National Corporation JOGMEC (no detailed reference about shareholding ratio)	Production of petroleum alternative fuels (GTL) from natural gas, demonstration plant construction and joint R&D (10 years). In the form of LLP of 36 billion yen
• Securing Resources	September 28, 2006	Nikkei page 9	Shell, Mitsui & Co., Ltd., Mitsubishi Corporation (Sakhalin 2 Project) (no detailed reference about shareholding ratio)	Russian government revoked the oil production licenses of three companies (for the Sakhalin 2 project) in order to promote the national interest; Russia's Foreign Minister explained that those acts did not constitute a dispossession. Follow-up story about existing JV's business
• Facility Sharing	September 26, 2006	Nikkei page 13	Tokyo FM Broadcasting Co., Ltd., KDDI (no detailed reference about shareholding ratio)	Music, video distribution in mobile digital radio
• Facility Sharing • Utilization of Sales Channels	September 22, 2006	Nikkei page 13	JFE, China Guangzhou Iron and Steel Enterprises Holdings Ltd. (no detailed reference about shareholding ratio)	"Manufacture and sale of automotive steel sheets is promising, but the blast furnace is difficult" (JFE president) Follow-up story about existing JV's business

Type of synergy	Date of article	News-paper	JV partners	Notes
• Securing Resources	September 22, 2006	Nikkei page 11	Shell, Mitsui & Co., Ltd., Mitsubishi Corporation (Sakhalin 2 Project) (no detailed reference about shareholding ratio)	Russian government revoked Sakhalin 2 Project oil production license of the three companies, aiming at Russian interest expansion. Follow-up story about existing JV's business
• Technology Introduction • Utilization of Sales Channels	September 21, 2006	Nikkei page 15	Duskin Co. Ltd. 58.38%, Mitsui & Co., Ltd. 34%, Taiwan President Chain Store Corporation 7.65%, etc.	Cleaning goods rental business in China
• Facility Sharing • Utilization of Sales Channels	September 21, 2006	Nikkei pages 1, 13	JFE, China Guangzhou Iron and Steel Enterprises Holdings Ltd. (no detailed reference about shareholding ratio)	Manufacture and sale of automotive steel sheets
• Securing Resources	September 20, 2006	Nikkei page 11	Shell, Mitsui & Co., Ltd., Mitsubishi Corporation (Sakhalin 2 Project) (no detailed reference about shareholding ratio)	Russian government revoked Sakhalin 2 Project oil production license of the three companies, aiming at Russian interest expansion. Follow-up story about existing JV's business
• Securing Resources	September 19, 2006	Nikkei pages 1, 9	Shell, Mitsui & Co., Ltd., Mitsubishi Corporation (Sakhalin 2 Project) (no detailed reference about shareholding ratio)	Russian government revoked Sakhalin 2 Project oil production license of the three companies, aiming at Russian interest expansion. Follow-up story about existing JV's business
• Facility Sharing • Utilization of Sales Channels	September 18, 2006	Nikkei page 6	Italy Fiat S.p.A., China Nanjing Automobile (Group) Corporation (no detailed reference about shareholding ratio)	To add a new different brand light truck vehicle to the existing JV line-up. Follow-up story about existing JV's business
• Facility Sharing • Utilization of Sales Channels	September 16, 2006	Nikkei page 11	Kasai Kogyo Co., Ltd. 75%, Malaysia Automotive plastic parts manufacturer Teck See Plastic Sdn Bhd 25%	Kasai Kogyo produces automotive interior resin member in Shiga prefecture and in Thailand, aims to expand sales channels in Nissan and other automotive makers
• Collaboration in lieu of Competition	September 15, 2006	Nikkei page 11	NTT Docomo, Inc., UK Vodafone Group Plc, China Mobile Ltd., etc. 7 companies (no detailed reference about shareholding ratio)	Coalition of leading mobile phone companies to discuss the new generation mobile technology founded in UK
• Facility Sharing	September 15, 2006	Nikkei page 11	Toshiba 49%→0%, US GE 51%→ 100%	Resin JV partnership to be broken off, to be a wholly owned subsidiary of GE

Type of synergy	Date of article	News-paper	JV partners	Notes
• Collaborative R&D • Facility Sharing	September 15, 2006	Nikkei page 11	Fujitsu Ltd. 55%, Advantest Corporation 45%	Advanced semiconductor low-cost production technology
• Utilization of Sales Channels	September 14, 2006	Nikkei page 13	Isuzu Motors Ltd. 80%, Mitsubishi Corporation 20%	Establish auto sales company in Germany
• Collaboration in lieu of Competition • Utilization of Sales Channels	September 13, 2006	Nikkei page 11	Nippon Oil Corporation, Idemitsu Kosan Co., Ltd., other petroleum wholesaler companies (no detailed reference about shareholding ratio)	Joint import and sale of bio-ethanol
• Facility Sharing • Utilization of Sales Channels	September 12, 2006	Nikkei page 12	Kagome Co., Ltd. 49%, Italy grocery sales companies (no detailed reference about shareholding ratio)	Full-scale entry into the frozen vegetable production of Italian-produced vegetables
• Utilization of Sales Channels	September 10, 2006	Nikkei page 7	Elpida Memory (Micron), Taiwan Powerchip Technology Corp (no detailed reference about shareholding ratio)	DRAM manufacturing sales in Taiwan
• Cost Sharing • Utilization of Sales Channels	September 9, 2006	Nikkei page 1	Sumitomo Mitsui Trust Bank, Ltd., JP Morgan Chase & Co. (no detailed reference about shareholding ratio)	Joint investment fund company of 140 billion yen fund corresponding to securities products in US
• Utilization of Sales Channels	September 9, 2006	Nikkei page 13	Furukawa Electric Co., Ltd. 50%→80%, Singapore firm 50%→20%	To get management rights of auto parts manufacturing and selling JV in China. Follow-up story about existing JV's business
• Utilization of Sales Channels	September 8, 2006	Nikkei page 13	Mold for plastic parts manufacturer ARRK Corporation 80%, China Jinbei Automobile Co., Ltd., 20%	Manufacturing mold for resin parts for automatic car and selling in China
• Collaborative R&D • Utilization of Sales Channels	September 8, 2006	Nikkei page 12	Kirin Beverage Company, Ltd. 55%, Yakult Honsha Company, Ltd. 45%	To enter into health food field by utilizing two companies' biotechnology
• Securing Resources	September 6, 2006	Nikkei page 1	Shell, Mitsui & Co., Ltd., Mitsubishi Corporation (Sakhalin 2 Project) (no detailed reference about shareholding ratio)	Russian government has brought suit against 3 companies of Sakhalin 2 Project to obtain a production stoppage court order, aiming at their own interests' expansion. Follow-up story about existing JV's business

Type of synergy	Date of article	News-paper	JV partners	Notes
• Alleviation of Friction • Utilization of Sales Channels	August 31, 2006	Nikkei page 13	Nissan 65%, China Dongfeng Group 35%	Founded auto loans, sales finance subsidiary in China
• Securing Resources	August 26, 2006	Nikkei page 7	Shell, Mitsui & Co., Ltd., Mitsubishi Corporation (Sakhalin 2 Project) (no detailed reference about shareholding ratio)	Russian government has orchestrated against three companies of Sakhalin 2 Project, aiming at their own interests expansion. Follow-up story about existing JV's business
• Facility Sharing	August 23, 2006	Nikkei page 12	SoftBank Corp. subsidiary Movida Japan Inc. 81%, Kyodo Printing Co., Ltd. 19%	Internet Comics service
• Facility Sharing • Utilization of Sales Channels	August 21, 2006	Nikkei pages 1, 13	Shin Nippon Steel 50%, Netherlands Mittal Steel Company, N.V. 50%	US new plant construction for steel plate for cars
• Facility Sharing • Utilization of Sales Channels	August 13, 2006	Nikkei page 1	Honda Group 26%, India Corporate group and others (no detailed reference about shareholding ratio)	Motorcycle production and sales JV in India
• Facility Sharing	August 12, 2006	Nikkei page 11	Sanyo Electric Co., Ltd. 100%→81%, Taiwan an electronics manufacturer 19%	Flat-screen TV joint manufacturing in Taiwan
• Utilization of Sales Channels	August 8, 2006	Nikkei page 12	Yomiko Advertising Inc. 60%, Hakuhodo DY Holdings Inc. 40%	Using Chinese TV magazine, advertising activities in China
• Facility Sharing • Collaborative R&D	July 28, 2006	Nikkei page 9	NEC 50%, Panasonic 50%, and NEC 44%, Panasonic 44%, US Texas Instruments Inc. 12%	Development company of mobile phone terminal
• Brand Introduction • Utilization of Sales Channels	July 26, 2006	Nikkei page 9	Italy Fiat S.p.A., Tata Motors Ltd. (no detailed reference about shareholding ratio)	Fiat brand automobile production and sales
• Facility Sharing • Utilization of Sales Channels	July 26, 2006	Nikkei page 12	Nissan Chemical Industries, Ltd., Mitsui Chemicals Incorporated, Marubeni Corp., Mitsui & Co., Ltd. (no detailed reference about shareholding ratio)	Fertilizer business integration new company
• Facility Sharing • Collaborative R&D	July 25, 2006	Nikkei page 13	NEC 50%, Panasonic 50%, and NEC 44%, Panasonic 44%, US Texas Instruments Inc. 12%	Development company of mobile phone terminal

Type of synergy	Date of article	News-paper	JV partners	Notes
• Technology Introduction • Utilization of Sales Channels	July 21, 2006	Nikkei page 11	Secom Co., Ltd. 80%, Vietnam Royal Security Services Co., Ltd. 20%	Japanese-style security system company in Vietnam
• Facility Sharing • Utilization of Sales Channels	July 19, 2006	Nikkei page 11	Ube Industries, Ltd., 25%, Marubeni Corp. 20%, Taiwan Synthetic rubber company TSRC 55%	Production of synthetic rubber in Guangdong, China
• Facility Sharing • Utilization of Sales Channels	July 17, 2006	Nikkei pages 1, 9	Shin Nippon Steel, Netherlands Mittal Steel Company, N.V. (no detailed reference about shareholding ratio)	Based upon basic agreement of the alliance between companies, JV will be established in North America and other areas
• Utilization of Sales Channels	July 15, 2006	Nikkei page 12	Sony 50%, Germany Bertelsmann AG 50%	JV, which was established in EU for purpose of music business integration. News of the fact that the judgment of anti-trust law court in the EU decided that integration by the JV violates the law, has had a large impact on the music world. Follow-up story about existing JV's business
• Facility Sharing	July 15, 2006	Nikkei page 11	Sony 50%, South Korea Samsung 50%	Liquid crystal new plant construction in South Korea
• Utilization of Sales Channels	July 14, 2006	Nikkei page 9	Sony 50%, Germany Bertelsmann AG 50%	Anti-trust law court in the EU decided that music business integration by the JV violates the law. Follow-up story about existing JV's business
• Utilization of Sales Channels	July 11, 2006	Nikkei page 13	SoftBank Telecom Corp. 51%, Daiichikosho Co., Ltd. 49%	Karaoke equipment sales for restaurants and pubs
• Utilization of Sales Channels	July 11, 2006	Nikkei page 7	Sumitomo Life Insurance Company 47.5%, Mitsui Life Insurance Company Ltd. 47.5%, Sumitomo Mitsui Banking Corporation 5%	Visit-type insurance sale stores. Dealing with 15 different kinds of insurance, including foreign insurance
• Collaborative R&D	July 11, 2006	Nikkei page 12	Toyota 51%, Mitsubishi Corporation 49%	Establishment of medical mall, a collection of clinics on different medical subjects, Toyota has experience and know-how obtained in the Toyota hospital
• Brand Introduction • Obtaining Local Expertise	July 6, 2006	Nikkei page 15	Lotte Co., Ltd. 70%, corporate rehabilitation company Revamp Corporation 30%	Specialized company in crispy donuts, entering into franchise agreement with Krispy Kreme Doughnuts, Inc.

Type of synergy	Date of article	News-paper	JV partners	Notes
• Utilization of Sales Channels	July 4, 2006	Nikkei page 13	Digital Garage, Inc. 51%, Dentsu Inc. 17%, Dentsu Inc. subsidiary 17%, Asatsu-DK Inc. 15%	Advertising company for SNS
• Technology Introduction • Brand Introduction • Utilization of Sales Channels	July 2, 2006	Nikkei page 7	Toshiba China subsidiary 90%, China TCL Corporation 10%	Toshiba OEM products manufacturing company
• Collaboration in lieu of Competition • Facility Sharing • Utilization of Sales Channels	June 30, 2006	Nikkei page 12	Yamato Holdings Co., Ltd. 70%→56.8%, Seino Holdings Co., Ltd. 15%, Nippon Express Co., Ltd. 15%, 12 local transportation companies 1.1% each	The grand coalition by local companies equity participation in Yamato/Seino Transportation logistics JV
• Facility Sharing	June 30, 2006	Nikkei page 13	Ichikoh Industries, Ltd. 50%, French Valeo S.A. Group 50%	Joint construction of a car lamp factory in Australia
• Technology Introduction • Utilization of Sales Channels	June 29, 2006	Nikkei pages 1, 13	Takeda Pharmaceutical Company Ltd., US pharmaceutical companies (no detailed reference about shareholding ratio)	As undue income transfer to the JV, 120 billion yen taxation US transfer pricing taxation is imposed
• Facility Sharing	June 28, 2006	Nikkei page 13	Nippon Light Metal Company, Ltd., Marubeni Corp., Vietnam aluminum alloy companies (no detailed reference about shareholding ratio)	The construction of aluminum raw materials factory in Vietnam
• Utilization of Sales Channels	June 27, 2006	Nikkei page 9	Sony 50%, Germany Bertelsmann AG 50%	Will anti-trust law court in the EU decide that the music business integration by the JV violates the law? Shareholding ratio may be reviewed. Follow-up story about existing JV's business
• Facility Sharing • Brand Introduction	June 27, 2006	Nikkei page 1	Japan Post, Netherlands TNT (no detailed reference about shareholding ratio)	Withdrawal of logistics business partnership JV announcement
• Facility Sharing	June 27, 2006	Nikkei page 11	Toagosei Company, Ltd. 0%→51%, Mitsui Chemicals, Inc. 100%→49%	Polymer flocculant business integration JV. Toagosei participate in JV.
• Technology Introduction • Utilization of Sales Channels	June 27, 2006	Nikkei page 11	KDDI 50%, UK BT Group plc 50%	Provision of line services across countries taking advantage of the know-how of BT

Type of synergy	Date of article	News-paper	JV partners	Notes
• Utilization of Sales Channels	June 26, 2006	Nikkei page 9	JV co. (Itochu Corp./ Marubeni Corp.) 33%, Canada two companies (balance) (no detailed reference about shareholding ratio)	Sale of pipeline steel for Canadian resource development companies
• Facility Sharing • Collaborative R&D	June 23, 2006	Nikkei page 12	Sanyo Electric Co., Ltd., Finland Nokia Corporation (no detailed reference about shareholding ratio)	Withdrawal announcement of mobile business partnership JV negotiations
• Collaborative R&D • Utilization of Sales Channels	June 23, 2006	Nikkei page 13	Shinko Electric Co., Ltd. 49%→4.9%, US Assist Technology 51%→95.1%	Liquid crystal transport equipment manufacturing and sales
• Utilization of Sales Channels	June 20, 2006	Nikkei page 13	Fujifilm Corporation 66%, Dentsu Inc. 34%	Ecommerce site construction acting company
• Facility Sharing	June 14, 2006	Nikkei page 11	Hitachi, Toshiba, Renesas Electronics Corporation (no detailed reference about shareholding ratio)	Dissolved the planned company for the joint manufacturing of semiconductors. Follow-up story about existing JV's business
• Collaborative R&D • Utilization of Sales Channels	June 14, 2006	Nikkei page 11	Isuzu Motors Ltd. 50%, US GM 50%	Joint R&D, joint manufacturing and joint sales of pickup truck
• Collaborative R&D • Utilization of Sales Channels	June 14, 2006	Nikkei page 11	Mitsubishi Electric, China Local Companies (no detailed reference about shareholding ratio)	Change the company mission from joint R&D of elevator equipment technology to that of production, sales and maintenance of elevator equipment
• Collaboration in lieu of Competition • Facility Sharing	June 10, 2006	Nikkei pages 1, 11	Sony group, Panasonic, Mitsubishi Electric, Hitachi, Toshiba, NHK, Japan Victor and others (no detailed reference about shareholding ratio)	Major companies established a patent management company in the JV (patent pool)
• Utilization of Sales Channels	June 9, 2006	Nikkei page 11	Nippon Valqua Industries, Ltd. 51%, US Garlock Sealing Technologies 49%	Manufacture and sale of gas leak prevention highly functional sealing material
• Collaboration in lieu of Competition • Facility Sharing	June 6, 2006	Nikkei page 11	Sony 35%, Panasonic 35%, Sharp 10%, Toshiba 10%, Hitachi 10%	TV for net service billing system integration
• Collaborative R&D • Utilization of Sales Channels	June 6, 2006	Nikkei page 12	Mitsui & Co., Ltd., Shochiku Co., Ltd. (no detailed reference about shareholding ratio)	Cinema complex business

Type of synergy	Date of article	News-paper	JV partners	Notes
● Collaborative R&D ● Utilization of Sales Channels	June 6, 2006	Nikkei page 12	Mitsubishi Corporation, Dentsu Inc. (no detailed reference about shareholding ratio)	Animation production business
● Utilization of Sales Channels	June 3, 2006	Nikkei page 11	Sony 50%, Germany Bertelsmann AG 50%	Will anti-trust law court in the EU decide that music business integration by the JV violates the law? Shareholding ratio may be reviewed. Follow-up story about existing JV's business
● Facility Sharing	June 2, 2006	Nikkei page 13	Asahi Kasei Group 50%, Kuraray Co., Ltd. 50%	Core parts production and sales of artificial kidneys
● Facility Sharing ● Collaborative R&D	June 1, 2006	Nikkei page 13	Chubu Electric Power Company, Incorporated, Electric Power Development Co., Ltd. (no detailed reference about shareholding ratio)	Electric power wholesale, retail
● Technology Introduction	June 1, 2006	Nikkei page 11	Vietnam National Maritime University (majority), Shin Kurushima Dockyard Co., Ltd. and its subsidiary Kanax corporation (balance) (no detailed reference about shareholding ratio)	Teamed up with the University of Vietnam, aiming at technician training, security of technicians
● Facility Sharing ● Utilization of Sales Channels	May 31, 2006	Nikkei pages 1, 11	Panasonic 23%→32%, Hitachi 50%, Toshiba 23%→16%, others (balance)	Proposal for capital increase of liquid crystal production JV (30 billion yen). Panasonic and Hitachi accepted it but Toshiba did not. Follow-up story about existing JV's business
● Utilization of Sales Channels	May 28, 2006	Nikkei page 7	Tokushukai Group 70%, Bio-venture OTS 30%	Investigational new drug analysis using gene analysis technology
● Technology Introduction ● Facility Sharing ● Utilization of Sales Channels	May 27, 2006	Nikkei page 11	Nippon Electric Glass Company, Ltd. 65%, Sumitomo Corporation Group 15%, China SVA Electron Co., Ltd. 20%	The manufacture and sales of glass substrate for liquid crystal
● Technology Introduction ● Utilization of Sales Channels	May 27, 2006	Nikkei page 11	Mitsubishi Electric 50%, China Electrical equipment manufacturer Zhuzhou Electric Locomotive Research Institute Co., Ltd. 50%	Production base of rail electrical equipment in China

Type of synergy	Date of article	News-paper	JV partners	Notes
• Utilization of Sales Channels	May 26, 2006	Nikkei page 13	Sony 50%, Germany Bertelsmann AG 50%	Bertelsmann AG is to sell a part of its music business to others, intending to maintain the JV co. in EU
• Facility Sharing • Utilization of Sales Channels	May 26, 2006	Nikkei page 1	Nisshin Steel Co., Ltd., Spain stainless steel manufacturing company Acerinox, S.A. (no detailed reference about shareholding ratio)	First step to advance into Indian market
• Alleviation of Friction	May 25, 2006	Nikkei page 13	Marubeni Corp. 49%, Malaysia insurance system's largest company 51%	Malaysia insurance system sales, management
• Facility Sharing • Utilization of Sales Channels	May 24, 2006	Nikkei page 13	Yamato Holdings Co., Ltd. 70%, Seino Holdings Co., Ltd. 15%, Nippon Express Co., Ltd. 15%	Nippon Express Co., Ltd. invested in Yamato/Seino JV
• Cost Sharing • Obtaining Local Expertise	May 22, 2006	Nikkei page 11	Kadokawa Group Holdings, Inc., Development Bank of Japan Inc., (no detailed reference about shareholding ratio)	2 billion yen of fund for animation producers
• Cost Sharing • Utilization of Sales Channels	May 22, 2006	Nikkei page 1	Mitsubishi UFJ Financial Group, Inc. approx. 10%, US fund companies (balance)	Established investment bank in US
• Facility Sharing • Utilization of Sales Channels	May 22, 2006	Nikkei page 1	Sony 50%, UK Ericsson 50%	Mobile phone manufacturing and sales in Europe
• Collaborative R&D • Utilization of Sales Channels	May 22, 2006	Nikkei page 11	Game company Square Enix Co., Ltd. 50%, Internet shopping Xavel,Inc. 50%	Site management services for women
• Securing Resources • Cost Sharing	May 21, 2006	Nikkei page 1	Mitsubishi Corporation, Mitsubishi Chemical Corporation, (no detailed reference about shareholding ratio)	Bank delegation, such as Mitsubishi UFJ Financial Group, Inc., executes huge loan in Saudi Arabia petrochemical JV
• Obtaining Local Expertise	May 16, 2006	Nikkei page 17	Sotec former president Mr. Hirasawa (individual) 51%, real estate fund 15%, and its subsidiary 34%	Asset management investment firm, JV between companies and the individual
• Technology Introduction	May 14, 2006	Nikkei page 1	Asahi Breweries, Ltd./ Itochu Corp. subsidiary ABIH 25%, Itochu Corp. subsidiary in China 75%	Introducing ASAHI's production technology in China, and establishing local production plants

Type of synergy	Date of article	News-paper	JV partners	Notes
• Facility Sharing • Cost Sharing	May 12, 2006	Nikkei page 11	Mitsubishi Heavy Industries, Ltd., and Mitsubishi Group companies (no detailed reference about shareholding ratio)	The acquisition of local firms, and aiming to expand business of metals machinery manufacturing and sales in China
• Collaborative R&D • Utilization of Sales Channels	May 12, 2006	Nikkei page 11	Isuzu Motors Ltd. 75%, Itochu Corp. 25%	Business planning consultant company for track sales, repair and sales-related business
• Facility Sharing	May 11, 2006	Nikkei page 11	Mitsubishi Chemical Corporation, US Exxon Mobil Corporation (no detailed reference about shareholding ratio)	Resin production and sales 2 JV companies partnership to be broken off, to be a wholly owned subsidiary of Mitsubishi
• Facility Sharing • Utilization of Sales Channels	May 10, 2006	Nikkei page 11	Nippon Steel Corporation Group; Suzuki Metal Industry Co., Ltd. 60%, Sumitomo Electric Industries, Ltd. subsidiary 40%	Stainless steel wire business integration JV
• Facility Sharing • Utilization of Sales Channels	May 10, 2006	Nikkei pages 1, 11	Yamato Holdings Co., Ltd. 50%, Nippon Yusen Kabushiki Kaisha 50%	International logistics JV to take advantage of the two companies' infrastructure, aiming at a comprehensive business alliance
• Facility Sharing	May 10, 2006	Nikkei page 7	Volkswagen AG, and its Chinese subsidiary (no detailed reference about shareholding ratio)	Enhanced parts procurement in China
• Technology Introduction • Brand Introduction • Utilization of Sales Channels	May 9, 2006	Nikkei page 13	Suntory Holdings Ltd., China local corporations (no detailed reference about shareholding ratio)	Manufacture and sales of soft drink JV in China, JV partnership to be broken off, to be a wholly owned subsidiary of Suntory
• Collaborative R&D • Utilization of Sales Channels	May 7, 2006	Nikkei page 5	Meidensha Corporation, Agritech Marketing Co., Ltd., Thailand Palm Oil Company Southern Group (no detailed reference about shareholding ratio)	Coconut shell biomass-fuel power plant construction
• Facility Sharing	May 2, 2006	Nikkei page 11	Fuji Television Network, Inc. (240 million yen), Transcosmos Inc. subsidiary (160 million yen), LLC (no detailed reference about shareholding ratio)	Video posting site management

Joint venture strategies

Type of synergy	Date of article	News-paper	JV partners	Notes
• Securing Resources	May 2, 2006	Nikkei page 11	Shell 55%, Mitsui & Co., Ltd. 25%, Mitsubishi Corporation 20%	The prospects of the Sakhalin 2 LNG sales project are improved
• Utilization of Sales Channels	April 26, 2006	Nikkei page 9	Luxembourg Arcelor 65%, Mitsui & Co., Ltd. 35%	Automotive steel processing in South Africa
• Securing Resources	April 22, 2006	Nikkei page 11	Sumitomo Corporation, Sojitsu Corporation (no detailed reference about shareholding ratio)	Acquire LNG interests in Nigeria
• Collaborative R&D • Cost Sharing	April 20, 2006	Nikkei page 13	Fujitsu Ltd. fund subsidiary 61%, Mitsui & Co., Ltd. fund subsidiary 39%	Technological development of light electrical parts based on the joint developed technology by Fujitsu Ltd. and the University of Tokyo, using VC fund assistance
• Collaborative R&D • Cost Sharing	April 16, 2006	Nikkei page 5	Oracle Corporation's subsidiary Miracle Linux 25%, China Red Flag Software 37.5%, South Korea Haansoft, Inc. 25%, others (balance)	Development of Asian version Linux in China
• Cost Sharing • Utilization of Sales Channels	April 14, 2006	Nikkei page 11	Mitsui & Co., Ltd. 40%, US electric power company AES 60%	Power generation business contractors in Jordan, total project cost of 33 billion yen, 70% of it is to be on external funding
• Technology Introduction • Facility Sharing • Utilization of Sales Channels	April 12, 2006	Nikkei page 1	Kobe Steel, Ltd., US Electric Furnace Steel Dynamics, Inc., US ore company Cleveland-Cliffs Inc. (no detailed reference about shareholding ratio)	New furnace construction in US to produce high-quality steel at low cost
• Technology Introduction • Facility Sharing • Utilization of Sales Channels	April 11, 2006	Nikkei page 17	Animation planning and production DLE 50%, India animation company Toon Boom Animation Inc. 50%	Animation production and sales for India and the US. Toons are strong in CG skill, and have a track record of working as subcontractors of the US movie CG
• Facility Sharing • Brand Introduction	April 5, 2006	Nikkei page 13	Mazda Motor Corporation 15%→ 30%, US Ford Motor Company 50%→35%, China Changan Automobile 50%	MAZDA invested in JV co. (Ford/ Changan Automobile 50:50) in China

Type of synergy	Date of article	News- paper	JV partners	Notes
• Securing Resources	April 5, 2006	Nikkei page 13	Mitsui & Co., Ltd/ Mitsui Oil Exploration Co., Ltd. subsidiary 15%, US big oil company Occidental Petroleum Corp. 70%, UAE investment firm Liwa Energy 15%	JV for the acquisition of new mining area in Oman
• Facility Sharing	April 4, 2006	Nikkei page 11	Hitachi Displays, Ltd. 50%, Panasonic 22%, Toshiba 22%, others (balance)	Expansion of Hitachi panel display production
• Collaborative R&D • Cost Sharing	April 3, 2006	Nikkei page 9	Fuji Biomedix Co., Ltd. 64.25%, Yokohama City University 10.75%, Institute of Accelerator Analysis Ltd. 12.5%, VC SBIHD 12.5%	New drug candidate component R&D based on the research results of Yokohama City University professor, joint research judgment whether the drug candidate component reached the affected area or not
• Collaborative R&D • Utilization of Sales Channels	April 3, 2006	Nikkei page 11	Hakuhodo Inc. (majority), Toppan Printing Co., Ltd. approx. 40%, others (balance) (no detailed reference about shareholding ratio)	Undertake customer information management company. Support advertising, promotion management
• Facility Sharing	March 31, 2006	Nikkei page 13	NEC 51%→100%, Fuji Heavy Industries Ltd. 49%→0%	Automotive battery JV partnership to be broken off, to be a wholly owned subsidiary of NEC
• Technology Introduction • Facility Sharing	March 30, 2006	Nikkei page 9	South Korea Ssangyong Motor, China Shanghai Automotive Industry Corporation (no detailed reference about shareholding ratio)	As South Korea Ssangyong Motor fear technology leakage, JV negotiations broken off
• Securing Resources	March 22, 2006	Nikkei page 7	China Russian governments agreed JV formation (no detailed reference about shareholding ratio)	Agreed to establish JV to secure oil resources of Siberia and other areas
• Collaborative R&D • Utilization of Sales Channels	March 22, 2006	Nikkei page 11	Square Enix Co., Ltd. 60%, Gakken Holdings Company, Ltd. 40%	Learning, vocational training software development (such as for firefighters)
• Securing Resources • Cost Sharing	March 20, 2006	Nikkei page 11	Tokyo Electric Power Company subsidiary 50%, Mitsubishi Corporation 50%	Purchase of Oman LNG supply to Tokyo Electric and Mitsubishi

Type of synergy	Date of article	News-paper	JV partners	Notes
• Technology Introduction • Utilization of Sales Channels	March 11, 2006	Nikkei page 9	Yamato Holdings Co., Ltd. 51%, Germany logistics world's leading company Deutsche Post AG 49%	Yamato is to enter the DM market in the know-how of Deutsche Post AG
• Securing Resources • Cost Sharing	March 3, 2006	Nikkei pages 1, 13	Sumitomo Chemical Company, Ltd. 50%, Saudi Aramco 50%	Japan leading bankers, such as Japan Bank for International Cooperation, and Saudi Arabia bankers decided on 667 billion yen loan to the JV. Huge Project of 1.1 trillion yen financing
• Collaborative R&D • Facility Sharing	March 2, 2006	Nikkei page 12	Toppan Printing Co., Ltd., China IC card companies (no detailed reference about shareholding ratio)	Using magnetic card production technology and IC card technology of Toppan Printing, letterpress IC card production JV
• Collaboration in lieu of Competition • Facility Sharing • Utilization of Sales Channels	February 27, 2006	Nikkei pages 1, 9	Yamato Holdings Co., Ltd. 85%, Seino Holdings Co., Ltd. 15%	Major logistics companies Yamato and Seino to form grand coalition in the Logistics JV
• Securing Resources	February 25, 2006	Nikkei page 11	Sojitsu Corporation 51%, Russia Forestry Company Flora 49%	Veneer plywood manufacturing from raw wood and exports JV in Russia to enjoy tariff incentives of Russia
• Facility Sharing	February 24, 2006	Nikkei page 13	Sumitomo Chemical Company, Ltd. 50%, Okura Industrial Co., Ltd. 50%	Gas shut-off film business JV. Unitika Ltd. announced to take over the JV. Follow-up story about existing JV's business
• Securing Resources	February 23, 2006	Nikkei page 1	Asahi Kasei Group, Thailand state-owned oil company (PTT) (no detailed reference about shareholding ratio)	Using cheaper raw materials made from natural gas for acrylic production. Natural gas procured from PTT, production plants JV in Thailand
• Technology Introduction • Utilization of Sales Channels	February 23, 2006	Nikkei page 15	Hakuhodo Inc. 60%, major US advertising company TBWA's subsidiary in Japan 40%	Taking advantage of TBWA's advertising production know-how
• Securing Resources	February 19, 2006	Nikkei page 7	Shell 55%, Mitsui & Co., Ltd. 25%, Mitsubishi Corporation 20% (Sakhalin 2 Project)	JV partner companies jointly do business assessment of Sakhalin 2 Project
• Utilization of Sales Channels	February 15, 2006	Nikkei pages 3, 13	Sanyo Electric Co., Ltd. 50%, Finland Nokia Corporation 50%	Headquarters JV of third-generation mobile technology business in North America., Sanyo Electric try to enter the market
• Utilization of Sales Channels	February 14, 2006	Nikkei pages 1, 11	Sanyo Electric Co., Ltd. 50%, Finland Nokia Corporation 50%	Headquarters JV of third-generation mobile technology business in North America

Type of synergy	Date of article	News-paper	JV partners	Notes
• Facility Sharing • Utilization of Sales Channels	February 14, 2006	Nikkei page 15	Pharmaceutical venture LTT Bio-Pharma Co., Ltd. 50%, clinical trial support company I'rom Holdings Group 50%	Anti-aging medical mall – open business
• Cost Sharing	February 10, 2006	Nikkei page 12	Inaba Foods Co., Ltd. 49%, Mizuho Group investment firms 41%, investment firm 10%	Inaba Foods start canning and sales in Thailand, using the Thai tax incentives available under the free trade agreement
• Technology Introduction • Collaborative R&D	February 2, 2006	Nikkei page 1	Toyota, China First Automobile Works Group (no detailed reference about shareholding ratio)	Development of an automobile that suits Chinese tastes; Toyota's technology transfer
• Facility Sharing	February 1, 2006	Nikkei page 13	Mitsubishi Rayon Co., Ltd. 50%, South Korea Lotte Chemical Corporation 50%	Production of equipment to increase the intensity of the liquid crystal panel
• Technology Introduction • Facility Sharing	February 1, 2006	Nikkei page 13	Customer management system sales company Synergy Marketing, Inc. 49%, Internet advertising company Opt, Inc. 51%	E-mail magazine advertising
• Facility Sharing	January 26, 2006	Nikkei pages 1, 13	Sony 50%, South Korea Samsung 50%	300 billion yen investment in production JV of next-generation liquid crystal panel (using a large glass substrate) for liquid crystal new plant construction
• Obtaining Local Expertise • Utilization of Sales Channels	January 25, 2006	Nikkei page 15	Sogo Rinsho Holdings Co., Ltd. (majority), healthcare system development company MED Support Systems Co., Ltd. (balance) (no detailed reference about shareholding ratio)	Support of local clinic (patient referrals to specialists)
• Cost Sharing • Technology Introduction • Alleviation of Friction	January 22, 2006	Nikkei pages 1, 5	Sumitomo Corporation, UK Electric Power International Power plc, Belgium power company Tractebel Engineering GDF-Suez (no detailed reference about shareholding ratio)	Joint investment in power generation business investment in Bahrain (150 billion yen)
• Utilization of Sales Channels	January 20, 2006	Nikkei page 13	Konami Corporation 70%, Internet Initiative Japan Inc 30%	Portal site management company

Type of synergy	Date of article	News-paper	JV partners	Notes
• Utilization of Sales Channels	January 19, 2006	Nikkei page 13	Mazda Motor Corporation, Mitsubishi Corporation (no detailed reference about shareholding ratio)	JV to sell power. Technology introduction
• Utilization of Sales Channels	January 19, 2006	Nikkei page 9	China Shanghai Automotive Industry Corporation 50%, Fiat S.p.A.'s China subsidiary 50%	Introduction of technology from Fiat, automobile manufacturing and sales in China
• Facility Sharing	January 17, 2006	Nikkei page 13	Ajinomoto Company, Incorporated Group 65.1%, China Xiamen Royi Group Co., Ltd. 30%, others (no detailed reference about shareholding ratio)	To produce the ingredients of dehydrated vegetables for e.g. instant soup
• Utilization of Sales Channels	January 13, 2006	Nikkei page 15	Catalog shopping DeNA Co., Ltd. 51%, Senshukai Co., Ltd. 49%	Business partnership in electronic trading field using mobile phone
• Facility Sharing	January 8, 2006	Nikkei page 7	Shin Nippon Steel 21%, Brazil Steel company Usinas Siderúrgicas de Minas Gerais S.A. (balance) (no detailed reference about shareholding ratio)	To increase production of automotive plated steel to automobile manufacturers in e.g. North America
• Securing Resources	December 26, 2005	Nikkei page 7	UK BP 50%, National Iranian Oil Company 50%	JV covers E&P in the North Sea to secure natural gas and crude oil of Iran, barter business purpose
• Facility Sharing	December 25, 2005	Nikkei page 7	Sumitomo Corporation 60%, Kobe Steel, Ltd. 37%, others (no detailed reference about shareholding ratio)	Coil steel processing company, for integration rationalization of prior related plant
• Obtaining Local Expertise	December 21, 2005	Nikkei page 15	Japan Alcohol Trading Co., Ltd 50%, Brazil Petrobras 50%	The sugar cane-derived ethanol Japan export base in Tokyo
• Utilization of Sales Channels	December 20, 2005	Nikkei page 13	Fujitsu General Ltd. 85%, China General Trading Company Oriental International group 15%	Integrated streamlining of sales channels of household air conditioner
• Utilization of Sales Channels	December 20, 2005	Nikkei page 13	Unicharm Corporation, South Korea LG Electronics Inc. (no detailed reference about shareholding ratio)	Rationalization of traditional agency sales channels

Type of synergy	Date of article	News-paper	JV partners	Notes
• Utilization of Sales Channels	December 20, 2005	Nikkei page 15	Aeon group of companies 51%, Yamaya Corporation 49%	Liquor import and sale
• Utilization of Sales Channels	December 19, 2005	Nikkei page 11	Yahoo Japan Corporation 60%, Index Corp. 35%, Connect Holdings Corp. 5%	Mobile phones Internet sales site management JV
• Cost Sharing	December 17, 2005	Nikkei pages 1, 9	Advantage Partners, Unison Capital, Inc., MKS Partners, 1/3 each	Aim to help Kanebo restructuring; fund firms union founded the JV holding company. Industrial Revitalization Corporation of Japan agrees to this plan
• Cost Sharing	December 15, 2005	Nikkei page 15	Advantage Partners, Unison Capital, Inc., MKS Partners, 1/3 each	Aim to help Kanebo restructuring, fund firms union founded the JV holding company
• Facility Sharing	December 8, 2005	Nikkei page 1	Sanyo Electric Co., Ltd., China consumer electronics major company Haier Group (no detailed reference about shareholding ratio)	Discussion about JV of white goods business in China
• Facility Sharing • Utilization of Sales Channels	November 29, 2005	Nikkei pages 1, 13	NEC 60%, Netherlands Royal Philips 40%	NEC to integrate with Philips by separating its office communication equipment business in EU
• Collaboration in lieu of Competition • Collaborative R&D • Facility Sharing • Utilization of Sales Channels	November 25, 2005	Nikkei page 11	Hitachi 18%, MasterCard Worldwide, US investment firm Oak Hill Capital Partners, IC general-purpose software owner company K.K. Bamboo etc. (no detailed reference about shareholding ratio)	Companies union of IC card world deployment
• Facility Sharing	November 23, 2005	Nikkei page 11	Sony 50%, South Korea Samsung 50%	New liquid crystal plant in South Korea, liquid crystal production increase
• Utilization of Sales Channels • Obtaining Local Expertise	November 22, 2005	Nikkei page 12	Mitsui & Co., Ltd. 30%, Chile waste acceptance operators Lepanto 70%	Greenhouse gas reduction projects, procurement buying and selling of emission rights
• Utilization of Sales Channels	November 7, 2005	Nikkei page 11	Excite Inc. 66.6%, NTT Resonant Inc. 33.4%	Search keyword-linked advertising
• Utilization of Sales Channels	November 3, 2005	Nikkei page 13	Isuzu Motors Ltd. 60% →100%, GM 40% →0%	JV partnership to be broken off, to be a wholly owned subsidiary of Isuzu Motors

Type of synergy	Date of article	News-paper	JV partners	Notes
• Utilization of Sales Channels	November 3, 2005	Nikkei pages 1, 13	Nippon Yusen Kabushiki Kaisha 12.5%, Mitsui O.S.K. Lines, Ltd. 12.5%, China 3 logistics companies (balance) (no detailed reference about shareholding ratio)	To advance Guangzhou as China logistics base for Japan automakers
• Utilization of Sales Channels	November 1, 2005	Nikkei page 13	Mitsubishi Corporation 75%, Nissin Kogyo Co., Ltd. 25%	Aluminum secondary alloy manufacturing plant in Thailand, for automotive parts
• Facility Sharing	October 29, 2005	Nikkei page 13	Panasonic 65%, Nippon Steel & Sumikin Pipe Co., Ltd. 35%	Manufacture and sale of steel conduit
• Facility Sharing • Utilization of Sales Channels	October 28, 2005	Nikkei page 13	Sky Perfect Communications Inc. 50%, NTT Group 50%	Video distribution using a fiber-optic line
• Facility Sharing	October 26, 2005	Nikkei page 15	IHI Corporation 2/3, Germany Siemens-owned steel plant leading company Vöest–Alpine AG 1/3	Catch-up of steel plant which depressed market
• Utilization of Sales Channels	October 25, 2005	Nikkei page 15	GEO Corporation 45%, leading publishing agency company TOHAN Co., Ltd. 55%	AV, sales, game software rental FC business
• Utilization of Sales Channels	October 24, 2005	Nikkei page 1& 9	Isuzu Motors Ltd. 60% →100%, US GM 40%→0%	JV partnership to be broken off, to be a wholly owned subsidiary of Isuzu Motors Ltd.
• Alleviation of Friction	October 21, 2005	Nikkei page 13	Mitsui & Co., Ltd. 30%, leading UK power company International Power plc 70%	Australia's largest coal power plant acquisition joint fund business 400 billion yen
• Facility Sharing • Utilization of Sales Channels	October 20, 2005	Nikkei page 12	Stationery Plus Corporation 50%, China fax paper roll manufacturing Hanhong Company 50%	Paper file local production in China
• Facility Sharing • Utilization of Sales Channels	October 19, 2005	Nikkei page 13	NEC, US Hewlett-Packard Company (no detailed reference about shareholding ratio)	Article in which JV is discussed for China business partnership
• Securing Resources • Cost Sharing	October 18, 2005	Nikkei page 13	Osaka Gas Co., Ltd. 70%, Sumitomo Corporation 30%	JV is to take over the mining area of joint petroleum development projects formerly owned by Idemitsu Kosan Co., Ltd. and Osaka Gas Co.

Type of synergy	Date of article	News-paper	JV partners	Notes
• Utilization of Sales Channels	October 18, 2005	Nikkei page 15	Kadokawa Group Holdings, Inc. 45%, Hong Kong Sun Wah Group 55%	Kadokawa operates five-cinema complex business in China
• Facility Sharing	October 18, 2005	Nikkei page 13	Sharp 70%→100%, China Nanjing Panda Electronics Co., Ltd. 30%→0%	JV partnership to be broken off, to be a wholly owned subsidiary of Sharp
• Utilization of Sales Channels	October 17, 2005	Nikkei page 11	Nihon Enterprise Co., Ltd.'s China subsidiary 56%, Tokyo Broadcasting System Television 34%, China information search company Serachina Co., Ltd. 10%	Mobile phones video, music, information transmission in China
• Facility Sharing	October 17, 2005	Nikkei page 7	US Apple Inc., South Korea Samsung (no detailed reference about shareholding ratio)	iPod for memory JV negotiations broken off
• Collaboration in lieu of Competition • Facility Sharing	October 15, 2005	Nikkei page 13	Pharmaceutical wholesalers 9 companies (Toho Pharmaceutical Co., Ltd., Vital-Net, Inc., Hokuyaku Inc., etc.)11.1% each	Business alliance management JV
• Utilization of Sales Channels	October 12, 2005	Nikkei page 11	Rakuten, Inc. 60%, NTT Docomo, Inc. 40%	Mobile phones Internet auction site
• Utilization of Sales Channels	October 8, 2005	Nikkei page 11	Sojitsu Corporation 40%, Malaysia car sales company DRB-HICOM and West Star Motor Sports, Inc. 60%	Manufacture and sale of car navigation system in Malaysia
• Collaborative R&D	October 7, 2005	Nikkei page 13	Mitsubishi Heavy Industries, Ltd. 50%, Konica Minolta, Inc.'s subsidiary 20%, Mitsubishi Corporation 15%, Seika Corporation 15%	Medical equipment business. Medical equipment joint R&D
• Securing Resources	October 5, 2005	Nikkei page 13	Sumitomo Metal Industries, Ltd., Sumitomo Corporation 15%, US Phelps Dodge Corporation 85%	Joint investment in Arizona mine
• Utilization of Sales Channels	October 4, 2005	Nikkei page 15	Cyber Agent, Inc. 60%, Cybozu, Inc. 40%	Management of portal site that specializes in business persons

Type of synergy	Date of article	News-paper	JV partners	Notes
● Collaborative R&D	October 4, 2005	Nikkei page 13	Hitachi 66%, Takeda Pharmaceutical Company Ltd. 34%	JV agreement provides JV relationship to be resolved in 2 years' time, to be a wholly owned subsidiary of Hitachi
● Reputational Backing ● Cost Sharing ● Utilization of Sales Channels	September 29, 2005	Nikkei page 7	Mitsubishi Tokyo Financial Group, Inc. 50%, US Merrill Lynch & Co., Inc. 50%. Additional preferred stock investment is Merrill Lynch & Co., Inc. 100%	Established a securities company managing 3.5 trillion yen in assets. The creditworthiness of the company was boosted by its association with the two well-established company names.
● Collaborative R&D ● Utilization of Sales Channels	September 28, 2005	Nikkei page 15	Itochu Corp. 51%, Orient Corporation 49%	Home remodeling business, and developing a business that combines loans for customers of financial assistance
● Obtaining Local Expertise ● Alleviation of Friction	September 27, 2005	Nikkei page 15	OBARA Corp. (a well-established resistance welding equipment company) over 90%, the balance held by locally-hired officers	Local production in car manufacturing for welding equipment factory in India for Japan-based automobile manufacturers
● Securing Resources ● Cost Sharing	September 17, 2005	Nikkei page 7	Indonesia PT Perusahaan Minyak Nasional 45%, US Exxon Mobil Corporation 45%, national and local government 10%	Indonesia oilfield development JV of Exxon and the state-owned oil company ($2,000,000,000 investment)
● Utilization of Sales Channels	September 13, 2005	Nikkei page 12	SoftBank Corp. subsidiary 49%, French software development and markets company Avanquest Software 51%	Software distribution business throughout Japan, Asia, Europe also view to other areas
● Facility Sharing	September 13, 2005	Nikkei page 13	Isuzu Motors Ltd. 50%, China Qingling Motors Co., Ltd. 50%	Trucks engine production, carried out by expanding the existing JV
● Facility Sharing	September 12, 2005	Nikkei page 17	Kandenko Company, Ltd., Sato Kensetsu Kogyo Co., Ltd., Tokyo Electric Power Services Co., Ltd., Yasuda, Inc. (no detailed reference about shareholding ratio)	Fewer management company work orders of transmission line construction equipment, shared with management cost reduction purpose of construction equipment
● Collaboration in lieu of Competition ● Facility Sharing ● Cost Sharing	September 9, 2005	Nikkei pages 1, 13	Hitachi, Toshiba, Renesas Electronics Corporation., Panasonic etc. less than 20% each (no detailed reference about shareholding ratio)	Co-founded an LSI product company with 200 billion to 300 billion yen of investment, to recover lost territory in international markets

Type of synergy	Date of article	News-paper	JV partners	Notes
• Obtaining Local Expertise • Utilization of Sales Channels	September 8, 2005	Nikkei page 13	Staff service holdings 51%, Nakayama Hayao (individual) 49%	Marketing and sales positions staff service business
• Technology Introduction • Utilization of Sales Channels	September 8, 2005	Nikkei page 13	Dentsu Inc. 49%, US Internet advertising company Twenty Four Seven Search 51%	Dentsu Inc. aims to recover status in search advertising market in Japan by know-how introduction of Twenty Four Seven Search
• Facility Sharing	September 4, 2005	Nikkei page 7	Fukuyama Transporting Co., Ltd. 51%, China Run off Kobe International Trade 49%	Established cargo packing company in Shanghai
• Facility Sharing	September 3, 2005	Nikkei page 13	Daido Metal Co., Ltd. 30%→0%, US auto parts company 70% →100%	Auto parts production JV partnership to be broken off, a wholly owned subsidiary of US Auto parts company.
• Facility Sharing	September 2, 2005	Nikkei page 11	Tokyo Broadcasting System Television 50%, Mitsui & Co., Ltd. 50%	Mobile phones digital broadcasting content
• Alleviation of Friction	August 31, 2005	Nikkei page 13	Oji Paper Co., Ltd. 90%, China investment firm 10%	Due to foreign capital guidelines change in China, doing business individually is no longer possible, switch to a JV
• Brand Introduction • Utilization of Sales Channels	August 27, 2005	Nikkei page 17	The Sazaby League 81%, Isetan 19%	Sazaby, which holds a license for French apparel, begins apparel business
• Facility Sharing	August 27, 2005	Nikkei page 15	Tachi-S Co., Ltd. 49%, US sheet production company Lear Corporation 51%	Production plant construction in UK to produce car seat for Nissan plant in UK
• Facility Sharing	August 25, 2005	Nikkei page 11	Sony, South Korea Samsung (no detailed reference about shareholding ratio)	Liquid crystal panel production JV. Announced the introduction of the Bravia brand for supply to Sony and to expand the liquid crystal TV business
• Facility Sharing • Utilization of Sales Channels	August 23, 2005	Nikkei page 12	Suntory Holdings Ltd. 50%, UK Blavod Extreme Spirits Plc 50%	Distilled spirits plant in US, Suntory aims to expand the distilled liquor range.
• Utilization of Sales Channels	August 11, 2005	Nikkei page 13	Automotive forgings company Kotani Corporation 60%, Sumitomo Corporation 25%, NTN 15%	Automotive forgings company Kotani to advance its factory into Poland
• Facility Sharing • Utilization of Sales Channels	August 9, 2005	Nikkei page 15	Pharmaceutical venture LTT Bio-Pharma Co., Ltd. 50%, Clinical trial support I'rom Pharmaceutical Co., Ltd. 50%	Anti-aging and medical mall business

Type of synergy	Date of article	News-paper	JV partners	Notes
• Collaborative R&D • Utilization of Sales Channels	August 7, 2005	Nikkei page 7	Mitsui & Co., Ltd. US subsidiary company 50%, US pesticide company Sipcam S.p.A. 50%	Mitsui has a strong microorganism-based pesticides business; Sipcam has a strong fungicide business; for the purposes of selling the optimal combination of pesticides to customers
• Facility Sharing • Cost Sharing	August 5, 2005	Nikkei page 13	Kawasaki Heavy Industries, Ltd. 50%, China shipping company China Ocean Shipping (Group) Company 50%	For local shipping demand development, shipbuilding dock new 27 billion yen investment
• Reputational Backing • Cost Sharing	August 3, 2005	Nikkei page 13	Marubeni Corp. 30%, JGC Corp. 25%, Itochu Corp. 20.1%, other local firms (no detailed reference about shareholding ratio)	Power plant and desalination plant construction totaling 120 billion yen for the supply of power and water for supply to Saudi Arabia petrochemical JV
• Facility Sharing • Cost Sharing	August 3, 2005	Nikkei page 13	Auto parts medium-sized company Meidoh Co., Ltd. 35%, Sugiura Manufacturing Co., Ltd. 25%, Ondo Corporation 20%, Owari Precise Products Co., Ltd.10%, Shinsho Corporation 10%	Co-founded the automotive bolt nut manufacturing company of China in five companies. Meido and Shinsho lead the project.
• Obtaining Local Expertise • Utilization of Sales Channels	August 2, 2005	Nikkei page 17	Bio professional VC K.K. Trans-Science, recruitment company (no detailed reference about shareholding ratio)	Recruitment company for employees seeking to transfer to the legal departments of venture companies
• Securing Resources	August 1, 2005	Nikkei pages 1, 9	Mitsui & Co., Ltd. 50%, Saudi Aramco 50%	Follow-up story about existing JV's business Saudi Arabia petrochemical JV investment amount expansion burden in development under the influence of the material costs soaring (900 billion yen of twice the original budget)
• Alleviation of Friction • Utilization of Sales Channels	July 29, 2005	Nikkei page 13	Itochu Corp. 15%, pharmaceutical wholesalers Alfresa Holdings Corporation 15%, China pharmaceutical wholesale and retail 39 system pharmaceutical 70%	The first JV to get a drug wholesale license in China

Type of synergy	Date of article	News-paper	JV partners	Notes
• Facility Sharing • Collaborative R&D	July 27, 2005	Nikkei page 13	Elpida Memory (Micron) 33%, Advantest Corporation, US Kingston Technology Company, Inc., Taiwan Powertech Technology, Inc.. others (no detailed reference about shareholding ratio)	JV of semiconductor test
• Brand Introduction • Utilization of Sales Channels	July 26, 2005	Nikkei page 13	Nissan Diesel Motor Co., Ltd. 25%→50%, Shanghai Automotive Industry Corporation 50% (no detailed reference about shareholding ratio)	Nissan Diesel aims to expand sales of Japanese brand cars to gain the initiative of China truck production
• Technology Introduction • Alleviation of Friction	July 25, 2005	Nikkei page 7	Netherlands Mittal Steel Company 49%, India Oil and Natural Gas Corporation Ltd. (ONGC) 51%	Oil and gas JVs for Central Asia, Africa oil field development, and steel plant construction by Mittal technology
• Brand Introduction • Utilization of Sales Channels	July 22, 2005	Nikkei page 15	Japanese restaurant chain Ootoya Co., Ltd 40%, Sumitomo Corporation subsidiary 5%, Thailand chicken sales company Betagro-Agro 55%	In response to the delicatessen lunch takeaway store development-oriented Japanese food in Thailand
• Facility Sharing • Collaborative R&D	July 21, 2005	Nikkei page 11	Tokyo Broadcasting System Television 51%, rental video store network Culture Convenience Club Company, Ltd. (CCC) 49%	The content of the program on DVD and mobile site joint R&D, also viewing Internet delivery of television program
• Facility Sharing	July 20, 2005	Nikkei page 13	Isuzu Motors Ltd. above 20%, Sojitsu Corporation less than 30%, Ukraine bus manufacturer HD Bogdan 50% (no detailed reference about shareholding ratio)	Isuzu Motors aims at truck production in Ukraine

Type of synergy	Date of article	News-paper	JV partners	Notes
• Facility Sharing • Collaboration in lieu of Competition	July 16, 2005	Nikkei page 9	Tokyo FM Broadcasting Co., Ltd. 25%, Nippon Broadcasting System, Inc., 10%, Nippon Cultural Broadcasting, Inc. 10%, Tokyo Broadcasting System Television 10%, as the core investors to attract further investment from local broadcasting stations, and other cellular, electronic, and automobile manufacturers	Mobile digital radio, music on PC, video distribution
• Securing Resources	July 15, 2005	Nikkei page 3	Shell 55%, Mitsui & Co., Ltd. 25%, Mitsubishi Corporation 20% (Sakhalin 2 Project)	Sakhalin 2, follow-up story about existing JV's business Sakhalin 2 project of investment expected to swell to twice the initial budget (2 trillion 200 billion yen). Wall of profitability strictly against Japanese firm side, investors of Shell expressed distrust
• Alleviation of Friction	July 14, 2005	Nikkei page 13	NUMMI (Toyota 50%, GM 50%)	Follow-up story about existing JV's business 16 billion yen to invest facility sharing renewal marking strong performance
• Collaboration in lieu of Competition • Facility Sharing	July 14, 2005	Nikkei page 15	Pasona Group Inc. 60%, 30 staffing companies participation capital (no detailed reference about shareholding ratio)	Large coalition of management company among staffing companies that operate common registration office of temporary staffing service
• Securing Resources	July 14, 2005	Nikkei page 7	Shell 55%, Mitsui & Co., Ltd. 25%, Mitsubishi Corporation 20% (Sakhalin 2 Project)	Sakhalin 2, follow-up story about existing JV's business. Sakhalin 2 Project of investment expected to swell to twice the initial budget
• Utilization of Sales Channels	July 13, 2005	Nikkei page 15	Tempstaff Co., Ltd. 51%, Sony 40%, US Kelly Services, Inc. 9%	Starting from general staffing service, technicians staffing service is planned in future. Using Kelly's network to expand staffing service into Thailand
• Alleviation of Friction • Facility Sharing	July 7, 2005	Nikkei pages 1, 13	Toyota Daihatsu union, India car companies (no detailed reference about shareholding ratio)	Judgment of the JV is required for the foothold of India foray

Type of synergy	Date of article	News-paper	JV partners	Notes
• Facility Sharing	July 5, 2005	Nikkei page 13	JFE Chemical Corporation, China Shandong Haihua Group Co., Ltd (no detailed reference about shareholding ratio)	Production of tar that becomes dye raw material, as a part of coal chemical business
• Facility Sharing • Cost Sharing	June 22, 2005	Nikkei page 9	South Korea Hyundai Motor Company 50%, China Guangzhou Automobile Industry Group 50%	Manufacture and sale of commercial vehicles (135 billion yen investment) in China
• Facility Sharing • Utilization of Sales Channels	June 22, 2005	Nikkei page 11	Akebono Brake Industry Company, Ltd. 50%→100%, US Auto parts company Delphi Corporation 50%→0%	Brake manufacturing of North America production base for Honda Group, Toyota and GM JV partnership to be broken off, to be a wholly owned subsidiary of Akebono Brake
• Technology Introduction • Facility Sharing	June 21, 2005	Nikkei page 13	Kobe Steel, Ltd. 35%, China wire rope manufacturer 15%, Sugita Densen Co., Ltd., Mitsui & Co., Ltd. (balance)	Production of special steel used for automotive suspension
• Collaborative R&D	June 17, 2005	Nikkei page 13	JFE, Germany ThyssenKrupp AG (no detailed reference about shareholding ratio)	Promoting development of automotive steel sheets
• Utilization of Sales Channels	June 16, 2005	Nikkei page 13	Yahoo Japan Corporation 60%, Index Corporation 35%, Connect Holdings Corp. 5%	Mobile phones Internet sales site established management
• Technology Introduction • Utilization of Sales Channels	June 10, 2005	Nikkei page 15	Secom Co., Ltd. 90%, China IT company 10%	Security of IT systems of factory and store
• Technology Introduction • Utilization of Sales Channels	June 8, 2005	Nikkei page 13	Wire manufacturer Fujikura Ltd. 40%, China optical fiber FiberHome Technologies Group 60%	Manufacturing and sales of fiber optic cables in China

Type of synergy	Date of article	News-paper	JV partners	Notes
• Securing Resources	June 2, 2005	Nikkei pages 1, 13	Itochu Corp. 12%, Thailand The Siam Cement Public Company Ltd. and Thailand state-owned oil company PTT 48%, Iran National Iranian Petrochemical Company 40% (no detailed reference about shareholding ratio)	For petrochemical resources secure after Iran sanctions
• Brand Introduction • Utilization of Sales Channels • Facility Sharing	June 1, 2005	Nikkei page 11	Toyota , French PSA Peugeot Citroën (no detailed reference about shareholding ratio)	The new construction of automobile factory in Czech Republic for the Middle East market, construction cost 180 billion yen.
• Alleviation of Friction • Technology Introduction • Utilization of Sales Channels	May 31, 2005	Nikkei page 15	CM video production TYO 35%, China Dalian Intelligent Manpower Corp., 51%, others (no detailed reference about shareholding ratio)	Animation production JV
• Alleviation of Friction • Utilization of Sales Channels	May 25, 2005	Nikkei page 15	Ito-Yokado Co., Ltd. 36.75%→51.75%, China Huafu Trade Fair prix 51%→36%, Itochu Corp. 12.25%	JV partnership to be broken off, to accelerate the JV into supermarkets
• Securing Resources • Cost Sharing	May 25, 2005	Nikkei page 13	Mitsubishi Corporation 7%→21%, Mitsubishi Chemical Corporation and others (no detailed reference about shareholding ratio)	To take the initiative for Saudi Arabia petrochemical JV
• Collaborative R&D	May 25, 2005	Nikkei page 11	Sumitomo Chemical Company, Ltd. 50%, UK Cambridge Display Technology 50%	To accelerate the organic EL developed with Cambridge's excellent technology in organic EL panel
• Facility Sharing	May 21, 2005	Nikkei page 11	Isuzu Motors Ltd. 6.9% →above 20%, China Qingling Motors Co., Ltd. (no detailed reference about shareholding ratio)	The investment expansion policy with respect to the track engine production JV
• Technology Introduction • Alleviation of Friction	May 19, 2005	Nikkei page 15	Mitsuwa Co., Ltd 34.3%→22% (no detailed reference about shareholding ratio)	Mitsuwa investment in 1990 founded JV is listed on stock exchanges in China

Type of synergy	Date of article	News-paper	JV partners	Notes
• Securing Resources • Cost Sharing • Utilization of Sales Channels	May 18, 2005	Nikkei page 13	Mitsubishi Corporation 50%, US ConocoPhillips Company 50% (no detailed reference about shareholding ratio)	Huge investment of 420 billion yen to 525 billion yen for North America West Coast LNG receiving terminal construction
• Alleviation of Friction	May 12, 2005	Nikkei pages 1, 13	Toyota 50%, GM 50%, NUMMI	Follow-up story about existing JV's business Toyota and GM, triggered by the success of NUMMI, to comment NUMMI is designated to conduct the joint R&D work of fuel cell vehicle technology
• Reputational Backing • Cost Sharing	April 26, 2005	Nikkei page 13	Marubeni Corp., JGC Corporation, UAE Abu Dhabi Emirate Water and Electricity Authority (Adwea) (no detailed reference about shareholding ratio)	Power plant for the supply of power and water and desalination plant construction, Japan Bank for International Cooperation and others grant 230 billion yen loan to this huge investment
• Collaborative R&D • Facility Sharing • Utilization of Sales Channels	April 15, 2005	Nikkei page 13	Fujitsu Ltd. 40%, US Advanced Micro Devices, Inc. 60%	Follow-up story about existing JV's business. The integrated company of both companies in the flash memory business
• Technology Introduction • Alleviation of Friction	April 13, 2005	Nikkei page 13	Mitsuwa Co., Ltd. 34.3%→22% (no detailed reference about shareholding ratio)	MITSUWA investment in 1990 founded JV is listed on stock exchanges in China
• Utilization of Sales Channels	March 31, 2005	Nikkei page 13	Itochu Corp., Techno science Corporation (CTC) 80%, Itochu Corp. 20%	Consulting firm of information systems
• Alleviation of Friction • Brand Introduction • Utilization of Sales Channels	March 30, 2005	Nikkei page 13	Mitsukoshi, Ltd. 50%, China Beijing Hualian Group 50%	JV opened first store in Chongqing
• Facility Sharing	March 19, 2005	Nikkei page 13	NEC 25%, SVA Electron Co., Ltd. 75%	30 billion yen investment for large liquid crystal panel production
• Utilization of Sales Channels • Obtaining Local Expertise	March 17, 2005	Nikkei page 11	Ito-Yokado Co., Ltd. 60%, Mitsui & Co., Ltd. 40%	To invite distinctive stores, taking advantage of the network of shopping center development Mitsui
• Facility Sharing	March 15, 2005	Nikkei page 13	Toyoda Gosei Co., Ltd. 50%, Australia Zumtobel Group 50%	White LED production plant in Australia

Type of synergy	Date of article	News-paper	JV partners	Notes
• Facility Sharing • Utilization of Sales Channels	March 9, 2005	Nikkei page 1	Nippon Express Co., Ltd., Mitsubishi Corporation (no detailed reference about shareholding ratio)	Established joint investment holding company for 6 Chinese companies to obtain a distribution network in China
• Facility Sharing	March 5, 2005	Nikkei page 13	Nichiro Corporation 45%, China Dragon Food Group 55%	JV is to purchase existing frozen food production plant of Dragon food
• Reputational Backing • Utilization of Sales Channels	March 4, 2005	Nikkei pages 1, 7	Mitsubishi UFJ Financial Group, Inc. 50%, US Merrill Lynch & Co., Inc. 50%	10 billion yen scale founded securities company for wealthy people. To increase its creditability by using the two companies of company name.
• Facility Sharing	February 22, 2005	Nikkei page 13	NEC 50%→100%, Mitsubishi Electric 50%→0%	PCs for monitoring business JV partnership to be broken off, to be a wholly owned subsidiary of NEC
• Brand Introduction • Utilization of Sales Channels	February 16, 2005	Nikkei page 15	Sekisui Chemical Company, Ltd. 60%, US H.B. Fuller Mauritius Ltd. 40%	Adhesive business in Japan and China. To increase the competitiveness by expanding the range
• Facility Sharing	February 12, 2005	Nikkei page 9	Amada Co., Ltd. 50% →100%, Italy Schiavi 50%→0%	Sheet metal processing equipment JV partnership to be broken off, to be a wholly owned subsidiary of Amada
• Facility Sharing	February 10, 2005	Nikkei page 13	Toshiba 60%, Panasonic 40%	Small and medium-sized liquid crystal display business JV invests 50 billion yen in new plant construction
• Technology Introduction • Alleviation of Friction • Utilization of Sales Channels	February 7, 2005	Nikkei page 1	Sumitomo Life Insurance Company 29%, China insurance company Chinese People's Insurance Company 71%	To advance into life insurance business in China, Sumitomo to provide know-how
• Facility Sharing	February 6, 2005	Nikkei pages 1, 7	Fujitsu Ltd. 80% →100%, Taiwan liquid crystal company AU Optronics Corp. 20%→0%	JV partnership to be broken off, to be a wholly owned subsidiary of Fujitsu
• Utilization of Sales Channels • Cost Sharing	January 31, 2005	Nikkei page 11	Itochu Corp., US Time Warner Inc. (no detailed reference about shareholding ratio)	Japanese animation, promotion of character goods in Japan and the United States. 3 billion yen scale of fund
• Facility Sharing	January 22, 2005	Nikkei page 13	Nippon Paper Industries Co., Ltd., China Cheng (no detailed reference about shareholding ratio)	Nippon Paper increased concern about the broken off JV, because Chinese company fell into financial problems

Type of synergy	Date of article	News-paper	JV partners	Notes
• Facility Sharing	January 21, 2005	Nikkei page 13	Nippon Paper Industries Co., Ltd., China Cheng (no detailed reference about shareholding ratio)	Nippon Paper increased concern about the broken off JV, because Chinese company fell into financial problems
• Brand Introduction • Facility Sharing • Utilization of Sales Channels	January 18, 2005	Nikkei page 13	Mazda Motor Corporation 25%, China First Automobile Works Group 70%, First Automobile Works Group 5%	Manufacture and sale of Mazda brand vehicles in China, Chinese government approved the JV establishment
• Technology Introduction • Facility Sharing	January 18, 2005	Nikkei page 13	Toyota 70%, China Guangzhou Automobile Group Co., Ltd. 30%	Toyota cars for engine core parts production in China
• Facility Sharing • Utilization of Sales Channels	January 15, 2005	Nikkei page 13	DIC Corporation, US Eastman Kodak Company (no detailed reference about shareholding ratio)	Follow-up story about existing JV's business. DIC will withdraw from JV after its share transfer to Kodak
• Facility Sharing	January 14, 2005	Nikkei page 13	Mitsui Chemicals, Inc., Mitsui & Co., Ltd. (no detailed reference about shareholding ratio)	Dashboard molding compound manufacturing plant in China
• Utilization of Sales Channels	January 12, 2005	Nikkei page 11	Isuzu Motors Ltd., Malaysia local firms (no detailed reference about shareholding ratio)	Isuzu is to advance sales in partnership with Malaysia local firms
• Facility Sharing • Utilization of Sales Channels	January 12, 2005	Nikkei page 13	Video rental company GEO Holdings Corporation. 50%, information distribution company Index Corporation 50%	Index. Provides the movie video, delivered in sales channels of GEO
• Facility Sharing	January 12, 2005	Nikkei page 5	Hitachi, Panasonic (no detailed reference about shareholding ratio)	New liquid crystal panel factory, receiving Chiba Prefecture's public subsidies
• Facility Sharing	January 4, 2005	Nikkei page 9	Nippon Yusen Kabushiki Kaisha 49%, China Shanghai automotive industry corporation's logistics company Anji Automotive Logistics Co,. Ltd. 51%	China foray providing automotive logistics base in China
• Utilization of Sales Channels	December 31, 2004	Nikkei page 9	Marubeni Real Estate sales 60%, Marubeni Corp. 5%, US Morgan Stanley 35%	Office building management, trustee of operation

Type of synergy	Date of article	News-paper	JV partners	Notes
• Facility Sharing • Utilization of Sales Channels	December 28, 2004	Nikkei page 13	Nippon Steel Corporation 60%, Nakayama Steel Works, Ltd. 40%	Bars steel production for bolts and nuts
• Facility Sharing	December 23, 2004	Nikkei page 11	Shinnittetsu Chemical, Mitsubishi Chemical Corporation (no detailed reference about shareholding ratio)	JV partnership to be broken off, to be a wholly owned subsidiary of Shinnittetsu Chemical
• Collaborative R&D • Utilization of Sales Channels	December 22, 2004	Nikkei page 13	Nissan, China Dongfeng Motor Corporation (no detailed reference about shareholding ratio)	Nissan brand commercial vehicles production, engine development. 35 billion yen new plant construction in Guangzhou
• Technology Introduction • Collaborative R&D	December 15, 2004	Nikkei page 11	Sony 50%, South Korea Samsung 50%	Business alliance by JV as a premise of patent mutual open policy
• Brand Introduction • Facility Sharing	December 14, 2004	Nikkei page 1	Toyota 50%, China First Automobile Works Group 50%	Manufacturing Prius, the Camry brand vehicles in China
• Facility Sharing	December 10, 2004	Nikkei page 11	Sony 50%, South Korea Samsung 50%	Seventh-generation liquid crystal new plant construction, JV discussion stated
• Facility Sharing	December 6, 2004	Nikkei page 9	Panasonic, China local companies (no detailed reference about shareholding ratio)	New production air conditioning factory in China
• Facility Sharing	December 5, 2004	Nikkei page 5	Mitsubishi Motors Corporation 18%, Nissan Motor Corp. 82%	Common parts of the transmission manufacturer
• Collaborative R&D • Cost Sharing	December 4, 2004	Nikkei page 11	Ebara Corporation, Mitsubishi Heavy Industries, Ltd., Yokohama City Government, IHI Corporation, Toshiba, Meidensha Corporation, Yokohama City University (no detailed reference about shareholding ratio)	CO_2 reduction to oversee the entire region, joint research and business development for the construction of energy supply and management system, receiving subsidy of Ministry of the Environment
• Securing Resources	November 28, 2004	Nikkei pages 1, 7	Shell 55%, Mitsui & Co., Ltd. 25%, Mitsubishi Corporation 20%	Sakhalin 2. Follow-up story about existing JV's business. Russian government petroleum company Gazprom proposed three companies of Sakhalin 2 Project participants, its capital participation in the project

Type of synergy	Date of article	News-paper	JV partners	Notes
• Facility Sharing • Utilization of Sales Channels	November 24, 2004	Nikkei page 9	Kikkoman Corporation's Thailand subsidiary 75.1%, Thailand Samroiyod 17.4%, Thailand River Kwai International 7.5%	Kikkoman is to build a vegetable fruit processing plant in the Del Monte brand in Thailand, starts production and sales
• Brand Introduction • Utilization of Sales Channels	November 23, 2004	Nikkei page 9	China Shanghai Automotive Industry Corporation approx. 70%, UK MG Rover Group approx. 30% (no detailed reference about shareholding ratio)	Overcoming the slump in Rover sales with the financial power and distribution channels of Shanghai Automotive Industry Corporation
• Facility Sharing • Utilization of Sales Channels	November 23, 2004	Nikkei page 13	Sanyo Electric Co., Ltd. 30%→70% up to 90%, Thailand Premier Enterprise 70%→0%	Follow-up story about existing JV's business in order to reorganize the white goods production base
• Utilization of Sales Channels	November 16, 2004	Nikkei page 15	Prestige International Inc. 65%, insurance agent Advance Create Co., Ltd. 35%	Insurance telemarketing new service
• Facility Sharing • Utilization of Sales Channels	November 11, 2004	Nikkei page 15	Hitachi Group companies (no detailed reference about shareholding ratio)	New elevator production plant construction in China, anticipating Olympic demand
• Facility Sharing • Utilization of Sales Channels	November 10, 2004	Nikkei page 7	China Baosteel Group Corporation 38%, Luxembourg Arcelor 25%, Germany Volkswagenwerk GmbH 37%	Car steel plate processing plant established in Shanghai
• Technology Introduction • Utilization of Sales Channels	November 9, 2004	Nikkei page 13	KDDI 50%, UK BT Group 50%	Provision of line services across countries taking advantage of the know-how of BT
• Cost Sharing	November 8, 2004	Nikkei page 1	35 companies such as banks, funds, firms (no detailed reference about shareholding ratio)	35 companies establish fund to get global warming gas carry-out rights
• Facility Sharing • Brand Introduction • Utilization of Sales Channels	November 8, 2004	Nikkei pages 1, 9	Honda Group, China Guangzhou Automobile Group, China Dongfeng Motor Corporation, 3 JV Cos among 3 parties (no detailed reference about shareholding ratio)	Honda Group is shooting at local production capacity doubled by making full use of 3 Chinese JV companies

Type of synergy	Date of article	News-paper	JV partners	Notes
• Technology Introduction • Brand Introduction • Utilization of Sales Channels	November 5, 2004	Nikkei page 13	JV1: Toshiba 70%, China TCL Corporation 30%, and JV2: Toshiba 49%, China TCL Corporation 51%	Manufacture and sale of refrigerators, washing machines. 2 JV companies to be founded
• Technology Introduction • Cost Sharing	November 4, 2004	Nikkei page 9	• Singapore Tele-communications Ltd., SingTel, India Bharti Enterprises, Australia Optus, Malaysia Maxis, Indonesia Telkomsel, Philippines Globe Telecom, Inc. same amount invested	Mobile phone infrastructure unified coalition by 7 Pacific Ocean large communication companies
• Technology Introduction • Brand Introduction • Utilization of Sales Channels	November 4, 2004	Nikkei pages 1, 11	Toshiba, China TCL Corporation (no detailed reference about shareholding ratio)	Manufacture and sale of refrigerator, washing machine appliances. 2 JV companies founded. Manufacturing company Toshiba is (majority), sales company is TCL (majority)
• Utilization of Sales Channels	November 2, 2004	Nikkei page 7	Mizuho Trust & Banking Co., Ltd. 50%, Sumitomo Mitsui Trust Bank, Ltd. 50%	Pension management company
• Facility Sharing • Brand Introduction • Utilization of Sales Channels	November 2, 2004	Nikkei page 13	Nissan Motor Corp. 30%→51%, China Citic Automobile, China Haima Automobile 70% →49%	Nissan integrates the JVs of China, strengthens the automotive sector
• Facility Sharing • Utilization of Sales Channels	October 21, 2004	Nikkei page 12	Sankyo Aluminium Industry Co., Ltd. 25%, Shin Nikkei Co., Ltd. 25%, Tateyama Aluminum Industry Co., Ltd. 25%, Tokuyama Corporation's subsidiary Shanon Corporation 25%	Production and sales of building resin sash
• Technology Introduction • Alleviation of Friction • Utilization of Sales Channels	October 17, 2004	Nikkei page 1	South Korea SK Telecom, LG Electronics Inc. and Dongah Elecomm 3 companies union, Vietnam Saigon Post and Telecommunications (no detailed reference about shareholding ratio)	Vietnam government announced an open policy towards the participation of foreign capital for the mobile phone business and permits the JV with South Korea
• Technology Introduction • Cost Sharing	October 17, 2004	Nikkei page 3	Hitachi, small and medium enterprise agency (no detailed reference about shareholding ratio)	Consulting service based on the management know-how of Hitachi and SME funding provided a combination

Type of synergy	Date of article	News-paper	JV partners	Notes
• Facility Sharing • Utilization of Sales Channels	October 10, 2004	Nikkei page 15	Fujifilm Corporation, US Arch Chemicals, Inc. (no detailed reference about shareholding ratio)	Photosensitive resin business JV partnership to be broken off
• Brand Introduction • Utilization of Sales Channels	October 2, 2004	Nikkei page 13	Shiseido Co., Ltd. 54%, Saha Group Thailand 46%	To perform a beauty salon business to introduce Shiseido brand into Thailand
• Facility Sharing	September 27, 2004	Nikkei page 9	Hitachi 55%, Omron 45%	ATM business
• Facility Sharing	September 27, 2004	Nikkei page 9	Hitachi 60%, NEC 40%	Mission-critical router business
• Securing Resources	September 22, 2004	Nikkei page 11	Mitsubishi Gas Chemical, Itochu Corp., Brunei government firm (no detailed reference about shareholding ratio)	Production of methanol in Brunei (33 billion yen investment)
• Facility Sharing	September 19, 2004	Nikkei page 5	Mitsubishi Corporation 36%, Junsei Chemical Co., Ltd. 15%, China Shanghai Qunli processing 49%	Production and sales of agricultural chemicals, pharmaceutical products in China
• Securing Resources • Facility Sharing	September 14, 2004	Nikkei page 11	Mitsubishi Gas Chemical 51%, China Chongqing Medical 49%	China's largest methanol production and sales base for coating raw materials and synthetic fibers
• Alleviation of Friction • Brand Introduction • Technology Introduction	September 13, 2004	Nikkei page 1 evening edition	Suzuki Motor Corp. & Maruti Udyog Ltd. India (no detailed reference about shareholding ratio)	In addition to the existing JV, JV to build a second plant in India
• Facility Sharing • Utilization of Sales Channels	September 9, 2004	Nikkei page 13	South Korea Hyundai Motor Company 50%, China Automobile company JAC 50%	Manufacture and sale of commercial vehicles in China
• Alleviation of Friction	September 2, 2004	Nikkei page 9	Shell 40%, China National Petroleum Company 60%	Europe & US oil companies must have JV with a local firm to foray into China
• Facility Sharing • Cost Sharing	August 19, 2004	Nikkei page 7	South Korea SK Hynix Inc., Europe ST Microelectronics NV (no detailed reference about shareholding ratio)	Determine the investment of $2 billion to expand into China

Type of synergy	Date of article	News-paper	JV partners	Notes
• Facility Sharing • Utilization of Sales Channels	August 12, 2004	Nikkei page 9	JFE, China Guangzhou Iron and Steel Enterprises Holdings Ltd. (no detailed reference about shareholding ratio)	First blast furnace for steel plate integrated production and construction in China. Project cost is more than 100 billion yen.
• Facility Sharing • Utilization of Sales Channels	August 11, 2004	Nikkei pages 1, 3	JFE, China Guangzhou Iron and Steel Enterprises Holdings Ltd. (no detailed reference about shareholding ratio)	First blast furnace for steel plate integrated production and construction in China. Project cost is more than 100 billion yen.
• Facility Sharing • Cost Sharing	August 5, 2004	Nikkei page 13	Finished vehicles logistics company Zero Trans Co., Ltd. 25%, Sumitomo Corporation 20%, Mitsui O.S.K. Lines, Ltd. 20%, China CITIC subsidiary logistics company 35%	The finished car logistics undertaking starting with Nissan cars in China
• Cost Sharing	August 4, 2004	Nikkei page 15	Takeda Pharmaceutical Company Ltd., Daiichi Sankyo Company, Ltd., Yamanouchi Pharmaceutical Co., Ltd., Yokohama National University, etc. Industry-university cooperation 22 companies (no detailed reference about shareholding ratio)	Participated in industry-academia collaboration "protein structure analysis Consortium," interoperable the world's highest performance analysis machine
• Utilization of Sales Channels	July 16, 2004	Nikkei page 11	Mochida Pharmaceutical Co., Ltd. (majority), Germany Siemens AG (no detailed reference about shareholding ratio)	Integration of Japan ultrasonic diagnostic equipment business
• Facility Sharing	July 16, 2004	Nikkei page 11	Sony 50%, South Korea Samsung 50%	Production of next-generation liquid crystal panel (using a large glass substrate)
• Alleviation of Friction • Cost Sharing	July 14, 2004	Nikkei page 13	Mitsubishi Corporation (majority), US Oil company ConocoPhillips Company (no detailed reference about shareholding ratio)	Liquefied natural gas (LNG) acceptance base construction near Los Angeles. Positive effect on local residents and the government negotiation by using JV formation
• Utilization of Sales Channels	July 13, 2004	Nikkei page 3	Mitsubishi Estate Company, Ltd. 51%→40%, Singapore The Ascott Group Ltd. 49%→60%	Japanese-style luxury rental housing business of cleaning laundry, fully furnished

Type of synergy	Date of article	News-paper	JV partners	Notes
• Securing Resources	June 16, 2004	Nikkei page 13	Mitsubishi Gas Chemical, Itochu Corp. etc. firms group, Saudi Aramco (no detailed reference about shareholding ratio)	Methanol production
• Cost Sharing	June 11, 2004	Nikkei page 13	Mitsui O.S.K. Lines, Ltd. 25%, Itochu Corp. 25%, Algeria Sonatrach 25%, Sonatrach's subsidiary 25%	By SPC among 4 companies, the LNG ship building and operation (35 billion yen)
• Cost Sharing	May 16, 2004	Nikkei page 1	Panasonic 75%, Toray Industries, Inc. 25%	Plasma panel the world's largest factory construction JV (90 billion yen)
• Facility Sharing	May 14, 2004	Nikkei page 11	Ube Industries, Ltd. 50%, Maruzen Petrochemical Co, Ltd. 50%	Polyethylene production
• Securing Resources • Cost Sharing	May 8, 2004	Nikkei pages 1, 11	Sumitomo Chemical Company, Ltd. 50%, Saudi Aramco 50%	Ethylene production (300 billion yen investment)
• Utilization of Sales Channels	April 23, 2004	Nikkei page 18	SoftBank Corp. SBI Investment Co., Ltd. 51%, Hong Kong Sunwah Kingsway Capital Holdings Ltd. 49%	Companies foray support, listing support, business development support in China and Japan
• Utilization of Sales Channels	April 3, 2004	Nikkei page 11	Nissan Motor Corp. 25%→above 75%, Thailand The Siam Group 75%→less than 25%	Follow-up story about existing JV's business. While there has been utilization of the JV as an export base in Asia, after the management rights acquisition by Nissan to function as a production base
• Utilization of Sales Channels	March 30, 2004	Nikkei page 1 evening edition	NTT Docomo, Inc. 20%, UK Hutchison Whampoa Ltd. 80%	Third-generation mobile phone, DoCoMo to consider sale of its share to other partner
• Facility Sharing	March 25, 2004	Nikkei page 11	Seiko Epson Corporation 55%, Sanyo Electric Co., Ltd. 45%	Liquid crystal business integration for mobile digital camera
• Technology Introduction	March 25, 2004	Nikkei page 13	IHI Corporation 51%, Hong Kong SSAI 49%	Large compressor production in China, plans for a base for Asia
• Facility Sharing	March 9, 2004	Nikkei page 13	Sony approx. 50%, South Korea Samsung 50% + 1 share	Liquid crystal panel joint manufacturing JV partnership to be broken off, to be a wholly owned subsidiary of Samsung
• Facility Sharing	February 28, 2004	Nikkei page 9	NEC 49%, South Korea Samsung 51%	Organic EL business integration JV. NEC intends to transfer related patents to Samsung and to withdraw from JV

Type of synergy	Date of article	News-paper	JV partners	Notes
• Facility Sharing	February 23, 2004	Nikkei page 1	Toray Industries, Inc. 50%, Europe BASF 50%	High-performance resin production JV in Malaysia
• Technology Introduction	February 19, 2004	Nikkei page 1	Honda Group 50%, US TCM 50%	By using Honda Group airplane engine technology, to enter into propeller aircraft business in US
• Technology Introduction	February 17, 2004	Nikkei page 13	Honda Group 50%, GE 50%	By using Honda Group airplane engine technology, to enter into small jet engine commercial aircraft business in US
• Alleviation of Friction	February 16, 2004	Nikkei page 7	Toyota 50%, GM 50%	Follow-up story about existing JV's business. Significant emphasis on NUMMI 20th anniversary
• Alleviation of Friction	February 12, 2004	Nikkei page 8	Toyota 50%, GM 50%	Follow-up story about existing JV's business. Significant emphasis on NUMMI 20th anniversary
• Technology Introduction	February 5, 2004	Nikkei page 15	Taisho Pharmaceutical Co., Ltd. 49%, French Sanofi 51%	Introduction of arrhythmic drugs of Sanofi
• Technology Introduction	January 28, 2004	Nikkei page 13	Meidensha Corporation 55%, Switzerland ABB 45%	Leverage of the arrester business through the introduction of ABB technology
• Technology Introduction • Brand Introduction	January 20, 2004	Nikkei page 3	Yamato Transport Co., Ltd. 49%→9%, US UPS 51%→ US%	Policy changes as to aim of a comprehensive logistics company under the UPS brand. JV partnership to be broken off, to be a wholly owned subsidiary of UPS
• Technology Introduction • Brand Introduction	January 3, 2004	Nikkei page 1	Mazda Motor Corporation 25%, Ford Motor Company 25%, China Changan Automobile (balance) (no detailed reference about shareholding ratio)	Part of a comprehensive business alliance of small car production business between Mazda and Ford in Shanghai, each company of brand to be used
• Collaborative R&D • Utilization of Sales Channels	December 23, 2003	Nikkei page 10	Kai Corporation 50%, US Universal Razor Industries, Inc. 50%	Cutlery product development and sales in US market
• Utilization of Sales Channels	December 14, 2003	Nikkei page 7	Sumitomo Corporation 37%, Egypt Orascom Group 63%	IT business in the Middle East, Africa
• Collaborative R&D	December 4, 2003	Nikkei page 1	Cannon 50%, Toshiba 50%	Using the joint R&D achievements, production and sales of large screen power-saving flat-screen TV
• Collaborative R&D • Utilization of Sales Channels	November 25, 2003	Nikkei page 9	Nissan, China Dongfeng Motor Corporation (no detailed reference about shareholding ratio)	Commercial vehicles production, engine development of Nissan brand. 35 billion yen new plant construction in Guangzhou. Total investment 220 billion yen

Type of synergy	Date of article	News-paper	JV partners	Notes
• Collaborative R&D • Utilization of Sales Channels	November 4, 2003	Nikkei page 9	IHI Corporation 70%, Taiwan Chin Fong Machine Industrial Co., Ltd. 30%	Joint R&D and production of automotive press machinery for China
• Collaborative R&D	October 22, 2003	Nikkei pages 1, 13	Sony 60%→70%, NTT Docomo, Inc. (balance) (no detailed reference about shareholding ratio)	Joint R&D of wallet portable IC card visceral mobile terminal technology
• Technology Introduction	October 21, 2003	Nikkei page 3 evening edition	NEC 28.6%→less than 20%, Shanghai Huahong Group 71.4%, US TowerJazz Semiconductor Co., Ltd. 0%→11%	Semiconductor contract manufacturing factory in China, by the introduction of technology of Jazz
• Facility Sharing	October 17, 2003	Nikkei pages 1, 13	Sony approx. 50%, South Korea Samsung approx. 50%	JV partnership to be broken off, to be a wholly owned subsidiary of Samsung
• Collaborative R&D	October 15, 2003	Nikkei page 9	Olympus Corporation 50%, Riso Kagaku Corporation 50%	Commercial printer joint R&D
• Utilization of Sales Channels	July 18, 2003	Nikkei page 11	Sanyo Electric Co., Ltd., Toyota Tsusho Corporation, China Hefei Sakae Group (no detailed reference about shareholding ratio)	Article that announced plan of JV listing
• Brand Introduction	July 12, 2003	Nikkei page 11	Toyota, China Guangzhou Automobile (GAC) (no detailed reference about shareholding ratio)	Passenger car of Toyota brand production
• Utilization of Sales Channels	July 3, 2003	Nikkei page 13	NSK Ltd. 49%→98%, US The Timken Company 51%→2%	Automotive bearings production JV in US
• Facility Sharing	July 1, 2003	Nikkei page 1	Tokyo Gas Co., Ltd. 51%, Shell Gas & Power 24.5%, Showa Shell Sekiyu K.K. 24.5%	Construction and operation of LNG gas turbine power plant
• Technology Introduction • Utilization of Sales Channels	July 1, 2003	Nikkei page 1	JFE 10.3%, Mitsui & Co., Ltd. 10.1%, Mitsubishi Corporation 10.1%, BrazilArcelor 43.9%, steel company CVRD 20.5%, others (balance)	Iron and steel overseas production JV reviewed, Japanese companies will withdraw from JV by selling their holdings
• Facility Sharing	June 25, 2003	Nikkei page 15	Shionogi & Co., Ltd. 49%, Germany pharmaceutical company Degussa AG 51%	To transfer the industrial chemicals business of Shionogi to JV

Type of synergy	Date of article	News-paper	JV partners	Notes
• Brand Introduction	June 18, 2003	Nikkei page 13	Sony 50%, Italy Technogym 50%	Sales of fitness equipment that take advantage of technogym brand in Japan
• Utilization of Sales Channels	May 27, 2003	Nikkei page 13	Hino Motors, Ltd. 50%, Mitsui & Co., Ltd. 25%, US Automobile dealership Penske Automotive Group 25%	Entry into the car rental business by know-how of Pensuke and sales network enhancements and in US
• Utilization of Sales Channels • Collaborative R&D	May 22, 2003	Nikkei page 15	Kawaijuku Educational institution 70%, Pasona Group Inc. 30%	Qualification test, college entrance examination, venue arrangements, whole service
• Utilization of Sales Channels • Collaborative R&D	May 9, 2003	Nikkei page 7	Mizuho FG approx. 90%, Development Bank of Japan Inc. approx. 10%	Corporate rehabilitation specialist company
• Utilization of Sales Channels	May 7, 2003	Nikkei page 15	Snow Brand Milk Products Co., Ltd. 51% →41%, French wine-related business company SEPV 49% →59%	Snow Brand Milk Products wanted to make JV out of consolidated application
• Brand Introduction	April 19, 2003	Nikkei page 1	Daimler-Benz AG Chrysler Group, LLC 50%, Guangdong Provincial Government 50% (no detailed reference about shareholding ratio)	Passenger car production at Mercedes-Benz brand
• Collaborative R&D	April 15, 2003	Nikkei page 9	Denso Corporation 50%, Germany Robert Bosch GmbH 50%	Design of large-scale integrated circuit, the development company
• Brand Introduction	February 19, 2003	Nikkei page 13	Ajinomoto Company, Inc. 50%, Anglo-Dutch Unilever N.V./Unilever PLC 50%	Follow-up story about existing JV's business. JV partnership to be broken off, to be a wholly owned subsidiary of Unilever. Ajinomoto decided to withdraw and transferred its share ownership of seven companies in Asia; the companies became subsidiaries of Unilever
• Utilization of Sales Channels • Collaborative R&D	February 13, 2003	Nikkei page 13	Intec Inc. 49%, South Korea LG Electronics Incorporated, CNS 51%	Server system miniaturization support services
• Utilization of Sales Channels	January 28, 2003	Nikkei page 7	Nippon Life Insurance Company 50%, China Shanghai SVA Group 50%	To advance into Chinese life insurance market
• Utilization of Sales Channels • Collaborative R&D	January 24, 2003	Nikkei page 13	Kodansha Ltd. 50%, US Random House 50%	Translation of Random House's new publication; exporting the translation of Japanese Manga, etc.

Type of synergy	Date of article	News-paper	JV partners	Notes
● Utilization of Sales Channels	January 11, 2003	Nikkei page 1	Nippon Life Insurance Company 50%, China Shanghai SVA Group 50%	To advance into Chinese life insurance market
● Collaborative R&D	December 31, 2002	Nikkei page 7	Hitachi, US IBM (no detailed reference about shareholding ratio)	HDD research and manufacturing facilities. And oversees 7 Asian countries
● Utilization of Sales Channels	December 20, 2002	Nikkei page 13	Fuji Heavy Industries Ltd. 51%→100%, Isuzu Motors Ltd. 49%→0%	Automobile manufacturing and sales company in US. JV partnership to be broken off, to be a wholly owned subsidiary of Fuji
● Facility Sharing	December 7, 2002	Nikkei page 11	Kobe Steel, Ltd. 50%, Germany copper processed goods company Wieland 50%	Adding a new production line to Toshiba Oita factory, for promotion of effective utilization
● Collaboration in lieu of Competition ● Utilization of Sales Channels	November 25, 2002	Nikkei page 13	Kobe Steel, Ltd. 50%, Germany copper processed goods company Wieland 50%	Manufacture and sale of copper tube in the US
● Facility Sharing	November 24, 2002	Nikkei page 7	Sumitomo Metal Industries, Ltd., Taiwan China Steel Corporation (no detailed reference about shareholding ratio)	Operating company of blast furnace in Wakayama Prefecture
● Utilization of Sales Channels	November 13, 2002	Nikkei pages 1, 11	Shin Nippon Steel, China Baoshan Iron & Steel Co., Ltd. (no detailed reference about shareholding ratio)	Automotive steel sheet production and sales in China
● Facility Sharing	November 13, 2002	Nikkei page 11	Mitsubishi Chemical Corporation 65%→ 100%, Tonen Chemical Corporation 35%→0%	General-purpose resin business JV partnership to be broken off, to be a wholly owned subsidiary of Mitsubishi Chemical
● Facility Sharing	November 13, 2002	Nikkei page 11	Shin Nippon Steel, China Baoshan Iron & Steel Co., Ltd. (no detailed reference about shareholding ratio)	Automotive steel sheet production and sales in China
● Collaborative R&D	November 2, 2002	Nikkei page 9	Chubu Electric Power Company, Inc., Mitsubishi Heavy Industries, Ltd. (no detailed reference about shareholding ratio)	Cogeneration company of fuel cell technology

Type of synergy	Date of article	News-paper	JV partners	Notes
• Facility Sharing	October 24, 2002	Nikkei page 3	Sumitomo Metal Industries, Ltd. approx. 60%, Taiwan China Steel Corporation approx. 40%	Operating company of blast furnace in Wakayama Prefecture
• Utilization of Sales Channels • Brand Introduction	October 17, 2002	Nikkei page 11	NHK Spring Co., Ltd. 50%, French Faurecia Group 50%	Manufacture and supply of car seat
• Utilization of Sales Channels • Brand Introduction	October 16, 2002	Nikkei page 9	Teijin Ltd. 50% →100%, Du Pont 50%→0%	Nylon business JV partnership to be broken off, to be a wholly owned subsidiary of Teijin
• Facility Sharing	October 15, 2002	Nikkei page 15	NEC 50%, Hitachi 50%	Follow-up story about existing JV's business. JV Elpida Memory (Micron) president personnel changes
• Utilization of Sales Channels • Brand Introduction	October 12, 2002	Nikkei page 12	GM 42.1%, Zyle Motor Sales and its main banks 33%, Suzuki Motor Corp. 14.9%, Shanghai Automotive Industry Corporation 10%	Automobile manufacturing sales in China
• Facility Sharing	October 8, 2002	Nikkei page 11	Fuji Heavy Industries Ltd. 51%→100%, Isuzu Motors Ltd. 49%→0%	RV business JV partnership to be broken off, to be a wholly owned subsidiary of Fuji
• Utilization of Sales Channels • Brand Introduction	October 7, 2002	Nikkei page 7	Daihatsu Motor Co., Ltd., China First Automobile Works Group (no detailed reference about shareholding ratio)	Automobile manufacturing sales in China
• Obtaining Local Expertise • Alleviation of Friction	October 4, 2002	Nikkei page 12	SMBC Consumer Finance Co., Ltd. 70%, Taiwan TC Bank 30%	Consumer loans outsourcing
• Facility Sharing	July 16, 2002	Nikkei page 1	Sumitomo Metal Industries, Ltd. 40% →0%, US Steel company LTV 60% →100%	JV partnership to be broken off, to be a wholly owned subsidiary of LTV
• Utilization of Sales Channels	July 14, 2002	Nikkei page 7	US GM , China car company (no detailed reference about shareholding ratio)	Automatic transmission manufacturing JV
• Utilization of Sales Channels • Brand Introduction	July 12, 2002	Nikkei page 11	Asahi Breweries Ltd, China Tsingtao Brewery Company Ltd. (no detailed reference about shareholding ratio)	Japan sales of Tsingtao beer brand

Type of synergy	Date of article	News-paper	JV partners	Notes
● Collaboration in lieu of Competition ● Collaborative R&D	July 12, 2002	Nikkei page 13	NEC, Toshiba, Hitachi , Fujitsu Ltd., Sanyo Electric Co., Ltd. less than16%, Oki Electric Industry Co., Ltd., Rohm Co., Ltd., Sanyo Electric Co., Ltd., Sharp, Sony approx. 1% (no detailed reference about shareholding ratio)	Joint R&D of next generation semiconductor technology
● Facility Sharing	July 12, 2002	Nikkei page 15	Panasonic 52%, Nippon Express Co., Ltd. 48%	As a logistics professional company, Nippon Express is to cooperate with logistics department of Panasonic
● Collaboration in lieu of Competition ● Facility Sharing	July 4, 2002	Nikkei page 11	Mitsubishi Chemical Corporation 50% →27.5%, Asahi Kasei Group 50%→45%, Idemitsu Kosan Co., Ltd. 0%→27.5%	Polystyrene manufacturing and sales
● Collaboration in lieu of Competition ● Facility Sharing	July 3, 2002	Nikkei page 1	Mitsubishi Chemical Corporation 50% →27.5%, Asahi Kasei Group 50%→45%, Idemitsu Kosan Co., Ltd. 0%→27.5%	Polystyrene manufacturing and sales
● Collaborative R&D	June 24, 2002	Nikkei page 7	Toshiba, Fujitsu Ltd. (no detailed reference about shareholding ratio)	JV for the trigger of industry restructuring
● Technology Introduction	June 20, 2002	Nikkei page 13	Mitsui & Co., Ltd. 50% →47.2%, Singapore National Cancer Center 50%→47.2%, Shimadzu Corporation 0%→5.6%	Sales and database construction of cancer-related gene
● Technology Introduction	June 14, 2002	Nikkei page 11	Seiko Epson Corporation 60% →70%, UK Cambridge Display Technology (CDT) 40%→30% (no detailed reference about shareholding ratio)	Development of next-generation organic EL display device
● Utilization of Sales Channels ● Reputational Backing ● Alleviation of Friction	June 6, 2002	Nikkei page 1	Toyota, China First Automobile Works Group, Tianjin Automobile (no detailed reference about shareholding ratio)	Production and sales of luxury cars in China

Type of synergy	Date of article	News-paper	JV partners	Notes
● Technology Introduction	June 4, 2002	Nikkei page 1	Hitachi 70% to be increasing, US IBM 30% to be decreasing, Shimadzu Corporation 0%→5.6%	JV as a receiving tray of HDD-related business acquisitions
● Utilization of Sales Channels	May 25, 2002	Nikkei page 7	US Merrill Lynch & Co., Inc. 50%, UK Bank HSBC 50%	Online securities JV company for wealthy individuals
● Obtaining Local Expertise ● Alleviation of Friction ● Brand Introduction	May 20, 2002	Nikkei page 7	Suzuki Motor Corp. 50%→54.2%, India government agency 50%→45.8%	India largest automaker
● Utilization of Sales Channels ● Reputational Backing ● Obtaining Local Expertise	May 18, 2002	Nikkei page 9	Itochu Corp. 50%, Australia Proteome Systems 50%	Protein analysis for the support of new drug development that applies the genome
● Collaborative R&D ● Cost Sharing	May 17, 2002	Nikkei page 9	US Advanced Micro Devices, Inc. (AMD), Germany Infineon Technologies AG, US DuPont photomask 1/3 each	Joint R&D JV to develop photomask technology for transferring a circuit of a semiconductor on a silicon wafer base
● Utilization of Sales Channels ● Brand Introduction	May 15, 2002	Nikkei page 11	Suntory Holdings Ltd.'s subsidiary 50%, Italy Davide Campari 50%	Suntory 4 brand of Scotch whisky and Campari 3 brand such as "Campari," "Cinzano" sales
● Utilization of Sales Channels ● Brand Introduction	May 4, 2002	Nikkei page 9	Snow Brand Milk Products Co., Ltd. 50%, US Food company Dole Food Company, Inc. 50%	Follow-up story about existing JV's business Business partnership dissolution between Snow Brand and Dole
● Utilization of Sales Channels	May 2, 2002	Nikkei page 9	Yamato Transport Co., Ltd. 51%→100%, US United Parcel Service (UPS) 49%→0%	Air freight, customs clearance business JV partnership to be broken off, to be a wholly owned subsidiary of Yamato Transport
● Collaborative R&D	April 20, 2002	Nikkei pages 1, 13	Mitsubishi Heavy Industries, Ltd., Germany Daimler-Benz AG Chrysler Group, LLC (no detailed reference about shareholding ratio)	Passenger cars gasoline engine joint R&D
● Technology Introduction	April 20, 2002	Nikkei page 13	JECS Corporation 49% →100%, Germany Robert Bosch GmbH 51%→0%	Nissan engine control system production JV partnership to be broken off, to be a wholly owned subsidiary of JECS

Type of synergy	Date of article	News-paper	JV partners	Notes
• Collaborative R&D	April 12, 2002	Nikkei page 11	Tokyo Electron Ltd., Screen Holdings Co., Ltd., ULVAC, Inc., Ebara Corporation (no detailed reference about shareholding ratio)	Joint R&D for connection technology of semiconductor manufacturing equipment
• Collaborative R&D	April 12, 2002	Nikkei page 1	Sanyo Electric Co., Ltd., Honda Group (no detailed reference about shareholding ratio)	Joint R&D of hybrid battery development
• Collaborative R&D	April 10, 2002	Nikkei page 13	Sony, Tokyo Seimitsu Co., Ltd., Hitachi, Mitsubishi Electric, Seiko Epson Corporation (no detailed reference about shareholding ratio)	Semiconductor circuit exposure device (next generation stepper) development
• Utilization of Sales Channels • Technology Introduction	February 19, 2002	Nikkei page 13	HITACHI 60% →100%, Taiwan UMC 40%→0%	Semiconductor production
• Utilization of Sales Channels	February 14, 2002	Nikkei page 13	Orix Group 50%, Nippon Koei Co., Ltd. 50%	ESCO business to obtain a reward, depending on the outcome of the energy conservation measures of the building
• Utilization of Sales Channels • Reputational Backing • Obtaining Local Expertise	February 13, 2002	Nikkei page 12	Tsumura & Co., US daily necessities wholesale Paltac Corporation, Wakamoto Pharmaceutical Co., Ltd., Ohta's Isan Co., Ltd., Kinkan Co., Ltd. (no detailed reference about shareholding ratio)	Household medicines, health foods markets in US
• Collaborative R&D	February 12, 2002	Nikkei page 1	Fujitsu Ltd., US consultancy Accenture (no detailed reference about shareholding ratio)	Management information system development
• Utilization of Sales Channels	February 7, 2002	Nikkei page 13	NEC, French consumer electronics company Thomson Multimedia (no detailed reference about shareholding ratio)	Plasma display panel (PDP) production (JV negotiations abandoned)
• Utilization of Sales Channels	February 1, 2002	Nikkei page 13	Showa Denko K.K 50%→0%, US Cabot Corporation 50%→100%	Specialty chemicals, additional agents of automotive aluminum, tantalum powder business JV partnership to be broken off, to be a wholly owned subsidiary

References

BARNEY, JAY B., GAINING AND SUSTAINING COMPETITIVE ADVANTAGE (4th ed. 2011).

BRUNSVOLD, BRIAN G., DENNIS P. O'REILLEY & D. BRIAN KACEDON, DRAFTING PATENT LICENSE AGREEMENTS (6th ed. 2008).

CANNADY, CYNTHIA, TECHNOLOGY LICENSING AND DEVELOPMENT AGREEMENTS (3d ed. 2013).

CHISUM, DONALD S., CHISUM ON PATENTS (1977).

GIBBONS, ROBERT, GAME THEORY FOR APPLIED ECONOMISTS (1992).

Gilson, Ronald J., *Locating Innovation: The Endogeneity of Technology, Organizational Structure, and Financial Contracting*, 110 COLUM. L. REV. 885 (2010).

Gilson, Ronald J., Charles F. Sabel & Robert E. Scott, *Contracting for Innovation: Vertical Disintegration and Interfirm Collaboration*, 109 COLUM. L. REV. 431 (2009).

GOMPERS, PAUL A. & JOSH LERNER, THE VENTURE CAPITAL CYCLE (2d ed. 2004).

HALLORAN, MICHAEL J. ET AL., VENTURE CAPITAL AND PUBLIC OFFERING NEGOTIATION (3d ed. 2000).

Hauswald, Robert & Ulrich Hege, *Ownership and Control in Joint Ventures: Theory and Evidence* (2009) www1.american.edu/academic.depts/ksb/finance_realestate/rhauswald/papers/Ownership%20and%20Control%20in%20JVs.pdf.

HEWITT, IAN, HEWITT ON JOINT VENTURES (5th ed. 2011).

Ihara, Hiroshi, *Gobengaishi no Yakuin Jinji wo Meguru Funso* [*Disputes Regarding Joint Venture Director Appointments*], 974 NBL 40 (2012).

KEATINGE, ROBERT R., ANN E. CONAWAY & BRUCE P. ELY, KEATINGE AND CONAWAY ON CHOICE OF BUSINESS ENTITY: SELECTING FORM AND STRUCTURE FOR A CLOSELY-HELD BUSINESS (2012).

Kitazume, Masahiko, *M&A to Jointo Bencha no Zeimu* [*M&A and Joint Venture Taxation*], *in* 2 BIZINESU HOMU TAIKEI: M&A JOINTO BENCHA [2 BUSINESS LAWS: M&A AND JOINT VENTURES] 273 (Michiaki Nakano & Zenichi Shishido eds., 2006).

KLEIN, WILLIAM & JOHN C. COFFEE, JR., BUSINESS ORGANIZATION AND FINANCE: LEGAL AND ECONOMIC PRINCIPLES (10th ed. 2007).

Lerner, Josh & Robert P. Merges, *The Control of Technology Alliances: An Empirical Analysis of the Biotechnology Industry*, 46 J. INDUS. ECON. 125 (1998).

LEVIN, WILLIAM E., TRADE DRESS PROTECTION (2d ed. 2008–2012).

Levinson, Daniel P. & Jarod G. Taylor, *The Expansive Reach of the FCPA Extends to Japan Again: A Second Japanese Company Resolves FCPA Charges Related to a Nigerian Bribery Scandal*, Morrison & Foerster LLP Client Alert (February 2012) www.mofo.jp/topics/legal-updates/tlcb/20120210.html#E.

Manesh, Mohsen, *What is the Practical Importance of Default Rules under Delaware LLC and LP Law?*, 2 HARV. BUS. L. REV. Online 121 (2012).

MAYER, COLIN, FIRM COMMITMENT (2013).

McCahery, Joseph A. & Erik P.M. Vermeulen, *Conservatism and Innovation in Venture Capital Contracting,* 2 TOPICS IN CORP. L. & ECON. 16 (2013).

MCCARTHY, J. THOMAS, MCCARTHY ON TRADEMARKS AND UNFAIR COMPETITION (4th ed. 1998–2013).

MILGROM, PAUL & JOHN ROBERTS, ECONOMICS, ORGANIZATION AND MANAGEMENT (1992).

NIMMER, MELVILLE B. & DAVID NIMMER, NIMMER ON COPYRIGHT (1985).

NISHIMURA SOGO ED., M&A-HO TAIZEN [PERSPECTIVE OF M&A LAW] (2001).

Porter, Michael E., *The Five Competitive Forces that Shape Strategy*, HARV. BUS. REV 86–104 (Jan. 2008).

RAIFFA, HOWARD, THE ART AND SCIENCE OF NEGOTIATION (1982).

RAIFFA, HOWARD, JOHN RICHARDSON & DAVID METCALFE, NEGOTIATION ANALYSIS (2007).

Rajan, Raghuram G., *Presidential Address: The Corporation in Finance*, 67 J. FIN. 1173 (2012).

ROBERTS, JOHN, THE MODERN FIRM (1992).

Robinson, David T. & Toby E. Stuart, *Network Effects in the Governance of Strategic Alliances*, 23 J. L. ECON. & ORG. 242 (2006).

Robinson, David T. & Toby E. Stuart, *Financial Contracting in Biotech Strategic Alliances*, 50 J. L. & ECON. 559 (2007).

SHIN CATERPILLAR MITSUBISHI CORPORATE HISTORY COMPILATION COMMITTEE, SHIN KYATAPIRA MITSUBISHI 25-NENSHI [NEW CATERPILLAR MITSUBISHI'S 25-YEAR HISTORY] (1991).

Shishido, Zenichi, *Conflicts of Interest and Fiduciary Duties in the Operation of a Joint Venture*, 39 HAST. L. J. 63 (1987).

SHISHIDO, ZENICHI, DOKIZUKE NO SHIKUMI TOSHITENO KIGYO: INSEN-TIBU SHISUTEMU NO HOSEIDORON [THE FIRM AS AN INCENTIVE MECHANISM: THE ROLE OF LEGAL INSTITUTIONS] (2006).

Shishido, Zenichi, *Goben Godo Kaisha* [*Joint Venture LLCs*], *in* KIGYO-HO KINYU-HO NO SHINCHORYU [NEW TREND OF CORPORATE LAWS AND FINANCE LAWS] 213 (Atsushi Koide et al., eds., 2013).

Shishido, Zenichi, *Dai 3 Hen (Mochibun Kaisha) Zenchu* [*General Comments to Part 3 (Membership Companies)*], *in* 14 KAUSHA-HO KONMENTARU [14 COMMENTARY ON THE COMPANIES ACT] 5 (Hideki Kanda ed., 2014).

Shishido, Zenichi, *Introduction: The Incentive Bargain of the Firm and Enterprise Law: A Nexus of Contracts, Markets, and Laws, in* ENTER-PRISE LAW: CONTRACTS, MARKETS, AND LAWS IN THE US AND JAPAN 1 (Zenichi Shishido ed., 2014).

Shishido, Zenichi, *Godo Kaisha no Taishain no Mochibunhyoka* [*Valua-tion of Exiting LLC Members' Ownership Interests*], *in* KIGYOHO NO GENZAI [ENTERPRISE LAW TODAY] 427 (Masayoshi Deguchi et al., eds., 2014).

Shishido, Zenichi, *Legislative Policy of Alternative Forms of Business Organization: The Case of Japanese LLCs, in* RESEARCH HANDBOOK ON PARTNERSHIPS, LLCS AND ALTERNATIVE FORMS OF BUSINESS ORGANIZATIONS, Ch. 22 (Robert W. Hillman & Mark J. Loewenstein eds., 2015).

Shishido, Zenichi, *The Strategy behind the Organizational Game: A Comparison between the Joint Venture and the Venture Capital Invest-ment Negotiation, in* STRATEGIC ALLIANCES AND JOINT VENTURES: LAW, ECONOMICS AND MANAGEMENT (Joseph A. McCahery & Erik P. M. Vermeulen eds., forthcoming available at: http://ssrn.com/abstract= 2629019).

SHISHIDO, ZENICHI & ATSUSHI KUSANO, KOKUSAI GOBEN: TOYOTA – GM JOINTO BENCHA NO KISEKI [INTERNATIONAL JOINT VENTURES: A CASE STUDY OF THE JOINT VENTURE BETWEEN TOYOTA AND GENERAL MOTORS] (1988).

SMITH, GORDON V. & RUSSELL L. PARR, INTELLECTUAL PROPERTY: LICENSING AND JOINT VENTURE PROFIT STRATEGIES (1993).

Steele, Myron T., *Freedom of Contract and Default Contractual Duties in Delaware Limited Liability Partnerships and Limited Liability Com-panies*, 46 AM. BUS. L.J. 221 (2009).

Strine, Jr., Leo E. & J. Travis Laster, *The Siren Song of Unlimited Contractual Freedom, in* RESEARCH HANDBOOK ON PARTNERSHIPS, LLCS AND ALTERNATIVE FORMS OF BUSINESS ORGANIZATIONS, Ch.1 (Robert W. Hillman & Mark J. Lowenstein eds., 2015).

Takeda, Shiro, *Nihon Kigyo no Kokusai Teikei Kaisho ni Kansuru Ichikosatsu* [*Study of Dissolutions of Japanese Companies' International Alliances*] 17 YOKOHAMA NATIONAL UNIVERSITY MANAGEMENT RESEARCH REVIEW 31 (1996) http://kamome.lib.ynu.ac.jp/dspace/bitstream/10131/753/1/KJ00000160245.pdf.

Index

access sales channels 75
accounting auditor 35
accumulation of capital reserve 38
additional capital 39, 53–4, 155–6, 187
adjustment 3
affiliate 16, 156, 176
affiliated company 86, 103–4, 124, 178
after-tax cash flow 46
agency problem 122
agent 1, 95, 120
alleviation of friction 79
alter ego 179
ancillary agreement 6, 121, 125–7,
    129–30, 132, 134, 154, 171, 175–7
ancillary contract 53, 57, 64–5
ancillary return 3, 37, 48–51, 72, 74–5,
    100–101, 105, 185, 189
anti-bribery law 120
anti-tax haven rule 47
antitrust
  issue 22, 24, 92
  law 4, 82–3, 91, 93–4, 117, 123,
    128–9, 160, 178
  restriction 71, 128
appointee director 166
arbitration 7, 58, 168, 170–72, 191–2
arm's length 16, 43, 73
articles of incorporation 6, 17–8, 31–5,
    125–6, 132, 140, 175
assign-back 85, 108
at cost 159
audit right 16, 144
autonomy 163–7, 202
autonomy of human capital provider 2,
  163

bankruptcy 7, 46, 55–6, 102–3, 148,
    151–2, 153, 170, 174, 179
bargaining

over exit right 35, 54
over right to information disclosure
    34
over sharing control 27–9
over sharing of veto right 32
over sharing return on investment 32
over sharing total return 28, 37
over voting right 29
BATNA 116
board of directors 19, 31–2, 34, 44–6,
    56, 95, 125, 151–2, 165, 192
board resolution 17, 32
boomerang effect 81, 91
bounded rationality 146
brand introduction 80
brand license 66–7, 102–4
brand name 14, 19, 63, 80, 96, 106
buyout 7, 60–62, 151, 169, 173, 175,
    187, 191

call option 33, 59–60, 62, 170, 191
capital gain 3, 38, 72
capital increase 39, 126
capital provider 2, 29, 158, 163–4, 196
capital reserve 38,
cartel 46, 74, 76, 82, 128, 178
change
  in circumstance 25
  in price of transaction 157
  of control 56–7, 154
charter autonomy 6, 137, 139–42
class voting 31
classes of stock 30–31, 125
classified stock 34
collaboration in lieu of competition 76
collaborative R&D 75, 81
comfort letter 166
commitment 4, 27, 84, 89, 127, 136,
    139, 163–4

commitment risk 54, 121
common stock 31, 34
comparable uncontrolled price method 98
comparative analysis 37, 162
composition of the board of directors 31
confidentiality agreement 84, 118, 122
conflicts of interest 11, 46, 146, 165, 199, 207
contract culture 132–3
contractual alliance 4, 71, 84, 86, 135
contractual organization 7–8, 53, 194–5, 198–9, 201, 203
control right 30, 163
controlling shareholder 57, 61
control-sharing arrangement 30, 144, 187
conversion of joint venture 154
co-partner 12, 43, 57, 59, 65, 90, 121
corporate brand 100, 103–4, 106
corporate identity 104–6
corporate opportunity 2, 11–12, 16–17, 20, 23, 165, 199
cost-center 6, 42, 74, 158–63, 165, 167
cost plus 41, 45
cost plus method 98
cost sharing 82, 124, 159
country risk 151
credit guarantee 156, 164, 166
cross-license 108, 111
cross-shareholding relationship 78

database 177
de facto binding force 137, 139–40
de facto contribution 73
de facto decision-making authority 96
de facto return 42, 73
deadlock 3, 25, 30, 33, 56, 58, 148, 153, 168, 173, 190–91
debt 20, 65, 179–81
debt financing 47, 126, 156–7
decision-making authority 30, 96, 160–61, 165–6, 190, 202
decision-making paralysis 25
default rules 6, 136–7, 141
design 87, 95–6, 98, 101–2, 105, 110
dilution 21, 104, 106, 155–6

disclosure 2, 11–12, 15, 20–23, 26, 28, 34–5, 45–6, 50, 91, 123–4, 165
discounted cash flow (DCF) 61, 63
discovery 171, 202
dissatisfaction 7, 20, 187, 191
dissolution 7, 20, 187, 191
dividend
    distribution 28, 41
    payout ratio 38, 188
    policy 38, 126, 157, 188
    see also hidden dividend
domination by one partner 189
dual-class stock *see* classified stock
due diligence 94, 110, 116, 118–20, 123–5
durability of agreement 6, 137
duty of care 180
duty of confidentiality 35, 57, 91, 101, 107, 109, 123, 177
duty of loyalty 23

enforceability
    by the JV company's charter/articles of incorporation 132
    of joint venture agreement 134, 142
    of shareholders' agreement 34
entrepreneur 2, 195–6, 200
equity
    offering to a third party 155
    offering to existing shareholders 155
establishment stage 5, 115, 126–9, 185, 187
estoppel 13
exclusive distribution right 41
exclusive license 91
exit
    bargaining 39
    clause 58, 196
    conditions 28, 53–4, 58
    grounds for 53, 55
    means of 59, 196
    method 3, 58
    option 6, 138
    reason for 53
    restriction 27
    right 3, 28, 35, 52–4, 58, 120, 124, 139, 170

facility sharing 77, 82, 159
fair
  price 15
  value 48, 128
feasibility study 119
fiduciary duty 12–13, 15, 21–3, 46, 186
financial investor 204, 207
financial statements 33, 35
first offer 59
first refusal 59, 62
fixed term 55, 154
flow-back 85, 108
Foreign Corrupt Practices Act 120
foreign related party 48, 98, 100, 157
franchise agreement 66, 105
free-riding 22, 92, 104, 111

game-theoretic 1, 4, 71, 75
going-concern value 63, 147, 149
governing law 63, 143, 14
grant-back 43, 85, 97, 108
guaranteed dividend 156

hidden dividend 42, 72
hold-up problem 6, 25
human capital
  contribution 2, 8, 14, 28, 43, 46, 87,
      89, 92, 108, 128, 138, 195
  provider 2, 29, 158, 163–4, 196
  recovery of 64, 101
  resource 130
hybrid contractual organization 81, 95

imbalance 2, 8, 14–16, 28, 37, 42–6,
    101, 195–6, 207
implicit contract 127
incentive bargaining 1–2, 4–8, 11, 16,
    27–8, 37, 52, 87, 116, 132, 151–2,
    162–4, 195, 197, 202, 206
incomplete contract 25, 132–3, 146
indemnification 108, 156
independent director's swing vote 191
  see also swing vote
information disclosure 15, 21, 23, 28,
    34, 45–6, 165
in-kind
  capital 139

capital contribution 88–9, 92, 101,
    126, 139
  investment 128
insolvency 56, 173
intellectual property (IP) 2–4, 21, 36,
    41, 44, 50, 65–6, 81, 87
  holder partner 91
  right 5, 87–95, 97, 101–4, 121, 130,
      176
internal approval 51, 123
International Centre for Settlement of
    Investment Disputes (ICSID) 117,
    172
IP *see* intellectual property
IPO (initial public offering) 8, 59, 74,
    154, 157, 162, 166, 169, 196, 206

joint venture agreement 5–7, 19, 23, 27,
    29, 31, 35, 38–9, 52–3, 56–8,
    61–7, 92, 102, 107, 115–16,
    118–19, 123–30, 132–4, 136,
    140–42, 144–6, 148–54, 169–71,
    174, 177, 179, 187, 188–91,
    194–7, 199–201
joint venture corporation 173
judicial dissolution 7, 173
jurisdiction 4, 90, 108, 123, 128, 135,
    141, 173, 180, 192

keiretsu 86
key personnel appointment/dismissal
    31
know-how 4, 12, 21, 26, 35, 49–50, 63,
    65–6, 74, 80–81, 85, 88, 90–91,
    94, 101, 105–6, 108–10, 128, 151,
    175, 189

labor law 64–5, 117
learning effect 3, 109
legal entity 6, 53, 84–6, 95, 126, 135–6,
    152
letter of intent (LOI) 5, 118–19, 122,
    123–4
licensee partner 4, 84, 89–90, 100
licensor partner 4, 22, 43, 65–6, 81,
    84–5, 88–92, 94–7, 99–102, 104,
    106–9, 111, 189

limited liability 136, 178, 180
limited liability company (LLC) 12–13,
    23, 30, 39, 59, 135–7, 139, 173
limited liability partnership (LLP) *see*
    partnership
liquidation 49, 59, 63, 72, 149,
liquidation value 63, 149, 176
long-term relational contract 5
loss-sharing agreement 179

M&A 8, 57, 96, 169, 196
majority control 29–30, 111
majority-shareholder rule 31
management committee 152, 167, 191,
    203
management fee 44, 104
management resource 30, 40, 42–3,
    107–8, 166, 190, 192, 207
managing partner 34
mandatory disclosure 15
market entry 27, 79, 120
market value 63
markup 41, 44–5
mediation 178, 191
memorandum of understanding (MOU)
    5, 91, 119, 122–4
milestone 55, 119, 154, 196, 201–2
minority partner 19–20, 24–5, 31–5, 58
minority shareholder 29–31, 61, 173
monetary capital 1–3, 8, 14, 39, 58, 64,
    88, 97, 128, 139, 176, 195, 200
monetary capital provider 2, 29, 164,
    196
monitoring 2, 6, 29, 33, 35, 40, 44–5,
    48, 90, 92–4, 96, 106, 109, 144,
    160, 162–3, 165, 167, 202
moral hazard 1, 110, 185, 199
motivation 1, 5, 27, 130, 176

net present value 38
non-compete
    agreement 74
    clause 92
    duty 64–5
non-equity contractual alliance 135
nonexclusive
    license 85, 91, 103–5, 107
    right 91, 105

non-licensor partner 4–5, 99, 102, 109,
    111
non-managing partner 34
non-pro rata return 43
non-pro rata self-dealing transaction 15,
    41, 43, 73
non-voting stock 156
non-zero-sum
    bargaining 117, 151
    game 38
notification 16, 20, 45, 83, 95, 128–9,
    144
NUMMI 49–50, 61–2, 80

obtain local expertise 75, 79
one-off agreement 179
operating committee 152, 160–61,
    165–8, 191
operational management failure 185–6
operational stage 5, 128, 144, 149–50,
    157
opportunistic behavior 2, 7–8, 11, 13,
    18, 20, 25–6, 44, 57, 89, 94–5,
    110, 121, 127, 142, 148, 162, 164,
    189, 198
organizational management failure 7,
    53, 185–7, 189
other partner(s), the 4–5, 11, 13, 17, 20,
    24–7, 29–30, 32, 35, 39–45,
    48–50, 54, 56–60, 62–3, 65–6,
    73–4, 80–81, 84, 90–92, 94–5,
    101–2, 107–10, 118, 121, 124,
    141, 144, 148, 151–3, 160, 162,
    169, 170, 174–5, 177, 179, 187,
    188–9, 198
outsourcing agreement 31, 44, 65
ownership percentages 29–33, 35, 37,
    38–9, 42–3, 60, 72–3, 111, 117,
    121, 123, 137, 151, 155, 189

parent–subsidiary relationship 94
Pareto frontier 49
Pareto-optimal outcome 26
partner's solely owned business 18–19,
    63, 100–101, 154, 169, 186
partnership 23, 59, 135–7, 139
pass-through taxation 136
payoff 1–3, 30, 35, 49, 154

piercing the corporate veil 176
pitfall 7, 186
political, economic, sociological and
    technological (PEST) factors 186
post-contract bargaining 6, 144, 169
post-contractual opportunism 148
pre-contract bargaining 5, 52, 115–16,
    118
pre-emptive right 39
pre-liquidation renegotiation 149, 154
preparatory stage 5, 83, 91, 94, 115–17,
    119–22, 125–7
prisoner's dilemma 21, 26
pro rata self-dealing transaction 15,
    41–2, 72
product brand 96, 104–5
profit-center 6, 74, 157–8, 161–3, 166
provisional director 192
put option 33, 58, 60, 62–3, 129, 170,
    196

quality control 96, 106
quorum requirement for board meeting
    31

recall
    of employee 64
    of seconded personnel 64
related-party
    interest 47
    transaction 41
relation-specific
    human capital 1
    investment 27
relational contract 5, 74, 132–4, 146
relationship-specific asset 25, 98, 101,
    139, 147–9
remuneration of officer 44
renegotiation
    causes of 146
    revisionary 145, 150–52, 157
    seed of 145
    supplemental 145, 150, 154
    turnaround 149, 154
repeated-game 26
reputational
    assets 90
    backing 75, 78, 174

damage 103, 179
risk 103, 179
resale price method 98
residual asset 30, 39, 65, 72, 101,
    175–7, 192
residual profit split method 99
retained earnings 28, 156–7
return
    from transaction 3, 24, 37, 39–46, 48,
        51, 72–5, 97, 107–8, 185, 188–9,
        207
    on investment 2–3, 14, 28, 37–40,
        48–9, 51, 72–5, 92, 97, 185, 188,
        204
review clause 123
risk
    of deadlock 3, 33
    of opportunistic behavior 11, 13, 18,
        25, 127
    of other party refusing to renegotiate
        25
    of squeeze-out 3, 24
royalty 41, 92, 98–9, 107
Russian roulette 60–61

sale of stock 59, 129
secondment
    agreement 109, 127–8, 130, 176–7
    of personnel 128, 135
self-dealing transaction 8, 15–6, 41–2,
    45, 72–3, 196, 199, 201
    see also non-pro rata self-dealing
        transaction; pro rata self-dealing
        transaction
sellout 7
service agreement 77, 109
service fees 41, 44, 46, 104
settlement 175
shareholder
    agreement 6–7, 33–5, 125, 194–5
    class meeting 31, 34
    derivative action 180
    voting agreement 125
    see also voting agreement
sharing control 3, 5, 27–9, 35–6, 111,
    121, 123, 165, 202
sharing total return 2–3, 11, 28, 37, 39,
    73, 95, 123

Silicon Valley model 196
single-round game 187, 192
special-purpose company (SPC) 47, 82
special resolution 34, 174
spillover 92
squeeze-out 3, 24, 30, 33, 60, 140, 170
stage-by-stage design 201
staged bargaining 1–2, 5
staged financing 8, 196
steering committee 152, 167, 191
stakeholder 37, 45, 46, 122, 166
stock
    transfer 191
    transferability 27
    transferability restriction 39
stock corporation 3, 12, 39, 58–60, 128,
    136–7, 139
strategic alliance 1, 8, 197–9, 201, 204,
    206
strategic investor 8, 204–7
sub-license 111
success of joint venture 24
supply chain 49
swing vote 191
synergy 1–2, 8

tax
    avoidance 47
    haven 47
    planning 51
    treatment 46, 48, 65
technology
    introduction 80
    license 14, 106–7
    transfer 4, 135
termination
    stage 2, 5–6, 153
    upon unforeseen event 55
territory 91–3
Texas shootout 60
threat

of exit 3, 5, 27, 33, 35–6, 52–4, 87–8,
    101, 111, 122, 192
of withdrawing human resource 64
of withdrawing monetary capital 36
of withdrawing personnel 178
three types of return 3–5, 37, 74,
    116–17, 185
three-player bargaining 6
Toyota production system (TPS) 49
trade dress 66, 105–6
trademark 4, 65–6, 87, 96, 100, 104–6
trade secret 87, 106, 110
transaction cost 37, 197
transactional net margin method 99
transfer price 16, 42, 44, 46, 48, 97
transfer price taxation 100, 157
turnaround renegotiation 149, 151, 154

unfair
    method 93
    trade practice 93
unitary taxation 47
United Nations Commission on
    International Trade Laws
    (UNCITRAL) 172
utilization of sales channels 78

valuation of ownership interest 28, 39,
    53, 60–61, 92
value chain 42, 158, 160–62
venture capital investment agreement 7,
    194–7, 200–202, 204
venture capitalist 2, 195–7, 200, 202,
    204–7
vertical relationship 14, 42
veto right 3, 16, 19, 20–21, 25, 27, 32–4,
    44, 56, 95, 121, 144, 149, 166,
    189–90
voting agreement 57, 125, 144
voting right 3, 29–30, 142, 155, 162

zero-sum bargaining 117, 151